Colloquial

Japanese

The Colloquial Series
Series Adviser: Gary King

The following languages are available in the Colloquial series:

	Afrikaans	*	Japanese
	Albanian		Korean
	Amharic		Latvian
	Arabic (Levantine)		Lithuanian
	Arabic of Egypt		Malay
	Arabic of the Gulf and		Mongolian
	Saudi Arabia		Norwegian
	Basque		Panjabi
	Bulgarian		Persian
*	Cambodian		Polish
*	Cantonese		Portuguese
*	Chinese		Portuguese of Brazil
	Croatian and Serbian		Romanian
	Czech		Russian
	Danish		Scottish Gaelic
	Dutch		Slovak
	Estonian		Slovene
	Finnish		Somali
	French	*	Spanish
	German		Spanish of Latin America
	Greek		Swedish
	Gujarati	*	Thai
	Hindi		Turkish
	Hungarian		Ukrainian
	Icelandic		Urdu
	Indonesian	*	Vietnamese
	Italian		Welsh

Accompanying cassette(s) (*and CDs) are available for the above titles. They can be ordered through your bookseller, or send payment with order to Taylor & Francis/Routledge Ltd, ITPS, Cheriton House, North Way, Andover, Hants SP10 5BE, UK, or to Routledge Inc, 29 West 35th Street, New York NY 10001, USA.

COLLOQUIAL CD-ROMs
Multimedia Language Courses
Available in: Chinese, French, Portuguese and Spanish

Colloquial
Japanese

The Complete Course for Beginners
Second edition

**Hugh Clarke and
Motoko Hamamura**

Routledge
Taylor & Francis Group

LONDON AND NEW YORK

First published 2003
by Routledge
11 New Fetter Lane, London EC4P 4EE

Simultaneously published in the USA and Canada
by Routledge
29 West 35th Street, New York, NY 10001

Routledge is an imprint of the Taylor & Francis Group

Typeset in Times New Roman by
Newgen Imaging Systems (P) Ltd, Chennai, India
Printed and bound in Great Britain by
TJ International Ltd, Padstow, Cornwall

British Library Cataloguing in Publication Data
A catalogue record for this book is available from the British Library

Library of Congress Cataloging in Publication Data
A catalog record for this book has been requested

ISBN 0-415-19478-4 (Book)

  0-415-27911-9 (CDs)

  0-415-19479-2 (Tapes)

  0-415-19480-6 (Pack)

Contents

Preface   vii

Introduction to the Japanese language   1

1 名刺の交換 **Meishi no kookan**   11
Exchanging business cards

2 自己紹介 **Jiko-shookai**   28
Introducing yourself

3 家族の話 **Kázoku no hanashi**   41
Talking about families

4 買い物 **Kaimono**   58
Shopping

5 月曜日に会いましょう。   75
Getsuyóobi ni aimashóo.
Let's meet on Monday!

6 鈴木さんの会社へどうやって
行きますか。   90
**Suzuki san no kaisha e dóo
yatte ikimásu ka.**
How do I get to your office, Mr Suzuki?

7 どんな感じの人ですか。   111
Dónna kanji no hito désu ka.
What does he look like?

8 市内観光に行きましょう。   130
Shinai-kánkoo ni ikimashóo.
Let's take the city tour!

9 ホテルで **Hóteru de**   145
At the hotel

10 競馬を見に行きませんか。   160
Keiba o mí ni ikimasén ka.
Would you like to come to the races?

11 日本に行くならどの季節が い
いでしょうか。 **178**
**Nihón ni ikú nara, dóno kísetsu
ga íi deshoo ka.**
If you're going to Japan, which is the best season?

12 どうも風邪を引いたようです。 **193**
Dóomo kaze o hiita yóo desu.
Somehow I seem to have caught a cold.

13 車にぶつけられた。 **211**
Kuruma ni butsukerareta.
Another car ran into me!

14 もしもし秋元先生いらっしゃい
ますでしょうか。 **229**
**Móshimoshi, Akimoto sensei
irasshaimásu deshóo ka.**
Hello, may I speak to Professor Akimoto?

15 上達の秘訣はこれです。 **248**
Jootatsu no hiketsu wa kore desu.
The secret road to progress!

Key to the exercises **258**
Grammar summary **289**
Appendix: hiragána, katakána and kanji **306**
Japanese–English glossary **312**
Index of grammar and language functions **383**

Preface

In this completely new edition of *Colloquial Japanese*, we have integrated the writing system into the course from Unit 1. This has resulted in the unusual, dare we say unique, feature of combining romanised transcription and the Japanese script in the first five units. Instead of learning **hiragána** and **katakána** syllabaries mechanically by rote before embarking on your study of Japanese, running the risk of losing your enthusiasm before you have begun, you are introduced gradually to the Japanese writing system as you acquire useful phrases and expressions you can use immediately. From the beginning we introduce the three components of the Japanese script – **kanji**, **hiragána** and **katakána** – within a context of partly romanised, natural spoken Japanese. We hope this innovation will help you learn how to read and write Japanese as quickly and painlessly as possible. From Unit 6 the basic conversations and dialogues are given in **kana** and a restricted number of **kanji**. Students who apply themselves diligently to the study of the Japanese script should be able to learn the 200 **kanji** introduced in the fifteen units. For those who cannot afford the time to master all the **kanji**, however, it will be possible to complete the course with a knowledge of the script introduced in the first seven units.

In addition to the introduction of the Japanese script, the new edition adopts a more interactive, communicative approach to the learning of Japanese. The language is introduced through a series of practical dialogues simulating the actual situations a learner of Japanese is likely to encounter. We have been careful, however, not to sacrifice the comprehensive coverage of grammar and vocabulary which were the hallmarks of earlier editions of *Colloquial Japanese*.

We have received encouragement and advice from many friends and colleagues, too numerous to mention here. We are particularly grateful to our copy editor, Diane Stafford, whose excellent command of Japanese and meticulous eye for detail has purged the manuscript of many typographical errors and inconsistencies. Special thanks must also go to our editors Sophie Oliver and James Folan of Routledge, whose patience and understanding encouraged us to go on when it seemed at times we would never finish the manuscript. We hope their faith in us will be rewarded with this volume.

Hugh Clarke and Motoko Hamamura
May 2001

Introduction to the Japanese language

Japanese, with over 127 million speakers in Japan, large emigrant communities in North and South America and a rapidly growing body of fluent non-native speakers, is one of the world's major languages. Outside the languages of Europe, it is probably the most studied foreign language, with about a million learners in China, a similar number in Korea and around 300,000 in Australia and New Zealand. It is the most studied foreign language in Australian secondary schools and is now also becoming very popular in Britain and America. Japan is the world's second-largest economy, a major provider of foreign aid and a significant force in world affairs, particularly in Asia. It has a rich, distinctive culture combining native elements with influences from the Asian mainland and, more recently, from Europe and America. A fascinating blend of tradition and modernity, Japan has a literary tradition extending back 1,200 years, yet is one of the most modern, some would say post-modern, high-tech, post-industrial societies in the world. The Japanese language is the key to understanding Japanese culture and society. Studying Japanese can be a very rewarding experience in its own right, but, more important, it has great practical value for anyone wishing to do business with the Japanese or planning to visit Japan.

Pronunciation and romanisation

Japanese has a relatively simple sound system. It does not have a strong stress accent as we have in English, preferring instead to use high and low pitch contrasts to mark the boundaries between phrases. For practical purposes, you will find that you can produce natural-sounding Japanese by giving each syllable equal stress and prominence (loudness).

Romanisation

The romanisation used in this book is a modification of the Hepburn system which is the most practical for speakers of English. We have indicated long vowels by writing the short vowel twice, e.g. **oo**, **uu**, etc. The acute accent has been added to indicate the pitch accent. The following descriptions of Japanese sounds are approximations based on the pronunciation of south-eastern British English.

The vowels

Japanese has five short vowels **a, e, i, o, u** and five long vowels romanised here **aa, ee, ii, oo** and **uu**. The short vowels are all the same length, very short and crisp, giving Japanese its characteristic staccato rhythm.

a   like the *u* in *cut*
e   like the *e* in *get*
i   like the *i* in *hit*
o   like the *au* in *taught* but shorter, like the *o* in *hot*
u   like the *u* in *put* but without the lip-rounding (pull the corners of your mouth back slightly when you pronounce this vowel).

The long vowels, indicated by double letters in our romanisation, are exactly the same sounds as their short counterparts, but are given twice the duration. A difference in the length of the vowel can make a difference in the meaning of a word. To avoid confusion and embarrassment, care must be taken to distinguish between long and short vowels. Take, for example, **shujin** '*husband*' and **shuujin** '*prisoner*' or, potentially even more dangerous, **komon** '*adviser*' and **koomon** '*anus*'.

When two or more vowels come together in Japanese each retains its original pronunciation. The sequence is pronounced without a pause in the middle, but each vowel is given its full value and duration, unlike the diphthongs in English which tend to coalesce the vowels together into a single sound. Note that the sequence **ei** is usually replaced in pronunciation by the long vowel **ee**, e.g. **senséi** '*teacher*' is pronounced **sensée**.

Devoicing of vowels

Under certain circumstances the vowels **i** and **u** are omitted, reduced or whispered. This phenomenon, known as devoicing, is particularly marked in the speech of Tokyo. You will notice it in the pronunciation recorded on the tapes which accompany this volume. It generally occurs when the vowels **i** or **u** are sandwiched between two of the consonants, **p, t, k, s, sh, ts, ch, f** and **h** (voiceless consonants), or when **i** or **u** follow one of these consonants at the end of a sentence (i.e. before a pause).

Consonants

The consonants **p, b, t, d, k, h, m** and **y** are pronounced pretty much the same as they are in English.

ch like *ch* in *church*, but for many speakers with the tip of the tongue down behind the lower front teeth.

j like *j* in *judge*, but for many speakers with the same tongue position as *ch* above.

ts like the *ts* in *cats*. Note that this sound occurs at the beginning of the syllable in Japanese. You will need to practise this sound to avoid confusing it with s.

z like the *z* in *zoo*. Many Japanese speakers pronounce this sound like the *ds* in *cards* at the beginning of a word and like *z* elsewhere.

f differs slightly from English *f*. The lower lip does not touch the upper teeth. It is like the sound we make blowing out a candle.

n before a vowel like *n* in *now*. At the end of a word the sound is midway between the *n* in *man* and the *ng* in *sang*. Try pronouncing *man* without touching the roof of your mouth with the tip of your tongue. When **n** occurs at the end of a syllable it is influenced by the following consonant. It is pronounced *n* when followed by **n, t, d, s, z, r** or **w**. Before **m, p** or **b** it is pronounced *m*, e.g. **shinbun** (pronounced **shimbun**) *'newspaper'*, **Nihón mo** (pronounced **nihom mo**) *'Japan too'*. When followed by **g** or **k**, **n** is pronounced like the *ng* in *singer*. Note that this last sound change also occurs in English, the *n* in *think* is actually pronounced *ng*.

g like the *g* in *get*. Some speakers, particularly in Tokyo, pronounce this sound as the nasal *ng* (like the *ng* in *singer*) when it occurs between vowels. Although the nasal pronunciation still enjoys considerable prestige in the media, the tendency seems to be towards using the stop pronunciation ('the hard g') in all positions.

r this sound does not occur in English. To our ears it often sounds like a blend of *d*, *l* and *r*. Actually it is made by flapping (or tapping) the tip of the tongue against the gum ridge behind the upper teeth.

The effect can be achieved by pronouncing the *r* of English word *rat* while placing the tip of the tongue in the position to form a *d*.

w   like the *w* in *wonderful*, but with the corners of the mouth pulled back slightly. This sound occurs only before **a**. Take care to pronounce **wa** like the *wo* in *wonder* and not like the *wa* in *war*.

Double consonants

Just as Japanese distinguishes short and long vowels it also makes a distinction between single and double consonants. Making these distinctions is the major difficulty English speakers encounter in pronouncing Japanese. The double consonants **pp**, **tt**, **tts**, **tch**, **ss**, **ssh**, **kk**, **nn**, **nm** (pronounced *mm*) take twice the time to pronounce of their single counterparts. Where the first element is **p**, **t** or **k** the sound is begun, then held for a syllable beat before being released. Double consonants occur in Italian and can be heard in English at word boundaries, as in *take care* or *about time*. Failure to distinguish single and double consonants can result in misunderstanding. Note, for example, **káta** '*shoulder*', **kátta** '*won*' or **bata** '*butter*', **batta** '*grasshopper*'.

Japanese also has syllables beginning with a consonant followed by **y**. This **y** is always pronounced as a consonant, like *y* in '*yes*'. We can hear a similar combination of a consonant plus y in English words like *new*, *cue*, *amusing*, etc. One combination English speakers find difficult is the initial **ry** in words like **ryokan** '*a traditional Japanese inn*'.

The apostrophe

An apostrophe is required in the romanisation to distinguish initial **n** from syllable-final **n**, which, you will recall, undergoes various sound changes according to the sound which follows. Compare **tan'i** '*unit*' with **tani** '*valley*' or **kin'en** '*no smoking*' with **kinen** '*memorial*'.

Pitch

In the romanised vocabulary lists in the early units, the grammatical summary and the glossaries, we have indicated the Japanese pitch accent. A fall from high to low pitch, where it occurs in a word, is marked with the acute accent mark ´. This mark on what we call 'the accented syllable' indicates that all preceding syllables of the word or phrase, except the first syllable, are pronounced on a high, level pitch. In the pronunciation of Tokyo words always begin with a low-pitched syllable unless that syllable carries the pitch accent mark. Where the final syllable of a word carries the accent mark it indicates that a following particle or ending begins with a low-pitched syllable. For example: **hana** '*nose*' is pronounced **ha^na** (low–high) and, as it has no accent mark, any following particles also continue on a high pitch. **hana ga takái** '*his nose is high, he is arrogant*' is pronounced **ha^nagataka_i**. In contrast, while **haná** '*flower*' is pronounced the same as **hana** in isolation, in connected speech it is followed by a low-pitched particle, e.g. **haná ga akai** '*the flower is red*' is pronounced **ha^na_ga a^kai**. On the other hand **háshi** '*chopsticks*', with its initial accented syllable is pronounced, **ha_shi** (high–low).

You may prefer to ignore the pitch notation used in our system of romanisation and simply model your pronunciation on the native speakers recorded on the tape which accompanies this volume. Unless you are keen to sound like a native of Tokyo you need not worry unduly about the pitch accent of Japanese. There is considerable regional variation in pitch tolerated within the definition of **kyootsuugo** or '*the common language*'.

Words of foreign origin

Japanese has borrowed many words from foreign languages, particularly from English. It is important to pronounce these words with the modifications they have undergone to accommodate them to the Japanese sound system and not in their original English, or other, pronunciation. As the Japanese writing system permits only very restricted consonant sequences, many loan-words in Japanese end up with more syllables than they have in their original languages, e.g. **supúun** '*spoon*', **fóoku** '*fork*', **gasorin sutándo** '*gasoline stand* (petrol station)'.

Pronunciation practice

Listen carefully to the pronunciation of these famous Japanese brand names, then try repeating them after the speakers. The bold forms in brackets indicate that our romanisation differs from the conventional spelling.

Sony (**Sónii**)	*Toyota* (**Tóyota**)	*Mitsubishi* (**Mitsúbishi**)
Kawasaki	**Suzuki**	*Toshiba* (**Tooshiba**)
Matsushita	*Subaru* (**Súbaru**)	*Mazda* (**Matsuda**)

Now listen to these Japanese words which have been borrowed into English. Notice the difference between the Japanese and English pronunciations.

karate   **karaoke**   *ikebana* (**ikébana**)   *origami* (**orígami**)
sashimi (**sashimí**)   **tsunami**   **kabuki**

Now some Japanese place names:

Yokohama   **Hiroshima**   *Nagoya* (**Nágoya**)
Okinawa   *Fukuoka* (**Fukúoka**)   *Nagano* (**Nágano**)

Here are some more place names, personal names and well-known words which contain long vowels:

Tokyo (**Tookyoo**)   *Osaka* (**Oosaka**)   *Honshu* (**Hónshuu**)
Kyushu (**Kyúushuu**)   *Kyoto* (**Kyóoto**)   *Sato* (**Sátoo**)
Kato (**Kátoo**)   *Noh* (**noo**)   *sumo* (**sumoo**)
judo (**júudoo**)

And some more with double consonants, vowel sequences and syllabic **n**:

Nihon (**Nihón**) '*Japan*'   *Nippon* (**Nippón**) '*Japan* –
                                      formal pronunciation'
Hokkaido (**Hokkáidoo**)   **Sapporo**   **Tottori**
Nissan   **Honda**   *Sendai* (**Séndai**)
sensei (**senséi**)   **geisha**   **ninja**
samurai   *tempura* (**tenpura**) *aikido* (**aikídoo**)
banzai (**banzái**)   *kampai* (**kanpai**) 'cheers!'

Listen to the following examples of devoiced vowels:

Nagasaki (**Nágasaki**)   *Shikoku* (**Shikóku**)   *sukiyaki* (**sukiyaki**)
sushi (**súshi**)   *Tsuchida* (**Tsuchida**)   *Chikamatsu*
Makita (**Mákita**)   (**Chikámatsu**)

Examples of consonants followed by **y** are given below.

ryokan *Japanese inn*   *Kyushu* (**Kyúushuu**)
kyúuri *cucumber*   **okyakusamá** *guest, customer*

Note the pronunciation of the following words of foreign origin.

tákushii *taxi* **térebi** *television* **náifu** *knife* **fóoku** *fork*
supúun *spoon* **supóotsu** *sport* **sákkaa** *soccer* **supagéttii** *spaghetti*

Pitch accent

Compare these accented and unaccented names listed below. Repeat the names after the native-speaker on the cassette tape.

Unaccented

(First syllable low, all following syllables high.)

Abe, Ono, Sano, Mori, Wada
Yoshida, Aoki, Ikeda, Nomura
Kimura, Murata, Matsumoto, Ishikawa, Sugiyama, Inoue, Ookubo,
    Saitoo

Accented

(Unless it carries the accent mark, the first syllable is low, then all syllables up to the accent mark are high. Syllables after the accent mark are low.)

Súgi, Óka, Háta, Míki, Séki
Sátoo, Kátoo, Fújita, Sákai, Támura, Mórita, Nishímura, Akíyama,
Ichikáwa, Takáhashi, Yamáguchi

The writing system

The Japanese writing system has been shaped by the historical accident of Japan's proximity to China. The Chinese language began to be used extensively in Japan after the introduction of Buddhism in the sixth century. Unfortunately, however, the characters which provided an ingenious solution to the representation of the largely monosyllabic, uninflected tonal language spoken in China were quite unsuitable as a means of writing Japanese which was, and is, a highly inflected poly-syllabic language. Some time around the beginning of the eighth century Chinese characters, known in Japan as **kanji**, were adapted to the writing of Japanese. This was achieved by ignoring the meaning of the Chinese characters and simply borrowing their sounds. This system was refined further by abbreviating or simplifying those Chinese characters used phonetically, resulting in the invention of the native syllabaries, **hiragána** and **katakána** some time in the tenth century. Japanese is still written with a combination of these three separate writing systems. **Kanji** are used for writing most nouns, and the roots of verbs and adjectives. They are used in their pseudo-Chinese pronunciation (called the **on-**reading) to convey the sounds of words borrowed from Chinese and in the native-Japanese, **kun-**reading to write original Japanese words. This means that you will learn at least two different pronunciations (readings), for most of the **kanji** introduced in this book. **Hiragána** is used for writing particles, suffixes and words with difficult or unusual characters, while **katakána** is used for writing words borrowed from languages other than Chinese.

In this book **kanji**, **hiragána** and **katakána** are introduced together in gradual stages from the very first unit. By the end of the book you should have an active mastery of **hiragána**, **katakána** and approximately 250 **kanji**. In addition, where appropriate, the glossary provides **kanji** transcriptions of all the words used in the book and other important vocabulary items.

Writing kanji

Kanji are made up of a relatively small number of distinct strokes, written, for the most part, from left to right or from top to bottom. As the classification of **kanji** is based on the number of strokes they contain and this is the principle upon which character dictionaries are arranged, it is important to learn how to count the number of strokes in a character and to execute them in the correct order. The glossaries also list the **kanji** used for writing vocabulary items introduced in the book, even where the characters they contain have not been introduced for specific study. The secret of learning **kanji** is to be aware of the discreet elements which form the character, linking them in your mind with a mnemonic of your own making, and practising writing them over and over again. The movements of hand and eye as you trace over the strokes of the character help to etch the image onto your memory.

How to use this book

The course has been designed to meet the needs of those who wish to acquire a thorough grounding in Japanese in a relatively short time.

The primary focus of the course is on the spoken language. It is indeed possible to work through the book without attempting to learn the written language at all. One the other hand, if your goal is to be able to read Japanese as well as speak it, it is important that you familiarise yourself with the Japanese script as early as possible. We have tried to design a book which will simultaneously meet the needs of these two different groups of learners. If you have decided not to tackle the written language you must rely more on your ears than your eyes. You will find the accompanying tapes an indispensable part of this course. The romanised text should be taken merely as a guide to the pronunciation of Japanese and an aid to help you remember the vocabulary. All the grammatical points are explained with romanised examples and all the glossary entries are given in both Japanese script and romanised transliteration.

We recommend, however, that serious students should at least learn the two Japanese syllabaries, **hiragána** and **katákana**. You acquire the new symbols gradually over the first seven units. By the time you reach Unit 8 you should be able to follow most of the material without looking at the romanised versions. If literacy in Japanese is your ultimate goal you must get into the habit of reading and writing the Japanese script. Don't fall into the trap of romanising everything before you try to work out what it means. Your aim should always be the comprehension of written texts as Japanese, not the laborious decoding of a series of abstract signs to produce an English translation.

If you need a high level of proficiency for business or other professional communication you should be prepared to learn a fair number of Chinese characters. You will find as you acquire more and more **kanji** that these are the building blocks of the Japanese vocabulary. You should learn how to read and write the 200 or so basic characters introduced in this course. In the first ten units new **kanji** are given with an indication of the number of strokes and the order in which they should be written. If you practise writing the **kanji** following the correct order of strokes you will soon acquire the basic principles of writing and counting strokes. For this reason we felt it was not necessary to continue giving the stroke order after Unit 10. From Unit 11 we have included a large number of **kanji** not included in the lists to be learnt by heart. We have shown the pronunciation of these additional characters with small superscript **hiragána** syllables known as **furigana.** This traditional system will help you to recognise a large number of **kanji** compounds in context even though you may not be able to write the individual characters. Advanced students might like to learn the new **kanji** compounds as they are introduced, whiting out the **furigana** readings when they are confident they can read the words without them.

Another major turning point you will notice in Unit 11 is that we no longer give lists of new vocabulary. This is partly to save space, but also because we believe that it is important that you become more actively involved in the learning process. You will find that making your own vocabulary lists and looking up the meanings of new words in the glossaries will speed up your acquisition of the language.

We have designed the course so that you can use it as a practical, direct-method language course, as a grammar handbook or as a basic dictionary. The glossaries, grammar index, **kanji** lists and grammar summary have been included so that you can find your way around the book with minimum effort. Although the course progresses in sequence from Unit 1 to Unit 15 you will often need to return to earlier units or jump to an explanation given in the grammar summary at the end of the book. The numbering system used in the main text, the Key to the Exercises and the recordings makes it easy for you to navigate from one part of the course to another.

1 名刺の交換
Meishi no kookan
Exchanging business cards

By the end of this unit you should be able to:

- Greet somebody
- Introduce yourself and respond to introductions
- Introduce others
- Thank someone and respond to thanks
- Apologise and respond to an apology
- Enquire about the jobs people do
- Say goodbye.

You will also learn:

- 16 **hiragána** symbols:
  さんてすかはこにちとのまそういえ
- 7 **kanji** characters: 田 本 中 川 山 上 下
- 3 **katakána** symbols: ス ミ ー
- To use the voicing marks, **nigori**.

Dialogue 1 ■■■

At an office reception for a visiting Japanese trade delegation you exchange business cards and practise your few words of Japanese. You are surprised to discover that you can identify some of the **kanji** used to write the visitors' names. The Japanese guests are impressed and flattered by your efforts to learn Japanese.

As you listen to the tape follow the text carefully to see if you can identify any of the Japanese characters below. Then look at the romanised text and the English translation. Come back to the Japanese text when you have studied the section on the script.

A. スミス: こんにちは。
　 本田: こんにちは。
　 スミス: 本田さんですか。
　 本田: はい、そうです。本田です。
　 スミス: はjimeまshiて、スミスです。どうぞyoroshiku.
　 本田: こちraこそ。

B. 田中: ミミさんですか。
　 スー: いいえ、スーです。
　 田中: どうmoすmiまseん。
　 スー: いいえ。

A. SÚMISU:	Konnichi wa.	SMITH:	*Hello.*
HONDA:	Konnichi wa.	HONDA:	*Good afternoon.*
SÚMISU:	Honda san désu ka.	SMITH:	*Are you Mr Honda?*
HONDA:	Hái, sóo desu. Honda désu.	HONDA:	*Yes, that's right.* *I'm Honda.*
SÚMISU:	Hajimemáshite. Súmisu desu. Dóozo yoroshiku.	SMITH:	*How do you do?* *I'm Smith. Pleased to meet you.*
HONDA:	Kochira kóso.	HONDA:	*The pleasure is mine.*
B. TANAKA:	Mími san desu ka.	TANAKA:	*Are you Mimi?*
SÚU:	Iie, Súu desu.	SUE:	*No, I'm Sue.*
TANAKA:	Dóomo sumimasén.	TANAKA:	*I'm sorry.*
SÚU:	Lie.	SUE:	*That's all right*

Vocabulary

こんにちは	**konnichi wa**	*hello, good day, good afternoon*
さん	**san**	*Mr, Mrs, Miss, Ms* (polite term of address)
…ですか	**désu ka**	*is it?, are you?,* etc.
はい	**hái**	*yes*
いいえ	**iie**	*no, don't worry* (reply to an apology)
そうです	**Sóo desu**	*that's right* (literally, 'it is so')
hajimeまshiて	**hajimemáshite**	*how do you do?* (literally, 'for the first time')

どうぞyoroshiku	dóozo yoroshiku	*pleased to meet you*
こちraこそ	kochira kóso	*me too, the pleasure is mine, etc.*
doうmo	dóomo	*very, really* (grateful, sorry, etc.)
すmiまseん	sumimasén	*I'm sorry*

Grammar points

In many ways Japanese grammar is less complex than that of the European languages. There are no changes indicating singular or plural nouns and no definite or indefinite articles. You will already have gathered from the example dialogues introduced in this unit that the verb comes at the end of the sentence and that the question marker, **ka** か, follows the verb.

You will also have noticed that **no** の is used to join nouns to indicate that the word preceding **no** possesses, or describes in some way, the following noun, e.g. **Tanaka san no hón** '*Mr Tanaka's book*', **yama no náka** '*in the mountains*' (literally, 'inside of the mountains', 'the mountains' inside'), **náka no hito** '*the person inside*' or '*the person in the middle*'. It is worth noting here that nouns with an accent on the final vowel lose that accent when followed by **no**. For example, **yamá** loses its accent in the phrase **yama no náka**, above.

These little words which show the grammatical relationship between the various components of a Japanese sentence are called 'particles', or sometimes, because they follow the nouns to which the refer, they are called 'postpositions' in contrast with English 'prepositions' which precede the noun. We refer to them as 'particles' in this book. In addition to the possessive particle **no** and the question marker, **ka**, in this unit we meet the topic particle, **wa**. This particle is used to indicate the topic of the sentence and means something like, '*as for ...*' or '*speaking of...*'. Of course, it is used far more frequently in Japanese than we would use these expressions in English. Notice, too, that the particle **wa** is written with the **hiragána** symbol for **ha**, は. This is one of the rare cases in which the **kana** spelling reflects an earlier stage of the Japanese language and does not coincide with the modern Japanese pronunciation. The particle **to** と, '*with*' or '*and*' is also used for joining nouns. And the tag question marker **ne** operates in the same way as **ka**.

Japanese names

Japanese usually have two names, the family name, **séi** or **myóoji**, which comes first and the given name, **namae**. Given names are generally used only within the family or between close friends. Most family names and place names in Japanese are compounds of two **kanji**. Here are some names which can be written with the seven characters introduced in this unit. Notice that the **t** and **k** at the beginning of a word often change to **d** and **g** respectively when that word occurs as the second element of a compound. This phenomenon is known as 'sequential voicing' (**rendaku**). It is a common feature of Japanese but occurs somewhat unpredictably, so learn each new compound as a new vocabulary item.

Pronunciation practice ■

田中	**Tanaka**	山本	**Yamamoto**
中田	**Nakada**	中本	**Nakamoto**
下田	**Shimoda**	川本	**Kawamoto**
山田	**Yamada**	山中	**Yamanaka**
本田	**Honda**	上山	**Ueyama**
上田	**Ueda**	中山	**Nakayama**
田山	**Táyama**	山下	**Yamáshita**
川田	**Káwada**	田川	**Tágawa**

The polite suffix **san**, さん, meaning Mr, Mrs, Miss or Ms, must be used when addressing anyone but a family member or a very close friend.

It can follow either the family name, the given name or the family name plus the given name, e.g. **Tanaka san**, 'Mr Tanaka', **Jiroo san**, 'Jiro' or **Tanaka Jiroo san**, 'Mr Jiro Tanaka'. Never use **san** to refer to yourself.

Business cards or Meishi

In Japan the exchange of business cards is an important ritual accompanying introductions. You offer your card with your name turned to face the recipient of the card. You make a slight bow, **ojígi** in Japanese, as you hand over your card. Usually you will also receive a card from the person to whom you are presenting your card. Having received the card you should take it in both hands and read it carefully, noting the **katagaki**, literally 'shoulder writing', the details of the company, position, rank, etc., written to the right or above the name. This information tells you a lot about the social standing of the person you have just met so you can choose the appropriate level of language when addressing him or her.

Writing

In this unit we introduce sixteen **hiragána** syllables, seven Chinese characters or **kanji** and three **katakána** syllables. If you are still unsure how these three different scripts are used for writing Japanese you can reread the section on the Japanese writing system in the introduction. The language can be written in the traditional fashion, i.e. in vertical columns starting from the upper right-hand corner of the page, or horizontally, left to right, as in English.

Hiragána

The **hiragána** symbols themselves, like **kanji**, are generally written from left to right and from top to bottom. The syllables introduced in Unit 1 are given below with the order and direction of the strokes indicated with a number placed at the beginning of each stroke.

sa   n   te   su

ka	ha (wa)	ko	ni
chi	to	no	ma
so	u	i	e

You will notice that with the addition of two dots in the upper right-hand corner, a syllable starting with **t**– is transferred into a syllable beginning with **d**–. Similarly, syllables with an initial **s**– or **k**– are transformed into **z**– or **g**– syllables with the addition of the same two dots. These are the voicing marks, known as **nigori** (or **dakuten**) in Japanese. For example:

てで	とど	さざ
te de	**to do**	**sa za**
そぞ	かが	こご
so zo	**ka ga**	**ko go**

The voicing mark is used with syllables beginning with **h**– to indicate an initial **b**– sound. For example:

は becomes ば as in こんばんは **konban wa** '*good evening*'.

Notice, too, that the second element of the long **oo** vowel is spelt with the **hiragána** symbol for **u**, う. For example:

そう in そうですか。 **Sóo desu ka.** '*Is that so?*'

From the outset it is very important to ensure that characters are written with the correct number of strokes performed in the correct order. This is particularly so in the case of **kanji** because they are arranged in dictionaries according to the number of strokes they contain. Besides, cursive handwriting is very difficult to decipher unless you have a sound knowledge of the principles of stroke order.

Exercise 1.1

Next time you go to eat **sushi**, perhaps you might like to try these delicacies. Imagine you are sitting at the **sushi** counter confronted by a menu written in **hiragána** and English. How would you order these from the **sushi** chef, who, incidentally, is called **itamae** or, more politely, **oitamae san** in Japanese.

A transliteration of the items on this menu, and answers to all the exercises in the book, can be found in the 'Key to the Exercises' that starts on p. 258.

Sushi Menu
Today's Specials

かに	いか	かずのこ	うに	はまち
Crab	Squid	Salted herring roe	Sea urchin	Yellow-tail kingfish

---

Kanji

The **kanji** introduced in this unit are all basic characters based on the original pictographs depicting natural phenomena or spatial relationships. These characters are particularly common in Japanese place names and family names. The **kanji** introduced in Unit 1 are given below in the square handwritten style with numbers indicating the order and starting point of each stroke. As a general rule **kanji** are written from left to right and from top to bottom. Often, however, a high central element will have precedence over

the left hand stroke, as in **yamá** and **ue** and there are some characters like **náka**, in which a final down-stroke bisects the rest of the character.

Katakána

As we mentioned in the section on the Japanese writing system in the Introduction, **katakána** is used nowadays for writing foreign names and words borrowed from languages other than Chinese. In this book we introduce **katakána** gradually a few syllables at a time. When you have learnt all the **hiragána** characters we will speed up the introduction of the remaining **katakána**. Unit 1 gives you just two syllables **su** and **mi** and the length mark, called **boo**, which is used in **katakána** script to indicate that the preceding vowel is lengthened. The length mark is written horizontally in horizontal writing, but in vertical script it would be written as a vertical line from top to bottom.

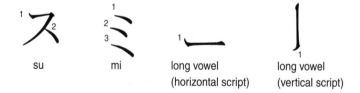

Foreign words

Modern Japanese uses many words which have been borrowed from foreign languages, mostly from English. These words, however, are often quite unrecognisable to native speakers of English because they have been adapted to the Japanese writing system and obey the Japanese rules of pronunciation. Because **katakána**, the script used for writing foreign loan words, is a syllabary and not an alphabet, it is not usually possible to write sequences of two or more consonants. Consequently, the *Sm–* at the beginning of *Smith* becomes **Sumi–** with the addition of the dummy vowel **–u**. As Japanese has no 'th' sound 's' is substituted, again followed by the dummy vowel **–u**. The Japanese equivalent of the one-syllable name, *Smith*, then, has three syllables, **su–, mi–, –su**. Note that **u** is the weakest of the five Japanese vowels and is hence the one usually used as a dummy vowel, but after **t–** or **d–** the dummy vowel is **o** and after **ch–** or **j–** it is **i**. More will be said of these spelling conventions as you learn more **katakána** words. As a general rule, however, you should treat **katakána** words as you would any new vocabulary item and only use words you have seen or heard before.

Exercise 1.2

The following reading exercise will test your knowledge of the meanings of the characters introduced in this unit and the use of the particles **no** and **to**. Match the Japanese phrases on the left with the English equivalents on the right. Read the Japanese phrases aloud as you go. Then cover up the Japanese and practise writing the phrases from the English cues. Check your answers with the Key to the Exercises on p. 258. For example:

1. 山の上   a. the top of the mountain   **yama no ue**

Now you are on your own.

2. 川と田   b. in the river
3. 山の下   c. mountains and rivers
4. 川の中   d. the river at the bottom of the mountain
5. 山の本   e. the rice-field up on the mountain
6. 本の山   f. the mountain above the river
7. 山の下の川   g. a book about mountains
8. 山の上の田   h. below the mountain
9. 山と川   i. a mountain (i.e. pile or stack) of books
10. 川の上の山   j. rivers and rice-fields

Exercise 1.3

Some Japanese girls write their family names, **séi** or **myóoji**, in **kanji** and their given names, **namae**, in **hiragána**. What are the names of the girls listed below? Notice that many girls' names end in –**ko** or –**e**.

1. 上田さちえ   2. 山本まちこ   3. 下田かのこ
4. 川田さとこ   5. 本田ちえ

How would these girls write their names in **kanji** and **hiragána**?

6. Táyama Masue   7. Tanaka Hámako   8. Nakayama Sónoko

Dialogue 2 ■

Greetings used in Japanese vary according to the time of day. To a lesser extent the same is true of expressions of leave-taking. When greeting someone the Japanese are far less inclined to use the name of the person they are addressing than we do in English. In this section the pronunciation guide and the English gloss appear beneath each dialogue.

A *Mr Yamanaka greets Mr Smith as he arrives at the office at 8:30 a.m. one Monday morning. He thanks Mr Smith for inviting him to play golf the day before. When you make a greeting in Japanese you often include a reference to the last time you met.*

山中: oはyoう ございます。
スミス: oはyoう ございます。
山中: kiのうは　どうmo ariがとうございまshita。
スミス: どういtashiまshiて。

YAMANAKA:	Ohayoo gozaimásu.	*Good morning.*
SMITH:	Ohayoo gozaimásu.	*Good morning.*
YAMANAKA:	Kinoo wa dóomo arígatoo gozaimashita.	*Thanks for yesterday.*
SMITH:	Dóo itashimashite.	*Not at all.*

B *Even Japanese sometimes get names wrong. Mr Honda recognises one of his customers on the platform at Shinjuku station when he is on his way home from work at about 8:00 p.m. In the dark he mistakes*

Mr Nakada for Mr Tanaka. Mr Honda apologises for his mistake and there are no hard feelings.

本田: こんばんは。
中田: こんばんは。
本田: 田中さんですか。
中田: いいえ、ちがいます。中田です。
本田: どうmo shitsureい shiまshita。
中田: いいえ。

HONDA:	Konban wa.	HONDA:	*Good evening.*
NAKADA:	Konban wa.	NAKADA:	*Good evening.*
HONDA:	Tanaka san désu ka.	HONDA:	*Are you Mr Tanaka?*
NAKADA:	Iie, chigaimásu. Nakada désu.	NAKADA:	*No, I'm not. I'm Nakada.*
HONDA:	Dóomo shitsúrei shimashita.	HONDA:	*I'm very sorry.*
NAKADA:	Iie.	NAKADA:	*That's all right.*

C *Mr Nakagawa tentatively approaches a young man at the reception for the visiting trade delegation. Someone has told him there is a man called John from one of the British firms who can speak Japanese. Relieved to find he has the right man, Nakagawa introduces himself.*

中川: shitsureい ですが、onaまえは？
JÓN: Jonです。
中川: hajimeまshiて、中川です。
JÓN: どうぞ yoroshiku。

NAKAGAWA:	Shitsúrei desu ga, onamae wa?
JOHN:	Jón desu.
NAKAGAWA:	Hajimemáshite. Nakagawa désu.
JOHN:	Dóozo yoroshiku.

NAKAGAWA:	*Excuse me, but* (may I ask) *your name?*
JOHN:	*(It's) John.*
NAKAGAWA:	*How do you do? I'm Nakagawa.*
JOHN:	*Pleased to meet you.*

D *Sue Smith is so thrilled that she can write her name with the only three **katakána** symbols she knows she decides to have her name in*

Japanese put on her business card. Mr Yamamoto who runs a beach resort hotel in Shimoda looks a little bemused as he reads the card Sue has given him.

スミス:	watashiのmeいshiです。
山本:	aa、スー・スミスさんですne。
スミス:	はい、そうです。
山本:	山本です。どうぞ　yoroshiku。

SÚMISU:	Watashi no meishi désu.
YAMAMOTO:	Áa, Súu Súmisu san désu ne.
SÚMISU:	Hái, sóo desu.
YAMAMOTO:	Yamamoto désu. Dóozo yoroshiku.

SMITH:	(This) *is my business card.*
YAMAMOTO:	*Ah, you are Sue Smith, aren't you?*
SMITH:	*Yes, I am.*
YAMAMOTO:	*I'm Yamamoto. Glad to meet you.*

E *The following exchange is between Sue Smith and her close colleague Mr Tanaka. Sue picks up a book left on the table and asks Mr Tanaka if it is his. Notice how Sue uses Mr Tanaka's name where in English we would use the pronoun 'you'. The tone is rather casual and informal.*

スミス	田中さんの本ですか。
田中	はい、watashiの本です。
スミス	どうぞ。
田中:	どうmo。

SÚMISU:	Tanaka san no hón desu ka.
TANAKA:	Hái, watashi no hón desu.
SÚMISU:	Dóozo.
TANAKA:	Dóomo.

SMITH:	*Is this your book, Mr Tanaka?*
TANAKA:	*Yes. It's my book.*
SMITH:	*Here you are, then.*
TANAKA:	*Thanks.*

F *Mr Yamanaka introduces his workmate Mr Nakada to Ms Yamamoto, a customer from Shimoda on the Izu Peninsula south-west of Tokyo.*

山中:	ごshoうかい shiます。
	こちraは中田さんです。
	かいshaの とmodaちです。
中田:	中田です。どうぞyoroshiku。
山本:	はjimeまshiて。下田の山本です。

YAMANAKA:	Goshookai shimásu.	*Let me introduce you.*
	Kochira wa Nakada	*This is Mr Nakada.*
	san désu.	
	Kaisha no tomodachi désu.	*He is a friend from the company.*
NAKADA:	Nakada désu. Dóozo	*I'm Nakada. Pleased to*
	yoroshoku.	*meet you.*
YAMAMOTO:	Hajimemáshite.	*How do you do?*
	Shimoda no Yamamoto désu.	*I'm Yamamoto from Shimoda.*

G *After a fruitless few hours trying to interest Mr Yamamoto in new sail-board technology our friends Yamanaka and Nakada decide to finish the day with a **sake** or two at their favorite **izakaya** or Japanese pub. They part at about 10:30 p.m. so they will be fresh for another day at the office tomorrow.*

山中:	ja, さyonara。
中田:	oyaすmi naさい。
山中:	まta ashita。
中田:	ja, まta。

YAMANAKA:	Ja, sayonará.
NAKADA:	Oyasumi nasai.
YAMANAKA:	Mata ashita.
NAKADA:	Ja, mata.

YAMANAKA:	*Well, goodbye.*
NAKADA:	*Good night.*
YAMANAKA:	*See you tomorrow.*
NAKADA:	*See you, then.*

Vocabulary

oはyoうございます	**ohayoo gozaimásu**	*good morning*
こんばんは	**konban wa**	*good evening*
oyaすmi naさい	**oyasumi nasai**	*good night* (before retiring)
さyoうnara	**sayoonara**	*goodbye* (formal pronunciation)
さyonara	**sayonara**	*goodbye* (casual pronunciation)
まta ashita	**mata ashita**	*I'll see you again tomorrow*
jaまta	**ja mata**	*see you! I'll see you again* (casual)
ちがいます	**chigaimásu**	*that's not right, that's incorrect, no*
ariがとうございます	**arígatoo gozaimasu**	*thank you*
ariがとうございまshita	**arígatoo gozaimashita**	*thank you* (past tense)
どういtashiまshiて	**dóo itashimashite**	*not at all, don't mention it* (in reply to thanks)
shitsureいshiまta	**shitsúrei shimashita**	*pardon me, I'm sorry, it was rude of me, etc.*
shitsureい ですが、	**shitsúrei desu ga**	*excuse me, but …* (may I ask …, etc.)
どうぞ	**dóozo**	*please, go ahead, take one, etc.*
meいshi	**meishi**	*business card* (*note*: **ei** is pronounced **ee**)
本	**hón**	*book*
かいsha	**kaisha**	*company, firm*
ごshoうかいshiま	**goshookai shimásu**	*let me introduce*
onaまえ	**onamae**	*(your, his/her) name* (honorific)
naまえ	**namae**	*(my) name* (neutral)
とmodaち	**tomodachi**	*friend*
watashi	**watashi**	*I, me*
こちra	**kochira**	*this side, this person*

kiのう	**kinóo**	*yesterday*
ashita	**ashita**	*tomorrow*
また	**mata**	*again*
こそ	**kóso**	*indeed* (**kochira kóso** *I'm pleased to meet you, too*)

Particles

は	**wa**	*as for, speaking of* (topic particle)
の	**no**	*'s, belonging to* (possessive or descriptive particle)
と	**to**	*with, and*
か	**ka**	*?* (question particle)
ne	**ne**	*isn't it?, didn't we? aren't you?* (a tag question, seeks agreement from the listener)

Exercise 1.4 ■

Imagine the voice on the tape is talking to you. Listen carefully and give an appropriate answer. Turn off your cassette between questions if you need more time to respond. You will find the English prompts given below helpful, but remember they are not necessarily in the same order as the answers you'll need.

ENGLISH PROMPTS: *Don't mention it. Bye, I'll see you again tomorrow. My name is ...* (your name, but pronounced in a Japanese way if you can manage it). *How do you do? I'm* (your name). *Good night.*

Exercise 1.5

Copy out the following printed sentences and phrases in appropriate handwritten characters following the correct stroke order shown in the models given on pp. 15–18. Read them over several times until you are sure of the pronunciation and the meaning of each example. If you get stuck look up the readings in the Key to the Exercises.

1. 田中さんですか。はい、そうです。田中です。
2. 川本さんですか。いいえ、ちがいます。山本です。
3. 山と川と田
4. 山の中の田
5. 本田さんと田山さん

Exercise 1.6

Choose an appropriate response from the list on the right to the phrases on the left.

1. スミスさんの本ですか。 a. さyonara。
2. また ashita. b. はい、そうです。
3. どうそ yoroshiku. c. ちがいます。中田さんの本です。
4. こんばんは。 d. こちra こそ。
5. そうですか。 e. こんばんは。

Exercise 1.7 ■■

A comprehension

There is an optional barbecue lunch arranged for the Japanese guests and people from your company. As husbands and wives are also invited the gathering includes a range of occupations. Over lunch there is a lively discussion about the kind of work each of them is doing.

Listen to the tape and identify the occupations of all the guests mentioned. Write down the names with their respective occupations and check your answers with the key in the back of this book.

You will need some new vocabulary items for this exercise.

Occupations

かいshaいん	**kaisháin**	*company employee*
shacho う	**shachoo**	*director, company president, CEO*
bucho う	**buchoo**	*department head*
がkuseい	**gakusei**	*student*
こうmuいん	**koomúin**	*civil servant*
shufu	**shúfu**	*housewife*
kyo う shi	**kyóoshi**	*teacher*
いsha	**isha**	*doctor*
naん	**nán**	*what*
shi ごと	**shigoto**	(my) *job*, *work* (neutral)
oshi ごと	**oshígoto**	(your, his/her) *job*, *work* (honorific)

Dialogue

田中: 上田さんの　oshi ごとは naん ですか。
上田: kyo う shi です。田中さんは?

田中: が kuse いです。
山田: 本田さんの oshi ごとは na ん ですか。
本田: い sha です。 山田さんは かい sha いんですか。
山田: いいえ、こう mu いんです。
本田: そうですか。

B Practice

Now try asking some of your friends, real or imaginary, the following questions.

1. What is your occupation?
2. Are you a company employee?
3. Are you a housewife?
4. Ms Smith is a company director, isn't she?
5. Is Mr Yamada a student?

Exercise 1.8

You are waiting in the lobby of the hotel for your Japanese guests to come down to meet you. How will you greet them, assuming the time is:

1. 9:00 a.m.?   2. 1:00 p.m.?   3. 7:00 p.m.?
4. What would you say to them after you had brought them back to the hotel at 11:00 p.m.?
5. How would you say goodbye to your guests at the airport?
6. How many cultural keywords do you remember? **Katagaki**, **nigori**, **izakaya**, **myóoji**, **ojígi** and **itamae** were all introduced in Unit 1. Could you explain these concepts to your friend who is planning a trip to Japan?

2 自己紹介
Jiko-Shookai
Introducing yourself

In this unit you will learn how to:

- Say who you are and where you come from
- Say where you live and ask people where they live
- Tell people you are learning Japanese
- Discuss nationality, country and language
- Express your likes and dislikes.

You will also acquire:

- 15 more **hiragána:** あ り せ お よ し た な ら き く も わ み れ
- 5 more **kanji:** 日 国 人 語 英
- 5 more **katakána:** ア メ リ カ ラ

Dialogue 1 ■

You are at an international health conference. The chair person, Dr Nakayama, is getting the members of your panel to introduce themselves. You recognise a lot of the vocabulary introduced in Unit 1. You realise listening to the material over and over again gives you confidence. Practice makes perfect.

中山せんせい: スミスさん、じこしょうかい o お ne がい します。
スミスさん: はい、わかりました。
みなさん、おはよう ございます。
わたしはメアリー・スミスです。
Rondon から きました。

英国人です。
いま、日本語o　なら t ています。
どうぞよろしく。

中山せんせい：　ありがとう　ございました。
　　　　　　　Tsu ぎは リーさんを ごしょうかい します。

リーさん：　　どうも。
　　　　　　　はじ me まして。
　　　　　　　わたしは リーです。
　　　　　　　中国の Pekin からです。
　　　　　　　日本語がすこしできます。

中山せんせい：　リーさんのご shúmi は なんですか。

リーさん：　　Sak カーと　ラ gubiーです。
　　　　　　　りょうりも　すきです。

中山せんせい：　どうも ありがとう　ございました。

NAKAYAMA SENSÉI:	Súmisu san, jiko-shóokai o onegai shimásu.
SÚMISU SAN:	Hái, wakarimáshita.
	Minásan, ohayoo gozaimásu.
	Watashi wa Méarii Súmisu desu.
	Róndon kara kimáshita.
	Eikokújin desu.
	Íma, Nihongo o narátte imasu.
	Dóozo yoroshiku.
NAKAYAMA SENSÉI:	Arígatoo gozaimashita.
	Tsugí wa Ríi san o goshookai shimásu.
RÍI SAN:	Dóomo.
	Hajimemáshite.
	Watashi wa Ríi desu.
	Chúugoku no Pékin kara désu.
	Nihongo ga sukóshi dekimásu.
NAKAYAMA SENSÉI:	Ríi san no goshúmi wa nán desu ka.
RÍI SAN:	Sákkaa to rágubii desu.
	Ryóori mo sukí desu.
NAKAYAMA SENSÉI:	Dóomo arígatoo gozaimashita.

DR NAKAYAMA:	*Ms Smith, I'd like you to introduce yourself.*
MS SMITH:	*Yes, certainly.*
	Good morning everyone.
	I'm Mary Smith.
	I come from London.
	I'm British.
	Now I am learning Japanese.

DR NAKAYAMA:	*Next, let me introduce Mr Lee.*
MR LEE:	*Thanks. I'm Lee. I'm from Beijing in China.*
	I can speak a little Japanese.
DR NAKAYAMA:	*What are your interests, Mr Lee?*
MR LEE:	*Soccer and rugby. I'm also fond of cooking.*
DR NAKAYAMA:	*Thank you very much.*

Vocabulary

せんせい	**senséi**	*teacher, Dr, Mr, etc.* (title for teachers, doctors, etc.)
じこしょうかい	**jiko-shóokai**	*self-introduction*
お ne がい しま す	**onegai shimásu**	*please give us…, I'd like to ask you for…*
わかりました	**wakarimáshita**	*I understand, certainly*
みなさん	**minásan**	*everyone, all of you* (honorific)
から	**kara**	*from* (particle)
きました	**kimáshita**	(I) *came*
英国人	**Eikokújin**	*Briton, English* (person)
いま	**íma**	*now*
日本語	**Nihongo**	*Japanese*
なら t て いま す	**narátte imasu**	*is/am/are learning*
tsu ぎは	**tsugí wa**	*next*
中国	**Chúugoku**	*China*
Pekin	**Pékin**	*Peking, Beijing*
すこし	**sukóshi**	*a little*
できます	**dekimásu**	*can* (speak), *can do*
shu み	**shúmi**	*hobby, interest, pastime*
なんですか	**nán desu ka**	*what is it*
…が すきです	**…ga sukí desu**	(I) *like…*
sak カー	**sákkaa**	*soccer*
ラ gubi—	**rágubii**	*rugby* (union football)
りょうり	**ryóori**	*cooking*
も	**mo**	*also, too, even*

Hiragána

In this unit we learn fifteen more **hiragána** symbols. You have now seen 31 of the 46 **hiragána** symbols you will need to read and write Japanese. Practise writing them on squared paper following the examples below. Make sure you write the strokes in the correct order.

With the addition of the **nigori**, or voicing mark, this basic list can be extended to include:

ぜ **ze**   じ **ji**   だ **da**   ぎ **gi**   ぐ **gu**

Notice that the symbol for **sho** しょ is made up of the two **hiragána** characters for **shi** し and **yo** よ with the **yo** written smaller to indicate it should be pronounced as a single syllable with the preceding symbol. This in turn can be combined with the **nigori** mark to produce the syllable **jo**, じょ. As we have not yet learnt how to write double consonants, in this unit the first element of a double consonant is left in romanisation, e.g. **narátte** is written ならって. Similarly, most syllables that would be written in **katakána** will have to remain in romanised script until the symbols have been introduced. Of course many of the words written in **hiragána** in the early units will gradually be replaced with **kanji**.

Katakána

In this unit you learn five more **katakána** symbols, ア **a**, メ **me**, リ **ri**, カ **ka** and ラ **ra**. You will notice the similarity between the **hiragána** and **katakána** symbols for **ri** and **ka**. Note too, the raised dot in リー・ミラー (Dialogue 1) which is often used to indicate a break between words borrowed from foreign languages. Normally Japanese does not have spaces between words as the alternation of **kanji**, **hiragána** and **katakána** tends to break up the text into easily identifiable units. In textbooks such as this one and in material written for young children, however, spaces are often used to break up a sentence. Note that where spaces are used particles are always written attached to the preceding noun.

| a | me | ri | ka | ra |

Kanji

In this unit we introduce five more **kanji** characters. You will notice that some characters have two or more pronunciations, or readings. The readings written in capital letters are the pseudo-Chinese pronunciations, or **on**-readings, which are mostly used in compound words of two or more **kanji** characters. Contrasting with the **on**-readings are the native Japanese pronunciations, or **kun**-readings, given in lower case, which are most often used when a **kanji** character stands alone. There are, however, exceptions to this general rule, as we saw in Unit 1 with the **kun**-compounds which are common in personal names and place names. As we shall see in the next unit, the **kanji**, for '*person*', 人, also has the reading –**ri**, but only when combined with the numbers for 'one' and

NICHI	KOKU,	JIN	GO	EI
hi	–GOKU	hito	language	England,
sun, day	kuni	person		Britain
	country			

'two' in the words **hitóri** '*one person*' and **futari** '*two people*', so this reading is not listed separately below.

Exercise 2.1

Write these sentences in Japanese script, combining **hiragána**, **katakána** and **kanji** as appropriate.

1. Kawada san wa Nihonjín desu.
2. Rárii Miraa san wa Chúugoku ni súnde imasu.
3. Nihongo mo Chuugokugo mo dekimásu.
4. Ríi san wa íma Eigo o narátte imasu.
5. Yamamoto san wa Amerika ni súnde imasu.

Grammar points

The simple sentence introduced in Unit 1 is extended to include the present continuous tense of the verbs, 'to live', and 'to learn'. These sentence patterns should be learnt at this stage as vocabulary items without worrying too much about their grammatical structure. In due course you will understand the various forms and functions of the Japanese verbal system.

Sentence patterns

... **ni súnde imasu**	(s/he is, I am, you are, we are, they are) *living in...*
... **o narátte imasu**	(s/he is, I am, you are, we are, they are) *learning...*
... **ga wakarimásu**	(I, you, s/he, we, they, etc.) *understand...*
... **ga dekimásu**	(I) *can do, can speak...* (used with languages)
... **ga dekimasén**	(I) *can't do, can't speak...* (used with languages)
... **ga sukí desu**	(I) *like...*
... **ga sukí ja arimasén**	(I) *don't like...*
or ... **ga sukí dewa arimasén**	(I) *don't like...*
... **ga dáisuki desu**	(I) *love...*

You will notice that some verbs mark their objects with **o** and others with the particle **ga**. Actually, there is only a small group of verbs in this latter category, but it is convenient to introduce some of them now as they occur very frequently in everyday conversation. At this stage just be aware that different verbs require different particles. In the meantime, use the expressions introduced here simply as set phrases to add a little variety to your conversation.

Here are some more sports, hobbies and pastimes you will be able to work into your conversations. Most of these should not cause you any problems as they are borrowed from English. They would normally be written in **katakána**, but, as our main purpose at this point is to enrich your Japanese conversation, the vocabulary is provided here only in romanised form. Go through this list saying aloud either, 'I like …' or 'I don't like … very much' – only in Japanese, of course, i.e. … **ga sukí desu** or … **ga amari sukí ja arimasen**. As in these suggested sentence patterns it is usual to leave out the first person pronoun '**watashi wa**'.

ténisu *tennis*	**júudoo** *judo*
suiei *swimming*	**háikingu** *hiking*
basukétto (booru) *basketball*	**takkyuu** *table-tennis*
báree (booru) *volley ball*	**sáafin** *surfing*
hókkee *hockey*	**booringu** (10 pin) *bowling*
sukíi *skiing*	**jooba** *horse-riding*
karaóke *karaoke singing*	**ópera** *opera*
sukéeto *skating*	**shibai** *theatre*
yakyuu *baseball*	**éiga** *film, movie*
górufu *golf*	**kaimono** *shopping*
sumoo *sumo wrestling*	**ryokoo** *travel*
dókusho *reading*	

Perhaps you have an even stronger passion or affection for something else, which will require the use of **dáisuki** (or '*big like*'). This expression has a very wide usage ranging from food to people and most things in between. For example:

Watashi wa chokoréeto ga dáisuki desu.	*I love chocolate.*
Nihonjín wa yakyuu to sákkaa ga dáisuki desu.	*Japanese love baseball and soccer.*
Nihongo no senséi ga dáisuki desu.	*I love our Japanese teacher.*

Exercise 2.2 ■

Here is another passage demonstrating these structures. Read it out aloud before checking your understanding of the passage with the key at the back of the book. You will probably have to refer to the vocabulary list which follows the passage.

Paku さんと　リーさんは　かん国人です。かん国の Sóoru から
きました。いま、アメリカに　すんでいます。fu たりとも 英
語が　よく できます。日本語もすこしできます。
Paku さんは　rókku と　ス pootsu が　すきです。
リーさんは　rókku が　あまり すきではありません。
kurashikkū と　どくしょが　すきです。Paku さんと
リーさんはいま、ラリー・ミーアズさんの　うちに　すんで
います。ミーアズさんはアメリカ人です。アラスカに
すんでいます。いま、日本語 o なら t て います。
ミーアズさんの　shu みは　アメリカ n futtobooru と
ア i ス hokke一です。Teni スも すきです。

Vocabulary

かん国	**Kánkoku**	*Korea*
かん国人	**Kankokujín**	*Korean* (person)
So—ru	**Sóoru**	*Seoul*
ふたりとも	**futari tomo …**	*both of them*
よく	**yóku**	*well*
rokku	**rókku**	*rock* (music)
おんがく	**óngaku**	*music*
あまり	**amari**	(not) *much*, (not) *very*
こてんおんがく	**koten-óngaku**	*classical music* (more often **kuráshikku**)
どくしょ	**dókusho**	*reading*
うち	**uchi**	*house*
ス pootsu	**supóotsu**	*sports*
ア i ス hokke一	**ais uhókkee**	*ice-hockey*
アメリカ n futtobo一oru	**Amerikan fúttobooru**	*American football*

Country, language and nationality

Japanese uses the suffixes –**go** 語 and –**jin** 人 after the name of a country to express the language or a national of that country. Here is a list of countries, languages and nationals.

COUNTRY	LANGUAGE	PERSON
Eikoku 英国 *England, Britain*	**Eigo** 英語 *English*	**Igirisújin Igiri** ス人 (regular form, **Eikokújin**, not often used) *the British*
Nihón 日本 *Japan*	**Nihongo** 日本語 *Japanese*	**Nihonjín** 日本人 *Japanese*
Kánkoku かん国 *Korea*	**Kankokugo** かん国語 *Korean*	**Kankokujín** かん国人 *Korean*
Chúugoku 中国 *China*	**Chuugkugo** 中国語 *Chinese*	**Chuugokújin** 中国人 *Chinese*

Note that **Kánkoku** refers only to South Korea. North Korea is generally called **Kita Choosen**.

Here are some more continents, countries and cities. How is your **katakána** reading coming along?

Yooróppa		*Europe*
Ájia	ア ji ア	*Asia*
Afurika	ア fu リ カ	*Africa*
Amerika	アメリカ	*America*
Oosutorária	Oo ス to ラリア	*Australia*
Tái	Tai	*Thailand*
Furansu	Fu ラ n ス	*France*
Róndon	Rondon	*London*
Pári	Pa リ	*Paris*
Itaria	Ita リア	*Italy*
Supéin	ス pein	*Spain*
Airurándo	ア iru ラ ndo	*Ireland*
Kánada	カ nada	*Canada*
Nyuujiirándo	Nyuujii ラ ndo	*New Zealand*
Indo	Indo	*India*
Róoma	Ro―ma	*Rome*
Suéeden	ス e―den	*Sweden*
Shídonii	Shidoni―	*Sydney*
Doitsu	Doitsu	*Germany*
Arasuka	アラスカ	*Alaska*

Exercise 2.3

Using the written cues below, ask each member of your group which country he or she comes from. Then take the part of the other person and make an appropriate response, again relying on the cues given. Some of the cues will also test your ability to read **kanji** and **katakána**. Remember in Japanese it is usual to use the name of the person you are talking to rather than the pronoun, 'you'. For example:

Cue: **Paku** Korea

Q: **Paku san wa dóchira kara kimashitaka** or **Paku san wa dóchira kara desu ka.**

A: **(Watashi wa) Kánkoku kara kimáshita** or **(watashi wa) Kánkoku kara desu.**

1. 山川   日本   2. ア リ   India   3. Han   Korea
4. ミ ラ ー 英国   5. メ ア リ ー ア ラ ス カ   6. リ ー   中国

Exercise 2.4

A new Japanese student has joined your aerobics class. You decide to use the opportunity to practise your Japanese by introducing her to the members of your cosmopolitan group. You give the nationality of each member of your class and mention what other languages they speak. Use the following cues to guide your Japanese explanations. For example:

Cue: Kim Korea Spanish

Kochira wa Kímu san desu. Kímu san wa Kankokujín desu. Supeingo mo dekimásu.

1. Wang   2. Baker   3. Braun
   China   England   Germany
   Japanese   French   Chinese
4. Rani   5. Gordon
   India   America
   Thai   Russian

Exercise 2.5

How would you ask someone where he or she lives? When you have asked the question, make an appropriate reply using the word supplied in brackets. For example:

Cue: **Honda** (Tokyo)

Q: **Honda san wa dóko ni súnde imasu ka.**

A: **Tookyoo ni súnde imasu.**

1. 山本	2. 国本	3. スミス	4. リー
(Nagoya)	(Sapporo)	(London)	(Beijing)
5. Leclerc	6. カー	7. メカリ	8. Kim
(Paris)	(Sydney)	(Rome)	(Seoul)

Exercise 2.6 ▮▮

Listen carefully to the tape. One of the students in your Japanese class is telling you where her friends come from. See if you can match all the names and nationalities correctly.

Hérena san wa watashi no Nihongo no kúrasu no tomodachi désu. Suéeden kara kimáshita. Érikku san mo Nihongo ga sukóshi dekimásu. Doitsújin desu. Píitaa san wa Nyuujiirandójin desu. Kímu san wa Sóuru kara kimáshita. Kankokujín desu. Méarii san wa Amerikájin desu. Edouíina san wa Igirisu kara kimáshita. Bóbu san wa Oosutorária kara desu. Minna watashi no Nihongo no kúrasu no tomodachi desu. Watashi wa Nihongo ga sukí desu. Kurasuméeto mo minná sukí desu.

Vocabulary

kúrasu	*class*
kurasuméeto	*classmate*
minná	*all, everyone*

Exercise 2.7 ▮▮

Now, using the English prompts below, tell your new Japanese friend about the hobbies of the various members of your class. This time the prompts will be given on the tape and there will be a short pause to give you time to answer. A model answer for each question will be provided on the tape and in the key at the back of the book. Follow this example:

Cue: Helena   movies   rock-music

Hélena san no shúmi wa éiga to rokku desu.

1. Michael	2. Robert	3. Anne
surfing	horse-riding	music
basketball	soccer	hiking

4. Karl
   reading
   travel

5. Gordon
   swimming
   baseball

6. you
   shopping
   tennis

Exercise 2.8 ■■

Listen to Dialogue 2 on the tape and see if you can answer the following comprehension questions. Only turn to the written text after you have made two or three attempts to answer the questions after listening to the tape.

1. Where does Mr Miller live?
2. Does Mr Kim live in Korea?
3. What language does Mr Miller speak a little?
4. Does Mr Kim speak Thai?
5. What is Mr Kim's hobby?

Dialogue 2 ■■

During the morning tea break at the conference Mr Kim finds himself in a long queue waiting for coffee. To pass the time he talks to the person in front of him. Listen to the dialogue and answer the questions which follow this passage.

KÍMU: はじ me まして、わたしは Kim です。どうぞよろしく。

ミラー: はじ me まして、ミラーです。
こちらこそ、どうぞよろしく。

KÍMU: ミラーさんのお国はどこですか。

ミラー: O—ス to ラリアです。でも、いま中国にすんでいます。
Kim さんは どちらからですか。

KÍMU: わたしは かん国人ですが、
いま Tái にすんでいます。

ミラー: そうですか。Tai 語が できますか。

KÍMU: いいえ、できません。
ミラーさんは 中国語が できますか。

ミラー: ええ。すこし だ ke。
とこ ro で Kim さんの ご shu みは なんですか。

KÍMU: ス po—tsu です。
Górufu がすきです。

ミラー: わたしも górufu がすきです。

Vocabulary

お国	**okuni**	*your country* (honorific)
どこ	**dóko**	*where*
どちら	**dóchira**	*which one, where* (polite)
できません	**dekimasén**	*can't speak, can't do*
ええ	**ée**	*yes*
だ ke	**dake**	*only*
とこ ro で	**tokoró de**	*by the way ...*

3 家族の話
Kázoku no hanashi
Talking about families

In this unit you will learn how to:

- Use neutral and honorific terms for family members
- Count people with the numeral classifiers **–ri** and **–nin**
- Say 'this', 'that' and 'that over there'
- Tell the time
- Name the months of the year
- Count from 1 to 99
- Give and ask for telephone numbers.

You will also acquire:

- 15 more **hiragána:** け つ ぬ ね ひ ふ へ ほ む め や ゆ る ろ を
- 20 more **kanji:** 一 二 三 四 五 六 七 八 九 十 男 女 子 大 小 好 時 何 月 半
- 5 more **katakána:** タ ク シ イ ハ

Dialogue 1 ▣

Mr Cooper is visiting his neighbour Mr Yamashita, who has invited him in for a cup of tea. After a while Mr Yamashita produces a pile of photos, which he proceeds to spread out on the coffee table in front of them.

クーパー: それは 何ですか。
山下: これは ちちの かんれきの しゃしんです。
クーパー: かんれき?
山下: 六十さいの たんじょうびです。
クーパー: そうですか。

山下:　　　これは　ちちと　ははです。
クーパー:　おとうさんは　わかい　ですねえ。
山下:　　　ええ、げんきです。teni スと gorufu が　好きです。
クーパー:　それは　だれの　しゃしんですか。
山下:　　　これは　あにと　あねです。
　　　　　　あには　どくしん　ですが、あねは　けっこん
　　　　　　しています。
クーパー:　にて　いますねえ。あれは　だれですか。
山下:　　　どれですか。ああ、　あれは　いもうとの　子ども
　　　　　　です。
クーパー:　かわいいですねえ。何さい　ですか。
山下:　　　二さい　です。
クーパー:　女の子　ですか。
山下:　　　いいえ、女の子　では　ありません。男の子です。

KÚUPAA:　　Sore wa nán desu ka.
YAMÁSHITA:　Kore wa chichi no kanreki no shashin désu.
KÚUPAA:　　Kanreki?
YAMÁSHITA:　Rokujússai no tanjóobi desu.
KÚUPAA:　　Sóo desu ka.
YAMÁSHITA:　Kore wa chichí to háha desu.
KÚUPAA:　　Otóosan wa wakái desu née.
YAMÁSHITA:　Ée, génki desu.
　　　　　　Ténisu to górufu ga sukí desu.
KÚUPAA:　　Sore wa dáre no shashin desu ka.
YAMÁSHITA:　Kore wa áni to ane désu.
　　　　　　Áni wa dokushin désu ga, ane
　　　　　　wa kekkon shite imásu.
KÚUPAA:　　Nite imásu née.
　　　　　　Are wa dáre (no shashin) desu ka.
YAMÁSHITA:　Dóre desu ka.
　　　　　　Áa, are wa imooto no kodomo désu.
KÚUPAA:　　Kawaíi desu née. Nánsai desu ka.
YAMÁSHITA:　Nísai desu.
KÚUPAA:　　Onnánoko desu ka.
YAMÁSHITA:　Iie, onnánoko dewa arimasén. Otokónoko desu.

COOPER:　　*What's that?*
YAMASHITA:　*These are my father's kanreki photos.*
COOPER:　　*Kanreki?*
YAMASHITA:　*It's the 60th birthday.*

COOPER:	*Really?*
YAMASHITA:	*This one's my mother and father.*
COOPER:	*Your father's young, isn't he?*
YAMASHITA:	*Yes. He's fit.*
	He likes tennis and golf.
COOPER:	*Whose photo is that?*
YAMASHITA:	*This is my elder brother and elder sister.*
	My brother is a bachelor,
	but my sister is married.
COOPER:	*They look alike, don't they?*
	Who's (or whose photo is) that?
YAMASHITA:	*Which one?*
	Oh, that's my younger sister's child.
COOPER:	*Cute, isn't it? How old?*
YAMASHITA:	*Two years old.*
COOPER:	*Is it a girl?*
YAMASHITA:	*No, it's not a girl. It's a boy.*

Vocabulary

それ	**sore**	*that* (near addressee)
これ	**kore**	*this* (close to speaker)
あれ	**are**	*that* (over there)
ちち	**chichi**	*father* (neutral)
かんれき	**kanreki**	*60th birthday*
しゃしん	**shashin**	*photograph*
六十さい	**rokujússai**	*60 years old*
たんじょうび	**tanjóobi**	*birthday*
はは	**háha**	*mother* (neutral)
おとうさん	**otóosan**	*father* (honorific)
わかい	**wakái**	*young*
げんき	**génki**	*fit, well, healthy*
あに	**áni**	*elder brother*
あね	**ane**	*elder sister*
どくしん	**dokushin**	*bachelor, single/ unmarried person*
けっこん しています	**kekkon shite imásu**	(is) *married*
にています	**nite imásu**	*looks like, resembles, look alike*
だれ	**dáre**	*who?*
どれ	**dóre**	*which one?*

いもうと	**imootó**	*younger sister*
子ども	**kodomo**	*child*
かわいい	**kawaíi**	*cute, appealing*
何さい	**nánsai**	*how many years old?*
二さい	**nísai**	*two years old*
女の子	**onnánoko**	*girl*
男の子	**otokónoko**	*boy*
ねえ/ね	**née/né**	*isn't it*, etc. (question markers; the former is slightly more formal)

Hiragána

In this unit we meet a further 15 **hiragána** symbols.

You have now been introduced to the 46 **hiragána** symbols. The full chart included in the Appendix (see p. 306) lists all the **hiragána** syllables. The shaded rows indicate the basic symbols in the traditional order. Read across the page from the upper left hand corner. You can remember the order of the rows with the mnemonic, '*a kana syllabary, think now how much you really want* (to learn it)'.

One more rule you will need to learn is how to form a double conso-nant sequence with the use of the **hiragána** symbol for **tsu** つ, written smaller to indicate that it is pronounced without its usual vowel as the first element of a double consonant. For example:

tta った, **kko** っこ, **sshi** っし, etc.

The first element of –**nn**–, however, is ん:

e.g. おんなの人 **onnánohito**, *a woman*

Note the following combinations with the **y**– syllables. Here the **y**– sylla-bles are written smaller to indicate they are to combine with the preced-ing **hiragána** and are pronounced as a single syllable. We have already learnt the **hiragána** syllables **sho** しょ and **jo** じょ in Unit 2.

kya きゃ	**kyu** きゅ	**kyo** きょ
gya ぎゃ	**gyu** ぎゅ	**gyo** ぎょ
sha しゃ	**shu** しゅ	**sho** しょ
ja じゃ	**ju** じゅ	**jo** じょ
cha ちゃ	**chu** ちゅ	**cho** ちょ
nya にゃ	**nyu** にゅ	**nyo** にょ
hya ひゃ	**hyu** ひゅ	**hyo** ひょ
mya みゃ	**myu** みゅ	**myo** みょ
rya りゃ	**ryu** りゅ	**ryo** りょ

Syllables with b and p

The syllables beginning with **b**– or **p**– are formed from the symbols in the **h**– line. **b**– is made with the **nigori** mark and **p**– with a small raised circle, known as **maru**, for example:

は	ひ	ふ	へ	ほ	ひゃ	ひゅ	ひょ
ha	**hi**	**fu**	**he**	**ho**	**hya**	**hyu**	**hyo**
ば	び	ぶ	べ	ぼ	びゃ	びゅ	びょ
ba	**bi**	**bu**	**be**	**bo**	**bya**	**byu**	**byo**
ぱ	ぴ	ぷ	ぺ	ぽ	ぴゃ	ぴゅ	ぴょ
pa	**pi**	**pu**	**pe**	**po**	**pya**	**pyu**	**pyo**

P in particular, is only rarely found in native Japanese words. You will normally encounter it in loan words, e.g. パス **pásu** '*a pass*', スーパー **súupaa** '*a supermarket*', when, of course, it is written in **katakána**.

Katakána

Here are five more **katakána** symbols.

These can be combined with the eight **katakána** symbols you have learnt so far to write a large number of loan words from English and other languages. Remember that the **katakána** symbols follow the same spelling conventions outlined above for **hiragána**.

Exercise 3.1 ■

Look at the list of **katakána** words below and see if you can guess what each one means (we have used romaji where you have not yet learnt the **katakána**). When you have read through the list a few times, try listening to the tape and imitating the pronunciation of your Japanese instructor.

1. タクシー
2. イタリア
3. アイス
4. pa スタ
5. バー
6. カラー・**terebi**
7. メーカー
8. カメラ
9. ライター
10. クーラー

Now, using the words introduced above, see if you can translate the following phrases into Japanese, then write them with **katakána** words or **kanji** joined by the particle **no** の.

11. Italian pasta
12. a camera manufacturer
13. a Japanese colour television
14. an American lighter
15. air-conditioner for a taxi

Kanji

In this unit we introduce more **kanji** than usual to include the numbers from 1 to 10, in addition to ten more basic characters.

ICHÍ hito- one	NI futa- two	SAN three	SHI yon four	GÓ five
ROKU six	SHICHÍ nana- seven	HACHÍ eight	KÚ, KYÚU nine	JÚU ten
otoko man	onna woman	ko child	DAI oo (kii) large	SHOO chii (sai) small
su (ki) like	JI toki o'clock hours	nán, náni what	–GATSU month	HAN half

Numbers and counting ▮

Just as we say, 'two bottles of milk', 'three planks of wood' or 'three head of cattle', in which 'bottles', 'planks' and 'head' might be regarded as numeral classifiers appropriate to the kind of object we are counting, Japanese employs a number of classifiers for counting objects depending on their shape and size. We have included a fairly comprehensive list of these numeral classifiers in the Grammar Summary (see p. 302).

Up to 10, Japanese has two sets of numbers, one a native Japanese set and the other borrowed from Chinese. In this unit the **kanji** for the numbers 1 to 10 are introduced with a few simple counters or units of measurement which require the pseudo-Chinese pronunciation, or the **on**-reading.

Although the **kanji** for the numbers are used frequently with small numbers and in telling the time or enumerating the months of the year, etc., the Arabic numerals are commonly used in everyday communication and, of course, are used exclusively for mathematics or finance.

You will notice that the numbers 4, 7 and 9 each have two pronunciations. **Yón** is often used instead of **shi**, which has the same pronunciation as the Japanese word for 'death'. **Nána** often replaces **shichí** as this latter is too easily confused with 1 **ichí**, 4 **shí** and 8 **hachí**. The pronunciations **kú**– and **kyúu**– are both common. Which one is used seems to be largely a matter of convention and depends on just what is being counted, though at times it seems either of the two pronunciations can be used. **Kú** like **shí** has an inauspicious meaning as it is a homophone for **kú** meaning '*suffering*'.

With the ten number **kanji** you can count from 1 to 99. '*Eleven*' is **juuichí** 十一 or '*ten-one*', fifteen is '*ten-five*' or **júugo** 十五, '*twenty*' is '*two-ten*' or **níjuu** 二十, and '*ninety-eight*' is **kyúujuu-hachí** 九十八 or '*nine-ten-eight*'. '*Forty*' is generally **yónjuu** rather than **shijúu**, though you will also hear this form, '*seventy*' is **nanájuu** and '*ninety*' is **kyúujuu**.

Exercise 3.2

Identify the following numbers. Pronounce them all in Japanese and write in **kanji** those numbers given in Arabic numerals.

1. 6	2. 5	3. 18
4. 27	5. 62	6. 四
7. 四十五	8. 九	9. 七十六
10. 十三		

The months of the year ■■

The months from January to December are formed with the ending –**gatsú** which is used for naming, but not counting, the months of the year. In this case April, the fourth month is pronounced **shigatsú** (**yón** is not used in this case) and July (the seventh month) is **shichigatsú**.

January	February	March	April	May	June
一月	二月	三月	四月	五月	六月
ichigatsú	**nigatsú**	**sangatsú**	**shigatsú**	**gogatsú**	**rokugatsú**

July	August	September	October	November	December
七月	八月	九月	十月	十一月	十二月
shichigatsú	**hachigatsú**	**kugatsú**	**juugatsú**	**juuichigatsú**	**juunigatsú**

Nángatsu 何月 means 'which month'.

Telling the time

The **on**-readings of the numerals are also used for telling the time, but sound changes occur when the word for minute, **–fun**, combines with the numerals other than **go** '*five*'. So in this unit we introduce only, **–ji**, '*o'clock*', used for counting the hours of the day, **hán**, which means '*half*' and is used to indicate time half-past the hour, and **–fun**, which means '*minute*' in combination with **–go**, '*five*'. There is one slight irregularity in combination with **–ji**, when **yón** loses its final **–n** to form the word for 4 o'clock, **yóji**.

The words for '*a.m.*' and '*p.m.*' are, respectively, **gozen** and **gógo**. In accordance with the structure of Japanese sentences, which run from the general to the particular, hours come before minutes. Here are some examples of how you tell the time in Japanese. Notice the question word **nán** in **nánji desu ka**, 何時ですか, '*What time is it?*'

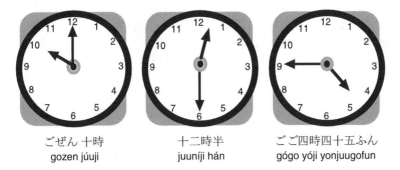

ごぜん 十時
gozen júuji

十二時半
juuníji hán

ごご四時四十五ふん
gógo yóji yonjuugofun

Telephone numbers

The numbers introduced in this unit are also used for telephone numbers, serial numbers, account numbers and so on. Zero is either **réi** or the

English word **zéro**. Sometimes a telephone number can be broken up into smaller components, such as its area code etc., with the addition of the particle **no**. When giving a telephone number Japanese usually lengthen the short vowels in **ni** ('*two*') and **go** ('*five*') to give **níi** and **góo** respectively. Here are some examples of telephone numbers, bank account numbers and computer passwords.

1. 三四六一 の 二七〇八   2. 三五九四 七七〇二   3. 三二〇八
   San yón rokú ichi no   **San góo kyúu yón (no)**   **San níi**
   níi nána zéro hachí   **nána nána zéro níi**   **zéro hachí**

Exercise 3.3 ■■

Practise pronouncing these times, telephone numbers and account codes after the instructor. Write down the first five examples from dictation. The answers are given in the key at the end of the book (p. 262).

6. 三四六一 の 二七〇八   7. 三五九四 七七〇二   8. 三二〇八
9. 26-3465-8791   10. (03) 9786-3342

Age

One way to express age in Japanese is by adding the ending –**sai** to the **on**-readings of the numbers. Japanese generally feel no compunction about asking you how old you are regardless of your sex. Although the old Confucian values are breaking down in modern Japan, it is still true that older people are afforded a good deal more respect and consideration than they are generally in most western societies. The point of asking your age is often to determine whether you are older or younger than the questioner, thereby establishing the degree of respect and deference you should be given. In addition to the expression, **nánsai desu ka**, introduced in this unit, you may also hear, **oikutsu désu ka**, which means the same thing, but is more polite. Notice the sound changes which occur when –**sai** follows the numerals 1, 8 and 10, **íssai** '*one year old*', **hássai** '*eight years old*' and **jússai** '*ten years old*'. Of course, these affect all the numbers which end in 1, 8 or 10, e.g. **nanajússai**, '*70 years old*'.

Family members

Japanese generally has two terms, an honorific term and a neutral term, for each family member. The honorific term is used for referring to or addressing people outside your own family circle or for addressing senior members of your own family. The neutral term is used when you are talking to others about members of your family. Here is a family tree with the honorific terms of reference or address written in bold with the neutral terms given in parentheses beneath. When addressing your younger brother or sister the given name is used, but when referring to someone else's younger brother or sister it is usual to attach the polite address form **san**, e.g. **imootó san** '(your) *younger sister*', **otootó san** '(your) *younger brother*'. Notice that there is no general term for brother or sister in Japanese. You have to indicate whether you are dealing with an older or a younger sibling. The term

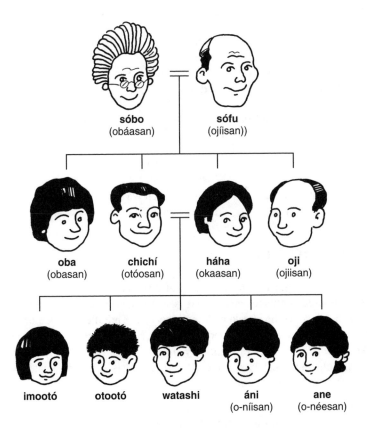

kyóodai means '*brothers and sisters*'. In Japanese you usually include yourself when counting **kyóodai**, e.g. **uchi wa yonin kyóodai desu** '*there are four children in our family*' or '*I have three brothers and sisters*'.

In Japanese you refer to your own wife as **kánai**, but to someone else's wife as **ókusan**. Similarly, '*my husband*' is **shújin**, but '*your husband*' or '*her husband*' is **goshújin** with the honorific prefix, **go–**, attached. You refer to your own children as **kodomo**, but other people's children as **okósan**.

Exercise 3.4 ■

Respond to the questions on the tape using the cues given below and the appropriate term for the family relationship. For example:

Q: **Ojisan wa oikutsu désu ka.** (35)
A: **Oji wa sanjuugósai desu.**

1. Otóosan wa nánsai desu ka. (65)
2. Onéesan wa nánsai desu ka. (29)
3. Okáasan wa oikutsu désu ka. (48)
4. Oníisan wa nánsai desu ka. (32)

The following are not recorded on the tape. Check your responses in the Key to the Exercises on p. 262.

5. Otootó san wa nánsai desu ka. (23)
6. Ojíisan wa oikutsu désu ka. (92)
7. Obáasan wa oikutsu désu ka. (87)
8. Imootó san wa nánsai desu ka. (17)

This and that

Japanese distinguishes three degrees of distance from the speaker. **Kore** '*this*' is used pretty much as 'this' is in English, referring to objects or persons close to the speaker. Something in the middle distance or close to or associated with the listener, or addressee, is **sore**, '*that*' (by you). **Are**, '*that over there*' or '*that by him*' is used to refer to objects away from both the speaker and the addressee and is often associated with a third person. For example:

Q: **Sore wa nán desu ka.** *What's that?*
A: **Kore wa chichi no shashin desu.** *This is a photo of my father.*

Q: **Are wa nán desu ka.** *What's that* (over there)?
A: **Are wa Nihongo no hón desu.** *That's a Japanese book.*

Dialogue 2 ■

You ask Mr Tanaka about his family and tell him about yours. It's reassuring to learn that a Japanese businessman is as concerned about his family as he is about his work. There is a transcription of this dialogue in the Key to Exercises.

スミス:　田中さん、お子さんは　何人　いらっしゃいますか。
田中:　うちは三人です。男の子二人と女の子一人います。
　　　おたくは?
スミス:　うちも三人です。女の子が二人と男の子が一人います。
　　　上の子は男の子で、下と まん中は女の子です。
　　　田中さんの上のお子さんはどちらですか。
田中:　上は女の子です。大がくせいです。まん中の男の子はこ
　　　うこうせいです。下の 子 はまだ中がくせいです。
スミス:　うちの子どもはまだ小さいです。上の男の子は小がくせ
　　　いです。二人の女の子は まだようちえんです。
田中:　それじゃあ、おくさんは　まいにち　おいそがしい　で
　　　しょうね。
スミス:　そうです。わたしも大へんですよ。

SMITH:　*How many children are in your family, Mr Tanaka?*
TANAKA:　*We have three children, two boys and a girl. What about you?*
SMITH:　*We also have three children, two girls and a boy. The eldest is a boy. The youngest and the middle are girls. What's your eldest, Mr Tanaka?*
TANAKA:　*The eldest is a girl. She is a university student. The middle boy is in high school. The youngest is still in junior high school.*
SMITH:　*Our children are still small. The eldest boy is in primary school. The two girls are still in kindergarten.*
TANAKA:　*Then, your wife must be very busy every day.*
SMITH:　*Yes. It's tough on me too!*

Vocabulary

| いらっしゃいます | **irasshaimásu** | *to be, to have* (honorific verb, cannot be used to refer to oneself or one's own family) |

子	ko	*child, son* (sometimes daughter)
お子さん	okosan	*child, your child* (honorific expression, not used to refer to one's own children)
まん中	mannaka	*middle*
大がく	dáigaku	*university*
大学せい	daigákusei	*university student*
こうこう	kookoo	*high school* (short for **kootoo-gákkoo**)
こうこうせい	kookóosei	*high school student*
中がっこう	chuugákusei	*junior high school student* (literally, 'middle school student')
小さい	chiisái	*small, little* (young, of children)
小がくせい	shoogákusei	*primary school pupil*
ようちえん	yoochíen	*kindergarten*
おくさん	ókusan	(your) *wife* (honorific)
まい日	mainichi	*everyday*
おいそがしい	oisogashíi	*busy* (honorific)
おたく	otaku	*your house*; *you*
よ	yo	*I'm telling you!, you know,* etc. (emphatic or assertive particle)

Exercise 3.5 ■

Listen to this passage on the tape, check the new vocabulary listed below and then answer the questions.

Harry Clark is having a chat with his university classmate, Kazuo Honda about their respective families. Coming from a small family himself, Harry Clark is surprised to hear how large Honda san's family is. You will find a romanised version of this passage in the Key to the Exercises (p. 263).

本田一男: うちのかぞくは　そふと　そぼ、ちちと　はは、
　　　　　あにと　あね、
　　　　　いもうとと　おとうと、それに わたしです。
　　　　　ぜんぶで　九人です。
　　　　　ちちは　こうむいんで、ははは　しゅふです。
　　　　　あには　かいしゃいんです。りょこうがいしゃの
　　　　　しゃいんです。

あねは 大がくせいです。かいものが
好きです。
いもうとは ちゅうがくせいです。
おとうとは しょうがくせいです。
いもうとも おとうとも ス po一ツが
好きです。

ハリー・クラーク:	たくさん ですね。
本田一男:	ええ。クラークさんは きょうだいが いますか。
ハリー・クラーク:	いいえ、いません。ひとりっこです。

Vocabulary

一男	**Kazuo**	*a common boy's name* (note irregular readings of **kanji** in names)
それに	**sore ni**	*and, in addition*
ぜんぶで	**zénbu de**	*altogether, in total*
で	**de**	*is … and is … and* (linking clauses, cf. **to** between nouns)
りょこうがいしゃ	**ryokoo-gáisha**	*travel company*
たくさん	**takusán**	*many, a lot*
きょうだい	**kyóodai**	*brothers and sisters, siblings*
一人っ子、ひとりっこ	**hitoríkko**	*only child*
しゅふ	**shúfu**	*homemaker*

Questions

1. How many in Kazuo Honda's family?
2. How many children in Harry Clark's family?
3. What does Mr Honda's younger brother like doing?
4. What is his father's job?
5. Where does his elder brother work?
6. What does his elder sister enjoy doing?
7. What work does his mother do?
8. What kind of school does his younger brother attend?

Exercise 3.6

Imagine you are Kazuo Honda answering Harry Clark's questions about the hobbies and pastimes of the various members of his family. Frame your answers using the English cues provided. For example:

Q: **Ojíisan no shúmi wa nán desu ka.**
Cue: golf
A: **Sófu no shúmi wa górufu desu.**

1. Obáasan no shúmi wa nán desu ka.	travel (**ryokoo**)
2. Otóosan no shúmi wa nán desu ka.	kendo (**kéndoo,** *Japanese fencing*)
3. Okáasan no shúmi wa nán desu ka.	tennis
4. Oníisan no shúmi wa nán desu ka.	soccer

The following are not recorded on the cassette tape. Check your answers with the Key to the Exercises (p. 263).

5. Otooto san no shúmi wa nán desu ka.	surfing (**sáafin**)
6. Onéesan no shúmi wa nán desu ka.	shopping
7. Ojíisan no shúmi wa nán desu ka.	reading books
8. Imooto san no shúmi wa nán desu ka.	basketball

Exercise 3.7

Harry Clark decides to investigate the business hours of the shops and businesses he will be using during his stay in Japan. How would he ask the business hours of the following places and what answer would he expect to receive? Use the cues below to generate the questions and provide the answers. For example:

Cue: post-office (**yuubínkyoku**), 10:00 a.m., 5:30 p.m.
Q: **Yuubínkyoku wa nánji kara nánji made desu ka.**
A: **(Yuubínkyoku wa) gozen júuji kara gógo goji-hán made desu.**

1. Bank, 10:00 a.m., 4:30 p.m.
2. Shops, 10:30 a.m., 7:00 p.m.
3. Supermarket, 7:00 a.m., 8:00 p.m.
4. Department store, 10:30 a.m., 9:00 p.m.
5. Convenience store, 6:00 a.m., 11:30 p.m.

You will need some more vocabulary items to complete this exercise.

Vocabulary

ぎんこう	**ginkoo**	*bank*
ゆうびんきょく	**yuubínkyoku**	*post office*
re ス to ラ n	**résutoran**	*restaurant*
スーパー	**súupaa**	*supermarket*
みせ	**misé**	*shop, shops*
de パ—to	**depáato**	*department store*
konbini	**konbíni**	*convenience store*
から	**kara**	*from*
まで	**máde**	*until, to, up to*
何時から何時まで	**nánji kara nánji made**	*from what time until what time?*

Exercise 3.8

Ask what month someone's birthday falls in, then answer the question using the cues given below. For example:

Cue: 山田、　十二月
Q:　山田さんの　たんじょうびは　何月ですか。
A:　(山田さんの　たんじょうびは)　十二月です。

1. おとうさん、　四月
2. 山川せんせい、　八月
3. クラークさんの　おくさん、　十月
   (in answering pretend you are Harry Clark)
4. お子さん、　六月
5. おばあさん、　九月

4 買い物
Kaimono
Shopping

In this unit you will learn how to:

- Ask how much things are
- Describe things
- Say where things are located
- Use the demonstrative adjectives
- Make simple requests
- Count the storeys in a building
- Use larger numbers.

You will also acquire:

- 10 more **kanji**   百 千 万 円 高 安 学 校 先 生
- 10 more **katakána** フ コ ン ヒ キ ユ マ モ ツ ヘ

Dialogue 1 ■■

Browsing in one of Tokyo's famous department stores you overhear this conversation at a specialist counter selling scarves. You recognise Mr Yamada, whom you met in Unit 1. He is talking to a young woman behind the sales counter.

山田:	きれいなスカーフですね。
てんいん:	ええ、めずらしい　いろです。
山田:	いくらですか。
てんいん:	一万円　です。いい　ものですよ。
山田:	もうすこし安いのは　ありませんか。

てんいん:	はい、ございます。
	そのスカーフは いかがですか。
山田:	どのスカーフですか。
てんいん:	その小さいのです。
山田:	いろが ちょっと。
	ともだちの たんじょうびの プreze ン to です。
てんいん:	おともだちは おいくつですか。
山田:	二十さい です。
てんいん:	では あのスカーフは いかがですか。
	おねだんは そう高く ありません。
山田:	いくらですか。
てんいん:	八千円です。
山田:	では、それを下さい。
てんいん:	かしこまりました。

YAMADA:	Kírei na sukáafu desu ne.
TEN'IN:	Ée, mezurashíi iró desu.
YAMADA:	Íkura desu ka.
TEN'IN:	Ichiman'en desu. Íi monó desu yo.
YAMADA:	Moo sukóshi yasúi no wa arimasén ka.
TEN'IN:	Hái, gozaimásu.
	Sono sukáafu wa ikága desu ka.
YAMADA:	Dóno sukaafu desu ka.
TEN'IN:	Sono chiisái no desu.
YAMADA:	Iró ga chótto…
	Tomodachi no tanjóobi no purézento desu.
TEN'IN:	Otomodachi wa oikutsu désu ka.
YAMADA:	Nijússai desu.
TEN'IN:	Déwa, ano sukáafu wa ikága desu ka.
	Onédan wa sóo tákaku arimasen.
YAMADA:	Íkura desu ka.
TEN'IN:	Hassen'en désu.
YAMADA:	Déwa, sore o kudasái.
TEN'IN:	Kashikomarimáshita.

YAMADA:	*It's a beautiful scarf, isn't it?*
SHOP ASSISTANT:	*Yes. It's an unusual colour.*
YAMADA:	*How much is it?*
SHOP ASSISTANT:	*It's ten thousand yen. It's a good one!*
YAMADA:	*Don't you have any a bit cheaper?*

SHOP ASSISTANT:	*Yes, we do, Sir.*	
	How about that scarf there?	
YAMADA:	*Which scarf?*	
SHOP ASSISTANT:	*That small one.*	
YAMADA:	*The colour is a bit …*	
	It's a birthday present for a friend.	
SHOP ASSISTANT:	*How old is your friend?*	
YAMADA:	*She's twenty.*	
SHOP ASSISTANT:	*Well, what about that scarf over there? It's not so*	
	expensive.	
YAMADA:	*How much is it?*	
SHOP ASSISTANT:	*It's eight thousand yen.*	
YAMADA:	*Give me that one, then.*	
SHOP ASSISTANT:	*Certainly, Sir.*	

Vocabulary

スカーフ	**sukáafu**	*scarf*
いくら	**íkura**	*how much?*
一万円	**ichiman'en**	*ten thousand yen*
もの	**monó**	*thing*
もうすこし	**moo sukóshi**	*a little more…, a little —er*
ありませんか	**arimasén ka**	*don't you have, aren't there any…*
ございます	**gozaimásu**	*there is, there are; we have* (formal)
いろ	**iró**	*colour*
ちょっと	**chótto…**	*a little, a bit…, not really to my liking*
プ reze ン to	**purézento**	*present*
ねだん (おねだん)	**nedan**	*price*
…を下さい/ください	**(…o) kudasái**	*please give me…*
かしこまりました	**kashikomarimáshita**	*certainly, Sir/Madam*
高い	**takái**	*high, expensive*
めずらしい	**mezurashíi**	*rare, unusual*
いい	**íi, yói**	*good*

きれい (な)	**kírei (na)**	*beautiful*
安い	**yasúi**	*cheap*
いかが	**ikága**	*how much?*

Adjectives

In Japanese, adjectives and other descriptive words and phrases always precede the noun they describe. We have already seen how a noun followed by **no** can be used to describe another noun (**Tokyo no hóteru** *'hotels in Tokyo'* or *'Tokyo hotels'*, **watashi no tomodachi** *'my friend'*).

Japanese has two types of adjective: 'TRUE ADJECTIVES' and 'NA ADJECTIVES' or 'DESCRIPTIVE NOUNS'. A list showing examples of both types can be found below.

true adjectives	na adjectives
takái *expensive*	**kírei na** *pretty, beautiful*
yasui *cheap*	**hadé na** *gaudy*
wakái *young*	**génki na** *fit, healthy*
sugói *great*	**sukí na** *favourite (like)*
ookíi *big*	**ookíi na** *big*
chiisái *small*	**chíisa na** *small*

True adjectives always end in a vowel followed by the suffixes –i, that is, –ai, –ii, –ui, or –oi (but not –ei) and behave in many respects like verbs. They directly precede the noun they describe. For example:

takái hon *an expensive book*   **chiisái kodomo** *a small child*

Na adjectives, on the other hand, can be thought of as nouns which require **na** to link them to the noun they describe. For example:

shízuka na kawá *a quiet river*   **hadé na sukáafu** *a gaudy scarf*

Both true adjectives and **na** adjectives can be used before **désu**, e.g. **sono hón wa takái desu** *'that book is expensive'*, **ano kodomo wa chiisái desu** *'that child is small'*, **kono sukáafu wa kírei desu** *'this scarf is beautiful'*. Note that in the latter case there is no **na** between the **na** adjective and **desu**. In Unit 3 we met the vocabulary items, **wakái** *'young'* and **génki** *'fit, healthy'*. We can see now that these are a true adjective and a descriptive noun, respectively, e.g. **wakái onnánoko** '*a young girl*' and **génki na kodomo** '*a healthy child*'. **Sukí**, which we met in the expression, **górufu ga sukí desu** '*(I) like golf*', is also a descriptive noun, e.g. **watashi no sukí na hón** '*my favourite book*' or '*a book I like*'.

In negative sentences, true adjectives appear in an adverbial form, also called the –**ku** form, e.g. **kono sukáafu wa tákaku arimasen** '*this scarf is not expensive*'. To make the adverbial form of any true adjective simply change the final –**i** of the dictionary form, so-called because this is how adjectives are listed in dictionaries, to –**ku**. Note too, that the position of the high-pitched syllable of an accented adjective shifts to the left in the adverbial form, e.g. **takái desu** '*it is expensive*', but **tákaku arimasen** '*it is not expensive*'. Actually, there are two possible negative forms of true adjectives: either –**ku arimasen** as we have just seen, or the more colloquial –**ku nai desu** as in **kono sukáafu wa tákaku nai desu** '*this scarf is not expensive*'. Descriptive nouns do not undergo any change when they appear in negative sentences. The negation is simply indicated by putting the copula, **désu**, into one of the two possible negative forms, **dewa** (or **ja**) **arimasén** or **dewa** (or **ja**) **nai desu**, e.g. **ano sukáafu wa kírei ja arimasen, ano sukáafu wa kírei ja nai desu** '*that scarf is not beautiful*'. A small number of adjectives occur as both true adjectives and as descriptive nouns, e.g. **ookíi hóteru** and **óoki na hóteru** both mean '*a big hotel*', while '*a small child*' could be either **chíisa na kodomo** or **chiisái kodomo**. Here too, note the difference in the pitch accent of the alternate forms and the fact that the shortened forms never occur before **désu**.

The true adjective **yói** '*good*' is usually used in its more colloquial pronunciation **íi** '*good*', but it should be noted that in the adverbial form only the full form, **yóku**, is used, e.g. **sore wa yóku arimasen** '*that is not good*'.

Exercise 4.1

Give the negative equivalents of the following sentences. Take care to distinguish true adjectives, descriptive nouns and the copula. Make sure you know the meaning of each sentence as you work through the exercise. Follow the example below.

Cue: **Chichí wa wakái desu.**
     My father is young.
A: **Chichí wa wákaku arimasen** or …**wákaku nai desu.**

1. Kono hón wa takái desu.
2. Ano sukáafu wa kírei desu.
3. Kono monó wa íi desu.
4. Sono hón wa watashi no désu.
5. Háha wa génki desu.
6. Kono iro wa mezurashíi desu.
7. Górufu wa sukí desu.
8. Ano kámera wa yasúi desu.
9. Ríi san wa Chuugokújin desu.
10. Otooto no shúmi wa karaóke desu.

This and that revisited

In Unit 3 we met the demonstrative pronouns, **kore** *'this'*, **sore** *'that'*, **are** *'that over there'* and **dóre** *'which?'*. In Japanese these pronouns can only occur before a particle or directly before the copula, **désu**. If we want to say 'this book' or 'that building over there' we have to use one of the demonstrative adjectives, **kono, sono, ano** or **dóno**. For example: **Kono hón wa ikága desu ka**. *'How about this book?'*

The one

The particle **no** の which we met as a possessive marker or as a particle linking nouns in Unit 1 is used after an adjective in the sense of *'the... one'*, e.g. **takái no** *'the expensive one'*. Consider the following sentences:

Moo sukóshi yasúi no wa arimasén ka.	*Don't you have a slightly cheaper one?*
Ookíi no wa yasúi desu. Chiisái no wa takái desu.	*The large one is cheap. The small one is expensive.* (Perhaps the discussion here is about mobile phones **keitai-dénwa**.)

Note, with descriptive nouns, **na** must be used before **no** is added. For example:

Sukí na no wa kono hón desu.	*The one* (I) *like is this book, This book is the one* (I) *like.*

This construction is particularly useful for shopping, as we will see in Dialogue 2.

Dialogue 2 ■

Peter decides to test out his Japanese buying a pair of jeans in one of the department stores over Shinjuku station.

ピーター:	ちょっとすみません。
てんいん:	はい、なにか...
ピーター:	ジーンズを　かいたいんですが。
てんいん:	あおいのと　しろいのがあります。
ピーター:	あおいのを　みせて下さい。
てんいん:	どうぞ。これはアメリカせいで、とてもいいものですよ。
ピーター:	日本せいのもありますか。
てんいん:	はい、ございます。こちらです。
ピーター:	ああ、それはなかなかいいです。
	日本せいの　あおいのを下さい。

PÍITAA:	Chotto sumimasén.
TEN'IN:	Hái nánika.
PÍITAA:	Jíinzu o kaitain' désu ga …
TEN'IN:	Aói no to shirói no ga arimásu.
PÍITAA:	Aói no o mísete kudasai.
TEN'IN:	Dóozo. Kore wa Amerikasei désu.
	Totemo íi monó desu yo.
PÍITAA:	Nihonsei no mo arimásu ka.
TEN'IN:	Hái, gozaimásu. Kochira désu.
PÍITAA:	Áa, sore wa nakanaka íi desu.
	Nihonsei no aói no o kudásai.

PETER:	*Ah, excuse me?*
SHOP ASSISTANT:	*Yes, Is there something* (I can help you with)*?*
PETER:	*I'd like to buy some jeans…*
SHOP ASSISTANT:	*We have blue* (ones) *and white* (ones).
PETER:	*Please show me the blue ones.*
SHOP ASSISTANT:	*Here you are. These are made in America. They are very good ones.*
PETER:	*Do you also have Japanese ones?*

SHOP ASSISTANT: *Yes, we have. They're over here.*
PETER: *Ah, those are really good.*
                    Give me the blue Japanese ones, please.

Vocabulary

なにか	**nánika**	*something*
かいたいですが	**kaitai désu ga**...	*I would like to buy, but...*
あおい	**aói**	*blue*
しろい	**shirói**	*white*
みせて下さい	**mísete kudasai**	*please show me*
せい	**−sei**	*made in..., −made*
とても	**totemo**	*very*
なかなか	**nakanaka**	*very, really, extremely*
ジーンズ	**jíinzu**	*jeans*

Exercise 4.2 ■

Imagine you are in an elegant department store, **depáato**, in Tokyo's upmarket Ginza district. Using the words you have learnt and the additional vocabulary given below ask the shop assistant to show you the items given in the cues. For example:

Cue: Those black boots over there.
A: **Ano kurói búutsu o mísete kudasái.**

You will find extra vocabulary listed underneath this exercise.

1. that yellow tie over there
2. the navy suit
3. that red skirt over there
4. the green hat
5. those brown trousers
6. that blue shirt over there
7. the grey suit
8. the white jeans
9. that beautiful scarf
10. a slightly cheaper one.

Vocabulary

Colours

These are true adjectives:

くろい	**kurói**	*black*
あかい	**akai**	*red*
きいろい	**kiiroi**	*yellow*

These are nouns. They must be linked to the noun they describe with the particle, **no**.

ちゃいろ	**chairo**	*brown* (literally, 'tea colour')
はいいろ	**haiiro**	*grey* (literally, 'ash colour')
みどり	**mídori**	*green*
こん	**kón**	*navy blue*

Items of clothing

せびろ	**sebiro**	(man's) *suit*
スーツ	**súutsu**	*suit* (man's or woman's)
ズ bo ン	**zubón**	*trousers, pants*
半ズ bo ン	**hanzúbon**	*shorts*
スカーto	**sukáato**	*skirt*
マフラー	**máfuraa**	*muffler, woollen scarf*
ブーツ	**búutsu**	*boots*
ne クタイ	**nékutai**	*tie*
wa イシ ya ツ	**waishatsu**	*shirt*
ぼうし	**booshi**	*hat*

To be or not to be

In English we use the same verb, the verb 'to be', to express equivalence, e.g. 'John is a student' and location, 'John is in the kitchen'. Japanese, however, makes a distinction between these two categories. We have already met **désu**, which is assigned its own category, the copula, because it behaves rather differently from other Japanese verbs. **Désu**, like the equals sign in an equation, shows that the two noun phrases in the sentence are equivalent, e.g. **kore wa hón desu** *'this is a book'*. **Taroo san wa gakusei desu** *'Taro is a student'*. If we want to say where something is we generally use either **arimásu** or **imásu**. For the most part, **arimásu** is used to indicate the location of inanimate objects and **imásu** is used of people and animals. Note that the particle **ni** is used to indicate location as we would use the preposition 'in' in English. You have already seen the negative form of **arimásu**, **arimasén**, as it also occurs in the negative form of **désu**, **dewa** (or **ja**) **arimasén**. The negative form of **imásu** is **imasén**. The examples below show **arimásu** and **imásu** in context.

Keitai-dénwa wa rokkai no denkaseihin-úriba ni arimásu.	*Mobile phones are in the electronic products counter on the sixth floor.*
Tanaka san wa kaigíshitsu ni imásu.	*Mr Tanaka is in the conference room.*

We have seen that **désu** can also be used in certain expressions to indicate location, e.g. **Chuuoo-yuubínkyoku wa dóko desu ka** *'Where is the central post office?'* This common usage does not contradict the assertion that **désu** behaves as a copula showing the equivalence of two noun phrases in a sentence. A more literal translation of this sentence might be, *'As for the central post office, what place is it?'* The function of **désu** after adjectives and descriptive nouns, however, is more to indicate politeness than to indicate equivalence.

Yamanaka san wa górufu ga dáisuki desu.	*Mr Yamanaka loves golf.*
Kono iró wa mezurashíi desu.	*This colour is unusual.*

When **arimásu** is used, as it frequently is, in the sense of *'to have'*, it can also be used when the object is a person. In this case the object is marked with the particle, **ga**. More will be said about subjects and objects in Japanese in a later unit.

Tanaka san wa Kankokujín no tomodachi ga arimásu.	*Mr Tanaka has Korean friends.*
Sannin no kodomo ga arimásu or **kodomo ga sannin arimásu.**	*I have three children.*

If you compare the two versions in the last example you will notice that a numeral and the appropriate classifier can come before the noun to which it refers, in which case it is linked to the noun by the particle, **no**. Or the number expression can follow both the noun and its particle. The latter of these two constructions seems to be the more common.

Dialogue 3 ■

At the department store

マリア:　　ちょっと　おうかがいします。
てんいん:　はい、何でしょうか。
マリア:　　くつうりばは　何がいに　ありますか。
てんいん:　ふじんの　くつは　二がいに　あります。
マリア:　　しんしの　くつは?
てんいん:　三がいです。
マリア:　　ありがとう　ございました。
てんいん:　どうぞ　ごゆっくり。

MÁRIA:　　Chotto oukagai shimásu.
TEN'IN:　　Hái, nán deshoo ka.
MÁRIA:　　Kutsu-úriba wa nangai ni arimásu ka.
TEN'IN:　　Fujin no kutsú wa sangai ni arimásu.
MÁRIA:　　Shínshi no kutsú wa?
TEN'IN:　　Sangai désu.
MÁRIA:　　Arígatoo gozaimásu.
TEN'IN:　　Dóozo goyukkúri.

MARIA:　　　　　　*I wonder if you could tell me…*
SHOP ASSISTANT:　*Yes. What would you like to know?*
MARIA:　　　　　　*What floor is the shoe department?*
SHOP ASSISTANT:　*Ladies' shoes are on the second floor* (first floor).
MARIA:　　　　　　*What about gentlemen's shoes?*
SHOP ASSISTANT:　*They're the third floor* (second floor).
MARIA:　　　　　　*Thank you.*
SHOP ASSISTANT:　*Please take your time.*

Note that Japanese designates floor numbers in the same way as American English, i.e. ground floor = 'first floor', etc.

Vocabulary

おうかがいします	oukagai	*I wonder if you can help me*
	shimásu	*(literally, 'I'd just like to ask')*
何でしょうか	nán deshoo ka	*what is it, I wonder* (polite)
うりば	uriba	*department, counter*
くつうりば	kutsu-úriba	*shoe counter*
かい	kai	*floor, storey* (classifier)
何かい、何がい	nankai, nangai	*which floor*
くつ	kutsú	*shoes*
しんし	shínshi	*gentleman*
ふじん	fujin	*lady*
ごゆっくり	goyukkúri	*at leisure, taking time*
		(honorific)

Numeral classifier

In this unit we meet the numeral classifier **kai**, which is used for counting floors or storeys in a building. Note the sound changes which occur when it combines with 1, 3, 6, 8 and 10. Remember, Japanese count floors starting from 1 at ground-floor level. *'Which floor?'* is either **nankai** or **nangai**.

| *1ˢᵗ floor* | *2ⁿᵈ floor* | *3ʳᵈ floor* | *4ᵗʰ floor* | *5ᵗʰ floor* |
| **ikkai** | **nikai** | **sangai** | **yonkai** | **gokai** |

| *6ᵗʰ floor* | *7ᵗʰ floor* | *8ᵗʰ floor* | *9ᵗʰ floor* | *10ᵗʰ floor* |
| **rokkai** | **nanakai** | **hakkai** | **kyuukai** | **jukkai** |

Exercise 4.3

You ask the well-groomed young woman sitting at the first-floor information desk, **annaijo**, at Mitsukoshi department store, if she can direct you to various departments in the store. Using the cues (and vocabulary given below the exercise) ask her on which floor each sales counter is located, then repeat the answer to confirm that you have understood correctly. For example:

Cue: men's clothing, third floor

Q: **Shinshiyoofuku-úriba wa nangai ni arimásu ka.**

A: **Wakarimáshita. Sangai désu ne.**

1. electronic goods department, fifth floor
2. camera department, sixth floor
3. watch department, fourth floor
4. furniture department, seventh floor
5. sporting goods department, third floor
6. computer department, fifth floor
7. women's shoes, second floor
8. food hall, first-floor basement
9. parking, second-floor basement
10. plant nursery, roof

Vocabulary

でんかせいひん	**denka-séihin**	*electronic goods*
でんかせいひんう りば	**denkaseihin-úriba**	*electronic goods counter/department*
ちか	**chiká**	*underground, basement*
ちか一かい	**chika-íkkai**	*first-floor basement*
ちゅうしゃじょう	**chuushajoo**	*parking (station/ floor etc.)*
しょくりょうひん	**shokuryoohin**	*food*
しょくりょうひん うりば	**shokuryoohin-úriba**	*food hall*
コンピュータ	**konpyúuta**	*computer*
ようふく	**yoofuku**	*clothes*
しんし	**shínshi**	*gentleman*
ふじん	**fujin**	*lady*
かぐ	**kágu**	*furniture*
とけい	**tokei**	*watch, clock*
くつ	**kutsú**	*shoes*
おくじょう	**okujoo**	*roof*
うえきうりば	**ueki-úriba**	*plant nursery*

Bigger numbers

In Unit 3 we met the numbers from 1 to 99. Now we introduce the numbers from 100 to 100 million. Because the yen is a very small unit of currency you will soon become accustomed to using large numbers in

Japanese. The Japanese have a separate term for ten thousand which can make counting a little complicated for English speakers. Note the sound changes which occur in combination with other numbers.

100	200	300	400	500	600	700	800	900	?00
百	二百	三百	四百	五百	六百	七百	八百	九百	何百
hyakú	nihyakú	sánbyaku	yónhyaku	gohyakú	roppyakú	nanáhyaku	happyakú	kyúuhyaku	nánbyaku
1,000	2,000	3,000	4,000	5,000	6,000	7,000	8,000	9,000	?000
千	二千	三千	四千	五千	六千	七千	八千	九千	何千
sén	ni sén	sánzen	yónsen	gosén	rokusén	nanasén	hassén	kyuusén	nanzén
10,000	20,000	30,000	40,000	50,000	60,000	70,000	80,000	90,000	?0000
一万	二万	三万	四万	五万	六万	七万	八万	九万	何万
ichimán	nimán	sanmán	yonmán	gomán	rokumán	nanamán	hachimán	kyuumán	nanmán

Remember when pronouncing these numbers that **n** at the end of a syllable (i.e. **hiragána** ん), is pronounced **m** before **p**, **b** or **m**. '*One thousand*' is either **sén** 千、 or **issén** 一千, but you do not get the choice with 'one hundred' and 'ten thousand'. The former never has a 'one' in front of it and the latter always does.

Numbers over ten thousand require a little extra practice. Notice that Japanese does not have a separate term for a million, preferring to say, 'a hundred ten thousands' instead. If you remember that '*one million*' is **hyakumán** 百万, you should not have too much difficulty. Consider, for example, the following:

五万 **gomán** 50,000   五十万 **gojuumán** 500,000
五百万 **gohyakumán** 5,000,000   五千万 **gosenmán** 50,000,000

Although you have learnt the **kanji** for the numbers, remember that the Arabic numerals we use in English are usually used in Japan too. Even when **kanji** are used, as, for example, for price labels or for numbering the pages in a book, large numbers are frequently written with just the basic **kanji** from 1 to 9 with the addition of the sign for zero, 0, e.g. instead of 三百五十円 (**¥350**) written out in full, you might simply see, 三五〇円.

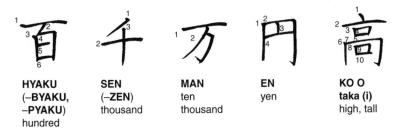

HYAKU
(**–BYAKU,**
–PYAKU)
hundred

SEN
(**–ZEN**)
thousand

MAN
ten
thousand

EN
yen

KO O
taka (i)
high, tall

yasu (i)
cheap

GAKU
learning

KOO
school

SEN
saki
ahead,
future

SEI
student; life

Exercise 4.4

Here are some words and phrases we have met before, but this time written in **kanji**. See if you can give the pronunciations and meanings of the following. You will need to refer to this unit's new **kanji** given below.

1. 小学校   2. 高校   3. 安い本   4. 英語の先生   5. 大学生

Exercise 4.5 ■■

See if you can follow this passage. First try to read it without listening to the cassette tape. Then listen to the tape without looking at the text to see if you can understand the gist of the passage. Finally, follow the text as it is being read on the tape. First just listen, then try reading along with the native speaker, trying to imitate the Japanese intonation and grouping of syllables.

田中さんと　山本さんは　ともだち　です。二人とも　日本人
す。でも　いまは　パリに　すんでいます。
田中さんはパリの日本人学校の先生です。
山本さんのごしゅ人は　日本の　ぎんこうの　パリしてんちょ
う　です。田中さんも　山本さんも　かいものが　大好きです。
パリに　きれいな　みせが　たくさんあります。高いみせも
安いみせも　あります。　きょうは　山本さんは　ブーツを
かいました。とてもいい　ブーツです。イタリアの　ものです。

Katakána

Now you have learnt all the **hiragána** syllables, you can concentrate your efforts into building up your store of **katakána**. We learn ten new **katakána** symbols in this unit.

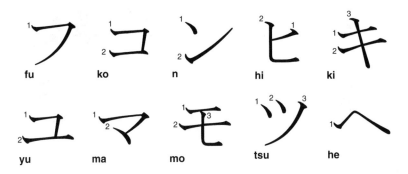

fu　　　ko　　　n　　　hi　　　ki

yu　　　ma　　　mo　　　tsu　　　he

Exercise 4.6

See if you can match the new **katakána** words with the appropriate illustrations on this and the next page. Some of the words might be a little difficult to guess. The Japanese word for 'bread', for example, is borrowed from the Portuguese. If in doubt, check with the key on p. 266.

a.　　　b.　　　c.　　　d.

e.　　　f.　　　g.　　　h.

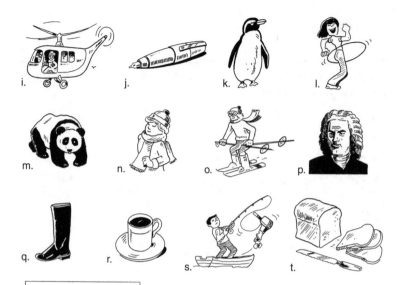

i.   j.   k.   l.

m.   n.   o.   p.

q.   r.   s.   t.

a. ペリカン
b. スーパーマン
c. マフラー
d. フラ・フープ
e. ツアー
f. コアラ
g. スキー
h. アフリカ
i. ペンギン
j. パンダ
k. モーター
l. マイク
m. バッハ
n. ヘリコプター
o. ブーツ
p. ペン
q. コーヒー
r. パン
s. マンモス
t. コンピュータ

5 月曜日に会いましょう。
Getsuyóobi ni aimashóo.
Let's meet on Monday!

In this unit you will learn how to:

- Make suggestions and issue invitations
- Offer to do something
- Say you are going to do something
- Talk about time – past, present and future
- Arrange the time and place for a meeting
- Say where something happens
- Count hours, days, months and years
- Say the days of the week
- Use the prefixes for this ..., last ..., next ... and every...

You will also acquire:

- 10 more **kanji**: 今 来 毎 週 年 火 水 木 金 土
- 10 more **katakána**: ウ オ サ ソ ホ チ ト ナ ニ ノ

Dialogue 1 ▮

*While taking a stroll along the Ginza, doing what the Japanese call a **Ginbura**, Bob Smith bumps into his friend Shuuji Imada whom he met some years ago in New York. After exchanging the usual greetings Bob suggests they both get together with their mutual friend Harry Wong for a meal later in the week.*

スミス:　しばらく ですね。おげんき ですか。
今田:　ええ、おかげさまで。おたくの みなさまも
　　　おげんきですか。
スミス:　ええ。ところで、今田さん、来週　ウォンさんと
　　　三人で　あいませんか。
今田:　いいですよ。来週は　いつでも　だいじょうぶ　です。
スミス:　そうですか。わたしは　火よう日が　だめで、
　　　ウォンさんは　水よう日が　だめです。
今田:　じゃ、月よう日に　しましょうか。
スミス:　あ、いいですね。時間は　いつが　いいですか。
　　　　　　　　かん
今田:　じゃ、みんなで　おひるを　たべましょうか。
スミス:　すしこう は　どうですか。
今田:　いいですねえ。では、来週の月よう日　十二時に
　　　あいましょう。
スミス:　はい。では、わたしは　ウォンさんにでんわします。
　　　さよなら。
今田:　じゃ。また　月よう日に。さよなら。

SUMISU:　Shibáraku desu ne.
　　　Ogénki desu ka.
IMADA:　É, okagesama de. Otaku no minásan mo ogénki desu ka.
SUMISU:　É. Tokoróde, Imada san, Wón san to sanin de aimasén ka.
IMADA:　Íi desu yo. Raishuu wa itsudé mo daijóobu desu.
SUMISU:　Sóo desu ka. Watashi wa kayóobi ga damé de, Wón san wa
　　　suiyóobi ga damé desu.
IMADA:　Ja, getsuyóobi ni shimashóo ka.
SUMISU:　A, íi desu née. Jikan wa ítsu ga íi desu ka.
IMADA:　Ja, minná de ohíru o tabemashóo ka.
SUMISU:　Sushikóo wa dóo desu ka.
IMADA:　Íi desu née. Déwa, raishuu no getsuyóobi juuníji ni aimashóo.
SUMISU:　Hái. Déwa, watashi wa Wón san ni denwa shimásu. Sayonará.
IMADA:　Ja, mata getsuyóobi ni. Sayonará.

SMITH:　*It's been a while, hasn't it?*
　　　Are you keeping well?
IMADA:　*Yes. Thank you. Is everybody well at your place?*
SMITH:　*Yes. By the way, Mr Imada, what say the two of us get*
　　　together with Mr Wong?
IMADA:　*Fine! Anytime next week is all right with me.*
SMITH:　*Tuesday is no good for me and Mr Wong can't make*
　　　Wednesday.

IMADA: *Shall we make it Monday, then?*
SMITH: *Mm, that's fine. What would be a good time?*
IMADA: *Then, what say we all have lunch together?*
SMITH: *What about Sushikóo?*
IMADA: *That would be nice. So, let's meet next Monday at twelve.*
SMITH: *Sure. Then I'll ring Mr Wong. Bye.*
IMADA: *Then, see you on Monday. Bye.*

Vocabulary

しばらく	**shibáraku**	*for a while, for a* (long) *time*
おげんき ですか	**ogénki desu ka**	*Are you well? How are you?* (honorific)
おかげさまで	**okagesama de**	*Thanks to you* (suggesting that my good health is the result of your being kind enough to ask after it)
おたく	**otaku**	*your place, you* (honorific)
みなさま	**minásama**	*all, all of you* (honorific)
ところで	**tokoróde**	*by the way*
三人で	**sannin de**	*the three of us/them*
いつでも	**itsudémo**	*any time at all*
だいじょうぶ	**daijóobu**	*all right, okay, no need to worry*
だめ	**damé**	*no good*
で	**de**	*is…and* (form of **désu** used to link clauses)
にしましょうか	**…ni shimashóo ka**	*Shall we make it…?, what about…?*
おひる	**ohíru**	*midday, midday meal, lunch*
たべましょうか	**tabemashóo ka**	*shall we eat*
でんわ	**denwa**	*telephone*

More verbs

So far we have met the Japanese copula, **désu**, which is used like the equals sign in an equation to equate one noun with another. In the last unit we were also introduced to the verbs **arimásu** and **imásu** which tell us where something, or, in the case of **imásu**, someone, is situated. We have also met one or two other verbs, which have been introduced as vocabulary items to add a little zest to your Japanese conversation without your needing to worry exactly how they perform in the sentence. We have met **kimáshita** '*came*' in expressions like **Kánkoku kara kimáshita** '*I come* (literally 'came') *from Korea.*' We also met **Wakarimáshita** '*I understand*' and **Róndon ni súnde imasu** '*I live in London.*' Apart from the obvious fact that the Japanese verb comes at the end of the sentence, you will have noticed that many sentences end in –**másu** or –**máshita**. Actually, this is the ending you use to show politeness to the person you are addressing. It is the form used in all conversation, except between close friends and among children, so it is the most appropriate form for foreign learners of the language to start with. Later we will also learn the plain verb forms used in the written language and in subordinate clauses.

Japanese marks the past tense with the ending –**máshita**. This indicates that the action of the verb is complete and contrasts with –**másu**, which is used for actions and states where the action is not yet completed. For this reason –**másu** doubles up to cover both present and future time and is hence often called the 'non-past form'. Of course, each of these forms has a negative equivalent, as shown below.

	Non-past affirmative	Non-past negative	Past affirmative	Past negative
Suffix:	–**másu**	–**masén**	–**mashita**	–**masén deshita**
Example:	**ikimásu**	**ikimasén**	**ikimáshita**	**ikimasén deshita**
	(I) go	*(I) don't go*	*(I) went*	*(I) didn't go*

Some verbs in Japanese which describe states rather than actions are generally used with some form of the auxiliary verb, **imásu**. The verb 'to live', for example, appears as **súnde imasu** '*I live*', **súnde imashita** '*I lived*', etc. More will be said of this construction in a later unit. In the meantime, remember these verbs in the contexts in which you have seen them so far. You will have noticed also that sometimes a Japanese adjective or descriptive noun is used where we would use a verb in English. Take, for example, the expressions in Japanese for liking or disliking something: **hambáagaa ga sukí desu** '*I like hamburgers*'.

Verbs with shimásu

Apart from its function as the freestanding verb '*to do*', **shimásu** combines with a number of nouns to form quasi compound verbs. Here are some common verbs with **shimásu**, and each one is followed by a sentence showing how it can be used.

benkyoo shimásu	*to study*
Mainichi nánjikan benkyoo shimásu ka.	*How many hours do you study every day?*
ryóori (o) shimásu	*to cook*
Píitaa san no ouchi de dáre ga ryóori o shimásu ka.	*Who cooks at your place, Peter?*
shokuji (o) shimásu	*to have a meal, eat*
Kyóo wa issho ni shokuji shimasén ka.	*Won't you join me for a meal today?*
kekkon shimásu	*to marry*
Onéesan wa ítsu kekkon shimashita ka.	*When did your elder sister get married?*
ryokoo shimásu	*to travel*
Rainen Amerika o ryokoo shimásu.	*Next year I'm going to travel through America.*

(*Note*: In this construction the course travelled is marked with the particle **o**.)

Dialogue 2 ▮▮

Yamada and Tanaka are hiring a car.

山田: あした reンタカーで ドライブに
　　　いきませんか。
田中: それは いいですねえ。どこへ いきましょうか。
山田: うみと 山と どちらが いいですか。
田中: わたしは どちらでも かまいません。
山田: それでは、山へ いきましょう。
田中: だれが うんてん しますか。
山田: ピーターさんに おねがい しましょう。
田中: そう しましょう。ピーターさんは うんてんが
　　　じょうず ですから。

YAMADA:　Ashita rentakáa de doráibu ni ikimasén ka.
TANAKA:　Sore wa íi desu née.
　　　　　Dóko e ikimashóo ka.

YAMADA:	Úmi to yamá to dóchira ga íi desu ka.
TANAKA:	Watashi wa dochira démo kamaimasén.
YAMADA:	Sore déwa yamá e ikimashóo.
TANAKA:	Dáre ga unten shimásu ka.
YAMADA:	Píitaa san ni onegai shimashóo.
TANAKA:	Soo shimashóo. Píitaa san wa unten ga joozú desu kara.

YAMADA:	*Let's hire a car and go for a drive tomorrow.*
TANAKA:	*That would be great!*
	Where shall we go?
YAMADA:	*Which do you prefer, sea or mountains?*
TANAKA:	*I don't mind which.* ('I'd be happy with either.')
YAMADA:	*In that case, let's go to the mountains.*
TANAKA:	*Who'll drive?*
YAMADA:	*Let's ask Peter.*
TANAKA:	*Let's do that. Peter's a good driver.*

Vocabulary

うんてん します	**unten shimásu**	*to drive*
re ンタカー	**rentakáa**	*car for hire, car rental*
で	**de**	*with, by, by means of* (instrumental particle)
へ	**e**	*to, towards* (directional particle written with **hiragána 'he'**).
うみ	**úmi**	*sea*
どちらでも	**dochira démo**	*either one*
かまいません	**kamaimasén**	*it doesn't matter*
おねがいします	**onegai shimásu**	*to request* (agent indicated by **ni**)
ですから	**désu kara**	*because ... is.* (Often used, as in the example here, in an incomplete sentence to indicate a reason.)

Exercise 5.1

How would the following statements be altered by the addition of the time expressions provided in the brackets (you can check their meaning in the table on p. 86)? Perhaps there are some sentences where no change is necessary. See the example below.

Cue: **Ikimasén (kinóo)**
A: **Kinóo ikimasén deshita.**

1. Tanaka san ni aimáshita. (ashita)
2. Nihón ni ikimáshita. (rainen)
3. Góhan o tabemáshita. (mainichi)
4. Atarashíi kuruma o kaimásu. (séngetsu)
5. Kyóo wa mokuyóobi desu. (kinóo)

Vocabulary

ごはん	**gohan**	*(cooked) rice; meal*
あたらしい	**atarashíi**	*new*
くるま	**kuruma**	*car, cart*

Exercise 5.2 ■

Here are some more time expressions to help you practise your tense endings. You can look up the days of the week on p. 85.

otótoi	*the day before yesterday*
asátte	*the day after tomorrow*
otótoshi	*the year before last*
sarainen	*the year after next*

Now tell your Japanese friend:

1. You came from London the year before last.
2. You are going to China the year after next.
3. The day after tomorrow is Saturday.
4. The day before yesterday was Tuesday.
5. What's today? That's right. It's Thursday.

'How about ...?'

In this unit we also meet the ending –**mashóo**, which is sometimes called the 'tentative', 'propositive' or 'hortative' suffix because it is used when you want to make a suggestion or put a proposition. In English we would normally say 'let's do' something or other where Japanese would use the –**mashóo** construction. If the suggestion is more tentative, or if you want to give the listener the opportunity to suggest something else, the –**mashóo** sentence can be framed as a question, –**mashóo ka** *'Shall we ...?'* *'What say we ...?'*, etc. Here are some examples and an exercise to help you get the hang of this useful expression.

Háyaku kaerimashóo.	*Let's go home quickly. Let's go back early.*
Yasúi no o kaimashóo.	*Let's buy the cheap(er) one.*
Nánji ni ikimashóo ka.	*What time shall we go?*

Funnily enough, this last example can also mean '*What time shall I come?*' in a context where the speaker is going to visit the listener. In Japanese **kimásu** is only used for movement towards the speaker or to a place associated with the speaker. In all other cases **ikimásu** is used. If we hear a knock at the door we might say, 'Just a minute, I'm coming' whereas a Japanese would say 'Just a minute I'm going.'

The –**mashóo** ending also provides a very convenient way to offer to do something for someone. For example:

Suutsukéesu o **mochimashóo ka.**	*Shall I carry your suitcase for you?*	(**mochimásu** *to hold, carry*)
Eigo de kakimashóo ka.	*Shall I write it in English?*	

Exercise 5.3 ■

Soften the following statements and questions by rephrasing the ideas as propositions or suggestions, retaining the **ka** ending when it occurs. If called upon to do so, could you also translate your new sentences into English and also write them in Japanese script? Some of the **kanji** you will need for this exercise are introduced later in this unit. Just in case you feel the urge to do so, the answers are included in the key at the end of the book.

Follow the example below:

Cue: **Sánji ni ikimásu.**
A: **Sánji ni ikimashóo.**

1. Íma kaerimásu ka.
2. Aói no o kaimásu.
3. Nánji ni aimásu ka.
4. Hachíji ni tabemásu.
5. Súgu ikimásu ka.

Knowing the object

Japanese shows the relationship between the various elements in a sentence by the use of particles. We have already met some such as **wa** (topic), **ga** (subject), **ni** (location) and so on. In this unit we meet **o**, written with the **hiragána** symbol を (once pronounced **wo**, but now indistinguishable in pronunciation from **o** お). This is another example of historical spelling, just as the topic particle pronounced **wa** is written with the **hiragána** character for **ha** は. The object is the noun, i.e. the thing, person or concept affected by the action of the verb. Not all verbs have objects, but those that do so are called 'TRANSITIVE VERBS'. Conversely, verbs which do not normally take an object are 'INTRANSITIVE VERBS'. As we shall see later, the distinction between transitive and intransitive verbs is an important one in Japanese grammar.

Here are some more examples illustrating the use of the particle **o**.

Nihonjín wa mainichi góhan o tabemásu.	*The Japanese eat rice every day.*
Dóno shinbun o yomimásu ka.	*Which newspaper do you read?*
Atarashíi kuruma o kaimáshita.	*I bought a new car.*

With verbs which indicate movement over a distance, or what we call 'verbs of linear motion', like 'to go', 'to walk', 'to fly' and 'to run', the object particle **o** is used to indicate the course of the movement and corresponds to English prepositions like 'along', 'through' and 'over'. We meet this construction again in the next unit.

Michi o arukimásu	*to walk along a road*
Sóra o tobimásu	*to fly through the sky*
Nihón o ryokoo shimásu	*to travel through Japan*

Note that some verbs, which are transitive in English and take a direct object, are intransitive in Japanese. One such verb is **aimásu**, '*to meet*', which takes an indirect object, marked by **ni**, in Japanese.

Kinóo Tanaka san ni aimáshita.	*Yesterday I met Mr Tanaka.*

Note that where the noun object forms a kind of compound verb with **shimásu**, as introduced on p. 78, the noun, which constitutes the first element, is not usually followed by the object particle **o**. For example:

Jón san wa Tookyoo de Nihongo o benkyoo shimáshita.	*John studied Japanese in Tokyo.*

Where the action is

We have seen how location, 'in', 'at' etc., with the verbs **imásu** and **arimásu** is indicated using the particle **ni**. For example:

Shachoo wa kaigíshitsu ni imásu *The director is in the conference room*

With more active verbs, however, the place of action is indicated with **de**. For example:

Mainichi kaisha de shinbun o yomimásu. *I read the newspaper every day at the company.*

Éki no kiósuku de zasshi o kaimáshita. *I bought the magazine at the kiosk at the station.*

Kanji

In this unit we introduce the **kanji** for writing the days of the week and a few other time expressions. All of these are used very frequently and some are basic elements that occur in a large number of other **kanji**. It is important, therefore, that you cannot only recognise them in context, but that you can write them confidently. Practise writing them following the stroke order shown below:

KON	RAI,	−MAI	SHUU	NEN
ima	ki (masu)	every, each	week	tóshi
now	come, next-			year

KA	SUI	MOKU	KIN	DO
hi	mizu	ki	kane	tsuchi
fire	water	tree, wood	gold, metal; money	earth

The days of the week

The days of the week are named after the five traditional Chinese elements of fire, water, wood, metal and earth with the addition of the sun (Sunday) and the moon (Monday) to make up the seven days of the week according to the western calendar. This solar calendar was introduced into Japan in 1872. The first **kanji** in the suffix –**yóobi**, used for naming days of the week, is rather complicated so it is given here with the reading indicated in small **hiragána** characters above the **kanji**. These **hiragána** symbols used to indicate the readings of difficult or unusual **kanji** are known as **furigana**. As we progress in this course we will be introducing more **kanji** with **furigana** to help you develop your reading skills in Japanese. Remember most **kanji** have both Chinese-style **on**-readings, used in compounds and other words borrowed from Chinese, and the native **kun**-readings, used when the character stands alone or forms part of a Japanese proper noun. There are exceptions to these rules of combination of **kanji** readings. Take, for example, the names of the days of the week where the first two **kanji** are read in the **on**-reading and the third –**bi**, is a variant **kun**-reading. Actually, the final –**bi** is optional. You will also hear **getsuyóo** '*Monday*', etc. for the names of the days of the week.

月曜日	**getsuyóobi**	*Monday*
火曜日	**kayóobi**	*Tuesday*
水曜日	**suiyóobi**	*Wednesday*
木曜日	**mokuyóobi**	*Thursday*
金曜日	**kin'yóobi**	*Friday*
土曜日	**doyóobi**	*Saturday*
日曜日	**nichiyóobi**	*Sunday*

Prefixes in time expressions

Although Japanese relies heavily on suffixes (i.e. endings) and particles, which follow the forms to which they refer, there are also a number of useful prefixes used with time expressions. The following chart shows how these are used. Note that there are some irregular forms.

	先 sen– *last ...*	今 kon– *this ...*	来 rai– *next ...*	毎 mai– *every ...*
週 –shuu *week*	先週 senshuu *last week*	今週 konshuu *this week*	来週 raishuu *next week*	毎週 maishuu *every week*
月 –getsu *month*	先月 séngetsu *last month*	今月 kongetsu *this month*	来月 raigetsu *next month*	毎月 maigetsu, maitsuki *every month*
年 –nen *year*	***	今年 kotoshi *this year*	来年 rainen *next year*	毎年 mainen, maitoshi *every year*
日 –nichi *day*	****	今日 konnichi, kyóo *today*	****	毎日 máinichi *every day*

Notes:

*先年 **sennen** does not mean 'last year', but '*in recent years*'. '*Last year*' is **kyónen** (去年).
先日 is pronounced **senjitsu and means, '*recently, the other day*'. 来日 **rainichi** does not mean 'tomorrow' but '*coming to Japan*'. Of course, '*yesterday*' is **kinóo** and '*tomorrow*' is **ashita**.

Time duration

The numeral classifier for counting hours is –**jíkan** 時間. The –**kan** of the suffix expresses duration and is also found in the classifiers for counting weeks, –**shúukan** 週間 and years, –**nénkan** 年間. Although the –**kan** is required when counting hours or weeks, for counting years either –**nénkan**, or simply –**nen** may be used. For example:

Nínen Nihón ni imáshita or   *I was in Japan for two years.*
   Ninénkan Nihón ni imáshita.

We have already met the suffix –**gatsu** 月, used for naming the months (**ichigatsú** 一月 '*January*' etc.), but for counting months, the numeral classifier –**kágetsu** か月 is used. For example:

Sankágetsu Tookyoo de Nihongo o   *I studied Japanese for three*
   benkyoo shimáshita.   *months in Tokyo.*

Incidentally, the permitted word order in Japanese sentences is very flexible. As long as the verb is at the end of the sentence, the order of the subject, object and expressions of time and place can be changed about freely. To illustrate, the example above would mean the same thing if it were **Tookyoo de sankágetsu Nihongo o benkyoo shimáshita** or **Nihongo o Tookyoo de sankágetsu benkyoo shimáshita**. Generally, the words towards the front of the sentence seem to carry a stronger emphasis.

Exercise 5.4 ■■

Here are some sentences to help you learn the Japanese script. First, read the sentences aloud, then check your results by comparing your voice with that on the tape. Then practise your comprehension skills by listening to the tape with your book closed. Finally, translate the sentences into English.

1. 今田先生は日本大学の英語の先生です。
2. 来週の土曜日八時半に来て下さい。
3. 山中さんの下の女の子は高校三年生です。
4. 毎週月・火・水に日本語のクラスがあります。
5. 水を下さい。
6. 今日はお金がありません。
7. 安いウイスキーはあまり好きじゃありません。
8. 先週の木曜日に金田さんは四国から来ました。

Exercise 5.5

Can you read this note Tom has left pinned to the door of his flat in Tokyo? He has been giving English lessons privately for about a year, while teaching himself Japanese with the aid of this book.

安子さん、
今日は英語のクラスがありません。ともだちと スキーに いきます。
来週の水よう日、ごご七時半に来てください。
よろしく。
八月二九日
トム

1. Which class has Tom cancelled?
2. Why?
3. What day did he say Yasuko should return?
4. What time will the class be held?
5. How do you think Yasuko feels about the note?

Katakána

The **katakána** symbols introduced in this unit will bring the total you have learnt to around thirty, leaving the final fifteen for the next two units. While it takes a bit of practice to remember **katakána**, you will find it a lot easier if you learn it in context rather than as isolated characters. You can usually guess the meaning of words written in **katakána** as the vast majority of them are borrowed from English.

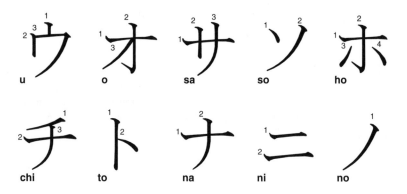

Exercise 5.6

Here is the menu of a little coffee shop or **kissáten** in the back blocks of Shinjuku. Or was it Shibuya? Or perhaps even Ikebukuro? Somewhere in Tokyo anyway.

ポニー

ジャズ喫茶店

メニュー

ホット・コーヒー	三六〇円
アイス・コーヒー	三八〇円
アメリカン・コーヒー	三五〇円
ジュース	一八〇円
コーラ	一八〇円
ウイスキー	四五〇円
チーズ・トースト	二〇〇円
ミックス・サンド	四〇〇円
ハム・サンド	三八〇円
トマト・サンド	三〇〇円
チキン・ピラフ	四八〇円
ホット・ドッグ	一八〇円
サラダ	二八〇円
アップル・パイ	二四〇円
バニラ・アイスクリーム	三二〇円

For the price of a cup of coffee you can sit there for an hour chatting with friends, writing letters or just listening to the music. Look at the menu and answer the questions below.

1. How much would you pay for an iced coffee?
2. What kinds of dessert are there?
3. What is the most expensive beverage?
4. How much would you pay for an orange juice and a hot dog?
5. How much would an American coffee (not as strong as a regular Japanese coffee), toasted cheese on toast and a salad cost?

6 鈴木さんの会社へどうやって行きますか。

Suzuki san no kaisha e dóo yatte ikimásu ka.

How do I get to your office, Mr Suzuki?

In this unit you will learn how to:

- Give and follow directions
- Make requests
- Ask and give permission
- Discuss existing states and actions in progress
- Make longer sentences
- Say what you want to do
- Say why you go somewhere.

You will also acquire:

- 10 more **kanji**:　　行 会 買 売 読 銀 社 書 聞 新
- 10 more **katakána**:　ケ セ テ ネ ヌ ヤ ヨ ル レ ロ

Dialogue 1 ■

*Not long after you arrive in Tokyo you decide to look up Mr Suzuki. You got his phone number and a letter of introduction from Mr Honda, whom you met in Unit 1. Mr Suzuki works in the Nihonbashi office of Mr Honda's trading company. You meet in a **kissáten** (coffee shop) in Shinjuku to discuss your proposed visit to Mr Suzuki's office. You may need to refer to the new **kanji** introduced later in this chapter.*

あなた: すずきさんの　会社へ　どう　やって　行きますか。

すずき: 日本ばしの　ちかてつの　えきの　ちかくに　あります。そのへんを　よく　ごぞんじ　ですか。

あなた: いいえ、　あまり　よく　しりません。ちずを　書いて　くださいませんか。

すずき: ああ、いいですよ。ちかてつの　Ａ　の２の　でぐちを　でてください。

あなた: Ａの２の　でぐちですね。はい、わかりました。

すずき: ええ。そして、そこを　ひだりへ　まがって　ください。

あなた: はい、わかりました。

すずき: すると　山田銀行があります。

あなた: ああ、そうですか。

すずき: ええっと、そのよこの　せまい　みちに　はいって、まっすぐ　百メートルぐらい　行きます。

あなた: 百メートル　まっすぐ　ですね。

すずき: すると　みぎがわに　毎日新聞か　読売新聞の　だいりてんが　あります。

あなた: はい、わかりました。

すずき: そこの　かどを　みぎに　まがって
二・三十メートルのところに　日英貿易という、小さな会社があります。

あなた: ああ、そうですか。

すずき: わたしの　じむしょは　そのビルの　二かい　にあります。

(*Looking at the map Mr Suzuki has drawn for you.*)

あなた: ありがとうございます。このちずで　よく　わかります。あした十二時ごろ　行っても　いいですか。

すずき: ええ、もちろん。いいですよ。何時でも　かまいません。いっしょに　おひるごはんを　たべましょうか。

あなた: はい、そう　しましょう。

ANÁTA: Suzuki san no kaisha e dóo yatte ikimásu ka.

SUZUKI: Nihonbashi no chikatesu no éki no chikaku ni arimásu. Sono hen o yóku gozónji desu ka.

ANÁTA: Iie, amari yóku shirimasén. Chízu o káite kudasaimasén ka.

SUZUKI: Áa, íi desu yo. Chikatetsu no éi no ní no déguchi o déte kudasai.

ANÁTA: Éi no ní no déguchi desu ne. Hái, wakarimáshita.

SUZUKI: Ée. Soshite, soko o hidari e magatte kudasái.

ANÁTA: Hái. Wakarimáshita.
SUZUKI: Suru to Yamada Gínkoo ga arimásu.
ANÁTA: Áa, sóo desu ka.
SUZUKI: Éetto, sono yoko no semái michi ni háitte, massúgu hyaku meetoru gúrai ikimásu.
ANÁTA: Hyaku meetoru massúgu desu ne.
SUZUKI: Suru to migigawa ni Mainichi-Shínbun ka Yomiuri-Shínbun no dairiten ga arimásu.
ANÁTA: Hái. Wakarimáshita.
SUZUKI: Soko no kádo o migi ni magatte, ni-sanjuu meetoru no tokoro ni Nichiei-Bóoeki to yuu, chíisa na kaisha ga arimásu.
ANÁTA: Áa, sóo desu ka.
SUZUKI: Watashi no jimúsho wa sono bíru no nikai ni arimásu.

(*Looking at the map Mr Suzuki has drawn for you.*)

ANÁTA: Arígatoo gozaimasu. Kono chízu de yóku wakarimásu. Ashita juuniji góro itte mo íi desu ka.
SUZUKI: Ée, mochíron. Íi desu yo. Nánji demo kamaimasén. Issho ni ohiru-góhan o tabemashóo ka.
ANÁTA: Hái, sóo shimashóo.

YOU: *How do I get to your office, Mr Suzuki?*
SUZUKI: *It's near the Nihonbashi underground station. Do you know that area well?*
YOU: *No, I don't know it at all well. Would you draw me a map?*
SUZUKI: *Yes, certainly. Come out of the underground at the A2 exit.*
YOU: *The A2 exit, is it? Yes, I see.*
SUZUKI: *Yes. And turn to the left there.*
YOU: *Yes, I see.*
SUZUKI: *Then you'll find the Yamada Bank.*
YOU: *Oh, is that right?*
SUZUKI: *Uh, 'um, go into the narrow road alongside and go straight ahead for about a hundred metres.*
YOU: *Straight ahead for one hundred metres…*
SUZUKI: *Then, on your right-hand side you'll see an agent for the Mainichi or the Yomiuri newspaper.*
YOU: *Yes, I see.*
SUZUKI: *Turn right at that corner and about twenty or thirty yards along there is a little company called Nichiei Trading.*
YOU: *Oh, I see…*
SUZUKI: *My office is on the first floor of that building.*

YOU: *Thank you very much. It will be clear with this map. May I come at 12 o'clock tomorrow?*

SUZUKI: *Yes, of course. That's fine. Any time will do. Let's have lunch together!*

YOU: *Yes, let's do that.*

Vocabulary

あなた	**anáta**	*you*
どうやって	**dóo yatte**	*how* (literally, 'doing what way?')
日本橋 ぱし	**Nihonbashi**	*district in central Tokyo*
ちかてつ	**chikatetsu**	*underground railway, subway*
えき	**éki**	*station*
ちかく	**chikáku**	*vicinity, area around ...*
ごぞんじですか	**gozónji desu ka**	*Do you know?* (honorific)
あまり	**amari**	(not) *much,* (not) *very*
よく	**yóku**	*well, often*
しりません	**shirimasén**	(I) *don't know*
ちず	**chízu**	*map*
書いて	**káite**	*writing, drawing*
くださいませんか	**kudasaimasén ka**	*Won't you?/Would you mind?*
でぐち	**déguchi**	*exit*
でて	**déte**	*going out, exiting*
ください	**kudasái**	*please* (give me)
ひだり	**hidari**	*left*
まがって　くださ い	**magatte kudasái**	*please turn*
そして	**soshite**	*and, after that*
すると	**suru to**	*then, next*
銀行	**ginkoo**	*bank*
ああ、そうですか	**áa, sóo desu ka**	*Oh, is that so? Really? I see*
ええっと	**éetto**	*uh, um* (hesitation form)
よこ	**yoko**	*side, alongside*
せまい	**semái**	*narrow*
みち	**michi**	*road, street*

はいって	**háitte**	*entering, going in*
まっすぐ	**massúgu**	*straight, straight ahead*
ぐらい	**gúrai**	*about*
みぎ	**migi**	*right*
みぎがわ	**migigawa**	*right-hand side*
毎日新聞	**Mainichi-shínbun**	*Mainichi Shimbun* (newspaper)
読売新聞	**Yomiuri-shínbun**	*Yomiuri Shimbun* (newspaper)
か	**ka**	*or* (particle)
だいりてん	**dairíten**	*agency*
そこの	**soko no**	*there* (not far away)
かど	**kádo**	*corner*
ところ	**tokoro**	*place, spot; where*
ぼうえき	**booeki**	*trade, trading*
会社	**kaisha**	*company, firm*
じむしょ	**jimúsho**	*office*
ビル	**bíru**	*building*
行ってもいいです か	**itte mo íi desu ka**	*may I go/come?*
もちろん	**mochíron**	*of course*
何時でも	**nánji demo**	*any time at all*
かまいません	**kamaimasén**	*it doesn't matter*
いっしょに	**issho ni**	*together*
おひるごはん	**ohiru-góhan**	*lunch*

Chiming in

In English, conversational etiquette demands that we do not butt in when others are speaking. In Japanese, however, the listener is expected to indicate that he or she is listening attentively to what is being said by chiming- in with comments, such as 'I see', 'really', 'you don't say?' etc. This feature of Japanese conversation is known as **aizuchi** (literally, 'pounding in unison', a reference to the cooperation required when two people are pounding rice in a mortar with large wooden mallets). Common examples of **aizuchi** are, **áa sóo desu ka**, **hái**, **wakarimáshita** and **sóo desu née**. There are several examples in Dialogue 1. Another feature of Japanese conversation is the frequent use of **hesitation forms**, like the **éetto** '*er*', '*um*', '*let me think*', etc., introduced in the dialogue. Other common hesitation forms are **anoo** '*er*' and **sóo desu nee** (pronounced in a drawn-out, level intonation) '*let me see*'. In addition to giving the speaker time to frame his or her thoughts, as do similar forms in English, Japanese hesitation forms, paradoxically, contribute to the flow of conversation. This is because they give the listener more time to become involved in the conversation and allow the speaker not to sound too abrupt or self-assertive, both of which are considered poor form in Japanese society.

Formation of the '–te form'

Another important form of the Japanese verb is the –te form, sometimes called the 'GERUND'. This is used in a number of constructions, either in conjunction with another auxiliary verb or as a linking form between clauses. We have already seen an example of the –te form (which sometimes appears as –de, as we shall see below) in the phrase, **Róndon ni súnde imasu** '*I live in London.*' The –te ending undergoes a number of sound changes depending on the type of verb concerned and the final consonant of the verb stem (what you have left when you cut off the –másu ending). The list that follows gives the –te forms of some verbs introduced in this or in previous units. Verbs in Japanese fall into three groups or conjugations, the 'CONSONANT-ROOT VERBS' (or '–u verbs'), the 'VOWEL-ROOT VERBS' (or '–ru verbs') and a small group of irregular verbs. More will be said about verb roots and the verb conjugations in the next unit (see p. 117 if you want to read ahead for more detail now). It is not generally possible to tell the conjugation of a verb when you see it with the –másu ending. If there is an –e before the –másu, however, you can be sure you are dealing with a vowel-root verb. The verb, **tabemásu** '*eats*', is a case in point. Vowel-root verbs simply add –te to the same verb stem to which –másu is attached. For example, **tabemásu** '*eats*', **tábete** '*eating*' (the English gloss here is more a convenient label than an indication of the literal meaning of the verb). Another vowel-root verb we have met is **mimásu** '*sees*', '*watches*', which has the –te form **míte**. Similarly, the irregular verbs **kimásu** '*comes*' and **shimásu** '*does*', have the predictable –te forms, **kíte** '*coming*' and **shite** '*doing*' respectively. Of the consonant-root verbs, only those which have –shi before the –másu ending add –te directly without undergoing any sound change. For example, **hanashimásu** '*speaks*' becomes **hanáshite** '*speaking*'. In all other consonant-root verbs, however, the –te ending is assimilated to the final consonant of the stem, resulting in the endings –ite, –ide, –tte or –nde.

kakimásu *writes*   **káite**   *writing* (–ki plus –te becomes –ite)

isogimásu *hurries*	**isóide**	*hurrying* (–**gi** plus –**te** becomes –**ide**)
kaimásu *buys*	**katte**	*buying* (–**ai** plus –**te** becomes –**atte**)
machimásu *waits*	**mátte**	*waiting* (–**chi** plus –**te** becomes –**tte**)
torimásu *takes*	**totte**	*taking* (–**ri** plus –**te** becomes –**tte**)
yomimásu *reads*	**yónde**	*reading* (–**mi** plus –**te** becomes –**nde**)
asobimásu *plays*	**asónde**	*playing* (–**bi** plus –**te** becomes –**nde**)

Uses of the '–te form'

Perhaps the most common use of the –**te** form is with the auxiliary verb **imásu** to express either an action in progress or a completed state. Generally, with transitive verbs, i.e. those verbs which take a direct object, the –**te** form followed by **imásu** is used to convey the idea that an action is in progress, like the present continuous tense in English. For example:

Shachoo wa íma shinbun o yónde imasu.	*The managing director is now reading the newspaper.*

With intransitive verbs the –**te imásu** construction describes a completed state. For example:

Otootó wa íma Nyuu Yóoku ni itte imásu.	*My younger brother is now in New York* (i.e. he is in a state of having gone to New York).

Japanese verbs generally designate actions. In order to describe a state most Japanese verbs use the –**te imásu** construction, as shown below.

kekkon shimásu *to marry*	**kekkon shite imásu** *to be married*
futorimásu *to get fat*	**futótte imasu** *to be fat*
yasemásu *to get thin*	**yasete imásu** *to be thin*
tsukaremásu *to become tired*	**tsukárete imasu** *to be tired*
okorimásu *to get angry*	**okótte imasu** *to be angry*
yorokobimásu *to rejoice*	**yorokónde imasu** *to be happy*
onaka ga sukimásu *to get hungry*	**onaka ga suite imásu** *to be hungry*
nódo ga kawakimásu *to get thirsty*	**nódo ga kawaite imásu** *to be thirsty*

The literal meaning of **onaka ga sukimásu** is '*the stomach becomes empty*' and **nódo ga kawakimásu** means '*the throat becomes dry*'. In either case a plain past tense verb can be used to convey much the same idea as the **–te imásu** form. For example:

Onaka ga sukimáshita or	*I'm hungry*
Nódo ga kawakimáshita	*I'm thirsty*

Some verbs seem to occur only in the **–te imásu** construction, for example:

Ásako san wa Jiroo san o ái shite imásu.   *Asako loves Jiro.*

The verb **shirimásu** *to get to know*, occurs in the **–te imasu** form in the affirmative, but not in the negative.

Yamamoto san o shitte imásu ka.	*Do you know Mr Yamamoto?*
Iie, shirimasén.	*No, I don't.*

The honorific expression **gozónji desu ka** '*do you know?*', introduced in this unit, is a safer alternative if you are addressing an older person or a social superior of little acquaintance. If you are addressed this way yourself you must not reply using the honorific prefix **go–**. You can say either **shitte imásu** or **zonjimásu** if you are replying in the affirmative and **shirimasén** or **zonjimasén** if your answer is negative.

Exercise 6.1 ■

Imagine you are having a telephone conversation with a Japanese friend. Your friend asks you what you are doing now. Just as in English we would not expect the reply 'I'm talking to you over the phone' so too in Japanese – the **–te imásu** form refers more generally to what we have been doing recently or how we have been spending our time these days. The point about the activity described in the **–te imásu** form is that it is not finished. Using the cues given below tell your friend what you are doing. Follow the example below:

Cue: reading a magazine (**zasshi**)
Q: **Íma náni o shite imásu ka.**
A: **Íma zasshi o yónde imasu.**

1. washing the car (**kuruma, araimásu, arratte**)
2. writing a letter (**tegami**)
3. studying Japanese
4. cleaning the room
5. watching television (**térebi**)

The following are not recorded on the cassette tape.

6. waiting for a friend (**machimásu, mátte**)
7. listening to the radio (**kikimásu, kitte**)
8. reading a novel (**shoosetsu**)
9. drinking coffee (**nomimásu, nónde**)
10. making a cake (**kéeki, tsukurimásu, tsukútte**)

Exercise 6.2

Match the following pictures with the appropriate captions.

a.   b.   c.   d.   e.

1. futótte imasu
2. okótte imasu
3. tsukárete imasu
4. yasete imásu
5. yorokónde imasu

Requests using the '–te form'

The –te form followed by **kudasái** is a very useful way to request someone to do something for you. Actually, this auxiliary is a form of the verb, 'to give', which will be treated in greater detail in the discussion of verbs of giving and receiving in Unit 12 (see p. 195). For the time being, you can think of **kudasái** as being close to the idea of 'please' in

English. Here are some requests that any language learner would find indispensable. Listen to the examples from the list below recorded on the cassette tape.

Moo ichido itte kudasái.   *Please say it again.*
Mótto yukkúri hanáshite kudasai.   *Please speak more slowly.*

And if all that fails you could try:

Eigo de itte kudasái.   *Please say it in English.*

Another very useful phrase is **...o oshiete kudasái** '*please teach me*' or '*please tell me*':

Nihongo o oshiete kudasái.   *Please teach me Japanese.*
Yuubínkyoku e no michi o   *Please tell me the way to the post office.*
    oshiete kudasái.

While these –**te kudasái** forms make perfectly acceptable requests for most situations, there are times when you might need a more polite expression. Generally, you can make a request more polite by framing it as a question. A negative question is politer still. It is interesting to see how a similar pattern can be seen in both the Japanese sentences below and their English translations.

Chízu o káite kudasai.   *Please draw me a map.*
Chízu o káite kudasaimasu ka.   *Would you draw me a map?*
Chízu o káite kudasaimasen ka.   *Wouldn't you draw me a map?*

A very polite request form, which you are likely to hear and perhaps even use yourself, is –**te itadakemásu ka**, which we shall gloss for the time being as '*would you be so kind as to...*' or '*would you mind...*', but which we shall see later is also bound up with the idea of giving and receiving.

Shitsúrei desu ga, onamae o   *Excuse me, but would you mind*
    oshiete itadakemásu ka.   *telling me your name?*

The particle o with verbs of motion

You will recall that intransitive verbs which describe movement from one place to another often mark the location through which the motion occurs with the particle **o**. The English gloss for this **o** might be a preposition like 'along', 'through', 'over', etc.

Sono semái toorí o massúgu itte kudasái.	*Please go straight along that narrow road.*
Tsugí no kádo o migi e magatte kudasái.	*Turn right at the next corner.*
Densha ga nagái tonneru o toorimashita.	*The train went through a long tunnel.*

Exercise 6.3

Using the request form introduced above, ask your friend to do the following for you.

1. Write it in romanised Japanese (**roomáji**).
2. Wait a minute (use **chotto**).
3. Say it again.
4. Ring you at three o'clock.
5. Draw (write) you a map.

Dialogue 2 ■

A stranger is asking directions to the central post office. In the written text of this dialogue we have introduced some additional **kanji** compounds for recognition only. From this point on we will indicate with **furigana** the pronunciation of any words written with **kanji** not previously introduced.

男の人: すみません。

女の人: はい。

男の人: ちょっとおうかがいしますが、中央
　　　　郵便局はどちらでしょうか。

女の人： つぎの　かどを　ひだりへ　まがって、ひろい　みちを
　　　　　ずっとまっすぐ行ってください。
男の人： そこのかどを　ひだりですね。
女の人： はい、そうです。そして三つめの　しんごうを　みぎへ
　　　　　まがってください。すると
　　　　　すぐあります。東京駅、丸の内の　みなみぐちの　ま
　　　　　えに　あります。
男の人： あるいて、何ぷんぐらい　かかりますか。
女の人： そうですねえ。四五ふん　かかります。
男の人： どうもありがとうございました。
女の人： あめですから、とちゅうから　ちかどうを　とおって行
　　　　　ってください。
男の人： はい。どうも、ごしんせつに。
女の人： どういたしまして。

OTOKÓNOHITO:	Sumimasén.
ONNÁNOHITO:	Hái.
OTOKÓNOHITO:	Chotto oukagai shimásu ga、chuuoo-yuubínkyoku wa dóchira deshoo ka.
ONNÁNOHITO:	Tsugi no kádo o hidari e magatte, hirói michi o zutto massúgu itte kudasái.
OTOKÓNOHITO:	Soko no kádo o hidari desu ne.
ONNÁNOHITO:	Hái, sóo desu. Soshite mittsume no shingoo o migi e magatte kudasái. Suruto, súgu arimásu. Tookyoo éki, Marunóuchi no minamiguchi no máe ni arimásu.
OTOKÓNOHITO:	Arúite nánpun gurai kakarimásu ka.
ONNÁNOHITO:	Soo desu nee. Shigofun kakarimásu.
OTOKÓNOHITO:	Dóomo arígatoo gozaimashita.
ONNÁNOHITO:	Áme desu kara tochuu kara chikádoo o tóotte itte kudasái.
OTOKÓNOHITO:	Hái. Dóomo, goshínsetsu ni.
ONNÁNOHITO:	Dóo itashimashite.

MAN:	*Excuse me.*
WOMAN:	*Yes?*
MAN:	*I wonder if you could tell me where the central post office is?*
WOMAN:	*Turn left at the next corner, and keep going straight along the wide road.*

MAN:		*Left at the corner there, is it?*
WOMAN :		*Yes, that's right. And turn right at the third set of traffic lights. Then it's right there. It is in front of the Marunouchi southern entrance to Tokyo Station.*
MAN:		*About how many minutes will it take on foot?*
WOMAN :		*Let me think. It'll take four or five minutes.*
MAN:		*Thank you very much.*
WOMAN :		*As it is raining, take the underground walkway part of the way.* (literally, 'from along the way')
MAN:		*Yes. It's very kind of you* (to suggest that).
WOMAN :		*Not at all.*

Vocabulary

ちょっと	**chótto**	*a little; just*
おうかがい します	**oukagai shimásu**	*excuse me, may I ask…?*
つぎ	**tsugí**	*next*
ひろい	**hirói**	*wide, broad, spacious (room)*
あめ	**áme**	*rain*
あめですから	**áme desu kara**	*because it is raining (literally, 'because it is rain')*
あるいて	**aruite**	*walking, on foot*
とちゅう	**tochuu**	*along the way, part of the way*
ちかどう	**chikádoo**	*underground walkway*

Exercise 6.4

A new flatmate has moved into your flat. You decide to show him around the town. Can you explain how to get from where you are standing to the following places? You'll need to familiarise yourself with some new vocabulary items first. Try to come up with your own directions first then check your answers in the Key to the Exercises (p. 268).

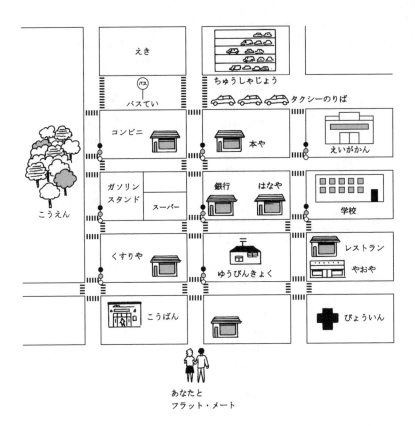

えき
バスてい
ちゅうしゃじょう
タクシーのりば
コンビニ
本や
えいがかん
ガソリン スタンド
スーパー
銀行
はなや
学校
こうえん
くすりや
ゆうびんきょく
レストラン
やおや
こうばん
びょういん

あなたと
フラット・メート

Vocabulary

えき	**éki**	*station*
バスてい	**basutei**	*bus stop*
タクシーのりば	**takushii-nóriba**	*taxi rank*
ちゅうしゃじょう	**chuushajoo**	*car park*
ガソリン・スタンド	**gasorin-sutándo**	*petrol station*
えいがかん	**eigákan**	*cinema, movie theatre*
こうえん	**kooen**	*park*
スーパー	**súupaa**	*supermarket*
コンビニ	**konbíni**	*convenience store*
びょういん	**byooin**	*hospital*
はなや	**hanáya**	*florist*
やおや	**yaoya**	*greengrocer*
くすりや	**kusuriya**	*chemist, pharmacy*

さいしょの	saisho no	*first*
はじめの	hajime no	*first, beginning*
一つめ	hitotsume	*first*
二つめ	futatsume	*second*
三つめ	mittsume	*third*
四つめ	yottsume	*fourth*
つきあたり	tsukiatari	*end of the road/corridor etc.; T-junction*
しんごう	shingoo	*signal, traffic lights*
こうさてん	koosaten	*intersection, junction*
とおり	toorí	*street, road*
おうだんほどう	oodan-hódoo	*pedestrian-crossing*
わたります	watarimásu	*to cross*
わたってください	watatte kudasái	*please cross*
わたると	wataru to	*when one crosses*
むこうがわ	mukoogawa	*opposite side*
むこう	mukoo	*opposite, beyond, overseas*
となり	tonari	*next to, neighbouring*
こうばん	kooban	*police box*
こうさてん	koosaten	*cross-roads, junction*
てまえ	temae	*in front of, before* (with location)
また	mata	*again; further*
つぎ	tsugi	*next, following*

Use the map and the vocabulary list supplied above and give her the directions she needs. For those of you without the tape we have given cues in English and sample answers in the key at the back of the book.

Q: **Dóo yatte gasorin-sutándo e ikimásu ka.**

A: **Kono michi o massúgu itte, futatsume no shingoo o hidari e magatte kudasái. Gasorin-sutándo wa migigawa de, súupaa no tonari désu.**

1. the post-office	2. the school	3. the taxi rank
4. the park	5. the hospital	6. the chemist
7. the florist	8. the restaurant	9. the station
10. the convenience store		

Make sure you can explain how to get to all of the destinations marked on the map.

Ordinal numbers

In addition to the quasi-Chinese set of numbers, **ichí**, **ní**, **san**, etc., Japanese has a set of native numerals which are used with the suffix –**tsu** to count miscellaneous objects with no obvious numeral classifier and also for counting age. The native numerals have been largely replaced by the Chinese numerals and are now generally found only up to ten. Here are the native Japanese numerals up to ten, paired with the numeral classifier, –**tsu**. Notice the word for 'ten' does not take the classifier.

1	2	3	4	5	6	7	8	9	10
hitótsu	futatsú	mittsú	yottsú	itsútsu	muttsú	nanátsu	yattsú	kokónotsu	tóo
一つ	二つ	三つ	四つ	五つ	六つ	七つ	八つ	九つ	十

It is this set of numbers, up to ten at any rate, which take the ordinal number suffix –**me** め. In the previous exercise we met **hitotsume** '*the first*', **futatsume** '*the second*', etc. It is also possible to use the Chinese set of numerals with the ordinal suffix, –**bánme**, as in **ichibánme** '*the first*', **nibánme** '*the second*', etc. After 10, of course, the –**bánme** alternative must be used, e.g. **sanjuuichibánme** '*the thirty-first*'.

Exercise 6.5

1. Listen to this dialogue we overheard in a department store. A middle-aged female customer is looking for the toilet. She asks a young shop assistant for help. You can find the romanised version of this passage and the translation in the key at the back of the book.

おきゃくさん: おてあらいは どこですか。

てんいん: はい、女性の おてあらいは このさきに
あります。
まず、ここを まっすぐ 行って ください。
そしてつきあたりを ひだりに まがって
ください。
女性の おてあらいは みぎがわに
あります。

おきゃくさん: 男性のは?

てんいん: は?

おきゃくさん: 男性の　おてあらいの　まえで　ともだちが
　　　　　　　まっていますから。

2. Now imagine you are working in a large resort hotel. A Japanese guest approaches and asks you the way to the gentlemen's toilet. Using the cues and vocabulary items given below, direct the guest to where he has to go. He is greatly relieved to find someone here who can speak Japanese. Tell him to go straight ahead down here until he reaches the end of the corridor. Then he should turn right and he will find the gents' on his left.

Vocabulary

josei	*woman, female*	**tsukiatari**	*end of the road/*
dansei	*man, male*		*corridor,* etc.
kono saki ni	*ahead, along in front*	**mázu**	*first, to start with*
		oteárai	*toilet*

This last is a rather genteel word. You will also hear **tóire** トイレ borrowed from English, **obénjo** or simply **benjo** (the form with the **o**- prefix is softer, more feminine) and **keshóoshitsu**, a euphemism equivalent to 'powder room'.

Expressing your wishes with –tai

One good way to say what you want to do is simply to use the suffix **–tai** on the verb stem. Another way of putting this might be to say that you replace the **–másu** ending with **–tai**, as the verb stem is what is left after **–másu** has been removed. The **–tai** ending is conjugated like an adjective, giving the negative forms, either **–taku arimasén** or **–taku nái desu**. As the **–tai** ending behaves like an adjective, you would expect the object of a verb with **–tai** to be marked by **ga**, but although purists still insist on **ga**, it is not at all uncommon to hear **o** used in this position instead.

Kyóo wa Chuuka-ryóori o tabetái desu.	*Today I want to eat Chinese food.*
Ashita wa ikitaku arimasén (or **ikitaku nai desu**).	*I don't want to go tomorrow.*

As –**tai** implies a degree of subjective judgement it is not usually used to refer to third persons and only refers to the second person in questions.

Nihongo de hanashitáku   *Don't you want to speak Japanese?*
  arimasen ka.

Coming or going to do something

The verb stem followed by the particle **ni** and a verb of coming or going is used to express a reason for going somewhere.

Pán o kai ni ikimáshita.   *I went to buy bread.*
Éiga o mí ni ikitai désu.   *I want to go to see a film.*
Shuumatsu ni asobi ni kite   *Please come to visit* (literally '*to play*')
  kudasái.   *at the weekend.*

In this construction the idea of going seems to have precedence over the other action, with the result that the place phrase, if mentioned, is followed by the directional particle **e** or **ni**.

Yokohama e Chuuka-ryóori o   *Shall we go to eat Chinese food in*
  tabe ni ikimashóo ka.   *Yokohama?*

Exercise 6.6 ■

Using the English cues given below, create a role-play dialogue in which Asako says she would like to do something and you respond suggesting that you both do it together. For example:

Cue: buy new clothes
Asako: **Atarashíi yoofuku ga kaitai désu.**
You: **Já, issho ni kai ni ikimashóo.**

1. eat Chinese food   2. see a film   3. buy a mobile phone
4. study English in   5. listen to rock
   London   music

Kanji

In this unit we introduce the **kanji** for some common Japanese verbs and adjectives, some of which we have met before. The letters in parenthesis are to be written in **hiragána**.

7 + 7 = 14 strokes

KOO
i (kimásu)
to go

KAI
ai (másu)
to meet

BAI
ka (imásu)
to buy

BAI
u (rimásu)
to sell

DOKU, TOKU
yo (mimasu)
to read

GIN
silver

SHA
company

SHO
ka (kimásu)
to write

BUN
ki (kimásu)
to hear

SHIN
atara (shíi)
new

Katakána

We have almost come to the end of the **katakána** syllabary. The five remaining symbols will be introduced in Unit 7. You should now be able to read and write almost all of the **katakána** words you come across and most of you should be able to write your names in **katakána**.

ke   se   te   ne   nu

ya   yo   ru   re   ro

Exercise 6.7

What do the items in each of the following lists of **katakána** words have in common? The answers plus the meaning and romanisation of the words appear in the Key to the Exercises (p. 271).

1. クラリネット、カスタネット、トロンボーン、フルート、クリスマス・キャロル
2. カクテル、ヌーガー、セロリー、ヨーグルト、チョコレート
3. カヌー、カヤック、ヨット、オール、ボート
4. ケニヤ、セネガル、ヨーロッパ、ブラジル、ローマ
5. バレンタイン・デー、セール、ケーキ、ルーレット、プレゼント

Exercise 6.8 ■■

First, read through the following passage silently to yourself. Then, following the written text with your eyes listen carefully to the voice on the cassette tape. Finally, read the passage aloud. Can you answer the questions below the passage? New vocabulary items are given below the passage.

先週の金曜日のばんに、会社の
カクテール・パーティーで高山さんと安田さんに会いました。
高山さんは新聞きしゃで、読売新聞につとめています。安田さんは銀行マンで、わたしのうちのちかくに すんでいます。
二人とも　むかし　ヨーロッパで　しごとを
していました。高山さんは　四年間　ロンドンに
いました。英語がとても上手です。安田さんは
ながくイタリアのいなかにすんでいました。
イタリアりょうりが大好きで、じぶんでよくつくります。
今イタリアのパスタとデザートについて本を書いています。

1. Where did I meet Mr Yasuda?
2. When did I meet Mr Takayama?
3. Why do you think Mr Takayama speaks such good English?
4. Where does Mr Takayama work?
5. What do Mr Yasuda and Mr Takayama have in common?
6. What project is Mr Yasuda engaged in at the moment?

Vocabulary

新聞きしゃ	**shinbun-kísha**	*journalist, newspaper reporter*
つとめています	**tsutómete imasu**	*works for, serves* (takes **ni**)
しごと	**shigoto**	*work*
むかし	**mukashi**	*formerly, in the past*
いなか	**inaka**	*country(side)*
について	**ni tsúite**	*about*
じょうすな	**joozú na**	*be skilled in, be good at*

7 どんな感じの人ですか。
Dónna kanji no hito désu ka.

What does he look like?

In this unit you will learn how to:

- Describe how things look or seem
- Ask, give and refuse permission
- Report what people say or think
- Explain when things happen
- Make compound sentences
- Give reasons
- Use plain-form verbs in subordinate clauses
- Form the plain past-tense form of verbs
- Describe sequences of events
- Say what happened before something else.

You will also acquire:

- 10 more **kanji**:　食　事　飲　車　分　早　白　青　手　私
- 5 more **katakána**:　ワ　ヲ　エ　ン　ヴ

Dialogue 1 ◼

Graham Short is due to arrive at Narita Airport tomorrow morning. Mr Abe, a division head with Nichiei Trading asks his young Australian assistant, Bruce, to go to the airport to meet him. Bruce wonders how he will recognise Mr Short.

阿部:　あした、イギリスからショートさんが来ますから、
　　　　くうこうへ　むかえに行ってください。あさ、
　　　　九時三十分の　ひこうきで　つくよていです。

ブルース: そうですか。ところで、ショートさんは どんないろの
ふくを きている でしょうか。

阿部<ruby>あべ</ruby>: ファックスによると、こんの せびろを きて、
青いネクタイを しめてくるそうです。

ブルース: そうですか。それでは どんなかんじの人か
おしえてください。

阿部<ruby>あべ</ruby>: そうですねえ。かおは ほそくて、かみのけは
ちゃいろだ そうです。

ブルース: めがねを かけていますか。

阿部<ruby>あべ</ruby>: いいえ、かけていません。

ブルース: せの高さは どうですか。

阿部<ruby>あべ</ruby>: せは高くて、やせている そうです。

ブルース: では、なまえと はんたいですね。

阿部<ruby>あべ</ruby>: ほんとうですねえ。それから、年れいですが、
四十ぐらいらしいです。

ブルース: はい。だいたい どんなかんじの人か 分かりました。

阿部<ruby>あべ</ruby>: それでは明日<ruby>あした</ruby>おねがいします。
ホテルにチェックインしてから会社に
つれて来てください。

ブルース: はい、わかりました。

ABE: Ashita, Igirisu kara Shóoto san ga kimásu kara, kuukoo e mukae ni itte kudasai. Ása kúji sanjúppun no hikóoki de tsukú yotei désu.

BURUUSU: Sóo desu ka. Tokoróde, Shóoto san wa dónna iro no fukú o kite iru deshóo ka.

ABE: Fákkusu ni yoru to, kón no sebiro o kite, aói nékutai o shímete kuru soo desu.

BURUUSU: Sóo desu ka. Sore de wa dónna kanji no hito ka oshiete kudasái.

ABE: Sóo desu née, kao wa hósokute, kaminóke wa chairo da sóo desu.

BURUUSU: Mégane o kákete imasu ka.

ABE: Iie, kákete imasen.
BURUUSU: Sé no takasa wa dóo desu ka.
ABE: Sé wa takákute, yasete iru sóo desu.
BURUUSU: Déwa, namae to hantai désu ne.
ABE: Hontoo desu nee. Sore kara, nenrei désu ga, yónjuu gurai
            rashíi desu.
BURUUSU: Hái. Daitai dónna kanji no hito ka wakarimáshita.
ABE: Sore déwa, ashita onegai shimásu. Hóteru ni chekkuín shite
            kara, kaisha ni tsurete kite kudasái.
BURUUSU: Hái, wakarimáshita.

ABE: *Tomorrow Mr Short is coming from England, so please go
            to the airport to meet him. He is scheduled to arrive in the
            morning on the 9:30 plane.*
BRUCE: *I see. By the way, what colour clothes will he be wearing?*
ABE: *According to the fax he'll be wearing a navy suit and a
            blue tie.*
BRUCE: *Oh really? Then could you tell me what he looks like?*
ABE: *Let me think, they say he has a narrow face and brown hair.*
BRUCE: *Does he wear glasses?*
ABE: *No, he doesn't.*
BRUCE: *What about his height?*
ABE: *Apparently he is tall and thin.*
BRUCE: *Then, he is the opposite of his name, isn't he?*
ABE: *That's right, isn't it! Then there's his age. Apparently he is
            around forty.*
BRUCE: *I see. Well then, I have a pretty good idea what he looks like.*
ABE: *Well then, I'm counting on you for tomorrow. Bring him to
            the office after he has checked in at the hotel.*
BRUCE: *Yes, certainly sir.*

Vocabulary

から	kara	*because…, …and so* (conjunction)
くうこう	kuukoo	*airport*
むかえ に 行って	mukae ni itte	*going to meet*
ふく	fukú	*clothes*
ファックス	fákkusu	*fax, facsimile*
…によると	… ni yoru to	*according to*

ひこうき	hikóoki	aeroplane, plane
つく	tsukú	arrive
よてい	yotei	schedule, plan
どんな	dónna	what kind of
かんじ	kanji	feeling, impression
ふく	fukú	clothes
でしょうか	deshóo ka	... do you think?
青	áo	blue (noun)
かお	kao	face
ほそくて	hósokute	slender and ..., thin and ...
かみのけ	kaminóke	hair (of head)
めがね	mégane	glasses, spectacles
せのたかさ	sé no takasa	height
やせている	yasete iru	is thin
そうです	... sóo desu	they say ..., apparently
ねんれい	nenrei	age
ぐらい	gurai	about
だいたい	daitai	more or less, approximately
チェックインする	chekkuín suru	check in (verb)
つれてくる	tsurete kúru	to bring (a person)

Compound sentences

The easiest way to expand on the simple sentence is to combine two contrasting sentences with **ga** or **keredomo** (**kedo** in informal colloquial speech), both of which carry the idea of 'but' in English. Generally, in these constructions the verb before **ga** or **keredomo** carries the same –**másu** ending as the verb at the end of the sentence. You should take care to pronounce these clause-final particles as if they were attached to the preceding verb and not as the first word of the second clause as we do in English.

Jikan wa arimasu ga, okane wa arimasen.   *I have the time, but I don't have the money.*

Note that in sentences of this kind, where a strong contrast is implied, the contrasting nouns are usually followed by the particle **wa**.

Abe san wa kimásu ga, Yamamoto san wa kimasén.   *Mr Abe is coming, but Mr Yamamoto is not.*

Nihongo wa mushikashíi desu keredomo, omoshirói desu.   *Japanese is difficult, but it is interesting.*

Giving reasons

Another common compound sentence is formed by two clauses linked by
kara, '*because*'. The clause preceding **kara** gives the reason for the
action described by the main verb at the end of the sentence.

Íma jikan ga arimasén kara, ashita shimásu.	*I haven't time now, so I'll do it tomorrow.*

Sometimes, a sentence ending in **kara** is tacked on as if it were an
afterthought.

Ashita ni shimashóo. Kyoo wa isogashíi kara.	*Let's make it tomorrow. I'm busy today.*

As in this example, Japanese tends to be more explicit, indicating the
reason with **kara**, whereas in English the reason is implied by simply
juxtaposing the two sentences.

Exercise 7.1

Match the consequences in the left-hand column with the most appropriate reasons on the right, joining them into a single sentence with **kara**.
Several new vocabulary items are introduced in this exercise. Follow the
example below:

Cue: **ashita shimásu**   **kyoo wa isogashíi desu**
A: **Kyoo wa isogashíi desu kara ashita shimásu.**

Consequences	Reasons
1. háyaku yasumimásu	a. onaka ga itái desu (*I have a stomach ache*)
2. tabemásu	b. onaka ga sukimashita (*I'm hungry*)
3. bíiru demo nomimashóo	c. okane ga arimasén
4. sen'en kashite kudasái	d. tsukarete imásu
5. kusuri o nomimásu	e. nódo ga kawakimáshita (*I'm thirsty*)

Vocabulary

onaka	*stomach, belly*	**kawakimásu**	*to become dry*
nódo	*throat*	**kasu**	*to lend*

sukimásu	*to become empty*	**kusuri**	*medicine*
tsukaréru	*to become tired*	**itai**	*hurts, aches, is painful*

Verbs in the plain form

We have seen Japanese verbs with the polite –**másu** ending and in the gerund or –**te** form. Another form of the verb is the PLAIN FORM, often also called the 'dictionary form' for the obvious reason that this is how verbs are usually listed in dictionaries. Here again it is necessary to revisit the four conjugations of Japanese verbs, the copula, consonant-root verbs, vowel-root verbs and irregular verbs. Here, using some verbs we have already met, are examples of the –**másu** form, –**te** form and the **plain** form of each of these verb conjugations:

Form Conjugation	–**másu** form	–**te** form	–**plain** form
copula	**désu** です	**de** で	**da (de aru)** だ(である)
consonant-root verb	**kakimásu** 書きます	**káite** 書いて	**káku** 書く
vowel-root verb	**tabemásu** 食べます	**tábete** 食べて	**tabéru** 食べる
irregular verb	**shimásu** します	**shite** して	**suru** する

All vowel-root verbs have dictionary forms ending in –**ru**, but not all verbs ending in –**ru** are vowel-root verbs. That is to say, it is not always possible to tell the dictionary form from the –**másu** form. Verbs ending in –**emásu** are all vowel-root verbs with plain forms ending in –**eru**, but with other verbs you can never be really sure. If you know the dictionary form you can accurately predict the –**másu** form, except in the case of verbs ending in –**ru**, where you need the additional information of the verb's conjugation before you can correctly assign its –**másu** form. Take, for example, the Japanese equivalents of the verbs '*to wear*' and '*to cut*', the vowel-root verb **kiru** and the consonant-root verb **kíru** (note the difference in pitch accent), which respectively have the –**másu** forms **kimásu** '*wears*' and **kirimásu** '*cuts*'. To form the –**másu** form from the plain form, then, vowel-root verbs simply drop the –**ru** ending and add –**másu**, whereas consonant-root verbs drop the final –**u** and add –**imásu**. In the process of adding the –**imásu** ending, verbs ending in –**tsu** and –**su** undergo slight sound changes becoming –**chimásu** and –**shimásu** respectively. For example, **mátsu** '*to wait*' becomes **machimásu** and **hanásu** '*to speak*' becomes **hanashimásu**.

Note that the plain-form equivalent of the copula, **désu**, is **da**.

The plain-form past tense

We have already met the past-tense marker, –**ta**, in the polite, final-verb endings –**máshita** and **déshita**. This ending attaches to the verb stem in the same way as the –**te** form does and undergoes all the same sound changes depending on the immediately preceding sounds. For practical purposes, then, all you need do to form the plain past tense is to substitute an '**a**' for the final '**e**' of the –**te** form.

káite *writing*	**káita** *wrote* (plain past tense form)
yónde *reading*	**yónda** *read* (plain past tense form)
itte *going*	**itta** *went* (plain past tense form)

Uses of the plain form

The plain form is used as a final verb in casual conversations between family members or close friends and when talking to children. As you become more fluent in Japanese you will learn when it is appropriate to switch to the plain form for final verbs. In the meantime, however, you should continue using the polite style, ending every sentence in –**másu** or **désu**. You cannot avoid learning the plain forms, however, as they occur frequently in non-final verbs (i.e. in subordinate clauses).

The various uses of the plain form will be introduced gradually over the next few units. In this unit we introduce the plain form as it is used in a number of time constructions and for quoting what one says or thinks.

Probability

The conjectural form of the copula, **deshóo**, is used after a plain-form verb to express probability, supposition or speculation.

Tanaka san wa ashita kúru	*Mr Tanaka will probably come*
deshoo.	*tomorrow.*

This same sentence with the final **deshóo** pronounced with a rising then falling question intonation means something like, '*Mr Tanaka will be coming tomorrow, won't he?*' or '*I'm right in thinking Mr Tanaka will be coming tomorrow, aren't I?*'

After a verb in the plain past tense, **deshóo**, usually expresses a supposition.

Abe san no hikóoki wa moo Tookyoo ni tsúita deshóo.	*Mr Abe's plane must have already arrived in Tokyo.*

Before

The plain form of the verb followed by the noun, **máe** *'front'*, is used to convey the idea of 'before'. The use of the time particle **ni** after **máe** seems to be optional. Where it is used it emphasises the point of time more precisely.

Irassháru máe ni denwa o kudasái.	*Please give me a ring before you come.*
Tookyoo ni kuru máe Róndon ni súnde imashita.	*Before I came to Tokyo I lived in London.*

After ... –ing ... '–te kara'

We have seen the particle, **kara**, used after a noun in the sense of *'from'*, e.g. **Tookyoo kara Shizuoka made Shinkánsen de ichijíkan kakarimásu**. *'It takes an hour on the Shinkansen ('bullet train') from Tokyo to Shizuoka.'* After the **–te** form of a verb, **kara** means *'after'*. In this construction the event in the main clause (i.e. the verb at the end of the sentence) generally follows on immediately after the verb in the subordinate clause and the sequence of events has been planned in advance by the subject of the main clause.

Shokuji shite kara térebi o mimáshita.	*I watched television after having my meal.*
Suzuki san ga kite kara soodan shimashóo.	*Let's discuss it after Mr Suzuki comes.*
Nihón ni tsúite kara súgu Nihongo no benkyoo o hajimemásu.	*I'll start studying Japanese immediately after I arrive in Japan.*

A sentence such as **Senséi ga káette kara Fújiko san ga kimáshita** *'Fujiko came after the teacher had gone home'*, would indicate that Fujiko had timed her arrival to occur after the teacher's departure. Where this sense of planning is absent, 'after' is expressed with the conjunction, **áto** *'after'*. More of this construction later.

Exercise 7.2 ▪

Listen to the pairs of sentences given on the cassette tape and join them
with **máe ni** or **–te kara** as the sense demands. You should have time to
give your answer before the correct answer comes on the tape. You
should keep the sentences in the same order when you combine them.

Cue: **dekakemásu**   **térebi o keshite kudasái**
A: **Dekakeru máe ni térebi o keshite kudasái.**

1. kaisha e dekakemásu   chooshoku o tabemásu
2. okane o iremásu   bótan o oshimásu
3. bótan o oshimásu   nomímono ga déte kimásu
4. denwa o shimáshita   denwa-bángoo o shirabemáshita
5. jogingu o shimasu   sháwaa o abimásu
6. nemásu   sutóobu o keshite kudasái

Vocabulary

dekakéru	to set out, leave (for = **e**)	**osu**	to push
kesu	to put out, turn off	**nomímono**	drink
		déte kuru	to come out
chooshoku or **asa-góhan**	breakfast	**sháwaa o abiru**	to have a shower, take a shower
chuushoku or **hiru-góhan**	lunch	**neru**	to sleep, go to bed
yuushoku or **ban-góhan**	dinner	**sutóobu**	stove, heater
bótan	button		

Indirect or reported speech or thought

To report what you or others have said or what you think, the Quotative
Particle, **to**, '*that*' or '*thus*', is used after the verb in the subordinate clause
(i.e. clauses containing a non-final verb) and the principal clause contains a verb of saying or thinking. In casual conversation, you will often

hear this particle pronounced **te** or **tte**, but for the time being you should stick to the standard pronunciation, **to**.

Suzuki san wa ashita kúru to iimáshita yo.	*Mr Suzuki said he is coming tomorrow, you know.*
Onamae wa nán to osshaimásu ka.	*What is your name?* (honorific)
Jón to mooshimásu.	*My name is John.* (formal)
Nihon-ryóori wa oishii to omoimásu ka.	*Do you think Japanese cooking tastes good?*

Another way to indicate that you are passing on what someone else has told you is to simply add **sóo desu** (the accent is lost after an accented verb) '*I hear*', '*they say*', '*the story goes*', etc., after the plain form of the verb.

Ashita kúru soo desu.	*Apparently he is coming tomorrow.*
Ano résutoran wa takái soo desu yo.	*They say that restaurant is expensive, you know.*

The expression **yóo desu** '*it seems*', '*it looks as if*' is similar to **sóo desu**, but tends to be used to indicate a judgement based on visible evidence rather than hearsay.

Kono térebi wa kowárete iru yoo desu.	*This television appears to be broken.*

Another expression used after a plain verb form, **rashíi desu**, '*it seems*', '*it appears*', can be used for either hearsay or appearance, thus combining the functions of **sóo desu** and **yóo desu**.

Anóhito wa máinichi gókiro hashíru rashíi desu yo.	*Apparently he runs five kilometres every day.*

Indirect questions

The quotative particle, **to**, is not generally used in reported or indirect questions. In this case the question particle, **ka**, follows the plain verb form in the subordinate clause in conjunction with a main verb of asking, telling, understanding, knowing or believing.

Kyoo nánji ni káeru ka wakarimasén.	*I don't know what time I'll* (or *'he'll'*) *be home today.*
Anóhito ga náni o itte iru ka sappári wakarimasén.	*I can't understand a word he is saying.*

It is usual to leave out the plain copula, **da**, before the question marker **ka**, as in the following examples taken from the opening dialogue, but you will sometimes hear the sequence **da ka**... in indirect questions.

Sore dewa, dónna hito ka oshiete kudasái.	*Then, tell me what sort of person he is?*
Taitei dónna kanji no hito ka wakarimáshita.	*I have a general idea of what kind of person he is.*
Nán da ka wakarimasén or **Náni ka wakarimasén.**	*I don't know what it is.*

When or whenever

We have met the particle **to** used to link nouns in the sense of '*and*' or '*with*' and we have seen in this unit how **to** can be used to mark the end of a quotation. Another clause-final particle, **to**, which follows the plain present tense (dictionary form) of the verb, expresses the idea of '*when*', '*whenever*' or '*if*' . When the final verb is in the present tense the main clause is a natural or habitual consequence of the clause ending in **to**. In this construction the main verb cannot be an imperative, request or verb expressing the speaker's determination.

Suzuki san ga kúru to tanoshíi desu.	*It's fun when Mr Suzuki comes.*
Íma súgu iku to básu ni ma ni aimásu yo.	*If you go straight away you'll be in time for the bus.*

When the final verb is in the past tense there is not necessarily an antecedent and consequent relationship between the clauses, but there is often a sense of surprise at the outcome expressed in the main verb.

| **Mádo kara sóto o míru to áme ga fútte imashita.** | *When I looked out of the window (I was surprised to notice that) it was raining.* |
| **Uchi ni káeru to kodomo ga byooki de nete imáshita.** | *When I got home my child was sick in bed.* |

The time when, toki

Another very common way of expressing time is simply to use a verb in the plain form followed by the noun **toki** 時 '*time*'. This last construction, however, is used only for 'when' and does not carry the sense of hypothetical or uncertain events conveyed by English 'if' or Japanese **to**.

| **Kaisha ni tsúita toki ni wa súgu watashi ni denwa shite kudasái.** | *When you get to the office please ring me at once.* |

Sequences of events

While nouns can be joined with **to**, verbs, adjectives and clauses are linked by putting all but the final element in the **–te** form. The **–te** form carries no tense in itself, the tense being conveyed by the final verb.

Kaisha e itte shinbun o yomimáshita.	*I went to the office and read the newspaper.*
Tookyoo e itte Nihongo o benkyoo shitai désu.	*I'd like to go to Tokyo and study Japanese.*
Kono résutoran no shokuji wa oishikute yasúi desu.	*The food at this restaurant is tasty and cheap.*

Permission and prohibition

A verb in the **–te** form followed by the particle **mo** means, '*even if one does…*'. Perhaps the most common use of this construction is in combination with **íi desu**, '*it is good*', '*it will be all right*', etc., to indicate permission.

| **Koko de tabako o sutte mo íi desu.** | *You may smoke here.* |
| **Kono hón o karite mo íi desu ka.** | *May I borrow this book?* |

Instead of **íi desu**, **kamaimasén** ('*it doesn't matter*') can be used to make the expression a little softer.

Kyoo wa háyaku káette mo kamaimasén.	*Today you may go home early* (literally, 'I don't mind even if you go home early').

The idea of prohibition is suggested with the use of –**te wa damé desu**, literally, '*as for doing…, it is no good*', or –**te wa ikemasén** '*as for doing…, it will not do*', etc.

Résutoran de tabako o sutte wa ikemasén.	*You must not smoke in the restaurant.*
Sono hón o karite wa ikemasén.	*You must not borrow that book.*

Exercise 7.3

A young Japanese on a working holiday is spending a week at your place to improve his English. You explain to him the rules of your house. Follow the example and use the lists below to tell your visitor what he can and cannot do.

Cue: **tabako o suimasu** (to smoke cigarettes)
A: **Sóto de tabako o sutté mo íi desu.**
    Náka de tabako o sutté wa damé desu.

1. keitai-dénwa o tsukaimásu (to use a mobile phone)
2. kakimásu
3. hanashimásu
4. haraimásu (to pay)
5. sháwaa o abimásu (abite) to take a shower

Permitted	*Prohibited*
sóto de (outside)	náka de
básu de (on the bus)	eigákan de (in the cinema)
pén de (with a pen)	enpitsu de (in pencil)
Eigo de (in English)	Nihongo de (in Japanese)
dóru de (in dollars)	en de (in yen)
ása	yóru (at night)

When you have finished making your pairs of dos and don'ts, try joining them into a single sentence with **ga** ('*but*'). For example:

Sóto de tabako o sutté mo íi desu ga, náka de sutté wa damé desu.

Now practise asking permission, approving or rejecting your own requests according to the instructions in the permitted and prohibited columns. Follow the two examples:

Q: **Keitai-dénwa o básu de tsukatté mo íi desu ka.**
A: **Hai, tsukatté mo íi desu.**
Q: **Keitai-dénwa o eigákan de tsukatté mo íi desu ka.**
A: **Iie, tsukatté wa damé desu.**

Exercise 7.4

You have just arrived at a traditional Japanese inn, or **ryokan**, in a hot spring (**onsen**) resort in the Japanese Alps. After changing into your summer kimono or **yukata** you come down to the front desk to sort out a few problems. Fill in the blanks in the following dialogue that you have with the manager.

MANAGER: Ohéya wa ikága desu ka. *How is your room, Sir/Madam?*
YOU: Íi héya de, nagamé mo subarashíi desu. *It is a nice room with a wonderful view.*
MANAGER: Oki ni itte itadaite ureshíi desu. *I'm glad you like it.*
YOU: Keredomo, 1. _____ (*the TV is broken*)
MANAGER: Dóomo sumimasén. Súgu naoshimásu. *I'm very sorry. We'll fix it at once.*
YOU: 2. _____ (*Are the shops [mise] in the hotel lobby [róbii] open now?*)
MANAGER: Iie, íma wa 3. _____ (*No, they are closed now.*)
YOU: Shokuji wa moo 4. _____ (*Is the meal ready yet?*)
MANAGER: Iie, máda 5. _____ (*No, it's not ready yet.*)
YOU: Ja, 6. _____ (*Is there an automatic vending machine, then?*)
MANAGER: Hái, dansei no ofúro no máe 7. _____ (*Yes, there is one in front of the men's bath.*)

You will need some vocabulary items to complete this exercise.

Vocabulary

ohéya	*your room, room* (honorific)
heyá	*room*
nagamé	*view*
subarashíi	*wonderful*
oki ni itte itadaite	*to have you like it, that you like it*
ureshíi	*happy, glad*
naósu	*to fix, mend*
akimásu	*to open* (intransitive)
shimarimásu	*to close* (intransitive)
kowaremásu	*to break, get broken* (intransitive)
dékite imasu	*to be ready, to be done*
moo	*already*
máda	*still* (not) *yet*
jidoohanbáiki	*automatic vending machine*
dansei	*men, male*
josei	*women, female*
ofúro	*bath*

Exercise 7.5 ▬

Listen to the passage on the tape then answer the following questions in English. You will need to learn a few more vocabulary items, listed below, before you can follow the passage. You will find the answers in the Key to the Exercises (p. 272). For those of you without the cassette tape, a romanised version of the passage appears in the Key to the Exercises.

1. Where was Mr Tanaka born?
2. How old is he now?
3. What does Mr Tanaka look like?
4. What sport did he play at university?
5. Which university did he attend?
6. When did he graduate?
7. How often does he play tennis these days?
8. Which company does he work for?
9. Where is Mr Tanaka working now?
10. What is happening next year?

Vocabulary

うまれる	**umareru**	*to be born*
ひくい	**hikúi**	*short, low*
すもうぶ	**sumóobu**	*the sumo club*
つとめる	**tsutoméru**	*to work for* (takes **ni**)
かわる	**kawaru**	*to change, move, transfer*
そつぎょうする	**sotsugyoo suru**	*to graduate*
せい	**sei**	*stature, height, build*
はいる	**hairu**	*rejoin, enter, fit*

Possession

Japanese makes a distinction between owning things which may be taken away by others (alienable possession) and things which are intrinsically part of the individual. So to express the idea of 'to have' with material objects, Japanese generally uses the verb **áru** '*to be*', '*to exist*', e.g. **Takayama san wa atarashíi kuruma ga arimásu.** '*Mr Takayama has a new car.*, On the other hand 'to have' with parts of the body, etc., is conveyed with the verb **suru** '*to do*'.

Séeraa san wa aói me o shite imasu.   *Sarah has blue eyes.*
Yásuko san wa kírei na te o shite imasu.   *Yasuko has beautiful hands.*

Wearing clothes

In Japanese a number of different verbs are used where we would use 'to wear' in English. As we have seen the general verb 'to wear' is the vowel-root verb **kiru** '*to wear*' or '*to put on*'. There are, however, more specific verbs for headwear, **kabúru**; footwear, trousers, skirts, etc., **haku**; glasses, necklace, pendant, etc., **kakéru**; tie or belt, **shiméru**; gloves or rings, **hameru**; jewellery, **tsukéru**. To have or wear a beard (**hige**) or moustache (**kuchihige**) is expressed with the verb **hayásu** '*to grow*'.

Exercise 7.6 ■

Read the description and match each sentence with the appropriate illustration.

1. Tanaka san wa kurói booshi o kabútte ite, mégane o kákete imasu.
2. Ueda san wa shirói booshi o kabútte ite, mégane o kákete imasen.

3. Tákushii no unténshu san wa shirói tebúkuro o hamete imásu.
4. Aóyama san wa kuchihige o hayáshite ite, kurói óbi o shímete imasu.
5. Yamamoto san wa kírei na buróochi o tsukéte imasu.
6. Aoki san wa gurée no sebiro o kite ite, shirói kutsú o haite imásu.

When you have identified all the people from the clues on the tape, try describing the characters in the pictures in Japanese. Finally see if you can write all their names in Japanese.

You will need a few more vocabulary items to complete this exercise.

Vocabulary

booshi	*hat*
óbi	*sash, belt*
buróochi	*brooch*
unténshu	*driver*
tebúkuro	*gloves*
gurée	*grey*

Katakána and kanji

With these five **katakána** symbols we have come to the end of both native Japanese syllabaries. You will rarely see two of these new syllables. ヲ is used exclusively for the grammatical function of indicating the object and is hence not used in writing words borrowed from other languages. The only time you might see it is in a text written entirely in **katakána**, as in a telegram or a computer game. ヴ has been manufactured artificially by combining the symbol for **u** and the **nigori** marks to convey the '*v*' sound of European languages, but, apart from its use in some names, it has been virtually abandoned in favour of **katakána** syllables beginning with **b**. For example, ヴァイオリン is now usually written バイオリン, '*violin*'. This unit's new **kanji** appear directly below the **katakána**.

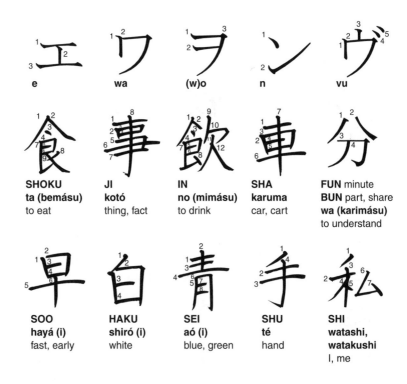

エ	ワ	ヲ	ン	ヴ
e	wa	(w)o	n	vu

食	事	飲	車	分
SHOKU	**JI**	**IN**	**SHA**	**FUN** minute
ta (bemásu)	**kotó**	**no (mimásu)**	**karuma**	**BUN** part, share
to eat	thing, fact	to drink	car, cart	**wa (karimásu)**
				to understand

早	白	青	手	私
SOO	**HAKU**	**SEI**	**SHU**	**SHI**
hayá (i)	**shiró (i)**	**aó (i)**	**té**	**watashi,**
fast, early	white	blue, green	hand	**watakushi**
				I, me

Exercise 7.7

Read the following sentences aloud. To make sure you have understood
what you have read check with the English equivalents in the Key to the
Exercises.

1. 山本さんと本田さんは毎日十二時十五分に会社のとなりのレス
   トランで会って、いっしょに食事しま す。
2. あの白いスポーツ・カーはエドワード・ヴィンセントさんの新
   しい車です。
3. 今日は車で来ましたから、アルコールを飲んではだめです。
4. 青山さんは大きな銀行につとめています。
5. 安子さんはきれいな手をしています。
6. 私はこのごろ毎日日本食を食べています。
7. 今日はどんな食事にしたいですか。
8. ここでたばこを飲んではだめです。

8 市内観光に行きましょう。
Shinai-kánkoo ni ikimashóo.
Let's take the city tour!

In this unit you will learn how to:

- Use the past tense of adjectives
- Give advice and suggest alternatives
- Use adjectival clauses
- Express ability to do something using **kotó ga dekíru**
- Express experience using **kotó ga áru**
- Make comparisons using the particle **yori**.

You will also acquire:

- 10 more **kanji**: 東 京 都 間 花 目 見 午 前 後

Dialogue 1 ■■

Miss Yamada is about to set off on a city tour. We overhear her discussing the day's schedule in the lobby with the tour guide. She seems to be more interested in shopping for souvenirs than seeing the city sights, however.

山田:　　今日は 何時に しゅっぱつしますか。
ガイド:　八時です。ちょう食を食べてからすぐロビーに
　　　　　あつまって ください。
山田:　　はい、分かりました。これから行くところは おもに
　　　　　しない ですか。
ガイド:　ええ、午前は しないかんこうです。午後は
　　　　　はくぶつかんと びじゅつかんを 見に行くよていです。

山田: そうですか。買いものを したいんですが、いつ
できますか。
ガイド: 買いものは ゆう食の前に できます。
山田: みせが しまる時間は だいたい 何時ごろ ですか。
ガイド: そうですねえ。だいたい 六時ごろです。
山田: たのまれた おみやげが たくさん あるんですが。
ガイド: 大じょうぶ ですよ。めんぜいてんは おそくまで
あいていますから。いつでも 買うことができます。
山田: ああ、よかった。

YAMADA: Kyóo wa nánji ni shuppatsu shimásu ka.
GÁIDO: Hachíji desu. Chooshoku o tábete kara súgu róbii ni
atsumátte kudasai.
YAMADA: Hái, wakarimáshita. Kore kara iku tokoro wa ómo ni shínai
desu ka.
GÁIDO: Ée, gózen wa shinai-kánkoo desu. Gógo wa hakubutsúkan to
bijutsúkan o mí ni iku yotei désu.
YAMADA: Sóo desu ka. Kaimono o shitái n' desu ga, ítsu dekimásu ka.
GÁIDO: Kaimono wa yuushoku no máe ni dekimásu.
YAMADA: Mise ga shimáru jikan wa daitai nánji góro desu ka.
GÁIDO: Sóo desu née. Daitai rokúji góro desu.
YAMADA: Tanomáreta o-miyage ga takusan áru n' desu ga.
GÁIDO: Daijóobu desu yo. Menzéiten wa osoku máde aite imásu
kara. Itsudemo kau kotó ga dekimásu.
YAMADA: Áa yókatta.

YAMADA: *What time do we leave today?*
GUIDE: *At 8 o'clock. Please assemble in the lobby straight after
breakfast.*
YAMADA: *Right. Will the places we go to now be mainly in the city?*
GUIDE: *Yes, in the morning we'll do a city tour. In the afternoon we
plan to go to see the museum and the art gallery.*
YAMADA: *I see. I'd like to do some shopping. When will I get the
chance to do it?*
GUIDE: *You will be able to do some shopping before dinner.*
YAMADA: *About what time do the shops close?*
GUIDE: *Let me see. Mostly around six o'clock.*
YAMADA: *I've got lots of presents I've been asked to buy.*
GUIDE: *It'll be all right. The duty-free shops are open until late. You
can buy them any time.*
YAMADA: *Ah. That's good.*

Vocabulary

しゅっぱつする	**shuppatsu suru**	*to leave, depart*
ロビー	**róbii**	*lobby*
あつまる	**atsumáru**	*to gather, assemble*
おもに	**ómo ni**	*mostly, mainly*
午前	**gózen**	*morning, a.m.*
午後	**gógo**	*afternoon*
しないかんこう	**shinai-kánkoo**	*city tour, city sight-seeing*
はくぶつかん	**hakubutsúkan**	*museum*
びじゅつかん	**bijutsúkan**	*art gallery*
見に行く	**mí ni iku**	*to go and see, go to see*
したいんですが...	**shitái n' desu ga**	*I would like to, but…*
できます	**dekimásu** (from **dekíru**)	*to be able to do; can*
みせ	**mise**	*shop*
しまる	**shimáru**	*to close*
ごろ	**góro**	*about*
たのまれた	**tanomáreta**	*have been asked, have been requested*
おみやげ	**omiyage**	*souvenirs, presents*
んですが	**n' desu ga**	*you see, the fact is…* (used to give an explanation)
めんせいてん	**menzéiten**	*duty-free shop*
おそく	**osoku**	*late* (adverb)
あいている	**aite iru**	*to be open*
よかった	**yókatta**	*Good! I'm glad* (past tense of adjective)

Past tense of adjectives

True adjectives in Japanese behave in much the same way as verbs. They can constitute predicates in their own right and they also occur in the past tense. In the Dialogue above we met the exclamation, **yókatta** '*Good! I'm glad*', etc. Actually, this is the past tense form of **yói** '*good*', the more formal form of **íi**, which we have seen several times before. It should be noted that **íi**, in fact, is rather restricted in its use. It does not occur in the adverbial form or in the past tense, being replaced by **yóku** and **yókatta** respectively. The past tense of true adjectives is formed by adding the suffix –**katta** to the adjective root, or, if you prefer, by replacing the –**i** of the present tense by –**katta**. In the polite speech style a past tense adjective in the principal clause is followed by a form of the copula, **désu**.

Kinóo no chuushoku wa oíshikatta desu.	*Yesterday's lunch was delicious.*
Senshuu wa zútto isogáshikatta desu.	*I was busy all last week.*

The negative past tense of true adjectives is formed by adding –**nakatta** (the past tense of the suffix **nai**, '*not to exist*', '*to be not...*', which is actually an adjective in form to the adverbial form (–**ku** form) of the adjective.

Ano éiga wa amari omoshíroku nakatta desu.	*That film was not very interesting.*

Remember that the –**tai**, '*(I) want to...*', ending introduced in Unit 6, also behaves like an adjective. Consequently, it forms its past tense with –**katta**:

Kono máe no nichiyóobi ni hanamí ni ikitákatta desu ga, áme ga furimáshita kara ikimasén deshita.	*Last Sunday I wanted to go and see the cherry blossom, but I didn't go because it was raining.*

Exercise 8.1

Read the sentences below then change the time expression as indicated, making any other changes the sense demands. For example:

Cue: **Kyóo wa isogashíi desu. (kinóo)**
A: **Kinóo wa isogáshikatta desu.**

1. Kyóo no shokuji wa totemo oishíi desu. (kinóo)
2. Kyóo no éiga wa amari omoshíroku nai desu. (senshuu)
3. Nihongo no shikén wa ítsumo muzukashíi desu. (sengetsu)
4. Kónban no páatii wa tanoshíi deshoo née. (yuube)
5. Kyóo no okyakusan wa amari óoku nai desu. (kinóo)

Vocabulary

shikén	*examination*	**yuube**	*last night*
ítsumo	*always*	**óoi**	*numerous*

Giving advice and suggesting alternatives

The noun **hoo**, '*direction*', '*side*' is used in comparisons and, after the plain past tense of a verb, to give advice.

Chooshoku o tábete kara súgu dekáketa hoo ga íi desu.	*You had better set out straight after breakfast. It would be better to leave straight after breakfast.*
Tanaka senséi ni kiita hoo ga íi desu.	*You'd better ask Dr Tanaka.*
Ashita háyaku ókita hoo ga íi desu.	*You'd better get up early tomorrow.*

Notice that a past-tense verb is used even where the reference is to an action in the future.

Exercise 8.2

Answer your Japanese friend's questions with a recommendation to do what is suggested in the question. Follow the example below:

Q: **Íma súgu kaerimashóo ka.**
A: **Ée, íma súgu káetta hoo ga íi desu.**

1. Koko de mátte mo íi desu ka.
2. Móo hajimemashóo ka.
3. Háyaku okimashóo ka.
4. Takai no o kaimashóo ka.
5. Nihongo de hanashimashóo ka.

Vocabulary

móo	*already*
hajiméru	*to start, begin*
okíru	*to get up*

Adjectival clauses

In Japanese descriptive words and phrases always precede the nouns they describe. We have seen how the descriptive phrase can be a noun followed by the particle **no**, as in **Tookyoo no hóteru**, '*hotels in Tokyo*'. It can be a **na** adjective, as in **kírei na haná** '*beautiful flowers*', or an adjective, **takái yamá** '*a high mountain*'. Actually, **takái yamá** means '*a mountain which is high*'. Sometimes a noun might be described by an adjective in the past tense, e.g. **isogáshikatta toki** '*when I was busy*'. In the same way, a verb can also be used to describe a following noun, e.g. **máiasa yómu shinbun** '*the newspaper I read every morning*' or **kinóo átta hito** '*the person I met yesterday*', **raishuu iku tokoro** '*the place I am going to next week*'. These clauses are generally equivalent to a relative clause in English, but because they precede rather than follow the noun they describe we prefer to call them 'adjectival clauses'. The time clauses (when something happens/happened, etc.) we met in the last unit with a plain tense verb followed by **toki**, '*time*' are actually adjectival clauses, literally, '*the time, when…*'. **Kinóo kaisha ni tsúita toki ni hoka ni dáremo imasén deshita** '*When I arrived at the company yesterday there was nobody else there*'. In adjectival clauses the subject particle, **ga**, is often replaced by **no**.

Kore wa Suzuki senséi ga káita hón desu or **Kore wa Suzuki senséi no káita hón desu.**	*This is the book Dr Suzuki wrote.*

Vocabulary

hoka ni	*besides, apart from*
dáremo	*nobody, anybody*

Exercise 8.3

Combine two simple sentences into a compound sentence using an adjectival clause as in the example below.

Cue: **Kore wa hón desu. (kinóo kaimáshita)**
A: **Kore wa kinóo katta hón desu.**

1. Anóhito wa Suzuki san desu. (senshuu Méari san no páatii de aimáshita)
2. Kore wa booshi désu. (ototoi depáato de kaimáshita)
3. Íma shinbun o yónde imasu. (kore wa Asahi-shínbun desu)
4. Kore wa tegami désu. (watashi ga Nihongo de kakimáshita)

Exercise 8.4

Using the English prompts combine the phrases given below into sentences containing adjectival clauses, following the example below.

Cue: 会う、今日の午後、山川先生、人、です、は
      (The person I am going to meet this afternoon is Dr Yamakawa.)
A: 今日の午後会う人は山川先生です。

1. は、買った、だそうです、本、きのう、ベストセラー
   (I hear the book I bought yesterday is a bestseller.)
2. きもの、だれ、人、ですか、きている、を、は
   (Who is the person wearing a kimono?)
3. あります、こと、そうだんしたい、が
   (There are things I wish to discuss.)
4. 見た、ですよ、えいが、おもしろかった、きのう、は
   (The film I saw yesterday was funny.)
5. もって行く、どれ、に、ですか、もの、中国、は
   (Which are the things you are taking to China?)

'Can do'

We have already met the verb **dekíru** in the sense of to be able to speak a foreign language, e.g. **Chuugokugo ga dekimásu ka** '*Can you speak Chinese?*' It is also used in a number of idiomatic expressions in which it has the basic meaning of '*to be done*', '*to be ready*', '*to be produced*'.

Shashin wa ítsu dekimásu ka.	*When will the photos be ready?*
Okinawa déwa paináppuru ga dekimásu.	*In Okinawa they can grow pineapples.*

Dekíru replaces **suru** in those verbs made up of a noun plus the verb 'to do', such as **benkyoo suru** '*to study*', **unten suru** '*to drive*', **kaimono suru**, '*to shop*', etc., to express ability or potential.

Kuruma no unten ga dekimásu ka.	*Can you drive a car?*
Koko de okane no ryoogae ga	*Can I change money here?*
dekimásu ka.	(**ryoogae suru** '*to change money*')

To make a potential form of a verb with **dekíru** it is necessary first to transform the verb into a noun phrase with the addition of **kotó** '*thing*', '*fact*'. That is to say, the plain present-tense form (or dictionary form) of the verb plus **kotó ga dekíru** expresses the idea, '*can do ...*'.

Nihongo o káku koto ga dekimasu ka.	*Can you write Japanese?*
Sashimí o tabéru kotó ga dekimásu ka.	*Can you eat sashimi (raw fish)?*

Experience

This same **kotó**, is also used with the verb **áru** '*to exist*', '*to have*', to express the idea of experience. When **kotó ga áru** is used after the plain past tense of a verb it means '*to have done...*'. After the plain present tense it means, '*to sometimes do...*'.

Nihón ni itta kotó ga arimásu ka.	*Have you* (ever) *been to Japan?*
Nihón no éiga o míru kotó ga	*Do you ever see Japanese*
arimásu ka.	*films?*

Exercise 8.5 ▉

The Japanese Embassy in London is seeking to employ a local member of staff who can drive, cook, use a computer and speak Japanese. The following is the text of the interview between the applicant and the Senior Consul, Mr Tanaka. Imagine you are the applicant responding to Mr Tanaka's questions. When you have finished filling in the blanks, listen to the complete interview on the cassette tape.

TANAKA: Kono shigoto ni wa kuruma no unten ménkyo ga hitsuyoo désu ga, unten dekimásu ka.

APPLICANT: (*Tell him you can. You have licences for both car and motorbike.*)

TANAKA: Tama niwa resépushon ga áru toki ryóori no tetsudái mo shimásu ga, ryóori ga dekimásu ka.
APPLICANT: (*Tell him you can. Explain that you used to work in a hotel in Paris.*)
TANAKA: Dónna ryóori ga dekimásu ka.
APPLICANT: (*Tell him you can cook Italian food. Say you can also cook Chinese and Thai food.*)
TANAKA: Parii no hóteru de Chuuka-ryóori o naraimáshita ka.
APPLICANT: (*Say no. You learnt from your mother.*)
TANAKA: Okáasan wa Chúugoku no katá desu ka.
APPLICANT: (*Tell him your mother isn't Chinese. She is Japanese.*)
TANAKA: Nihongo o joozu ni hanásu kotó ga dekimásu ga, káku kotó mo dekimásu ka.
APPLICANT: (*Tell him you can write only hiragána and katakána.*)
TANAKA: Konpyúuta wa dóo desu ka.
APPLICANT: (*Tell him you can use a computer.*)

You will need some more vocabulary items to do this exercise.

Vocabulary

ménkyo	*licence*	**katá**	*person (honorific, not used to refer to oneself or one's family)*
jidóosha	*automobile, car*		
ootóbai	*motorbike*		
tama níwa	*occasionally, sometimes*		
resépushon	reception	**... wa dóo desu ka**	*what about ...?*
dake	only (e.g. hiragána dake desu '(I know) only hiragana.')	**shika**	*only* (takes a negative verb, e.g. **Nihongo shika dekimasén** '*I can only speak Japanese.*')
tetsudái	*help, assistance*		
hataraku	*to work*		
tsukúru	*to make*		

Comparisons

There is no change in the form of adjectives to express the comparative or superlative degree. Instead, Japanese uses the particle **yóri** '*than*', the noun **hoo** '*side*', '*direction*' and a set of demonstrative pronouns **dótchi, kótchi**, etc.

Tookyoo wa Róndon yori ookíi desu.	*Tokyo is bigger than London.*
Sukiyaki yóri sushi ga sukí desu.	*I like sushi more than sukiyaki.*

A question of the type, 'Which is…er, A or B?' is expressed as **A to B to (déwa), dótchi ga…desu ka**.

Nihongo to Chuugokugo to déwa dótchi ga muzukashíi desu ka.	*Which is more difficult, Japanese or Chinese?*

Corresponding to the question word **dótchi** or its more formal equivalent **dóchira** '*which one of two?*' are the demonstrative pronouns **kótchi/kochira** '*this* (one of two)', **sótchi/sochira** '*that* (one of two)' and **átchi/achira** '*that* (one of two over there)'.

Sótchi o kudasái.	*Please give me that one* (of two).

These demonstrative pronouns are also used to indicate direction, '*this way*', '*that way*', etc. The forms ending in –**ra**, in particular, are more polite and are often used in invitations or instructions.

Kochira e dóozo.	*This way please.*

For emphasis the **hoo** we met earlier in the unit can be used.

Róndon yori Tookyoo no hoo ga zutto hirói desu.	*Tokyo is far larger than London.*

Where only one of the items in the comparison is mentioned, it is usual to use **hoo**.

Tookyoo no hoo ga hirói desu.	*Tokyo is the larger.*

Comparison can also be suggested by using the adverb **mótto**, '*more*'.

Mótto yasúi no ga arimasén ka.	*Don't you have a cheaper one?*

Superlatives are generally expressed with the aid of **ichiban**, '*number one, most*'.

Ichiban ookíi kutsú o mísete kudasai.　　　　*Please show me your biggest pair of shoes.*

Exercise 8.6

Using the data supplied below, fill in the blanks in the following sentences.

1. (山田 178 cm, 中川 174 cm)
2. (田中 170 cm 68 kg, 山本 160 cm 92 kg)
3. (本田 1930 年生まれ, 前田 1935 年生まれ)
4. (ちかてつ 三十分, タクシー 一時間)
5. (ビール 三八五円, コーラ 二九〇円)
6. (ラーメン 五百六十円, てんぷら 八百円)
7. (今日 26°C, きのう 22°C)
8. (今週 いそがしい, 来週 ひま)

1. _____wa _____ yori se ga takái desu.
2. _____wa _____ yori futótte imasu.
3. _____wa _____ yori toshiue désu.
4. _____yori _____no hoo ga hayái desu.
5. _____wa_____ yori yasúi desu.
6. _____wa_____ yori takái desu.
7. _____wa_____ yori atatakái desu.
8. _____no hoo ga tsugoo ga íi desu.

Vocabulary

se ga takai	せが高い	*to be tall* (literally, 'stature is tall')
... nen-umare	... 年生まれ	*born in...* (year)
toshiue	年上	*older, more senior* (person's age)
hima	ひま	*free time*
tsugoo ga íi	つごうがいい	*to be convenient, to be suitable*

Dialogue 2 ▇

Frank Anderson is talking to his business associate Mr Baba about his coming trip to Japan.

アンダーソン:	来週日本に行くよていですが、日本にいる間は さくらの花が見たいです。
馬場:	ちょうど今、花見の きせつ ですよ。
アンダーソン:	花見に どこが いいですか。
馬場:	京都の あらし山が 有名 ですが、東京でも 見ることができますよ。
アンダーソン:	東京では どこが いいですか。
馬場:	こうきょの まわりや めいじじんぐうやいの かしらこうえんなども にんきの ある ところですよ。
アンダーソン:	私が行く会社は こきょうの ちかく ですか ら。ちょうど よかったです。
馬場:	てんきがいいと いいですね。あめが ふると さくらはすぐちりますから。

ANDÁASON:	Raishuu Nihón ni iku yotei desu ga, Nihón ni iru aida wa sakura no haná ga mitái desu.
BABA:	Choodo íma hanamí no kísetsu desu yo.
ANDÁASON:	Hanamí ni dóko ga íi desu ka.
BABA:	Kyóoto no Arashiyama ga yuumei desu ga, Tookyoo démo míru kotó ga dekimásu yo.
ANDÁASON:	Tookyoo déwa dóko ga íidesu ka.
BABA:	Kóokyo no mawari ya, Meiji-jínguu ya, Inokashira-kóoen nádo mo ninki no áru tokoro désu yo.
ANDÁASON:	Watashi ga iku kaisha wa kóokyo no chikáku desu kara, choodo yókatta desu.
BABA:	Tenki ga íi to íi desu ne. Áme ga fúru to sakura wa súgu chirimásu kara.

ANDERSON:	*I'm going to Japan next week and while I'm there I'd like to see the cherry blossom.*
BABA:	*It's just the right season for viewing the cherry blossom.*
ANDERSON:	*Where is a good place for seeing the cherry blossom?*
BABA:	*Arashiyama in Kyoto is famous (for its cherry blossom), but you can also go blossom viewing in Tokyo.*
ANDERSON:	*I wonder where in Tokyo would be good?*
BABA:	*The area around the Imperial Palace, the Meiji shrine and Inokashira Park and so on are all popular spots.*

ANDERSON: *That's just fine for me. The company I'm going to is near the Imperial Palace.*

BABA: *I hope the weather is good. Cherry blossom scatters as soon as it rains.*

Vocabulary

…**yotei désu**	*to plan to…*
ga	*and* (when first clause is a general statement and second is explanation of detail)
iru aida	*while (I am) in*
sakura	*cherry (tree)*
hana	*flower*
chóodo	*just, precisely, exactly*
hanamí	*cherry-blossom viewing*
kísetsu	*season*
Arashiyama	*place name*
yuumei (na)	*famous*
kóokyo	*Imperial Palace*
mawari	*surrounds, area around*
Meiji-jínguu	*the Meiji Shrine*
Inokashira-kóoen	*the Inokashira park*
…**ya**…**ya**	*and, such things as … and…* (used to join similar items)
nádo	*et cetera, and so on*
ninki ga áru	*to be popular*
chikáku	*vicinity, nearby*
tenki	*weather*
…**to íi desu**	*(I) hope…, it will be good if…*
chiru	*to scatter, fall* (of blossom)

Exercise 8.7 ■

Listen to the dialogue on the cassette tape and answer the questions which follow. You will find a romanised transcription of this passage in the Key to the Exercises (p. 275).

ジェーン・ロバーツさんは一九八〇年にニュージーランドで生まれました。大学で四年間日本語をべんきょうしました。大学をそつぎょうしてすぐ日本に来ました。今は東京にある小さな新聞会社につとめています。りょこうしゃのための英じ新聞です。おも

にアメリカやイギリスやオーストラリアなどから日本に来るわか
いバックパッカーの人たちが読みます。ジェーンさんも来年かい
がいりょこうをしたいといっています。まだ中国に行ったことが
ないから、九月にペキンに行くつもりだそうです。

1. Where was Jane born?
2. In what year was she born?
3. What did she do when she graduated from university?
4. Where is she working now?
5. What does the company produce?
6. Who are the main users of the product?
7. What does Jane say she wants to do next year?
8. What does she intend to do in September?

Vocabulary

...**ni tsutómete iru**	*to be working in / for...*	**bakkupákkaa**	*back-packer*
ryokóosha	*traveller, tourist*	**hitotachi**	*people (–***tachi** *= plural suffix)*
...**no tame no**	*for..., for the sake of...*	**kaigai**	*overseas*
Eiji	*English script, English language*		

Kanji

In this unit we introduce ten more **kanji**. As many of them are used in Dialogue 2, we suggest that you read through the list of new characters, then go back to the Japanese script version of the dialogue.

TOO
higashi
east

KYOO
capital

TO
metropolis

KAN
aida
interval; between

KA
haná
flower

MOKU	**KEN**	**GO**	**ZEN**	**GO, KOO**
me	mi (mású)	zodiac sign of	máe	áto after
eye	to see	the horse;	front; before	ushi (ro)
		noon		behind

Exercise 8.8

Rewrite the following romanised sentences in Japanese script, using **kanji, hiragána** and **katakána** as appropriate. Check with the answers in the key at the back of the book to see if you have understood them correctly.

1. Senshuu Kyóoto e itte kimáshita.
2. Raigetsu Tanaka senséi to hanamí ni ikimásu.
3. Me no máe ni takusan no kírei na haná ga arimáshita.
4. Gógo gojihán ni Tookyoo-éki no máe de mátte ite kudasai.
5. Tookyoo wa Kyóoto yori ookíi desu.

9 ホテルで
Hóteru de
At the hotel

In this unit you will learn how to:

- Discuss conditions and consequences
- Use more numeral classifiers
- Narrate what happened in the past
- Talk about doing two or more things at the same time
- Talk about doing things frequently or alternatively using **–tari**
- Use the indefinite pronouns **dáreka**, **nánimo**, etc.

You will also acquire:

- 10 more **kanji**:　着 話 明 朝 海 門 休 紙 枚 台

Dialogue 1 ▨

*Come along with me as I check in with my family at a hotel in Kyoto. Just my luck! There has been a mix-up over my booking. This is the conversation I had with the young woman at the hotel front desk or **furónto**.*

フロント：　いらっしゃいませ。
クラーク：　クラークですが、チェックインを
　　　　　　したいんです...
フロント：　はい、かしこまりました。しょうしょう
　　　　　　おまち下さい。ただ今 おしらべ いたします。
クラーク：　ツインと ダブルの へやを よやくしましたが...
フロント：　はい、今日から あさってまで 三ぱく で、四人さま
　　　　　　ですね。

クラーク： そうです。
フロント： おへやは シャワーつきの へやですね。
クラーク： いいえ、よやくした時は、ふろつきの へやを
　　　　　おねがい したんですが…
フロント： もうしわけございません。今日は ちょっと
　　　　　ございませんが、あしたでしたらあるとおもいます。
クラーク： では、あした ふろつきの へやが あったら
　　　　　かえてください。
フロント： かしこまりました。それでは、こちらに
　　　　　ごじゅうしょと おなまえをおねがいします。
　　　　　それから、サインをこちらに おねがいします。
クラーク： はい、わかりました。

FURÓNTO: Irasshaimáse.
KURÁAKU: Kuráaku desu ga, chekkuin o shítai n' desu.
FURÓNTO: Hái, kashikomarimáshita. Shóoshoo omachi kudasái. Tadáima oshirabe itashimásu.
KURÁAKU: Tsúin to dáburu no heyá o yoyaku shimáshita ga.
FURÓNTO: Hai, Kyóo kara asátte made sanpaku de, yonin sama désu ne.
KURÁAKU: Sóo desu.
FURÓNTO: Ohéya wa sháwaa-tsuki no heyá desu ne.
KURÁAKU: Iie, yoyaku shita tokí wa, furó-tsuki no heyá o onegai shitá n' desu ga…
FURÓNTO: Mooshiwake gozaimasén. Kyóo wa chótto gozaimasén ga, ashita deshitara, áru to omoimásu.
KURÁAKU: Déwa, ashita furó-tsuki no heyá ga áttara kaette kudasái.
FURÓNTO: Kashikomarimáshita. Sore déwa, kochira ni gojuusho to onamae o onegai shimásu. Sore kara, sain o kochira ni onegai shimásu.
KURÁAKU: Hái, wakarimáshita.

FRONT DESK: *May I help you?*
CLARK: *My name is Clark. I'd like to check in, please.*
FRONT DESK: *Yes, certainly Sir. Just one moment please. I'll check your booking now.*
CLARK: *I booked one twin and one double room.*
FRONT DESK: *Three nights from tonight till the day after tomorrow for four people, isn't it?*

CLARK: *That's right.*
FRONT DESK: *Your room was a room with a shower, wasn't it?*
CLARK: *No. When I made the booking, I asked for a room with a bath.*
FRONT DESK: *I'm terribly sorry, Sir. We don't have anything today, but I think we could find you one tomorrow.*
CLARK: *Well then, if you have a room with a bath tomorrow please change the room for me.*
FRONT DESK: *Certainly, Sir. Well then, could you write your name and address here, please? Then sign here, please.*
CLARK: *Yes, I see.*

Vocabulary

フロント	**furónto**	*front desk, reception*
チェックインする	**chekkuin**	*to check in*
しょうしょう	**shóoshoo**	*a little* (formal)
おまち下さい	**omáchi kudasai**	*please wait* (honorific)
ただいま	**tadaima**	*just now; now* (formal)
おしらべ いたします	**oshirábe itashimasu**	*I'll check / investigate* (respectful)
よやくする	**yoyaku suru**	*to reserve, book*
ツイン	**tsúin**	*twin* (-*bed room*)
ダブル	**dáburu**	*double* (-*bed room*)
三ぱく	**sanpaku**	*three nights' stay* (**haku** = counter for nights' stay)
四名さま	**yonmeisama**	*four people* (very formal)
おへや	**oheya**	*your room* (honorific)
シャワーつき	**sháwaa-tsuki**	*with a shower*
ふろつき	**furo-tsuki**	*with a bath*
おねがいしたんですが	**onegai shita n' desu ga**	*I requested you know, but …*
もうしわけございません	**mooshiwake gozaimasen**	*We're terribly sorry* (very formal)
ございませんが	**gozaimasén ga …**	*There aren't any, I'm afraid.*

かえる	**kaeru**	*to change*
ごじゅうしょ	**gojúusho**	*address*
サインをおねがいします	**sáin o onegai shimásu**	*please sign* (formal request)

More ways to say 'if' and 'when': –tára

In Unit 7 we met the clause-final particle **to**, which expresses the idea of 'if, when or whenever'. It describes natural or habitual consequences beyond the control of the subject of the main verb and therefore cannot be used in sentences which contain a request or command. This restriction does not apply to the suffix –**tára** which is perhaps the most common ways of saying 'if' or 'when' in Japanese. It attaches to the stem of verbs, undergoing the same sound changes as with the –**te form** and the plain past tense. The accent of the first syllable of –**tára** is lost if the vowel stem already carries an accent. In essence you can form the –**tára** conditional by attaching **ra** to the plain past tense, e.g. **tábetara** '*if one eats*', **ittára** '*if one goes*'. This also applies to adjectives, which form their plain past tense by adding –**katta** to the adjective root, e.g., **isogáshikatta** '*was busy*' and the conditional by adding a further –**ra**, **isogáshikattara** '*if you are busy*'. The basic meaning of the –**tára** conditional is 'if or when the action of the subordinate verb is completed the action of the main verb follows'.

Yókattara chotto ocha demo nomimasén ka.	*If you like, what about having a cup of tea or something?*
Okane ga áttara ryokoo shitai desu.	*If I had the money, I'd like to travel.*
Okyakusan ga kitara watashi ni oshiete kudasai.	*Please let me know when the visitors come.*

When the main verb is in the past tense, the –**tára** construction, like **to**, usually carries a connotation of surprise.

Uchi ni káettara tomodachi ga kite imashita.	*When I got home* (I was surprised to discover) *my friend had come.*

The difference between the uses of **to** and –**tára** can be illustrated by comparing the following two sentences.

| **Fuyú ni náru to sukíi ni ikimasu.** | *When winter comes I go skiing.* (i.e. every year, habitual consequence.) |
| **Fuyú ni náttara sukíi ni ikimásu.** | *When winter comes I'm going skiing.* (i.e. this year, single event.) |

–(r)éba

Another conditional suffix, –(r)éba is attached to the verb root (the dictionary form of the verb minus the final **u** or, with vowel-root verbs and irregular verbs, –**ru**). The –(**r**) of this suffix drops when it is preceded by a consonant and the accent is lost with accented vowel roots, e.g. **káku** becomes **kákeba** '*if one writes*', **asobu** becomes **asobéba** '*if one plays*', **tabéru** gives **tabéreba** '*if one eats*', **akeru akeréba** '*if one opens*', **kúru kúreba** '*if one comes*', **suru suréba** '*if one does*', and so on. With true adjectives –**kereba** is added to the adjective root, **yókereba** '*if it is good*', **átsukereba** '*if you are hot*'. Remember **nái**, the plain form of **arimasén**, behaves like an adjective, so its –(**r**)éba conditional is **nákereba** '*if there is not*'. The meaning of –(**r**)éba overlaps a great deal with -**tára** and in most cases the two are interchangeable. There are, however, a number of idiomatic expressions in which the –(**r**)éba conditional is preferred. As these are associated with the plain negative form of the verb they will be introduced in the next unit. In the meantime familiarise yourself with the formation of the –(**r**)éba conditional and learn to recognise it in contexts such as those introduced in the next exercise.

Exercise 9.1

Complete sentences 1–8 by choosing an appropriate clause from the list below. You will probably need to refer to the vocabulary list at the end of the exercise.

1. _____ さきに 食べてください。
2. _____ 車と いえを 買いたいです。
3. _____ くつを ぬぎます。
4. _____ おまわりさんに 聞いてください。
5. _____ 車を うんてんしません。
6. _____ いえに 早く かえるようになりました。
7. _____ 一休み しましょうか。
8. _____ 中止です。

a. けっこんしたら
b. おさけを 飲んだら
c. これが おわったら
d. 日本のいえに 行ったら
e. みちが 分からなかったら
f. あめが ふったら
g. おなかが すいたら
h. たからくじに あたったら

Vocabulary

さきに	saki ni	*first, ahead, before*
ぬぐ	núgu	*to take off* (clothes, etc.)
おまわりさん	omáwarisan	*policeman, policewoman*
一休み	hitóyasumi	*a rest, a break*
中止	chuushi	*cancellation, calling off*

Exercise 9.2 ■

Listen to these examples on the tape and repeat, paying particular attention to the intonation patterns and the positions of pauses. Make sure you understand what the sentences mean by checking your translations against the Key to the Exercises (p. 275). You will need a few more vocabulary items, which you can find listed here below the exercise. Some of the **kanji** included here are those introduced later in this lesson.

1. 今、すぐ行けば 間にあいますよ。
2. 車がなければ あるいて行きます。
3. 日本人の ともだちが ほしければ しょうかいします。
4. 十時すぎれば でんしゃが すいています。
5. さむければ もうふを 一枚 たしてください。
6. 毎日 うんどうすれば はやく やせますよ。

Vocabulary

間にあう	ma ni áu	*to be in time* ('for' = **ni**)
ほしい	hoshíi	*to want*
すぎる	sugíru	*to pass, exceed, be more than*
でんしゃ	densha	*train* (electric)
すく	suku	*to become empty*
もうふ	móofu	*blanket*
たす	tasu	*to add*
うんどう	undoo	*exercise*

While – 'nagara'

The idea of someone doing two or more things at the same time is expressed by –**nagara** attached to the verb stem: **tabenágara** '*while eating*', **kakinágara** '*while writing*', **utainagara** '*while singing*'. With accented verbs the accent moves to the first syllable of –**nagara**, while unaccented verbs have unaccented –**nagara** forms. In Japanese, the major, or longer, activity tends to go into the main clause, and the subordinate, or shorter activity, into the clause with –**nagara**, which seems, to me at least, to be the reverse of what happens with the use of '*while*' in English.

Shinbun o yominágara asagóhan o tabemáshita.	*I read the newspaper while I was having breakfast.*
Koohíi o nominágara soodan o shimáshita.	*We discussed it over a cup of coffee.*

If the subjects of the clauses are different, '*while*' is expressed with **aida** '*interval of time*', or **aida ni** after the plain present tense of the verb.

Kánai ga kaimono o shite iru aida, kuruma de zasshi o yomimáshita.	*While my wife was shopping I read a magazine in the car.*

Exercise 9.3

How would you describe these situations in Japanese using –**nagara**?

1. Asako is eating potato chips as she reads a newspaper.
2. Last night my mother fell asleep while watching television.
3. The truck driver always listens to the radio while driving his truck.
4. Tsutomu is singing a song while having a bath.
5. My son often listens to music while he is studying.

Vocabulary

ポテトチップ	**potetochíppu**	*potato chips, crisps*
いねむりをする	**inemúri o suru**	*to fall asleep, doze off* (when not in bed)
ラジオ	**rájio**	*radio*
うた	**utá**	*song*

うたう	**utau**	*sing* (often used with うた, e.g., うたをうたう *to sing*)
むすこ	**musuko**	*son* (usually *my son*)
おふろに はいる	**ofúro ni háiru**	*to have a bath*

More numeral classifiers

When counting objects in Japanese you must be careful to use the right numeral classifier. We have met some already, but in most cases, as for example when we were counting hours or minutes or the floors of the department store, the Japanese categories had clear English equivalents. This is not the case when we are counting dogs or pencils or cars, all of which come with a numeral classifier in Japanese and no particular word in English. The **kanji** for some of these numeral classifiers are introduced in this unit. With some common exceptions, most of the classifiers combine with numerals from the pseudo-Chinese set, **ichí**, **ní**, **san**, etc., often undergoing sound changes in the process. You will find an extensive chart of these classifiers and the sound changes in the Grammar Summary at the end of the book (p. 299). For counting miscellaneous objects with no clear numeral classifier, you should use the native Japanese set of numbers, **hitótsu**, **futatsú**, **mittsú**, etc., or the Chinese numerals followed by –**ko**, e.g. **íkko**, **níko**, **sánko**, etc. The numeral and its classifier usually appear in the adverbial position before the verb, but it is also possible to place the number followed by **no** in front of the noun to which it refers. When the number and its classifier follow the noun, the subject, topic or object particles are often omitted. The usage should be clear from the following example sentences and phrases. Note that sound changes occur most frequently in combinations with 1, 3, 6 and 8.

Honda san wa ie ga níken to kuruma o sándai mótte imasu.	*Mr Honda has two houses and three cars.*
Buráun san wa mainichi koohíi o róppai nomimásu.	*Mr Brown drinks six cups of coffee every day.*
Inú ippikí to kanariya ichíwa kátte imasu.	*We have one dog and one canary.* (**káu** *to keep, have* (a pet))
'Shichínin no samurai' wa Kurosawa Ákira no ichiban yuumei na éiga desu.	*'The Seven Samurai' is Akira Kurosawa's most famous film.*

Here is a list of some of the more common numeral classifiers. We have met some of them before; others are being introduced for the first time. The various sound changes are somewhat irregular but you will pick them up gradually with practice. If in doubt about a particular combination of number and classifier check it in the Grammar Summary. When asking how many things are being counted, use **nán** plus the numeral classifiers (**nánbon, nánmai, nánbiki**, etc.) with the pseudo-Chinese numerals, and **íkutsu** with the Japanese numerals.

–**nin**	people (but **hitóri** '*one person*', **futarí** '*two people*')
–**dai**	vehicles, machines, telephones, etc.
–**ken**	houses, shops, etc. (1. **íkken**, 6. **rókken**, 8. **hákken**)
–**mai**	flat objects, sheets of paper, plates, etc.
–**hai**	'*glassful*', '*cupful*' (1. **íppai**, 3. **sánbai**, 6. **róppai**, 8. **háppai**)
–**hon**	cylindrical objects, bottles, pens, etc. (1. **íppon**, 3. **sánbon**, 6. **róppon**, 8. **háppon**)
–**satsu**	books, volumes (1. **issatsú**, 8. **hassatsú**)
–**hiki**	small to medium animals (fish, dogs, cats, etc.) (1. **ippikí**, 3. **sánbiki**, 6. **roppikí**, 8. **happikí**)
–**wa**	birds (1. **ichíwa**, 3. **sánba**, 6. **róppa**, 8. **hachíwa**)
–**too**	large animals (horses, cows, etc.) (1. **íttoo**, 8. **hátto**)
–**tsuu**	letters (1. **ittsuu**, 8. **hattsuu**)

Exercise 9.4

Change the English prompts into Japanese to make a complete sentence with an appropriate numeral classifier. Note that we have introduced some more classifiers in the list of **kanji** for this unit. Refer to the Key to the Exercises (p. 276) to check whether you have understood the meaning of the sentences.

Cue: あそこにいます。(one dog)
A: あそこに いぬが 一匹います。

1. えんぴつが いります。(twelve)
2. ください。(three tissues)
3. 毎日飲みます。(three glasses of milk)
4. かっています。(two dogs)
5. どうぶつえんで 生まれた。(two giraffes)
6. さかなやで 買いました。(three small fish)
7. ワインが のこっていますか。 (how many bottles?)
8. ゆうべ 手紙を書きました。 (three)

9. きのううれましたか。 (how many cars?)
10. ほしいですか。 (how many sheets of paper?)

Vocabulary

いる	**iru**	*to need*
ティシュ・ペーパー	**tishupéepaa**	*tissue paper*
ぎゅうにゅう	**gyuunyuu**	*milk*
いぬ	**inú**	*dog*
かう	**káu**	*to have, keep* (an animal)
どうぶつえん	**doobutsúen**	*zoo*
キリン	**kirin**	*giraffe*
生まれる	**umareru**	*to be born*
さかなや	**sakanaya**	*fish shop*
さかな	**sakana**	*fish*
ワイン	**wáin**	*wine*
のこる	**nokóru**	*to remain, be left*
うれる	**ureru**	*to be sold, sell* ((intrans.) often used instead of **uru** *to sell* (trans.))
手紙	**tegami**	*letter*

Counting the days

To count the days of the month Japanese uses two different numeral classifiers, –**ka** for the days up to ten and for the 14th and 24th, and –**nichi** with almost all of the other numbers. The 20th, **hatsuka**, also uses the same classifier, but combined with an old native Japanese numeral, which now survives only in this word and in **hátachi** which means, '*20 years old*'. –**ka** combines with the Japanese set of numerals and –**nichi** with the pseudo-Chinese numerals. The first day of the month is either **tuitachí** or **ichijitsu**. With the exception of these last two forms which mean '*the first day of the month*', these numeral classifiers for the days of the month can be used either to name the days of the month or count days' duration, i.e. **mikka** means either '*3rd of the month*' or '*three days*'. '*One day*' is **ichinichi**. As the combinations of number and classifier are a little irregular they are introduced here in some detail.

一日	**ichinichi**	*one day*
二日	**futsuka**	*2nd, two days*

三日	mikka	*3rd, three days*
四日	yokka	*4th, four days*
五日	itsuka	*5th, five days*
六日	muika	*6th, six days*
七日	nanoka	*7th, seven days*
八日	yooka	*8th, eight days*
九日	kokonoka	*9th, nine days*
十日	tooka	*10th, ten days*

The 14th of the month or fourteen days is **juuyokka** and the 24th or 24 days is **nijuuyokka**. The other days are quite regular, e.g. **juurokunichi** '*16th*', **sanjuuichinichi** '*31st*'. '*How many days?*' or '*What day of the month?*' is **nánnichi**. Japanese dates (and addresses on envelopes too) proceed from the general to the particular, year followed by month then finally the day.

Nánnen, nángatsu, nánnichi ni umaremáshita ka.	*What year, month and day were you born?*
Shóowa juukyúunen sangatsú kokonoka ni umaremáshita.	*I was born on the 9th March, 1944.*

Japanese dates

Although the western calendar is well understood and often used in Japan, the usual way to express dates is in relation to the periods of the emperor's reign. In the modern period there have been four emperors and four reign periods. They are the **Méiji** period which started in 1868, the **Taishoo** period from 1912, the **Shóowa** period from 1926 and the **Heisei** period from 1989. As these starting dates mark year one of each reign period, when converting Japanese dates to the western calendar remember to calculate from the year before, for example, **Shóowa** 19 is 1944 (1925 plus 19) and 1960 is **Shóowa** 35.

Exercise 9.5

Read the dates below and see if you can convert them to dates in the western calendar. You might find it easier to write the Japanese year period first and leave the calculations till later. When you have finished converting the dates to English try the exercise in reverse. Check your efforts against the romanised answers in the Key to the Exercises (p. 276).

1. へいせい三年十月三日。
2. しょうわ二十年八月六日。
3. しょうわ十六年十二月八日。
4. めいじ三十八年九月四日日ようび。
5. こどもの日は五月五日です。

Verb stem plus –tári

This suffix, which indicates that two or more actions are performed alternately or frequently, attaches to the verb stem in the same way as the –te form and plain past tense –ta ending do, undergoing the same sound changes. It brings together two or more actions which are taken as examples of a potentially longer list in much the same way as nádo '… *and so on, and the like*', does for nouns. When two or more verbs are linked with the –tari form, the last, that is the principal verb of the sentence, is usually followed by a form of the verb suru '*to do*'.

Yoaké made osake o nóndari sushí o tábetari shimashita.	*We drank sake and ate sushi (and did various other things) until dawn.*
Kono heyá de hón o yóndari tegami o káitari shimasu.	*In this room we read books, write letters and so on.*

Often this expression is heard with just a single verb.

Uchi de térebi o mítari shimasu.	*I stay home and watch TV or something.*

Sometimes the copula, **désu**, **da**, etc., replaces **suru**.

Sóbo wa konogoro chooshi ga wárukute netári ókitari desu.	*Lately my grandmother is out of sorts and is in and out of bed all the time.*

Vocabulary

よあけ	**yoaké**	*dawn, daybreak*
このごろ	**konogoro**	*lately, these days*
ちょうし	**chooshi**	*tune, tuning, condition*
わるい	**warúi**	*bad*

Exercise 9.6

You are showing a visitor over the dormitory where you are staying as an exchange student in Japan. Explain the facilities available and give examples of the various ways you use them. Use the example below as a guide.

Cue: my room, sleep, study

A: **Watashi no heyá desu. Koko de netári benkyoo shitári shimasu.**

1. bathroom, shower, take baths
2. lounge, chat, entertain visitors
3. kitchen, cook, eat
4. reading room, read newspapers, study
5. laundry, wash clothes, iron

Vocabulary

ふろば、おふろ	furobá, ofúro	bathroom
シャワーをあびる	sháwaa o abiru	to shower
おうせつ間	oosetsuma	lounge, drawing room
おしゃべりする	osháberi suru	to chat
せったいする	séttai suru	to entertain
だいどころ	daidokoro	kitchen
せんたくば	sentakuba	laundry
せんたくをする	sentaku (o) suru	to wash clothes, do the laundry
アイロンをかける	áiron o kakéru	to iron
としょしつ	toshóshitsu	reading room

Indefinite pronouns

Japanese has a series of indefinite pronouns formed by adding the suffix –**ka** to the various question words.

náni what	**nánika** something, anything
dáre who	**dáreka** someone
doko where	**dókoka** somewhere
dóre which one of many	**dóreka** any one (of many)
dótchira which one of two	**dótchiraka** either one (of two)
ítsu when	**ítsuka** sometime
ikura how much	**íkuraka** somewhat

The same question words can take the suffix –**mo** to give a negative connotation. These indefinite pronouns are often used in conjunction with negative verbs. For added emphasis the suffix –**demo** is used instead of –**mo**.

nánimo *nothing*   **nándemo** *anything at all, nothing at all*
dókomo *nowhere, everywhere*   **dókodemo** *anywhere at all*
ítsumo *any time, always*   **ítsudemo** *anytime at all*

Where the verb requires a directional particle like **e** or **ni** these are inserted between the question word and **mo**.

Dárenimo iimasén deshita.   *I didn't tell anyone.*
Dókoemo ikimasen.   *I'm not going anywhere.*

Exercise 9.7 ▆▆

This exercise will give you practice in the use of the indefinite pronouns. Rearrange the components into complete Japanese sentences, then translate them into English. You can hear the finished sentences on the tape and check your English translations against those in the Key to the Exercises (p. 277).

1. しました　あたらなくて　たからくじに だれも　がっかり
2. ありませんから　うちに　ものが　食べるも
    レストランで食事しましょう　何も
3. ドアを　ノック　から　しています 行って 見に ください だれか
4. しずかな　おちゃ　飲みましょう ところ どこか でも で
5. ひまな　いつか　うちに 時に あそびに来てください
6. あの　いつも　みせは こんでいます
7. こまった事が 何か いってください あったら いつでも
8. どこへも こんどの 行きません 週まつに

Vocabulary

たからくじ	**takarákuji**	*lottery*
あたらなくて	**ataranakute**	*not winning and…* (literally 'not hitting')
がっかりする	**gakkári suru**	*to be disappointed*
しずかな	**shízuka na**	*quiet*
ドア	**dóa**	*door*
ノックする	**nókku suru**	*to knock*

ひまな時	**hima na toki**	*spare time* (**hima no toki** also used)
こむ	**kómu**	*to become crowded*
こまる	**komáru**	*to get into trouble, to get into a fix*
こまった事	**komátta kotó**	*problem, getting into difficulty*

Kanji

In this Unit we introduce ten more **kanji**.

CHAKU
ki (ru) to wear
tsu (ku) to arrive

WA
haná (su)
to speak, talk

MEI, MYOO
aka (rui) bright

CHOO
ása morning

KAI
úmi sea

MON
gate

KYUU
yasú (mu)
to rest

SHI
kami paper

MAI
sheet (of paper
etc.)

DAI
stand, platform;
counter for
machines

Exercise 9.8

Read the following sentences aloud then translate them into English. Check your answers in the Key to the Exercises (p. 277).

1. 今朝山中さんは東京に着いたそうです。
2. 白い紙を三枚下さい。
3. 明日のりょこうにバスを二台よやくしました。
4. 英語の先生は大学の門の前で学生と話していました。
5. 明日の午後海へドライブに行きましょう。
6. リーさん、時間があったらいつか中国の話をしてください。
7. 日本では一年に十五日の休日があります。(**kyuujitsu** '*holiday*')
8. ショートさんはこんのせびろを着て来るそうです。
9. 明日会社を休みたいです。(Note: **yasúmu** can be used as a transitive verb meaning '*to take time off from.*')
10. むこうに着いたら でん話を 下さい。(**mukoo** '*over there*', '*the other side*')

10 競馬を見に行きませんか。
Keiba o mí ni ikimasén ka.
Would you like to come to the races?

In this unit you will learn how to:

- Talk about your intentions
- Talk about your plans for the future
- Give explanations
- List reasons
- Use the demonstrative adjectives **dónna**, **konna**, etc.
- Use the demonstrative adverbs **dóo**, **koo**, etc.
- Give advice
- Ask people what kinds of things they like to do
- Suggest what might happen
- Use the potential verbs to say what you can or cannot do.

You will also acquire:

- 10 more **kanji**: 口 耳 字 父 母 入 出 住 知 開

Dialogue 1 ■

On the train one evening you overhear a conversation between two Japanese businessmen. You turn around to recognise Mr Yamaguchi and Mr Maeda, whom you met the other day at an export forum. You can't make out all they are saying, but you pick out enough words to know they are discussing plans for the weekend.

前田: このごろはどうですか。あいかわらず おいそがしいんでしょうね。

山口: そうなんですよ。新しいけいやくがつぎからつぎへと入るし、出ちょうが おおいし、外国からの おきゃくさんが毎週のように来るから、ぜんぜん じぶんの 時間が ないんですよ。

前田: ところで、こんどの土曜日はおひまですか。

山口: ええっと、こんどの土曜日はちょっと...。

前田: じゃあ、日曜日は?

山口: 日曜日はべつによていがありませんが...

前田: それでは、日曜日はおひまなら、けいばを見に行きませんか。

山口: けいば! まさか前田さんみたいなえらい方はけいばへ 行かないでしょう。

前田: ああ、山口さんは かんがえかたが ふるいですねえ。このごろの けいばは けっこう しゃれていいますよ。とくに わかい OL の間で やきゅうより人気があるそうです。私はよく行くんですよ。お金をあまりかけなければたのしいですよ。

山口: そうですか。行ったことがありませんから、知りませんでした。ぜひ行って見たいですね。私はおおもうけするつもりです。

前田: そうかんたんに かてませんよ。

山口: やって見ないと分かりませんね。

前田: まったく そのとおりです。

MAEDA: Kono goro wa dóo desu ka. Aikawarazu oisogashíi deshoo ne.

YAMÁGUCHI: Sóo na n' desu yo. Atarashíi keiyaku ga tsugí kara tsugi e to háiru shi, shutchoo ga ooi shi, gaikoku kara no okyakusan ga maishuu no yóo ni kúru kara, zenzen jibun no jikan ga nái n' desu yo.

MAEDA: Tokoróde kóndo no doyóobi wa ohima désu ka.

YAMÁGUCHI: Ee tto, kóndo no doyóobi wa chótto…

MAEDA: Jáa, nichiyóobi wa?

YAMÁGUCHI: Nichiyóobi wa betsu ni yotei ga arimasén ga…

MAEDA: Sore de wa, nichiyóobi wa ohima nara, keiba o mi ni ikimasén ka.

YAMÁGUCHI: Keiba! Másaka Maeda san mítai na erái katá wa keiba e ikanai deshóo.

MAEDA:	Áa, Yamáguchi san wa kangaekáta ga furúi desu née. Konogoro no keiba wa kékkoo sharete imásu yo. Tóku ni wakái óoéru no aida de yakyuu yori ninki ga áru sóo desu. Watashi wa yóku ikú n' desu yo. Okane o amari kakénakereba tanoshíi desu yo.
YAMÁGUCHI:	Sóo desu ka. Itta kotó ga arimasén kara shirimasén deshita. Zéhi itte mitai désu ne. Watashi wa oomóoke suru tsumori désu.
MAEDA:	Sóo kantan ni katemasén yo.
YAMÁGUCHI:	Yatte mínai to wakarimasén ne.
MAEDA:	Mattaku sono tóori desu.

MAEDA:	*How are things these days? I suppose you're busy as usual, aren't you?*
YAMAGUCHI:	*Yes, you're right there. New contracts are coming in one after another, I've had lots of business trips and what's more we've had customers from abroad virtually every week, so the fact is I've had no time to myself at all.*
MAEDA:	*By the way, are you free this Saturday?*
YAMAGUCHI:	*Hmm (let me see). Saturday is a bit (inconvenient).*
MAEDA:	*Well, what about Sunday?*
YAMAGUCHI:	*I don't have any particular plans for Sunday.*
MAEDA:	*Well, if you're free on Sunday, would you like to come to the races?*
YAMAGUCHI:	*Horse races! Surely important people like you don't go to the races, Maeda san.*
MAEDA:	*Ah, Yamaguchi san, you're old fashioned in your thinking. These days horse racing is pretty stylish you know. In particular, they say it is more popular than baseball among young 'office ladies'. I often go. If you don't bet too much money it is enjoyable.*
YAMAGUCHI:	*That would be nice. I've never been so I had no idea. I'd love to come. I'm intending to make a big profit.*
MAEDA:	*It's not all that easy to win, you know.*
YAMAGUCHI:	*You never know till you try, do you?*
MAEDA:	*You're certainly right there.*

Vocabulary

あいかわらず	**aikawarazu**	*as usual*
けいやく	**keiyaku**	*contract*

つぎからつぎへと	**tsugí kara tsugi e to**	*one after the other*
入る	**háiru**	*to go in, come in, enter*
毎週のように	**maishuu no yóo ni**	*virtually every week* (literally, '*as if every week*')
こんどの	**kóndo no**	*this time, next time, this, next*
おひま	**ohima**	*free time* (honorific)
ぜんぜん	**zenzen**	*(not) at all, entirely*
ええっと	**ee tto**	*hmm, let me see* (hesitation form)
…はちょっと	**…wa chótto**	*is a bit* (difficult, inconvenient, etc.)
べつに	**betsu ni**	*in particular; separately, apart*
よてい	**yotei**	*plan, arrangement*
なら	**nára**	*if* (as you say…)
けいば	**keiba**	*horse racing, the races*
えらい	**erái**	*great, eminent, important, responsible*
けっこう	**kékkoo**	*splendid* (**na** adjective); *pretty, fairly* (adverb)
まさか	**másaka**	*surely* (not)
行かないでしょう	**ikanai deshóo**	*probably* (surely) *don't go*
しゃれている	**sharete iru**	*to be stylish*
とくに	**tóku ni**	*particularly, especially*
の間で	**no aida de**	*among*
見に行きませんか	**mí ni ikimasén ka**	*literally, won't* (you) *go and see, would you like to go/ come and see?*
ぜひ	**zéhi**	*definitely, without fail*
あまり	**amari**	*(not) too much*
かける	**kakéru**	*to bet*

たのしい	**tanoshíi**	*enjoyable, pleasurable*
おおもうけ	**oomóoke**	*a large profit*
...つもりです	**...–u tsumori désu**	*intend to...*
そうかんたんに	**sóo kantan ni**	*as easily as (all) that*
かてる	**katéru**	*to be able to win*
やってみる	**yatte míru**	*to try doing*
—ないと	**...–nai to**	*if you don't...*
まったく	**mattaku**	*entirely, completely*
そのとおり	**sono tóori**	*that way, like that*

Note: **tóori** is one of a small number of native Japanese roots where the last element of the long **oo** is written with **hiragána o** rather than **u**. Most long **oo** vowels occur in words borrowed from Chinese or in verbal suffixes. In these cases they are written with a final **u**.

Intention

A common way to express what you intend to do is to use the noun **tsumori** '*intention*' after the dictionary form of the verb.

Kyóo wa háyaku káeru tsumori désu.   *I intend to go home early today.*

As this is a rather subjective expression it is usually used to refer to one's own intentions. If you want to say someone else intends to do this or that it is usual to add a further qualification such as **sóo desu** '*it seems*', '*apparently*', etc.

Suzuki san wa rainen kara Róndon ni iku tsumori da sóo desu.   *I understand Mr Suzuki intends to go to London next year.*

The meaning is a little different when the main clause does not refer to the future.

Sonna tsumori déwa nakatta desu.   *That's not what I meant. That's not what I intended.*

Kore démo ganbátte iru tsumori désu.   *Even at this rate I feel I am giving it my utmost.*

Hito no kotó o kangáete iru tsumori désu.   *I am trying to consider others.*

We have already met another noun, **yotei** '*plan*', '*arrangement*', which is also often used in much the same way as **tsumori**. In the dialogue we met the expression **betsu ni yotei ga arimasén** '*I have no particular plans*', in which **yotei** is used as a noun in a main clause, but, like **tsumori désu**, **yotei désu** can also follow the dictionary form of a verb.

Nichiyóobi ni keiba o mí ni iku	*On Sunday I'm going to* (look at) *the*
yotei désu.	*races.*

Exercise 10.1

After a high school graduation ceremony you overhear a group of young people discussing what they intend to do in the future. Using the cues, the vocabulary list below and **tsumori désu**, say what each of the graduates intends to become in the future. Follow the example.

Cue: Yasuo kun is going to study acting.
A: **Yasuo kun wa haiyuu ni náru tsumori désu.**

1. Haruo kun is going to study journalism.
2. Rie san is going to study English and education in America.
3. Jun kun is going to study medicine.
4. Sachie san is taking up an apprenticeship in a restaurant.
5. Tomoko san is going to study music.

Vocabulary

náru	*to become*	**pianísuto**	*pianist*
haiyuu	*actor*	**kun**	term of address for boys
jaanarísuto	*journalist*		and young men. Used
shéfu	*chef*		mainly by men.
kyóoshi	*teacher*	**ongakka**	*musician*
isha	*doctor*		

Talking about your plans

Another common way to say what you are thinking of doing is to use the expression of –(y)óo to omou '*I'm thinking of doing…*'. We have actually met this –(y)óo suffix, sometimes called the propositive or hortative suffix on the ending –**mashóo** '*let's*', '*let me do something*'. The ending also attaches to the verb root, with the initial –(y) dropping after a consonant.

For example, **tabeyóo** '*let's eat*', **ikóo** '*let's* go'. The fall from high to low pitch always occurs after the first vowel of the suffix regardless of the accent of the verb root. In the polite style this ending often occurs with a verb of thinking to convey the idea of '*I'm thinking of doing…*'.

Rainen Nihón ni ikóo to omótte imasu.	*I'm thinking of going to Japan next year.*
Kónban éiga o miyóo to omótte imasu.	*Tonight I'm thinking of seeing a film.*

If you are finding it a little difficult at this stage to get your mind (and tongue) around this new construction, you can achieve the same effect with –**tai to omótte imasu**.

Shóorai náni ni naritái to omótte imasu ka.	*What would you like to do in the future?*

This same suffix is used with the verb **suru** '*to do*', to express the idea of '*trying to do something*' or, according to the context, being '*about to do something*'.

Kinóo ryóoshin ni renraku o shiyóo to shimáshita ga dekimasén deshita.	*Yesterday I tried to contact my parents, but was unable to do so.*
Kyoojuu ni owaróo to shite imásu.	*We are trying to finish today* (literally, '*within today*').
Choodo dekakeyóo to shite ita toki ni denwa ga narimáshita.	*The phone rang just as I was about to leave.*

The idea of being 'about to do something' is more often expressed with the noun **tokoro** '*place*', '*point*'.

Íma dekakéru tokoro desu.	*I'm about to leave* (set out).

Giving advice

We have already met the expression, **ikága desu ka** used when offering food to a guest, as in **Áisu koohíi wa ikaga desu ka**? '*May I offer you an iced coffee?*' The expression, centred around **ikága**, a polite word for '*how*,' is also used in conjunction with the conditional form of a verb to make suggestions, '*how about…?*' '*why not…?*'. The neutral equivalent of the honorific **ikága** is simply the demonstrative adverb **dóo,** introduced in this unit. In less formal situations **dóo** is used instead of **ikága.** But it is always possible, in any language, that suggestions and offers of advice may be misinterpreted, so it is wise to err on the side of politeness in these constructions.

Ashita irassháttara ikága desu ka.	*What say you come tomorrow?*
Shinkánsen ga takakéreba básu de	*If the Shinkánsen* (bullet train)
ittára dóo desu ka.	*is* (too) *expensive* (for you)
	why don't you go by bus?

In less formal contexts a suggestion can be made simply with the –**(r)éba** ending alone.

Hitóri de ikéba.	*Why don't you go by yourself?*
Osóba ni suréba.	*Why don't you have the soba* (buckwheat noodles)?

Of course, the most obvious way to give advice is with the –**ta hoo ga íi** construction introduced in Unit 8. As **hoo,** meaning '*side*' or '*direction*', is also used in comparisons, its use for making suggestions closely parallels the use of 'better' in English.

Háyaku itta hóo ga íi desu.	*You'd better go early.*

Exercise 10.2

Suggest an appropriate solution to the situation on the left by turning the clause into a conditional and combining it with one of the pieces of advice on the right. Follow the example. (You'll need to learn the new vocabulary items given below the exercise before you start.)

Cue: **atamá ga itái, kusuri o nómeba dóo desu ka.**
A: **Atamá ga itakereba kusuri o nómeba dóo desu ka.**

1. Shéfu ni naritái.
2. Okane ga takusán hoshíi.
3. Jikan ga nákereba.
4. Jibun de dekinákereba.
5. Nedan ga tákakereba.

a. Betsu no misé ni mo itta hóo ga íi deshoo.
b. Hito ni tanóndara ikága desu ka.
c. Minarai ni itta hóo ga íi desu.
d. Úmaku tooshi o shita hóo ga íi desu.
e. Áto ni shitára dóo desu ka.

Vocabulary

betsu no	*a different, a separate, another*	**jibun de**	*by oneself*
		úmaku	*skilfully*
nedan	*price*	**tooshi suru**	*to invest*
hito	*person; someone else*	**áto ni suru**	*to make it later,*
tanómu	*to ask*		*put off till*
minarai	*apprentice, apprenticeship*		*later, postpone*

Potential verbs

We have already seen how we can express the idea of 'can do…' by using **kotó ga dekimásu** after the 'dictionary' form of the verb.

Piano o hiku kotó ga dekimásu ka. *Can you play the piano?*

There is, however, a more common way of expressing potential by using yet another form of the Japanese verb. Japanese consonant-root verbs have corresponding vowel-root verbs which convey the idea of being able to do this or that. To form the potential form from any consonant-root verb simply replace the final **u** with **–eru**. For example:

káku '*to write*' becomes **kakéru** '*to be able to write*' and
utau '*to sing*' (verbs like this have roots ending in –w which is
  pronounced only before **a**, as we shall see in the next unit)
  becomes **utáeru** '*to be able to sing*'.

As these potential verbs are stative verbs rather than action verbs they generally mark their objects with the particle, **ga**.

Piano ga hikemásu ka. *Can you play the piano?*
Kanji ga kakemásu ka. *Can you write kanji?*

With vowel-root verbs the potential ending is **–rareru**, which, as we will see directly, is also the passive ending. The potential form of the irregular verb **kúru** '*to come*' is **koraréru** '*to be able to come*'. The other irregular verb **suru** '*to do*' does not have a potential form, **dekíru** being used instead.

Sashimi ga taberaremásu ka.	*Can you eat sashimi?*
Ítsu koraremásu ka.	*When can you come?*
Mínibasu o unten dekimasu ka.	*Can you drive a minibus?*

Often the idea of potential in Japanese is expressed not with a potential verb, but with an intransitive verb. These verbs are best learnt simply as vocabulary items. Here are three particularly useful ones.

miéru *to be able to see, to be visible*
Fuyu no háreta hi ni wa Tookyoo kara *On a fine winter's day*
Fújisan ga miemásu. *you can see Mt. Fuji from Tokyo.*

kikoeru *to be able to hear, to be audible*
Tonari no heya no kóe ga kikoemásu. *You can hear the voices from the room next door.*

mitsukaru *to be able to find, to be found*
Kuruma no kagí ga mitsukarimáshita. *I found* (was able to find) *the car keys.*

Exercise 10.3

You have as your house guest this weekend an Italian visitor Franco, who has spent many years in the Far East. You ask him if he can do various things, using your newly acquired potential verbs, of course.

1. Ask Franco if he can speak Chinese.
2. Ask him if he can make (**tsukuru**) pasta tonight.
3. Ask Franco if he can come with you to the zoo on Thursday to see the panda.
4. Ask if he can eat Japanese **shiokára** (salted squid guts) and **umeboshi** (salted plums).
5. Ask Franco if he can read Japanese.

Possibility

We know how to say that this or that probably happened or will probably happen, using **deshóo** after the plain forms of the verb.

Ashita kúru deshoo.	(He'll) *probably come tomorrow.*
Moo Igirisu ni káetta deshoo.	(He) *has probably already returned to England.*

If we are less sure about what might happen we move from the realms of probability to possibility and to Japanese uses of the expression **kámo shiremasen** (literally, '*whether or not we cannot know*') to convey the idea of '*might…*' or '*may…*'.

Ashita yukí ga fúru kámo shiremasen.	*It might snow tomorrow.*
Denwa-bángoo o wasureta kámo shiremasen.	*She may have forgotten the phone number.*

Because Japanese carries so much information in the verb at the end of the sentence, it often employs adverbs at or near the beginning of the sentence to give the hearer an inkling of what lies ahead. With conditional clauses it is common to start with **móshi** '*if*'. **Tabun** '*probably*' is often used with **deshóo** and with **kámo shiremasen** there is **moshikashitára** '*possibly*', '*perhaps*'.

Móshi jikan ga áttara kyóo no gógo kíte kudasai.	*If you have time please come this afternoon.*
Tabun kyóo wa osoku káeru deshoo.	*He'll probably be back late today.*
Moshikashitára wasureta kámo shiremasen.	*Perhaps he's forgotten.*

Giving explanations

To give an added connotation of explanation or elaboration to a sentence Japanese often ends a sentence in **n' desu** or the more formal **no desu** after the plain form of a verb. This means something like '*the fact is*' or '*let me explain that*', or just '*you see*' or '*you know*', and functions to link the sentence to the wider conversational context. Compare **ashí ga itái desu** and **ashí ga itái n' desu**. Although both have the basic meaning '*my foot hurts*', the former is a simple statement of fact, probably a piece of information with no particular connection to the present topic of conversation. The latter, however, is an explanation, perhaps in reply to the question '*Why are you walking so slowly?*'

Ashita shuppatsu surú n' desu.	*I'm leaving tomorrow, you see* (and that's why I'm busy packing).
Kaze o hiitá n' desu.	*I've got a cold, you see* (and that's why my voice is husky).

The use of **n' desu** is particularly common in questions beginning with **dóoshite** or **náze** (or the more colloquial **nánde**), all meaning 'why', and in answer to these questions. Note in the example below that **da**, the plain present form (dictionary form) of **désu**, becomes **na** before **n' desu**.

Dóoshite Nihóngo o benkyoo shite iru n' desu ka.	*Why are you studying Japanese?*
Kánai wa Nihonjín na n' desu.	*My wife's Japanese, you see.*

More demonstratives

We have met the demonstrative pronouns **kore** '*this*', **sore** '*that* (by you)', **are** '*that*' (over there) and **dóre** '*which one?*' and their corresponding demonstrative adjectives **kono, sono, ano** and **dóno**. We have also met the adverb **sóo** '*like that*' in the expression **Sóo desu ka** '*Is that so?*' As you may have suspected, **sóo** belongs to a series of demonstrative adverbs, **kóo** '*like this*', **sóo** '*like that*', **áa** '*like that*' (over there) and **dóo** '*how*'.

Kóo suréba dóo desu ka.	*What say we do it like this?*

In colloquial speech these adverbs are often replaced by the longer forms **koo yuu fúu ni** (literally, 'in this kind of manner'), etc.

Soo yuu fúu ni hanáshite wa damé desu.	*You mustn't talk like that.*

There is another set of demonstrative adjectives meaning '*this kind of*', '*that kind of*' and '*what kind of?*'. They are **konna, sonna, anna** and **dónna**. These, too, in informal colloquial language are often replaced by **koo yuu, soo yuu, aa yuu** and **dóo yuu**. **Yuu** is the verb '*to say*' and is written **iu** いう. These demonstrative adjectives can in turn be converted into adverbs by adding the particle **ni**, as in **konna ni** '*this much*', **dónna ni** '*how much*', etc.

Konna ryóori wa hajímete desu.	*This is the first time I've had this kind of food.*
Dónna hito to kekkon shitai désu ka.	*What sort of person do you want to marry?*
Shikén wa sonna ni muzukáshikatta désu ka.	*Was the exam* (really) *that difficult?*

Exercise 10.4 ■■

You are a university student working part-time at the reception desk of a large hotel in London. A Japanese tourist comes in and reports that she has lost her handbag. Ask her the details of her handbag and its contents using **dónna**. Some model questions and answers are provided for you on the cassette.

1. What colour is it?
2. What shape is it?
3. What sorts of things were inside it?

Now take the part of the tourist and answer your own questions. You will need the new vocabulary introduced below.

Vocabulary

dónna iro	*what colour* (**nániiro** is also used)	**choohóokei**	*rectangular*
		daenkei	*oval*
béiju	*beige*	**nakámi**	*contents*
pínku	*pink*	**saifu**	*purse, wallet*
katachi	*shape*	**kuréjitto káado**	*credit card*
marui	*round*	**teikíken**	*season ticket*
shikakú	*square*	**ie no kagí**	*house key*
sánkaku	*triangular*		

Listing reasons – 'and what is more ...'

We have learnt that verbs or adjectives in Japanese can be joined by putting the first in the –**te** form. So we have met expressions like **itte kimásu** '*goodbye*' (literally, '*I'm going and coming*') and **yásukute oishíi desu** '*it's inexpensive and tasty*'. Another way of joining clauses is with the emphatic particle **shi**, which is a more emphatic way of saying '*and*' than the –**te** form. It means something like, '*and what is more*' and '*moreover*'.

Ashita ane mo kúru shi otootó mo kimásu. *Tomorrow my sister is coming and my brother is coming too.*

Often **shi** is used for giving a number of reasons why something is, or should be, so.

Yúkiko san wa kírei da shi, atamá mo íi shi, kanemóchi desu kara, kánojo to kekkon shitai hito ga óoi sóo desu.

Yukiko is beautiful, intelligent and rich so apparently there are lots of people who would like to marry her.

Exercise 10.5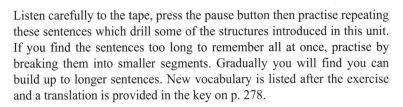

Listen carefully to the tape, press the pause button then practise repeating these sentences which drill some of the structures introduced in this unit. If you find the sentences too long to remember all at once, practise by breaking them into smaller segments. Gradually you will find you can build up to longer sentences. New vocabulary is listed after the exercise and a translation is provided in the key on p. 278.

1. *Tanaka Jiro is not feeling too well at work. He asks his boss if he can go home.*

A: のども いたいし せきも でるから、早く かえりたいん
　　ですが、よろしいですか。
B: ええ。もしかしたら、かぜかも 知れませんね。
　　お大事にどうぞ。
A: どうも ありあがとうございます。

2. *A conversation between doctor and patient.*

A: すべってころんだんですが、こんなに はれてきました。
B: こっせつかも 知れません。レントゲンを とって見ましょう。

3. *Trying to get something for a headache on a public holiday.*

A: きゅうに ずつうの くすりが いるんですけれど、どこで
　　売っているでしょう。
B: ああ、きょうは 休みですね。でも、コンビニで 売っている
　　かも 知れません。
A: じゃ、ちょっと 行って見ます。

Vocabulary

nódo	*throat*
sekí	*cough*
yoroshíi	*good* (formal, suggests approval by a social superior)
kaze	*a cold*

subéru	*to slip*
korobu	*to fall over*
hareru	*to swell*
kossetsu	*broken bone*

Dialogue 2 ■

Listen to the dialogue and see how much you can understand before learning the vocabulary. Then check the new vocabulary and listen again.

阿部: このごろる とてもつかれろんですよ。

馬場: そうですか。会社でおいそがしいんでしょう。

阿部: いそがしいというより 課長としての 責任が重いから、ストレスが たまるんです。

馬場: それは いけませんねえ。ストレス解消に何をしていますか。

阿部: いや、別に何もしていません。

馬場: 必ず時間を作って、何か好きな事をした方がいいですよ。

阿部: そうですね。本当にこのごろは運動不足という感じですよ。

馬場: それなら、今度の日曜日にゴルフでも一緒にしませんか。

阿部: いいですねえ。ぜひお供したいですね。

ABE: Kongoro totemotsukaréru n' desu yo.

BABA: Sóo desu ka. Kaisha de oisogashíi n' deshoo.

ABE: Isogashíi to yuu yori kachoo to shite no sekinin ga omói kara, sutorésu ga tamarú n' desu.

BABA: Sore wa ikemasén née. Sutoresu káishoo ni náni o shite imásu ka.

ABE: Íya, betsu ni nánimo shite imasén.

BABA: Kanarazu jikan o tsukútte, nánika sukí na kotó shita hóo ga íi desu yo.

ABE: Sóo desu ne. Hontoo ni konogoro wa undoobúsoku to yuu kanji désu yo.

BABA: Sore nara, kóndo no nichiyóobi ni górufu demo issho ni shimasén ka.

BABA: Íi desu nee. Zéhi otómo shitai désu ne.

Vocabulary

yóri	*than, rather than*
kachoo	*section head*
sekinin	*responsibility*
omoi	*heavy*
sutorésu	*stress*
tamaru	*to build up, accumulate*
sutoresu-káishoo	*stress relief*
betsu ni	*in particular*
kanarazu	*without fail*
tsukúru	*to make*
undoo-búsoku	*lack of exercise, getting insufficient exercise*
...to yuu	*that, of the kind that* (often used in adjectival clauses to link noun to its qualifier)
sore nára	*in that case*
kóndo no	*this, next*
otómo suru	*to join, accompany, go along with*

Kanji

The **kanji** charts introduced from Units 1 to 10 have been included primarily to help you learn to write and recognise the Chinese characters. Only one or two readings have been given for each character and you have not always had examples demonstrating both the **on** and **kun** readings of the **kanji**. We feel that now you have learnt how to read and write over 100 **kanji** you should have a good idea of the principles underlying the stroke order and a feel for the correct proportions of written **kanji**. From Unit 11 the information about how to write the character will be dropped in favour of including more readings and English meanings for each **kanji**. As there are several **kanji** in this list with a variety of readings not included in the chart we have set out some additional information below. You will need to have read through this section carefully before starting the remaining exercises.

KOO	JI	JI	FU	BO
kuchi	**mimí**	character	**chichí**	**háha**
mouth	ear		father	mother

NYUU	SHUTSU	JUU	CHI	KAI
hái (ru)	**dé (ru)**	**sú (mu)**	**shi (ru)**	**a (keru)**
to enter	to exit, leave	to live	to know	to open

Additional readings of this unit's kanji

入　**i(reru)** *'to put in'*. Note: 入れる could be either **ireru** *'to put in'* or **haireru** *'to be able to enter'*. Context will usually determine which is the correct reading. Remember the important distinction in Japanese between transitive (trans.) and intransitive (intrans.) verbs. **Hái(ru)** is intransitive, **i(reru)** is transitive.

出　**dá(su)** *'to put out'*, *'send out'*, *'take out'*, *'pay'* (trans.). The intransitive **dé(ru)** means *'to go out'*, *'come out'*, *'stick out'*, *'protrude'*, etc.

知　no extra readings to learn for this one, but remember that **shi(ru)** means *'to get to know'*, *'to become acquainted with'*. The equivalent of *'I know'* in Japanese is **shitte imásu** (literally, 'I am in a state of having got to know'). Just to make you thoroughly confused, however, *'I don't know'* is simply **shirimasén**.

開　In the chart we have just **a(keru)** (trans.) *'to open'*. There is also its intransitive partner, **a(ku)** *'to open, to come open'*, etc., as in *'the door opens'*. There is also another verb **hirá(ku)**, written in exactly the same way as **a(ku)**, which means *'to open'*, *'to uncover'*, *'spread open'*. This is a transitive verb like **a(keru)** and its partner **hirakéru** *'to become modern'*, *'become civilised'* is an intransitive verb like **aku**. Obviously the Japanese did not design their language with the needs of foreign learners uppermost in their minds!

Exercise 10.6

Read the following sentences aloud then translate them into English.

1. 山口くんのお父さんとお母さんを知っていますか。
2. 知りません。どこに住んでいますか。
3. よこから入れますか。いいえ、あそこは出口です。
4. 前の入口は開いていませんが。
5. それなら、前の門が開く時間までまつほかはありません。
   (**hoka wa arimasén** '*there is nothing for it but to...*')
6. 新聞の「聞」という字は「門」と「耳」をいっしょに書いたかん字です。
7. 安子さんの小さくて、白い耳が花のように見えました。
8. 口を大きく開いて、した (*tongue*) を出してください。

11 日本に行くならどの季節がいいでしょうか。

Nihón ni ikú nara, dóno kísetsu ga íi deshoo ka.

If you're going to Japan, which is the best season?

In this unit you will learn how to:

- Use the plain negative forms of verbs and adjectives
- Discuss obligation
- Say what will happen if something is not done
- Make decisions
- Talk about what you have done in the past
- Request people not to do certain things
- Use conditionals with **nara**
- Give reasons using **no de**.

You will also acquire:

- 20 more **kanji**:　北　南　西　春　夏　秋　冬　夕　方　多
　　　　　　　　　　少　歩　旅　天　気　雨　雪　風　暑　寒

Dialogue 1 ■■

Barbara who has been learning Japanese in London is talking to her friend about her plans to visit Japan next year. Can you follow the dialogue with the aid of the Japanese–English glossary (p. 312)? Making your own vocabulary list will help implant the words into your memory.

バーバラ： いろいろ 考えたんですが、 来年の旅行は日本に行く
　　　　　 ことにしました。

ともだち： いいですねえ。初めてですか。

バーバラ： いいえ、十年ぐらい前にちょっと行ったことが
　　　　　 あります。

ともだち： それで、いつ頃行く予定にしているんですか。

バーバラ： まだ決めていませんが行くなら、ど季節
　　　　　 がいいでしょうか。

ともだち： そうですねえ。春か秋ですねえ。

バーバラ： その外の 季節 はどうですか?

ともだち： 夏も冬も旅行には向ませんよ。夏は蒸し暑いし、
　　　　　 冬はかなり寒くなりますから...

バーバラ： 日本の春と秋はどんな感じですか。

ともだち： 春は桜がとてもきれいですよ。特に夜桜はロマンチ
　　　　　 ックで、若い人達に人気があります。春にいつたら
　　　　　 どうですか。いいですよ。

バーバラ： とてもよさそうですねえ。じゃ、春にしましょう。

BÁABARA: Iroiro kangáeta n' desu ga, rainen no ryokoo wa Nihón ni
iku kotó ni shimáshita.

TOMODACHI: Íi desu née. Hajímete desu ka.

BÁABARA: Iie, júunen gurai máe ni chotto itta kotó ga arimásu.

TOMODACHI: Sore de, ítsu goro iku yotei ni shite irú n' desu ka.

BÁABARA: Máda kimete imasén ga, ikú nara, dóno kísetsu ga íi
deshóo ka.

TOMODACHI: Sóo desu née. Háru ka **áki** desu née.

BÁABARA: Sono hoka no kísetsu wa doo desuka?

TOMODACHI: Natsú mo fuyú mo ryokoo ni wa mukimasén yo. Natsú
wa mushiatsúi shi, fuyú wa kánari sámuku narimásu
kara…

BÁABARA: Nihón no háru to áki wa dónna kanji désu ka.

TOMODACHI: Háru wa sakura ga totemo kírei desu yó. Toku ni yozákura
wa romanchíkku de, wakái hitotachi ni ninki ga arimasu
haru ni ittara doo desuka. íi desu yo.

BÁABARA: Totemo yosasóo desu née. Já, háru ni shimashóo.

The plain negative

We have been trying to put a positive spin on learning Japanese, but we cannot delay any longer the introduction of the plain negative forms. Actually we have already met a negative form in the shape of **nái** in **nái desu**, an alternative to **arimasén**, and, in the negative of adjectives, **tákaku nai** '*not expensive*', etc. What we already know about negatives is summarised in the following table.

Verb	Adjective	Copula	Descriptive noun
kakimasén	**tákaku nai desu** **tákaku arimasen**	**déwa arimasén**	**sukí dewa (ja) arimasén** **sukí ja nái desu**
(I) *don't write*	(it) *isn't expensive*	(it) *is not*	(I) *don't like*

The plain non-past negative ending **–(a)nai** is added to the verb root, the initial **–(a)** dropping with vowel-root verbs, e.g. **tabénai** '*to not eat*'. The irregular verbs **kúru** and **suru** become **kónai** and **shinai** respectively. Unaccented verbs have unaccented negative forms, e.g. **iku** '*to go*', **ikanai** '*to not go*'. With accented verbs the accent mark moves to the vowel before the **–n** of the suffix, **káku** '*to write*', **kakánai** '*not write*', **míru** '*to see*' **mínai** '*not see*'. Verbs with dictionary forms (plain non-past forms) ending in **–au** or **–ou** are really consonant-root verbs ending in **–w**. This final **–w** of the root now appears only before **–a**, that is, in the various negative forms of the verb, **omowánai** '*not to think*', **warawanai** '*not to laugh*', etc.

To recap, let us use the larger table to compare the non-past and past tense forms of the plain and polite-style negative in verbs, adjectives, descriptive nouns and the copula.

	Non-past affirmative	Non-past negative	Past affirmative	Past negative
C-root verb	**káku**	**kakánai**	**káita**	**kakánakatta**
V-root verb	**míru**	**mínai**	**míta**	**minákatta**
Irreg. (k)	**kúru**	**kónai**	**kíta**	**konákatta**
Irreg. (s)	**suru**	**shinai**	**shita**	**shinákatta**
Adjective	**takái**	**tákaku nai**	**tákakatta**	**takaku nákatta**
Copula	**da**	**ja nái**	**dátta**	**ja nákatta**
Des. noun	**sukí da**	**sukí ja nái**	**sukí datta**	**sukí ja nákatta**

Exercise 11.1

This exercise drills the negative forms of verbs and adjectives. How would you tell your friend,

1. that she had better go in a season which is not too hot?
2. that she had better take the train at a time when it is not too crowded?
3. that you like desserts that are not too sweet?
4. that Saturdays and Sundays are the days when you do not go to the gym?
5. that there are a few people who won't be coming tonight?

Double negatives and obligation

Although you will hear a lot of Japanese using plain forms like these as final verbs in casual conversation, for the time being most of us will use the plain forms as non-final verbs in polite-style speech. The uses of the negative verbs are obviously the same as those of their affirmative counterparts, but there are a number of negative endings that deserve special treatment. These are the negative –**te** form endings and the negative conditionals.

The negative forms of the conditional endings –**tára** and –**(r)éba** are –**(a)nákattara** and –**(a)nákereba**.

Kyóo dekínakattara, zéhi ashita madé ni yatte kudásai.	*If you can't do it today please be sure to do it by* (the end of) *tomorrow.*
Anáta ga ikanákereba watashi mo ikimasén.	*If you're not going, I'm not going either.*

A similar construction uses the clause final particle **to** meaning '*if*', '*when*' or '*whenever*' after a negative verb to mean '*if not*'.

Súgu dénai to básu ni ma ni aimasén.	*If we don't leave immediately we'll be late for the bus.*

One very useful construction using the negative conditional form is –**(a)nákereba narimasen**, a double negative form which literally means '*if one does not do something, it will not do*', which is the Japanese way of expressing obligation.

| Kyóo wa háyaku kaeránakereba narimasen. | *Today I have to go back early.* |
| Nihongo wa máinichi sukóshi zútsu benkyoo shinákereba narimasen. | *With Japanese you have to study a little every day* (**zútsu** '*each*', e.g., **Hitótsu zútsu** '*one each*' or '*one of each*'). |

Instead of **narimasén** in this construction you will sometimes hear **ikemasén**, literally, '*it cannot go*'. This also suggests obligation, but with perhaps a slightly stronger connotation of moral responsibility. **Ikemasén** alone means something like '*Don't!*' or '*Stop it!*' and is often used as a rebuke to mischievous children.

| Ashita wa shikén desu kara kónban wa isshookénmei benkyoo shinákereba ikemasen. | *Tomorrow's the exam, so I'll have to study for all I'm worth.* |

You may also hear expressions of compulsion with the descriptive noun **damé** '*no good*' instead of a negative verb. The construction with **damé** is more emphatic and carries an even heavier connotation of moral obligation.

| Mata ashita konákereba damé desu. | *You must come again tomorrow.* |

In addition to the conditional **–(a)nákereba narimasen** form, you will also hear **–(a)nákute wa narimasen** or the very colloquial **–(a)nákucha naranai**, which is sometimes contracted even further by dropping the final verb. This last is usually used in very informal casual conversation in plain-style speech.

| Minshuku no yoyaku o shinákute wa narimasen. | *I have to make the **minshuku** booking.* (*Note*: **Minshuku** is a private house which offers homestay or similar budget accommodation.) |
| O! Juuníji da. Móo kaeranákucha! | *Oh! It's twelve o'clock. I'll have to be going home.* |

Exercise 11.2 ■

You are having a party. From the list of sentences on the cassette tape say which are directly related to your preparations for the party.

1. 薬を飲まなくてはなりません。
2. 色々な食べ物を用意しなければなりません。
3. 使ったコップやお皿を洗ってしまわなければなりません。
4. 飲み物を冷蔵庫に入れなければなりません。
5. 部屋をかたずけなくてはなりません。
6. 買物をしなければなりません。
7. お手洗いに行かなければなりません。
8. 音楽を選ばなければなりません。

Vocabulary

iroiro na   *various* (*Note*: the **kanji** 々 sign indicating the previous **kanji** is to be repeated. A backward tick ゝ or a backward tick with the voicing marks ゞ performs the same function with **hiragána**, but its use is usually confined to writing in vertical script.)

sara   *plate* (*Note*: **osára** is a more genteel alternative used mainly by women.)

Prohibition

If, as we have seen, two negatives make a strong positive statement, 'must', then it follows that a single negative should convey a strong negative message. You will recall from Unit 7 that this is just what happens in Japanese. The idea of prohibition, 'you must not...' is expressed by a verb stem followed by **–te wa ikemasén**.

Hikóoki no náka de keitai-dénwa o tsukátte wa ikemasén.   *You must not use a mobile phone inside the aircraft.*

Remember the opposite construction, that is, to express permission, use **–te mo íi desu**.

Sóto de tabako o sutté mo íi desu.   *You may smoke outside.*

Exercise 11.3

Match the conditions in the left-hand column with the consequences set out in random order on the right. Then read the full sentences over two or three times each, making sure you understand what they mean. Finally, check your answers against those in the Key to the Exercises (p. 279).

1. 今すぐ行かないと	a. 分かりません。
2. お金がないと	b. すぐおなかが すきます。
3. 日本で日本語ができないと	c. 着るものがなくなります。
4. ちゃんと食べないと	d. 何も買えません。
5. せんたくを しないと	e. ふべんです。
6. じっさいに見ないと	f. バスにおくれるかもしれません。

Making decisions

In English the verb 'to make' can be used to convey the idea of making a decision. For example, we might say, 'I'm busy today. Let's make it tomorrow'. In Japanese this idea is achieved with the verb, **suru** '*to do*': **Kyóo wa isogashíi kara ashita ni shimashóo**. This construction, noun + **ni** + part of the verb **suru**, means to '*decide on*' something. If you want to say you have decided to do this or that, in other words if you want to use this construction with a verb or adjective, you must use the noun **kotó** '*thing*' after the plain form of the verb before you add **ni suru**. This **kotó** has the function of turning the verb into a noun so it can take the nominal particles, in this case **ni**, or be made the subject or object of another verb. In this respect its function is very similar to the –ing ending of the English gerund in expressions like, '*I like reading books*', **Hón o yómu kotó ga sukí desu**.

For practical purposes you can think of …–**koto ni suru** as being, '*to decide to …*' and …–**(a)nái kotó ni suru** as being '*to decide not to …*'.

Koosoku básu de iku kotó ni shimáshita.	*We decided to go on the expressway bus.*
Shinkánsen de ikanai kotó ni shimáshita.	*We decided not to go on the Shinkansen.*

Exercise 11.4 ■■

Haruo had not been feeling very well, so he decided to visit his doctor. The doctor diagnosed the trouble as **gendáibyoo** '*sickness of the modern lifestyle*' brought on by overwork, lack of exercise and poor diet. Haruo has decided to turn over a new leaf to get fit and healthy. How would you go about this task if you were Haruo? On the tape and written below is the doctor's advice. Use this, the vocabulary items beneath and the numbered cues to make a list of the things you would do. There is also one example to help you.

<ruby>肉<rt>にく</rt></ruby>の食べすぎです。<ruby>肉<rt>にく</rt></ruby>の<ruby>代<rt>かわ</rt></ruby>りにもっと <ruby>魚<rt>さかな</rt></ruby> や<ruby>野菜<rt>やさい</rt></ruby>
を食べる<ruby>方<rt>ほう</rt></ruby>がいいです。<ruby>毎日<rt></rt></ruby><ruby>運動<rt>うんどう</rt></ruby>するようにして
ください。 お<ruby>酒<rt>さけ</rt></ruby>はへらしてください。たばこはやめなければ
なりません。
お<ruby>腹<rt>なか</rt></ruby>がすいたら<ruby>甘<rt>あま</rt></ruby>いものの<ruby>代<rt>かわ</rt></ruby>りに<ruby>果物<rt>くだもの</rt></ruby>を食べると
いいです。

Cue: **nikú herasu**
A: **Nikú o herasu kotó ni shimásu.**

1. tabako, suwanai
2. amai monó, kawari ni, kudámono, tabéru
3. osake, ryóo, herasu
4. máinichi, undoo suru
5. mótto, sakana, yasai, tabéru

Vocabulary

kawari ni *instead of* **hóo ga ii** *it is better to…* **yóo ni suru** *to make it so that…, arrange to…, make sure that…*

'Please don't …'

The negative request is formed with the ending –**(a)naide kudasai**.

Shibafu ni hairánaide kudasái.	*Please don't walk on the grass* (**shibafu** '*lawn*').
Ki ni shináide kudasai.	*Please don't think anything of it. Don't worry. It's nothing,* etc.
Shinpai shináide kudasai.	*Please don't worry* (more serious than the above).

Often the negative request is dropped in favour of a more indirect approach. You might hear a tour guide, for example, say, **Kochira de no shashin wa goénryo kudasái** '*Please refrain from taking photographs here.*' Or something along the lines of '*please try not to*' **shinai yóo ni shite kudasái** or '*be careful not to…*' **shinai yóo ki o tsukéte kudasái**.

**Kása o wasurenai yóo ni ki o
tsukéte kudasai.**

*Please be careful not to forget your
umbrella.*

Exercise 11.5 ■

Each of the following role-play dialogues contains a negative request.
First read through the dialogue making sure you understand the meaning
of the sentences. Then find an appropriate answer to put into the blank
space. Finally, listen to the tape and try repeating the whole dialogue
yourself until you can memorise it. Repeat this procedure with each
dialogue.

1. You notice the caretaker of your building mopping the floor in the
   corridor outside your office.

   あなた：　　あのう、ここを通ってもいいですか。

   管理人：　　まだ床がぬれているので、＿＿＿＿＿ないように気
   　　　　　　をつけてください。

2. The tour guide is giving instructions about tomorrow's departure.

   ツアーコンダクター：　明日の朝六時半出発です。

   山本さん：　　　　　　随分、早いですねえ。

   ツアーコンダクター：　ええ、申し訳ありませんが、

   　　　　　　　　　　　六時までにロビーに集まって

   　　　　　　　　　　　ください。＿＿＿＿＿ようにお願い
   　　　　　　　　　　　します。

3. Tomoko and Yoko are sisters living together in an apartment in
   Tokyo. Tomoko is just about to go out to do some shopping.

   ともこ：　スーパーの買物に行ってくるね。

   よおこ：　お砂糖と塩を＿＿＿＿＿ないように買ってきてね。
   ともこ：　はい。

Vocabulary

osátoo　　*sugar* (*Note*: women's word, men use **satóo** without the
　　　　　　elegant **o–** prefix.)

More clause-final particles

Giving reasons with no de

Another useful way to show a cause and effect relationship between two clauses is to use the particles **no de**, '*because*' after a plain form of the verb. This is similar in use and meaning to **kara**, but is more formal and is used more often in writing. **no de** is more restricted in its use than **kara**. It tends not to occur in sentences in which the main verb is imperative, interrogative or implies obligation or prohibition. In speech the **no** is often contracted to just **n**'.

Yuki ga yandá no de yamá e sukíi ni dekakemáshita.	*As the snow had stopped we set out for the mountains to do some skiing.*
Kono hen ni kitá n' de, tsúide ni yotte mimáshita.	*I was in the area so I just dropped in while I was at it.*

Nára – *'if'*

Nára after the plain form of the verb provides yet another conditional expression in Japanese. It is usually found in contexts where it means something like, '*if as you say*' or '*if it is so that…*'. It picks up and expands an assertion made, or presumed to have been made, by the person you are addressing. In this respect it deals with factual rather than hypothetical situations.

Róndon ni iku nara watashi no tomodachi no tokoro ni yottára dóo desu ka.	*If you are going to London* (as you say you are) *why don't you drop in at my friend's place?* (**yoru** '*to drop in*' [at = **ni**].)

Exercise 11.6

Choose the most appropriate ending for each of the following **nára** clauses from the list of options on the right. When you have finished the exercise practise repeating the completed sentences.

1. 日本に行くなら

2. 京都に行くなら

a. ついでに奈良にも行くといいですよ。近いですから。

b. 夜、六時以降にしてください。

3. 無理<ruby>無<rt>む</rt></ruby><ruby>理<rt>り</rt></ruby>なら
4. 手みやげを<ruby>持<rt>も</rt></ruby>っていくなら
5. <ruby>電話<rt>でんわ</rt></ruby>をするなら

c. 春か秋の<ruby>方<rt>ほう</rt></ruby>がいいです。
d. <ruby>仕方<rt>しかた</rt></ruby>がありません。
e. 何がいいでしょうねえ。

Vocabulary

íkoo	*after, from … onwards*
tsuide ni	*incidentally, at the same time, while …*
Nára	*the ancient capital*
temíyage	*a gift* (usually of food) *taken when visiting someone*
shikata ga nái	*it can't be helped, never mind*

'Without doing …'

Perhaps a more common use of the –(a)**náide** construction is to join clauses.

Kyóo wa kaisha e ikanáide *Today I didn't go to the office and spent*
  ichinichijuu kaze de nete *all day in bed with a cold.*
  imáshita.

This –(a)**náide** is often equivalent to '*without*' in sentences like:

Asagóhan o tabénaide kaisha e *I went to the office without*
  ikimáshita. *having breakfast.*

There is another negative –**te** form, –(a)**nakute** which is used (without the initial –**a**) as the –**te** form of the verb **nái** '*to have not*'.

Íma wa okane ga nákute komátte *At the moment I'm in a fix*
  imasu. *because I've got no money.*

This is also the only form used with adjectives and descriptive nouns.

Shokuji ga óishiku nákute gakkári *We were disappointed the food*
  shimashita. *was not good.*

It is used for joining clauses, particularly when the subjects are different or there is a cause-and-effect relationship between the clauses.

Koko de kurejittokáado　　It's inconvenient not being able to use a
　ga tsukaenákute fúben　　credit card here.
　desu.

This is also the form used in the pattern –**(a)nakute mo íi** 'need not…'
(literally, 'even if not, it is good').

Nihongo ga ryúuchoo ja nákute　　It does not matter if you are not
　mo kamaimasén.　　　　　　fluent in Japanese.
Móo kusuri o nománakute mo　　You needn't take the medicine any
　íi desu.　　　　　　　　　　longer.

Dialogue 2

*Miss Abe, who is holidaying in Sydney, asks the concierge at her hotel if
he can suggest an interesting optional tour.*

阿部:　　　　すみません。ちょっとオプショナルツアーの
　　　　　　ことを 伺 いたいんですが。

コンシェルジェ:　はい。どんなツアーがよろしいですか。

阿部:　　　　まだよく 考 えていないんですが、
　　　　　　何かちょっと変わったツアー が ありますか。

コンシェルジェ:　そうですねえ。今日は天気もいいし、
　　　　　　ヘリコプターはいかがですか?

阿部:　　　　ヘリコプターですか。乗ったことはないんですが、
　　　　　　大丈夫かしら。それにちょっと高そうですねえ。

コンシェルジェ:　ヘリコプターは楽しいし、安全ですよ。それ
　　　　　　に、ヘリコプターから見る景色は最高です。せっか
　　　　　　くここまでいらっしゃったんですから。

阿部:　　　　実は、前から一度は乗ってみたかったんです。でも
　　　　　　日本では高くて、今までなかなか
　　　　　　機会がなかったんですよ。

コンシェルジェ:　日本の半額以下ですから、この機会に 乗ってみたら
　　　　　　いかがですか。

阿部:　　　　半額? 本当ですか。では、乗って みましょう。

Vocabulary

konsheruje	*concierge* (in a hotel)
… no kotó	*about…* (also… **ni tsuite**)
ukagaetái n' desu ga	*I would just like to enquire, but…* (a common polite opening gambit when requesting information)
kawatta	*unusual, different, strange* (from **kawaru** '*to change*')
sóo desu née	*let me think, hmm, I wonder,* etc.
káshira	*I wonder* (sentence-final particle used by women)
takasóo na	*looks/seems expensive*
–sóo na	*looking…, seeming…* (suffix attached to adjectives, forms a descriptive noun)
anzen na	*safe* (anzen dáiichi 安全第一 *safety first*)
sekkaku	*since you have gone to all the trouble of…, with difficulty*
ichidó wa	*once* (at least)
íka	*less than* (cf. **íjoo** 以上 '*more than*')
… te míru	*to try doing…, do… and see*

Exercise 11.7

Answer the following comprehension questions based on Dialogue 2.

1. What kind of optional tour is Miss Abe looking for?
2. Why does she have reservations about a helicopter flight?
3. Give three reasons the concierge put forward to convince Miss Abe to take the flight.
4. Why hadn't Miss Abe flown in a helicopter in Japan? Give two reasons.
5. Why did she finally decide to take the flight?

Kanji

From this unit we introduce the new **kanji** in a slightly different format. As you now know the principles of stroke order and stroke formation we no longer provide the stroke order for each character, though we do give the number of strokes in each character. It is important to practise writing the **kanji** as this process helps etch the correct balance and stroke count into your memory. The readings and meanings given for each **kanji** are far from complete. Where possible, both Chinese-style **on**-readings (in small capital letters) and native Japanese **kun**-readings (lower case) are given, but often it has not been possible to find appropriate examples of each reading.

Exercise 11.8 ■■

After you have tried reading these sentences aloud, repeat them after your tutor on the tape.

1. 雪の中を歩いてかえりましょう。
2. 南日本は北日本より暑いです。
3. 天気がわるかったら行かないことにしましょう。
4. 春休みに西日本を旅行しようと思っています。
5. 夕方から風がつよくなって雨がふりだしました。
6. 寒いからもう少しあったかいセーターを着た方がいいです。
7. 夏にはこのへんの海に来る人がひじょうに多いそうです。
8. むこうの高い山が秋の夕日をあびてとてもきれいに見えます。
9. 今年の冬は雪が少なかったのでスキーに行きませんでした。
10. 東京駅の南口から北口へ歩いて行って何分ぐらいかかりますか。

Useful expressions

Omachidoosama déshita.	*Sorry to have kept you waiting.*
Osewasamá deshita.	*Thank you for your help.*
Otsukaresama déshita.	*Thank you for your efforts* (literally, 'you must be tired').
Gokúroosama deshita.	*Thank you for your efforts.* (Not used towards people of higher social status)
Zannén deshita.	*What a pity!*
Ganbátte kudasai.	*Stick to it! Work hard!*

北	**HOKU** **kita** 4 strokes #11.103	north 北風 **kitakaze** north wind 東北 **toohoku** the north-east	南	**NAN** **minami** 9 strokes #11.104	south 南国 **nangoku** southern climes 南アフリカ **minami Áfurika** South Africa
西	**SEI, SAI** **nishi** 6 strokes #11.105	west 西日本 **nishi-Nihón** western Japan 西南 **seinan** south-west	春	**SHUN** **háru** 9 strokes #11.106	spring 来年の春 **rainen no háru** next spring 春の花 **háru no haná** spring flowers
夏	**KA** **natsú** 10 strokes #11.107	summer 夏休み**natsuyásumi** summer holiday 夏の海 **natsu no úmi** the sea in summer	秋	**SHUU** **áki** 9 strokes #11.108	autumn 秋の山 **áki no yamá** the mountains in autumn
冬	**TOO** **fuyú** 5 strokes #11.109	winter 冬のスポーツ **fuyu no supóotsu** winter sports 今年の冬 **kotoshi no fuyú** this winter	夕	**SEKI** **yuu** 3 strokes #11.110	evening 夕方 **yuugata** evening 夕日 **yuuhi** the setting sun
方	**HOO** **katá, –gatá** 4 strokes #11.111	direction, side, person (hono-rific) あの方 **anokatá** he, she (honorific) 先生方 **senseigata** teachers (honorific)	多	**TA** **óo(i)** 6 strokes #11.112	numerous, many 人が多い **hito ga ooi** there are many people 多くの人 **óoku no hito** many / most people
少	**SHOO** **suku(nái)** **sukó(shi)** 4 strokes #11.113	few, a little 少々 **shóoshoo** a little, a moment 少年 **shoonen** a boy	旅	**RYO** **tabi** 10 strokes #11.113	journey 旅行 **ryokoo** trip, journey 旅行会社 **ryokoogáisha** travel company
歩	**HO** **arú(ku)** 8 strokes #11.115	a step, to walk 歩いて **arúite** on foot 一歩 **íppo** one step	天	**TEN** 4 strokes #11.116	heaven, sky 天国 **téngoku** heaven 天気 **ténki** weather
気	**KI** 6 strokes #11.117	air, vapour, spirit 人気 **ninki** popularity 気分 **kíbun** mood, feeling	雨	**U** **áme** 8 strokes #11.118	rain 雨天 **úten** rainy weather 大雨 **ooáme** heavy rain
雪	**SETSU** **yuki** 11 strokes #11.119	snow 雪国 **yukíguni** the snow country 大雪 **ooyuki** heavy snow fall	風	**FUU** **kaze** 9 strokes #11.120	wind; fashion, way, style 中国風 **Chuugokufuu** Chinese style 海風 **umíkaze** sea breeze
寒	**KAN** **samú(i)** 12 strokes #11.121	cold 寒気 **kánki** a cold snap 寒い天気ですねえ。 The weather is cold, isn't it?	暑	**SHO** **atsú(i)** 12 strokes #11.122	hot 暑中見まい **shochuu-mímai** wishes for good health in the hot season

12 どうも風邪を引いたようです。

Dóomo kaze o hiita yóo desu.

Somehow I seem to have caught a cold.

In this unit you will learn how to:

- Talk about giving and receiving goods and favours
- Use more expressions with the **–te** form
- Discuss expectations using **hazu**
- Discuss obligation using the verbal auxiliary **–beki**
- Use concessive clauses with **no ni**.

You will also acquire:

20 more **kanji**:　外 心 思 急 酒 配 洋 様 電 部
　　　　　　　　　　曇 長 名 元 林 降 森 空 立 雲

Dialogue 1 ■

Akita san is concerned about his workmate Baba san, who has been unusually quiet during their regular Friday night round of drinks after work.

秋田：　馬場さん、顔色が良くないですね。

馬場：　どうも風邪を引いたようです。頭ものども痛いし、
　　　　咳も出るんです。

秋田：　お医者さんに診てもらったらどうですか。

馬場：　ええ、明日ちょっと医者に行って来ようと思っています。

They continue the conversation after lunch at work on Monday.

秋田: 薬か何かもらいましたか。

馬場: ええ、一応。でも効くかどうか分かりません。食後に
一錠飲まなくてはならないそうです。

秋田: じゃ、水を持って来てあげましょうか。

馬場: あ、どうもすみません。（心の中で：秋田さんは
親切だなあ。病気も悪くないなあ。時々病気になろう
かな。ゴホン、ゴホン。）

秋田: 馬場さん。もううちに帰った方がいいんじゃないですか。
咳もひどいし、だるそうだから。

馬場: じゃ、外の人にうつすといけないから、
帰て休むことにします。（心の中で：大した風邪じゃない
のに、何だか、悪いような気がするなあ。）

秋田: じゃ、お大事に。

馬場: ありがとうございます。じゃ、お先に失礼します。

AKITA: Baba san, kaoiro ga yóku nái desu ne.

BABA: Dóomo kaze o hiita yóo desu. Atamá mo nódo mo itái shi, sekí
mo déru n' desu.

AKITA: Oisha san ni míte morattara dóo desu ka.

BABA: Ée, ashita chótto isha ni itte koyóo to omótte imasu.

They continue the conversation after lunch at work on Monday.

AKITA: Kusuri ka nánika moraimáshita ka.

BABA: Ée, ichioo. Démo kiku ka dóo ka wakarimasén. Shokugo ni
ichijoo nomanákute wa naránai soo desu.

AKITA: Já, mizu o motte kite agemashóo ka.

BABA: Á, dóomo sumimasén. (Kokóro no náka de: Ákita san wa
shínsetsu da náa. Byooki mo wáruku nai náa. Tokídoki byooki
ni naróo ka ná. Gohón, gohón.)

AKITA: Baba san. Móo uchi ni káetta hoo ga íi n' ja nái desu ka. Sekí
mo hidói shi, darusóo da kara.

BABA: Já, hoka no hito ni utsusu to ikenai kara, káette yasumu kotó ni
shimásu. (Kokóro no náka de, táishita kaze ja nái no ni, nán da
ka, warúi yoo na ki ga surunaa.)

AKITA: Já, odaiji ni.
BABA: Arígatoo gozaimasu. Já, osaki ni shitsúrei shimasu.

Vocabulary

kaze o hiku	*to catch a cold*
míte morau	*get … to examine, have examined*
ichioo	*once, for the time being, tentatively, for what it's worth*
… ka dóo ka	*whether or not …*
kiku ka dóo ka wakarimasén	*I don't know whether it will work or not*
shokugo	*after meals* (cf. **shokuzen** 食前 '*before meals*')
ichijoo	*one tablet* (**–joo** is the numeral classifier for tablets)
motte kúru	*to bring*
–te agemashóo ka	*shall I … for you?*
wáruku nái náa	*it's not so bad, it's not bad at all* (e.g. being sick)
–(y)óo ka náa	*I think I'll …* (literally, '*shall I just …?*')
gohón gohón	*Cough! Cough!* (the sound of coughing, cf. **hákushon** '*Atishoo*'! for a sneeze)
darusóo	*seem drowsy, look tired, seem to lack vitality, seem lethargic*
yóo na	*as if*
ki ga suru	*to feel, have the impression* (*that …* = **yóo na** …)
warúi yóo na ki ga suru	*to feel bad, to feel one has done something wrong, to feel guilty*
odaiji ni	*look after yourself* (said to a sick person)
osaki ni shitsúrei shimásu	*Sorry to leave early, good bye*

Giving and receiving verbs

Japanese has a number of verbs for giving and receiving. Which is used depends on the relative status of the giver and receiver and whether the action is away from or towards the speaker. For in-giving, that is, for someone giving something to the speaker or a third person, the verb used is **kudasáru** where the giver is of higher social status than the speaker and **kureru** when the giver is of lower or equal social status.

When you are talking to someone you do not know well, it is usually safer to use **kudasáru**. In practice **kudasáru** often indicates a second-person subject and **kureru** a third-person subject.

Kore wa Suzuki san ga kudasátta yubiwa désu yo.	*This is the ring you gave me, Mr Suzuki.*
Tomodachi ga kureta inú ni 'Póchi' to yuu namae o tsukemáshita.	*I called the dog my friend gave me 'Pochi'.*

For out-giving, 'I give', 'he gives', etc., **ageru** is generally used regardless of the status of the recipient, though **sashiageru** can be used in situations calling for particular respect and decorum.

Kangófu wa kanja ni kusuri o agemáshita.	*The nurse gave medicine to the patient.*
Watanabe senséi ni omiyage o sashiagemáshita.	*I gave a souvenir gift to Professor Watanabe.*

There is a verb, **yaru** '*to give to an inferior*', but this seems to be used mainly for actions directed towards junior members of one's own family, particularly one's own children. It is also used with non-human indirect objects.

Musuko no tanjóobi ni táko o yarimáshita.	*I gave my son a kite for his birthday.*
Kíngyo ni esá o yarimáshita.	*I fed the goldfish.*

Paralleling the use of the giving verbs **kudasáru** and **kureru**, there are the receiving verbs: **itadaku** '*to receive from a superior*' and **morau** '*to receive from someone other than a social superior*'. **Itadaku** is often used when the receiver is the first person ('*I*' or '*we*') and the giver is the second person ('*you*'). Notice that the person from whom something is received is usually indicated with the particle **ni**, though you will also occasionally hear **kara** used instead.

Senséi ni itadaita hón wa totemo chóohoo desu.	*The book I got from you (professor) is very useful.*
Tároo kun ni moratta okáshi wa sukóshi amasugimásu.	*The cakes we got from Taro are a bit too sweet.*

Often there is little difference in meaning between giving and receiving sentences, such as the following:

Senséi ga kudasátta jibikí o hóndana ni okimáshita.	*I put the dictionary the professor gave me on the bookshelf.*

Senséi ni itadaita jibikí o hóndana ni okimáshita.	*I put the dictionary I got from the professor on the bookshelf.*

In purely neutral contexts where we are not concerned with the relative status of giver and receiver, **ataeru** is used for '*to give*' and **ukéru** for '*to receive*'.

Kono garasu wa sootoo no atsúryoku o ataete mo waremasén.	*This glass will not break even when subjected to considerable pressure.*
Atatakái kangei o ukemáshita.	*We received a warm welcome.*

For receiving letters, parcels, etc., **uketóru** is often used.

Sokutatsu o táshika ni uketorimáshita.	*I am in receipt of your express delivery letter* (formal cliché).

Giving and receiving verbs as auxiliaries

The giving and receiving verbs can also be used after the –te form to show the relationship between the instigator and recipient of an action.

Saitoo san wa furúi kataná o mísete kudasaimáshita.	*Mr Saito showed me an old sword.*

The –**te kudasáru** ending usually indicates that a social superior does something for me or someone closely connected with me. –**te kureru** also suggests that I have been the recipient of some favour, but this time from a person who is clearly not of higher social standing.

Kodomo ga michi o annái shite kuremáshita.	*The child showed me the way.*

To indicate that I, or we, have done or will do something for someone else, a verb in the –te form followed by **ageru** is used.

Tokei o shúuri ni dáshite agemashóo ka.	*Shall I put your watch in for repair for you?*

As with the simple verb **yaru**, –**te yaru** is generally used when the speaker is doing something for his own children. –**te yaru** is not normally used by women or by junior members of the family.

Musuko o tsuri ni tsurete itte   *I took my son fishing.*
yarimáshita.

–te yatte kudasái is used when one is asking for a favour to be done for a member of one's family, a subordinate or a pupil.

Kodomo no machigái o naóshite   *Please correct the child's*
yatte kudasái.   *mistakes for him.*

When the receiving verbs are used as auxiliaries after the **–te** form they often, but not necessarily, suggest that the subject of the sentence, 'I' or '*we*', instigated the action. Note that the agent is followed by the particle **ni**.

Dáiku ni yáne o naóshite   *I got the carpenter to fix the roof.*
moraimáshita.
Abe senséi ni subarashíi é o   *I was lucky enough to have Dr Abe*
káite itadakimáshita.   *paint a wonderful picture for me.*

In the last example there is no suggestion that I caused Dr Abe to paint the picture. It is very similar in meaning to:

Abe senséi ga subarashíi é o káite kudasaimáshita.

A very polite request form can be made with **–te itadakemásu ka**, or the even politer **–te itadakemasén ka** after the appropriate verb. In this case the potential form of the verb, i.e. 'can receive' is used in an affirmative or negative question.

Shió to koshóo o tótte   *Would you mind passing the salt and*
itadakemásu ka.   *pepper?*
–te itadakitái, –te moraitái   '*I'd like you* (him) *to ...*', '*I wish you*
                           (he) *would ...*'

The receiving verbs with the desiderative **–tái** ending can be used to express the idea that you would like someone to do something for you. **–te itadakitái** is usually used when referring to a second or third person present in the conversational situation and **–te moraitái** to an absent third person.

Kinóo katta yasai wa kusátte   *The vegetables I bought yesterday are*
imasu kara torikáette   *rotten so I'd like you to change them*
itadakitái n' desu ga.   *for me.*
Háyaku chichí ni káette kite   *I wish father would come back home*
moraitái desu.   *quickly.*

In neutral situations, where the relationship between individuals is not involved, **–te hoshíi** is often used instead of **–te moraitái**.

Moo sukóshi suzushiku nátte   *I wish it would get a bit cooler. Don't*
  hoshíi desu née.   *you?*

Exercise 12.1

Fill in the gaps with the appropriate form of the verbs, **morau**, **kudasáru**, **ageru** or **yaru** as the sense demands.

1. Chichi ni nékutai o katte _____.
   (I bought my father a tie.)
2. Suzuki senséi ga eigo o oshiete _____.
   (Mr Suzuki taught me English.)
3. Sumimasén ga, michi o oshiete _____tái n' desu ga.
   (Excuse me. Would you mind showing me the way?)
4. Isha ni míte _____.
   (I had myself examined by the doctor.)
5. Imootó o éki made kuruma de okutte _____.
   (I gave my sister a lift to the station in my car.)

Exercise 12.2 ■■■

Listen to the following letter from Kaya to her friend Yohko. Play the cassette tape several times until you feel you can understand the gist of what the letter contains. Take notes as you go so you can answer the questions that follow. When you have finished the exercise read the text of the letter (N.B. The recording employs a slightly longer version of the letter). Finally, turn to the Key to the Exercises and see if you can reproduce the Japanese from the English translation. Don't worry at this stage about reproducing the **kanji** with **furigana** readings. They are included here to get you used to reading longer texts in Japanese script. Notice in letter writing the polite **–másu** style is used even between close friends or family members.

1. かやは 洋 から_____。
2. 秋男はかやに_____。
3. 両 親 は私に_____。
4. ボーイフレンドから_____。
5. 母はバスデーケーキを_____。

陽子さん、お元気ですか。シドニーは段々春めいて来ました。庭には色々な

花が咲いていて大変きれいです。

今日は九月四日で、私の二十歳の誕生日です。誕生日に家族から色々なプレ

セントをもらいました。両親からはお金をもらいました。兄の洋はフラン

スの香水をくれました。弟の秋男はネックレスをくれました。私のボーイ

フレンドはきれいな花を持って来てくれました。母は誕生日ケーキを作って

くれました。私の好きなチョコレート・ケーキでした。夜は、家族と一緒に

中華料理を食べに行きました。とてもいい誕生日でした。

私の大学は来週から始まります。少し忙しくなりそうです。

それでは、又手紙を書きます。皆様によろしく。

かや

Vocabulary

haruméite kimashita	*there is a feeling of spring in the air* (conventional reference to the season at the beginning of a letter)
–meku	*to seem like* (a suffix added to season nouns, forms a consonant-root verb)
narisóo desu	*it looks as if it (I) will become…*
–sóo	*seemingly, it looks as if…* (a suffix which attaches to the verb stem)

minásama   *everyone* (polite form of **minásan** often used in letters or speeches)

More auxiliaries after the '–te form'

In Japanese it is very common to have more than one verb at the end of the sentence. We have seen how the giving and receiving verbs can be used as auxiliary verbs after the –**te** form to show who is doing what for whom, and we are now familiar with the use of the various forms of **iru** after the –**te** form to indicate an action in progress or a completed state. In this unit we meet several more verbs used as auxiliaries after the –**te** form.

Try doing, do...and see, '–te míru'

The verb **míru** '*to see*' is used after the –**te** form to convey the idea that the action was performed tentatively or casually in order to see what the outcome might be. The original meaning of **míru** is retained in this construction, which might be literally translated as 'to do something and see...'. The same idea is often conveyed in English with the verb, 'to try'.

Kazuko san ni denwa o kákete mimáshita.	*I tried giving Kazuko a call.*
Afurika ni itte mitái desu nee.	*I'd like to go and have a look at Africa.*

Because the –**te míru** form is indirect and tentative it is often used to make suggestions.

Okuchi ni áu ka dóo ka wakarimasén ga tábete mite kudasai.	*I don't know whether you'll like it, but just try some.*

The construction with –**te miru** should not be confused with the –**(y)óo to suru** form introduced in Unit 10, although both may often be translated by '*to try*' in English. The former conveys the idea that you do something to see what happens, in other words you succeed in doing what you set out to do. The latter construction is used when you attempt to do something, but for one reason or another your ambitions are frustrated and you fail to complete your task. Some speakers of English make a distinction between 'I tried doing... (to see what would happen).' and 'I tried to do... (but failed)'. Perhaps the point can be illustrated by comparing the following sentences.

Michi o watatte mimáshita ga mukoogawa ni mo éetíiému ga arimasén deshita.	*I tried crossing the road but there was no ATM* (cash dispenser) *on the other side either.*

Michi o wataróo to shimáshita ga kootsuu ga hagéshikute wataremasén deshita.	*I tried to cross the road but the traffic was so heavy I couldn't get across.*

To do beforehand – '–te oku'

This construction with **oku**, the verb '*to put*' carried out conveys the idea that an action has been carried out or has been done in preparation for something else.

Sono mama ni shite oite kudasái.	*Please leave it as it is* (like that).
Bíiru o reizóoko ni irete okimáshita.	*I put some beer in the fridge* (in preparation for tonight's party).
Nihón ni iku máe ni Nihongo o sukóshi benkyoo shite oita hoo ga íi desu yo.	*You should* (take the precaution of) *studying a little Japanese before you go to Japan.*
Kinoo denwa de setsumei shite okimáshita kara wakáru hazu desu.	*I explained it to him over the phone yesterday so he should know about it.* (*Note*: **hazu**, '*should*' is introduced later in this unit)

To end up doing – '–te shimau'

Zénbu ippen ni tábete shimaimashita.	*He ate it all up at once.*
Tabesugi de onaka o kowáshite shimaimashita.	*I ended up with an upset stomach from eating too much.*

In colloquial Japanese this –**te shimau** construction is sometimes abbreviated to –**chau**, particularly in Tokyo where some speakers seem to use it indiscriminately even when there is no particular connotation of finality or completion.

Sonna kotó o yuu to káetchau yo.	*I'll go home if you talk like that.*

To have been ...– '–te áru'

This construction is used with transitive verbs to convey the idea that the present state is the result of a completed action. It often strongly suggests a deliberate action by a human agent. The same kind of idea is often expressed with a passive verb in English. In Japanese too, this construction generally requires that the object of the transitive verb become the subject (or topic) of the –**te áru** construction.

Món ga akete áru kara náka de chuusha shimashóo.	*The gate has been opened* (for us) *so let's park inside.*

The negative of the –**te áru** construction is, naturally enough, –**te nái** or, in the polite style, –**te arimasén.**

Komugiko wa máda katte nái kara kónban okonomiyaki ga dekimasén.	*The flour hasn't been bought yet so we can't make okonomiyaki to-night.* (**Okonomiyaki** is a kind of savoury pancake.)

In the above example there is a strong suggestion that someone has deliberately opened the gate, which would not be conveyed by the neutral, **món ga aite iru** '*the gate is open*', i.e. by –**te iru** after the intransitive verb, **aku.**

In practice this construction is used in much the same way as the –**te oku** construction explained above.

Keeps on getting more ... – '–te kúru'

The verb, **kúru** '*to come*' after the –**te** form indicates that the action of the verb started at some point in the distance or at some time in the past and continued until the present location or time.

Mainichi kaisha kara káeru to inú ga mukae ni háshitte kimasu.	*Every day when I get home from work the dog comes running to greet me.*
Nihón demo isshoo kekkon shinai josei ga fúete kimashita.	*In Japan too there has been a continual increase in the number of women who never marry.*

Will go on getting more ... – '–te iku'

This construction is similar to –**te kúru** above, but the starting point of the action is the speaker or narrator's present location or time.

Tsugí kara tsugí e to furúi tatémono ga kiete ikimásu.	*The old buildings go on disappearing one after another.*

**Kore kara wa moo sukóshi rakú
ni nátte iku deshoo.**

*I expect it will get a little
easier for me from now on.*

Exercise 12.3 ◼

Listen to these questions on the tape and give your own answer to each
question. You may need to pause the tape to give yourself time to respond.

1. 京都に行ってみたいですか。
2. さしみを食べてみたことがありますか。
3. 将来、どんな仕事をしてみたいですか。
4. 日本酒を飲んでみたいですか。
5. 日本でどんなものを見てみたいですか。

Here are some new words which might help you answer these questions.

Vocabulary

shoorai	*the future, in the future*	**Nára no daibutsu**	*the Great Buddha in Nara*
eiga-kántoku	*film director*	**shiro**	*castles*
ongakka	*musician*	**matsuri**	*festival*
uchuu-hikóoshi	*astronaut*		
okuresóo	*it looks as if we'll be late* (see grammar notes on –**sóo** in Unit 13)		

Exercise 12.4

Complete the following sentences by choosing the most appropriate
clause from the list on the right.

1. Pán ga nái kara

2. Hóteru no heyá o

3. Okuresóo da kara

4. Tomodachi ga uchi ni asobi ni kúru no de

5. Chízu de iku basho o

a. heyá o kírei ni shite okitái desu

b. denwa o shite oita hoo ga ii to omoimasu

c. sukóshi katte oite kudasái

d. shirábete okimasu

e. yoyaku shite okimáshita

Exercise 12.5 ■

Paul has decided to invite a few friends around for a barbecue this weekend. Before he goes off to buy the food he makes a list of the things he has and does not have at home. As he is learning Japanese like you, for practice he writes his list in Japanese script. Paul's Japanese neighbour, Taro, has come around early to help with the shopping. With the list to guide you, imagine you are Paul answering Taro's questions, using **móo**, '*already*' or **máda**, '*not yet*' in your answers as appropriate. Press the pause button to give you time to supply the answer. You will find Paul's responses in the Key to Exercises. Here are Paul's list and Taro's questions.

ポールのバーベキュー　今週の日よう日

買ってあるもの
ソーセージ、ステーキ、ビール、
コーラ、ジュース、ポテトチップス

買ってないもの
たまねぎ、レタス、トマト、レモン、
きゅうり、マスタード、トマトソース

1. Potetochíppusu o kaimashóo ka.
2. Tomatosóosu ga irimásu ka.
3. Kyúuri wa takusán áru deshóo?
4. Uchi no niwa no rémon o motte kimashóo ka.
5. Sutéeki wa móo katte áru deshóo?

The plain style of speech

The plain style of speech is used among close friends and family members and when talking to children. It is in this form of speech where the differences between men's and women's speech become most pronounced. Women, in particular, use a number of sentence-final particles, like **no** (a question marker when pronounced with rising intonation, otherwise used for giving explanations, '*the fact is…*', etc.), **káshira** '*I wonder*' and **wa**, an assertive feminine particle. **Sóo yo** and **sóo na no yo** '*that's right*' are also typically feminine exclamations.

In the plain form men tend to use the colloquial first-person pronoun **boku** or even the somewhat vulgar **ore**, the corresponding second-person pronouns, **kimi** and **omae**, and the sentence-final emphatic particles, **ná(a)**, **zó** and **zé**, none of which are normally used by women. Of the final particles, **zé** differs from **zó** in that it can follow verbs in the plain hortative or propositive form, –(y)óo '*let's…*', e.g. **Ikóo ze** '*Let's go!*', whereas **zó** cannot.

Exercise 12.6 ■

Listen to the following exchange between Akiko and Haruo Yamaguchi, a young married couple. Like many such conversations the content is of no great import, but they provide us with examples of the plain style, some useful vocabulary and a number of new constructions using the **–te** form. How many **–te** forms can you find and what do they mean?

秋子: 何を探しているの?

春男: 車の鍵はどこかなあ。

秋子: さっきテーブルの上に置いておいたけど。

春男: あっ、あった、あった。じゃ、ちょっと行ってくるよ。

秋子: どこへ行くの?

春男: ビールがないから買ってこようと思って…

秋子: 冷蔵庫にカン・ビールが三本入れてあったけど…

春男: もう、ゆうべ田中さんと二人で全部飲んでしまったよ。

秋子: 遅いから、酒屋はもう閉まっているんじゃないの?

春男: いや、駅前のコンビニで酒類も売っているからそこに行ってみるよ。

秋子: じゃ、ついでに明日の朝食のパンと牛乳も買ってきて。

春男: うん、わかった。じゃ、行ってくるよ。

秋子: いってらっしゃい。

ÁKIKO:　　Náni o sagashite iru nó?

HARUO:　　Kuruma no kagí wa dóko ka náa.

ÁKIKO: Sákki téeburu no ue ni oite oita kedo.
HARUO: Á, átta, átta. Já, chótto itte kúru yo.
ÁKIKO: Dóko e iku nó?
HARUO: Bíiru ga nái kara katte koyóo to omotte.
ÁKIKO: Reizóoko ni kanbíiru ga sánbon irete átta kedo…
HARUO: Móo, yuube Tanaka san to futarí de zénbu nónde shimatta yo…
ÁKIKO: Osoi kara, sakaya wa móo shimatte iru n' ja nái no.
HARUO: Íya, ekimáe no konbíni de sakérui mo utte iru kara soko ni itte
         míru yo.
ÁKIKO: Já, tsuide ni ashita no chooshoku no pán to gyuunyuu mo
         katté kite.
HARUO: Ún, wakátta. Já itte kúru yo.
ÁKIKO: Itterasshái.

Vocabulary

ka náa	*I wonder* (masculine)	**íya**	*no* (when contradicting)
kedo	*but* (casual speech abbreviation of **keredomo**)	**wakátta**	*okay, right, I've got it.*
átta	*I've found it!*		

Expectation and obligation

Hazu désu is used after the plain form of a verb or adjective to indicate expectation. It often corresponds to the English, '*ought to…*' or '*should …*', etc., but without any suggestion of moral obligation.

Ashita kúru hazu desu.   *He should come tomorrow. / I expect he'll come tomorrow.*

Sono gurai no kotó o shitte iru   *He should at least know that.*
hazu désu.

Where a sense of moral obligation is implied **beki désu** is used instead.

Ashita kúru beki desu.   *He should come tomorrow.* (He owes it to us to come tomorrow.)

Mae mótte denwa suru beki   *I should have rung beforehand but…*
déshita ga…

Where the obligation is not to do this or that, it is the final verb which takes the negation, becoming **beki ja arimasén**, etc.

Shachoo ni sonna kotó o yuu　*I should not have said that to the*
beki ja arimasén deshita.　*director.*

Exercise 12.7

In the following sentences fill in the blanks with either **hazu** or **béki** as the sense demands.

1. Densha wa taitei juugófun-okí ni kúru ____ desu.
2. Wakái hito wa toshiyóri ni séki o yuzuru ____ desu.
3. Kyóo ginkoo wa aite iru ____ desu.
4. Supíido seigén o mamóru ____ desu.
5. Kinóo tegami o dashimáshita kara kanarazu nisánnichi de tsuku ____ desu.
6. Háyaku isha ni míte morau ____ desu.

Vocabulary

–okí	*every…, at… intervals* (suffix used with numbers and numeral classifiers)
nisánnichi	*two or three days*

Although

We have already learnt how to express concession using the coordinate particles **ga** and **keredomo**. These differ from most clause-final particles and resemble the particle **kara** '*because*' in that they follow the same form as the main verb at the end of the sentence, that is to say, for most of us, the polite **–másu** form. There is, however, a compound particle, **no ni** '*although*', which follows the plain form of the verb or adjective.

Nankai mo oshieta no ni, máda　*Though I taught him time and time*
obóete imasén.　*again he still doesn't*
　　remember it.

Takái no ni shitsu ga íi kara　*Although it's expensive, it's good*
kaimáshita.　*quality so I bought it.*

As we saw with the compound particle **no de** '*because*', the plain present form of the copula used before **no ni** is **na**.

Ano hóteru wa yuumei na no　*Although that hotel is famous I was*
ni sáabisu ga wárukute　*disappointed to find the service*
gakkári shimashita.　*is terrible.*

In formal written Japanese you may also come across the clause-final compound particle **mono no**, which has much the same meaning as **no ni**.

Sooridáijin wa atarashíi náikaku o kessei shita mono no, tsugi no sénkyo de katéru ka doo ka wa utagawashíi.

Although the Prime Minister formed a new cabinet it is doubtful whether he can win the next election.

Exercise 12.8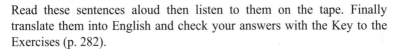

Read these sentences aloud then listen to them on the tape. Finally translate them into English and check your answers with the Key to the Exercises (p. 282).

1. 今日は雲一つない青空のすばらしい天気です。
2. 山下電気の海外部長は今青森と秋田の方を旅行しています。
3. 急に空が曇ってきて雨が降りそうになったので、急いでうちにかえりました。
4. 森田社長の後ろに立っている人の名前は小林洋子だと思います。
5. 空が曇っているのに雨の心配はないそうです。
6. 大林先生はお元気そうですねえ。
7. このお酒は秋田の名酒だそうです。
8. 国立大学の外国人学生が毎年ふえてきています。

Vocabulary

furisóo	*to look like rain, look as if it will rain*
genkisóo	*to look well* (more on the suffix –**sóo** in Unit 13)
Osóre irimasu ga.	*I am very sorry/grateful*, etc.
Goméiwaku desu ga.	*I'm sorry to bother you, but…*
Otesúu desu ga.	*I'm sorry to bother you, but…*
Dóozo okake kudasái.	*Please sit down.*
…o oshiete itadakemásu ka.	*Would you mind telling me…?*
Osumai wa dóchira desu ka.	*Where do you live?* (honorific)

Kanji

This Unit's new kanji are given in detail below.

Kanji	Readings	Meaning / Examples	Kanji	Readings	Meaning / Examples
外	**GAI** **sóto** hoka 5 strokes #12.123	outside; other, another 外国人 **gaikokujin** foreigner 外に出る **sóto ni déru** go outside 外の人 **hoka no hito** someone else	心	**SHIN** **kokóro** 4 strokes #12.124	heart; mind, spirit 安心 **anshin** peace of mind 心のやさしい人 **kokóro no yasashíi hito** a kind-hearted person
思	**SHI** **omó(u)** 9 strokes #12.125	thought; to think そう思います **sóo omoimasu** I think so 思わず **omówazu** without thinking	急	**KYUU** **isó(gu)** 9 strokes #12.126	sudden; steep; to hurry 急に **kyuu ni** suddenly 急ぎましょう **isogimashóo** let's hurry
酒	**SHU** **sake** 10 strokes #12.127	sake, rice wine, alcoholic drink 日本酒 **Nihonshu** Japanese sake 酒が好きな人 **sake ga sukí na hito** someone who likes sake	配	**HAI** **kubá(ru)** 10 strokes #12.128	distribution, to distribute 心配 **shinpai** worry 紙を配る **kamí o kubáru** to hand out the paper
洋	**YOO** 9 strokes #12.129	ocean; Western 大西洋 **Taiséiyoo** Atlantic O. 洋食 **yooshoku** western food 洋間 **yooma** western room	様	**YOO** **sama** 14 strokes #12.130	way, means; polite address 田中様 **Tanaka sama** Mr T. 様子 **yoosu** appearance, situation
電	**DEN** 13 strokes #12.131	electricity 電気 **dénki** electricity 電話 **denwa** telephone	部	**BU** 11 strokes #12.132	part, section; department 一部 **ichíbu** one part, some of 部分 **búbun** part
曇	**DON** **kumó(ru)** 16 strokes #12.133	to cloud over 曇り時々雨 **kumóri tokidoki áme** cloudy with occasional rain 今日は曇っている **kyóo wa kumótte iru** today it's cloudy	長	**CHOO** **nagá(i)** 8 strokes #12.134	chief; long 社長 **shachoo** president 部長 **buchoo** department head 長い **nagái** long
名	**MEI** **na** 6 strokes #12.135	name; reputation 名前 **namae** name 名高い **nadakái** famous, renowned 名人 **meijín** master, expert	元	**GEN** **motó** 4 strokes #12.136	origin 元にもどる **motó ni modóru** go back to the beginning 元気 **génki** fit, well, healthy
林	**RIN** **hayashi** 8 strokes #12.137	forest 小林先生 **Kobayashi senséi** Mr (Dr) Kobayashi 林の中 **hayashi no náka** in the forest	降	**KOO** **fú(ru)** o(ríru) 10 strokes #12.138	to fall (rain,etc); get off 雪が降る **yuki ga fúru** it snows バスを降りる **básu o oríru** to get off the bus
森	**SHIN** **mori** 12 strokes #12.139	wood, grove 森林 **shinrin** woods and forests 青森 **Aómori** place name in northern Honshu	空	**KUU** **sóra** kara 8 strokes #12.140	void; sky; empty 空気 **kúuki** air 空手 **karate** 青空 **aozóra** blue sky 空っぽ **karappo** empty (head)
立	**RITSU** **tá(tsu)** 5 strokes #12.141	to stand, establish 国立大学 **kokuritsudáigaku** a national university 立ちっぱなし **tachippana shi** standing all the way/time	雲	**UN** **kúmo** 12 strokes #12.142	cloud 雲が多い **kúmo ga óoi** there are many clouds 雲海 **unkai** sea of clouds

13 車にぶつけられた。
Kuruma ni butsukerareta.
Another car ran into me!

In this unit you will learn how to:

- Use the causative form of verbs
- Recognise and use the passive voice
- Recognise the causative-passive
- Use the suffix **–sóo**, '*it looks as if …*'
- Use the suffix **–gáru** to describe the behaviour of others.

You will also acquire:

- 20 more kanji: 色 物 牛 肉 映 画 館 店 待 力
  刀 切 親 友 右 左 有 言 近 家

Dialogue 1 ▮

Kitabayashi Yooko and Morita Yasuko, acquaintances from the same neighbourhood, meet on the street. We pick up their conversation after the usual bows, thanks and salutations have been exchanged.

北林：　森田さん。首が痛そうですねえ。どうしたんですか。

森田：　この間運転していた時、横から急に車が出て来てぶつけられたんです。

北林：　じゃ、一種のむち打ち症ですか。

森田: ええ、首と腰をやられて、今治療に
通っています。

北林: 大変ですねえ。それで車の方は?

森田: 今、修理に出してありますが、かなりやられています。

北林: そういう場合、保険はどうなるんですか。

森田: 早速、うちの保険会社に連絡して、 やっても
らっています。相手の不注意 によるので、
費用は全部出してもらえるんじゃな
いかと思いますが...

北林: 面倒ですねえ。

森田: ええ。それと車がないと買物の時とっても不便です。

北林: じゃ、次に行く時連れて行ってさしあげますよ。
遠慮なくおっしゃってください。

森田: どうもご親切に。

KITABAYASHI:	Morita san. Kubi ga itasóo desu née. Dóo shita n' desu ka.
MORITA:	Konoaida unten shite ita toki, yoko kara kyuu ni kuruma ga déte kite butsukeraretá n' desu.
KITABAYASHI:	Já, ísshu no muchiuchishoo desu ka.
MORITA:	Ée, kubi to koshi o yararete, íma chiryoo ni kayotte imásu.
KITABAYASHI:	Taihen désu née. Sore de kuruma no hóo wa?
MORITA:	Íma, shúuri ni dáshite arimásu ga, kánari yararete imásu.
KITABAYASHI:	Soo yuu ba'ai, hoken wa dóo náru n' desu ka.
MORITA:	Sassoku, uchi no hokengáisha ni renraku shite, yatte moratte imásu. Aite no fuchúui ni yorú no de, híyoo wa zénbu dáshite moraerú n' ja nái ka to omoimásu ga…
KITABAYASHI:	Mendóo desu née.
MORITA:	Ée. Sore to kuruma ga nái to kaimono no toki tottemo fúben desu.
KITABAYASHI:	Já, tsugí ni iku toki tsurete itte sashiagemásu yo. Enryonáku osshátte kudasai.
MORITA:	Dóomo goshinsetsu ni.

Vocabulary

itasóo	*looks sore*	**...ni yoru**	*to be the result of, to*
butsukerareru	*be hit*		*stem from*
yarareru	*be done in,*	**zénbu dáshite**	*I think we can proba-*
	take a blow	**moraeru n'**	*bly get them to pay*
sóo yuu ba'ai	*in that case,*	**ja nái ka to**	*the lot*
	in circum-	**omoimásu**	
	stances like	**enryo náku**	*without reserve,*
	that	**ossháru**	*don't hesitate to...*
			to say (honorific)

Exercise 13.1

Answer the following comprehension questions on Dialogue 1. The questions are in English, but you should be able to answer them in both English and Japanese. The Key to the Exercises has model answers in both English and Japanese (p. 283). Your answers may well be correct even if they don't correspond exactly to those in the back of the book.

1. What injury did Mrs Morita sustain in the accident?
2. What is she doing about it?
3. Is she still driving her car?
4. What is the situation regarding insurance?
5. What does Mrs Morita find inconvenient?
6. How does Mrs Kitamura offer to help?

Passive sentences

Dialogue 1 introduces a number of passive sentences. To form a passive verb from its active voice equivalent, the subject of the active sentence becomes the agent of the passive sentence and is indicated with the particle **ni**, in much the same as 'by' marks the agent of an English passive sentence. The passive ending –**(r)areru** (which you met as a potential verb ending in Unit 10) is added to the verb root, the initial –**(r)** dropping after a consonant. For example, the active sentence, **Senséi wa Tároo o homemáshita** '*The teacher praised Taro*' is transformed into the passive sentence, **Tároo wa senséi ni homeraremáshita** '*Tároo was praised by the teacher*'. Some more examples of passive verbs are

taberaréru '*to be eaten*', **miraréru** '*to be seen*', **kakaréru** '*to be written*' and **omowaréru** '*to be thought*' or '*to spring to mind*'. The passive forms of the irregular verbs **suru** '*to do*' and **kúru** '*to come*' are **sareru** (sometimes **serareru**) and **koráreru** respectively. You may find it puzzling to learn that **kúru** has a passive equivalent, because we do not make passives from intransitive verbs in English and we cannot imagine a context in which we might use a verb form meaning, 'to be come'. In Japanese, however, even intransitive verbs can occur in the passive. When they do, they often carry a connotation of inconvenience or discomfort experienced by the subject of the sentence, usually '*I*' or '*we*'. This construction is known as the 'INDIRECT PASSIVE' or the 'ADVERSATIVE PASSIVE'. A few examples should make the concept easier to understand.

Kinóo áme ni furaremáshita.	*I was caught in the rain yesterday.*
Kyuu ni tomodachi ni koráete komarimáshita.	*I was put out when my friend turned up suddenly.*
Kare wa háyaku ryóoshin ni shinarete shinseki ni sodateráreta.	*He suffered the early death of his parents and was raised by relatives.*

This indirect passive construction can also be used with transitive verbs, in which case it strongly suggests that someone has been affected by the action. This contrasts with the direct passive which is simply a neutral description of what happened. For example, the direct passive **saifu ga nusumaremáshita** '*the wallet was stolen*' merely tells us what happened to the wallet. On the other hand, the indirect passive, **saifu o nusumaremáshita** '*I had my wallet stolen*', strongly suggest the distress and inconvenience I suffered as a result of the theft. Notice that in the indirect passive the object of the active sentence remains the object in the passive sentence, the subject being the person who suffers the inconvenience.

Exercise 13.2

Complete the following sentences by choosing an appropriate ending from the list below (use the English cues as a guide). Then translate the completed sentences into English.

1. Shigoto ni iku tochuu (I was caught in the rain.)
2. Isha ni mótto (I was told to exercise.)
3. Sake wa kome kara (is made)

a. tsukurárete imásu.

b. homeraremáshita.

c. saifu o nusumaremáshita.

4. Nihongo ga joozu da to (I was praised.)

5. Gaikoku de (I had my wallet stolen.)

d. undoo suru yóo ni iwaremáshita.

e. áme ni furaremáshita.

Causative sentences

In Japanese the causative is formed with the suffix, **–(s)aséru** after the verb root, the initial **–(s)** dropping after a consonant. For example:

tabesaséru	*to make eat*
mataséru	*to make wait*
warawaseru	*to make laugh*

The irregular verbs **suru** and **kúru** have the causative forms **saseru** and **kosaséru**. In addition to the causative meaning, the **–(s)aseru** suffix is also often used to convey the idea of letting someone do something and is therefore sometimes called the 'PERMISSIVE'. We will retain the causative tag, but remember the form carries both connotations. Sometimes the distinction between causative and permissive can be shown by the use of **ni** after the object of the permissive clause. For example:

Watashi ni yarasete kudasái *please let me do it* as opposed to **shachoo wa Suzuki san o yamesasemáshita** *the boss gave Mr Suzuki the sack* (literally, '*made him stop work*').

This distinction cannot be made if there is another object in the sentence. In this case the person made or permitted to perform the action is always followed by **ni**.

Tanaka kun ni gaikoku kara no okyakusan o mukae ni ikasemáshita.	*I had* (or *let*) *young Tanaka go to meet the customer from overseas.*

Here are some more examples of the causative.

Warawasenáide kudasái.	*Please don't make me laugh.*
Abe san ni iwaseru to, Edomae no sushí wa ichiban oishii désu.	*If you let Mr Abe have his say,* (he'll tell you) *local Edo* (i.e. Tokyo) *sushi is the best.*

In casual colloquial speech a shortened causative form, –(s)asu, often replaces the longer suffix. This shorter form is particularly common in the plain past-tense and conditional endings.

Sonna íi nikú o inú ni	*We can't have you letting the dog eat*
tabesáshitara komáru yo.	*such good meat.*

The causative form should be used with caution as it usually implies a person in authority issuing orders or distributing privileges. For this reason it is often used in conjunction with another verb, such as **ageru** or the suffix –**tai**, to soften the blow.

Oishii jizake o nomásete	*I'll let you try some delicious local*
agemasu.	*sake.*
Koko no oishii unagi o sóbo ni	*I'd like to have my grandmother try*
tabesasetái desu.	*some of the delicious eel they*
	have here.

–sasete itadakimásu

This very polite verb ending is used in formal situations and is particularly favoured by certain types of middle-class ladies. It is formed with the causative form of a verb followed by the object honorific verb, **itadaku** '*to receive*' (from a social superior). Literally the expression means something like '*I receive the favour of being permitted to…*'. You will hear it mainly in set formal routines found in speech-making or in the context of elaborate greeting or leave-taking.

Minásan, kore kara Ákita	*Ladies and gentlemen, now I would like*
no min'yoo o utawasete	*to take the liberty of singing a folk*
itadakimásu.	*song from Akita.*

The causative-passive

When the causative suffix attaches to a verb root it forms a new vowel-stem verb which can take the various verb endings, including the passive suffix. However, as mentioned above, the short causative form is often preferred to the full form when other endings are to be added, and this is usually the case with the causative-passive. For example, the verb **mátsu** '*to wait*' forms the causative verb **matséru**, '*to make wait*', '*to keep waiting*', and we would expect the causative-passive, '*to be kept waiting*' to be **mataseráreru**, but, while this form is possible, **matasáreru** is far more common. The causative-passive of **suru** '*to do*', however, is **saserareu**. Here are some examples of the causative-passive form.

Byooin de zúibun nágaku matasaremáshita.	*I was kept waiting an awfully long time at the hospital.*
Kekkónshiki de supíichi o saseraremáshita.	*I was made to give a speech at the wedding ceremony.*

It is interesting to note that this causative-passive construction does not carry the connotation of permission commonly found in the –(sa)seru construction.

Exercise 13.3

Using the English cues given, change the verb in brackets to the appropriate causative form, then translate the whole sentence into English.

1. Jón san wa joodan o itte hito o (**warau** – makes laugh).
2. Yuushoku no shitaku wa watashi ni (**suru** – let do) kudasái.
3. Shinpai (**suru** – making) sumimasén.
4. Tsugí wa boku ni (**haráu** – let pay) kudasái.
5. Kono konpyúuta o chótto (**tsukau** – let use) kudasái.
6. Háisha de ichijíkan íjoo (**mátsu** – was kept waiting).
7. Kodomo no toki ni múri ni (**tabéru** – was made to eat) no de, yasai ga kirai ná n' desu.
8. Konogoro osoku made shigoto o (**suru** – made to).

'It looks as if it will ...'

We have already covered the use of **sóo desu** after the plain form of a verb or adjective to indicate hearsay or reported speech, when it is more or less equivalent to '*I hear that*', '*they say that*', '*apparently*', etc. Attached to the stem of the verb or adjective (remember the stem is what is left when you cut off the –**masu** ending of a verb or the final –**i** of a true adjective), –**sóo** (which loses its accent when attached to unaccented stems) means '*it looks...*' or '*it looks as if it will...*'. Here are some examples.

Ano konpyúuta wa takasóo desu né.	*That computer looks expensive.*

Kyóo wa gakkoo ni okuresoo　　*It looks as if he'll be late for school*
désu.　　　　　　　　　　　　　　*today.*

The adjective **íi** (or **yói**) '*good*' and the negative, **nái**, have irregular –**sóo**
forms, becoming **yosasóo** '*seems good*' and **nasasoo** '*seemingly not*',
respectively.

Háyaku itta hoo ga yosasóo　　*It looks as if it would be better to go*
desu.　　　　　　　　　　　　　　*early.*
Koko ní wa íi no ga nasasóo　　*It doesn't look as if there are any good*
desu.　　　　　　　　　　　　　　*ones here.*

Exercise 13.4 ■

Listen to these casual plain-form dialogues between Yumi and her friend
Yoshie. Notice the use of the –**sóo** suffix and the feminine final particles
káshira and **nó**. After each dialogue practise the question and response
taking the parts of each of the characters in turn. Pay particular attention
to the intonation of questions without the question particle, **ka**. Finally,
to make sure you have understood, use the vocabulary list to produce a
translation of the dialogues. You'll find a model answer in the Key to the
Exercises (p. 283).

1. ユミさんとよしえさんは友だちです。デパートの服売場
　　で一緒に洋服を見ています。
　　ユミ：　このコート似合うかしら?
　　よしえ：うん、似合いそうよ。ちょっと着てみたら?
2. ユミさんとよしえさんはお腹が空いてきました。
　　デパートのレストランのショーケースのメニューを覗いて、
　　何を食べようか相談しています。
　　ユミ：　　そうねえ、あれおいしそう。私、てんぷらにする。
　　よしえ：　じゃ、私はうなぎにする。
3. ユミさんはアパートを探しています。よしえさんに昨日見た
　　アパートのことを話しています。
　　よしえ：　昨日見たアパートどうだった?

ユミ：　バス・トイレ付きで、駅にも近くて便利
　　　　な所よ。

よしえ：　よさそうね。それに決める?

ユミ：　もう少し見てから決めようかと思っているの。

4. ユミさんとよしえさんは先生にあげるプレゼントを
選んでいます。

ユミ：　このスカーフどうかしら?

よしえ：　ああ、それ渋くて、先生が好きそうね。

ユミ：　ちょっと地味かしら?

よしえ：　うん、もう少し派手なのがいいかも知れないわね。

ユミ：　あッ!雨が降りそう。もうそろそろ帰ろうか。

Describing how others feel or behave

In Japanese a distinction is made between subjective information based
on our own opinions and feelings, and judgements and opinions about
others which are formed on the basis of observed evidence. In Japanese
samúi means, '*I am cold*' or '*I feel cold*', based on my own subjective
experience. If I want to say someone else is cold, however, I cannot use
the same subjective expression, but must make an objective judgement
based on what I have seen or heard. We can say, '*he looks cold*'
samusóo desu or '*he says he's cold*' **samúi soo desu** or '*he seems to be
cold*' **samúi yoo desu**. We can also use the suffix **–gáru**, which is used
to make an objective verb out of a subjective adjective, so **samugáru**
means '*to behave as if one feels cold*', **hazukashigáru** '*to be shy, behave
in an embarrassed manner*'. The same ending can be added to the suffix
–tái '(I) *want to…*' to give **–tagáru** '(he) *wants to…*'. Compare **watashi
wa onsen ni hairitái desu** '*I want to take a hotspring bath*' with **kare
mo hairitagátte imasu** '*he wants to take one* (i.e. a hotspring bath)
too'. The suffix can also be used with a small number of descriptive
nouns, like **iya na** in the list below. Here are some common pairs
consisting of a subjective adjective and an objective verb formed
with **–gáru**.

Subjective ('I')	Objective ('He', etc.)	
hoshíi	hoshigáru	*to want*
iya da	iyagáru	*to dislike, find repugnant,*
		be unwilling to
kowái	kowagáru	*to be frightened*
atsúi	atsugáru	*to feel the heat, be hot*
omoshirói	omoshirogáru	*to find interesting* or *amusing*
natsukashíi	natsukashigáru	*to feel nostalgic about*

According to and in accordance with

Two expressions often confused by learners of Japanese are **ni yoru to** and **ni yotte**. The confusion arises because the English translation '*according to*' is from time to time applied to each construction. For example, we can say in English 'according to Bill, it is going to rain tomorrow' and 'cultures differ according to the country', using 'according to' both times for what are actually two quite different concepts. In Japanese, the former, indicating reported speech or quoted opinion, is expressed with **ni yoru to** and the latter, which can be paraphrased as '*in accordance with*' or '*depending on*' is **ni yotte**. The Japanese equivalents of the two English sentences given above, therefore, are, **Bíru san ni yoru to ashita wa áme da sóo desu** and **kuni ni yotte búnka ga chigaimásu**. **Ni yoru to** usually occurs in a sentence which ends with **sóo desu** '*it seems*', '*it appears*', '*they say*'. We can also express the idea of 'according to' with…**no hanashi dé wa**, '*in the words of…*' or …**ni iwaseru to** '*if we let…have his/her say*'.

Degrees of probability

When we make a statement based on the evidence available to us, we indicate the degree to which we believe what we say to be true with adverbs like 'definitely', 'probably', 'perhaps', 'possibly' etc. The Japanese seem less inclined than we are to make dogmatic assertions. They qualify many of their statements with a final **deshóo** '*probably*' or **to omoimásu** '*I think…*'. When necessary, however, they can indicate certainty with **kanarazu** '*without fail*', '*certainly*' at the beginning of a sentence, though paradoxically even these strong assertions tend to finish in a final **deshóo** or **to omoimásu**.

Kanarazu nyuugaku-shíken ni gookaku suru deshóo.	*He is sure to pass the entrance exam.*

At the other end of the certainty scale we have met the construction of a plain verb + **ka mo shiremasen** *'perhaps'* (literally, 'whether or not we cannot know'). Another common expression which falls somewhere between these two, is formed with **n' ja nái ka to omoimásu** *'probably'* (literally, 'I think, is it not that...?'). In written Japanese and in more formal situations this contracted form is usually replaced by the full form **no dewa nái ka to omoimásu**:

Ashita kúru n' ja nái ka to omoimásu.	*He'll probably come tomorrow.*

Knowing how to do things

Japanese has a very convenient way of saying 'how to do something' or 'the way to do something'. The suffix **–kata** is simply added to the verb stem, so **tabekáta** means *'how to eat'* or *'way of eating'*, **tsukaikata** *'how to use'*, *'way of using'*, **ikikata** *'how to go'*, *'way of going'*, and so on. We have met this construction in the expression **shikata ga arimasén** *'it can't be helped'*, which we can see now actually means, *'there is no way of doing it'*.

Anóko no iikata wa otóosan to sokkúri desu.	*His way of speaking is just like his father.*
Kuni ni yotte kangaekáta ga chigaimásu.	*Ways of thinking differ from country to country.*
Kono ji no yomikáta o oshiete itadakemásu ka.	*Could you tell me how to read this character please?*

Difficult or easy to do

We have met the adjectives **muzukashíi** *'difficult'* and **yasashíi** *'easy'*. Japanese also has two suffixes **–nikúi** *'difficult to...'* and **–yasúi** *'easy to...'* which attach to the verb stem.

Mifune san no Nihongo wa nakanaka wakarinikúi desu.	*Mr Mifune's Japanese is difficult to understand.*
Kono hón wa yomiyasúi desu.	*This book is easy to read.*

Exercise 13.5 ▆

In this exercise we drill some of the new constructions introduced above. First listen to this short dialogue then answer the questions that follow it. Takeo and Haruo are waiting for Akiko in a **kissáten** (coffee shop).

たけお： 秋子さん、遅いですねえ。

春男： もしかしたら約束忘れたんじゃないかと思います。

たけお： ちょっと電話してみます。

Takeo returns a few minutes later.

　　　　 家に電話してみましたが、誰も電話にでませんでした。

春男： もう少し待ってみましょうか。

たけお： もう一時間近くも待っているのに、来ませんねえ。

春男： もう来ないんじゃないでしょうか。

たけお： じゃ、あきらめて行きましょう。

1. What did Haruo think was the reason why Akiko had not shown up?
2. Who rang her home?
3. Who answered the phone?
4. How long did they wait?

Now following the example below, use the cues to make similar dialogues of your own. Model answers are given in the Key to the Exercises (p. 284).

Cue: **tsukaikata, kantan**

A: **Chótto sumimasén. Kore no tsukaikata o oshiete kudasái.**

B: **Ée, íi desu yo. Kantan désu.**

5. yarikata, sukóshi fukuzatsu.
6. Éki e no ikikata, sukóshi yayakoshíi.
7. makizúshi no tsukurikata, kotsu o oshiete agemásu.
8. kippu no kaikata, koko ni okane o irete, kono botan o osu daké.

Dialogue 2 ▆

Mary has just arrived in Japan to spend a year as an exchange student at a university in Tokyo. She is discussing her accommodation problems with staff in the international office of her host university.

Listen to the dialogue and then move on to the comprehension questions in Exercise 13.6. This is primarily an aural comprehension exercise, but you should return to test your reading comprehension after you have learnt the new **kanji** introduced in this unit.

受け付け：　はい、次の方、どうぞ。

メアリー：　宿泊についてどなたかと相談したいです。

受け付け：　はい、わかりました。宿泊担当
　　　　　　は木村です。あそこの窓から二番
　　　　　　目の机にすわっています。

メアリー：　適当な宿泊を紹介していただけませんか。

木村：　　　そうですねえ。予算によりますが、大体
　　　　　　三種類の宿泊があります。大学の学生寮と
　　　　　　下宿と自炊のアパートです。

メアリー：　家賃はどのぐらいになりますか。

木村：　　　学生寮は一番安く、光熱費も含めて月一万五千円です。
　　　　　　下宿は二食付きで六万円ぐらいです。
　　　　　　アパートは八万円から二十万円ぐらいまであります。

メアリー：　下宿というのはどんなものですが。

木村：　　　まあ、二三人の外の大学生と一緒に暮らします。
　　　　　　自分の部屋がありますが、お風呂、トイレなどの
　　　　　　施設は共同で使います。日曜日を除いて毎日朝
　　　　　　食と夕食がついています。
　　　　　　日曜日は食事が出ないので、コンビニから何か買っ
　　　　　　てくるか、外食をするか、どちらかにします。
　　　　　　アパートは自由ですが、学生にとっては高すぎるで
　　　　　　しょう。家賃と別に敷金と礼金も払わなければな
　　　　　　りません。水道と光熱費ももちろん別です。

メアリー：　そうですか。日本政府から奨学金を
　　　　　　もらっているので、月に七万円位まで出せると思
　　　　　　います。下宿にしようかしら。

<ruby>木村<rt>きむら</rt></ruby>：　<ruby>下宿<rt>げしゅく</rt></ruby>なら大学のすぐ近くにいいところがあり
ますよ。歩いて十分ぐらいしかかかりません。

メアリー：　じゃあ、そこに連れていってください。中を見たいです。

<ruby>木村<rt>きむら</rt></ruby>：　はい、いいですよ。今から行ってみましょう。

UKETSUKE: Hái, tsugí no katá dóozo.

MÉARII: Shukuhaku ni tsúite dónataka to soodan shitai désu.

UKETSUKE: Hái, wakarimáshita. Shukuhaku tántoo wa Kimura désu.
Asoko no mádo kara nibanme no tsukue ni suwatte imásu.

MÉARII: Tekitoo na shukuhaku o shookai shite itadakemasén ka.

KIMURA: Sóo desu née. Yósan ni yorimásu ga, daitai sánshurui
no shukuhaku ga arimásu. Daigaku no gakuséiryoo to
geshuku to jisui no apáato desu.

MÉARII: Yáchin wa dóno gurai ni narimásu ka.

KIMURA: Gakuséiryoo wa ichiban yásuku, Koonetsúhi mo fukúmete
tsukí ichiman gosen'en désu. Geshuku wa nishoku-tsuki de
rokuman'en gurai désu. Apáato wa hachiman'en kara
nijuuman'en gurai máde arimásu.

MÉARII: Geshuku to yuu no wa dónna monó desu ka.

KIMURA: Máa, nisannin no hoka no dai to issho ni kurashimásu. Jibun
no heyá ga arimásu ga, ofúro, tóire nado no shísetsu wa
kyoodoo de tsukaimásu. Nichiyóobi o nozoite, mainichi
chooshoku to yuushoku ga tsúite imasu. Nichiyoo bi wa
shokuji ga denai no de, konbini kara nanika o katte kuruka
gaishoku o suruka dochiraka ni shimasu. Apáato wa jiyúu
desu ga, gakusei ni tótte wa takasugíru deshoo. Yáchin to
betsu ni shikikin to réikin mo harawanakereba narimásen.
Suidoo to koonetsúhi mo mochíron betsu désu.

MÉARII: Sóo desu ka. Nihon séifu kara shoogakukin o moratte
irú no de, tsukí ni nanaman'en gurai máde daséru to
omoimásu. Geshuku ni shiyóo kashira.

KIMURA: Geshuku nára daigaku no súgu chikáku ni íi tokoró ga
arimásu yo. Arúite júppun gurai shika kakarimásén.

MÉARII: Jáa, soko ni tsurete itte kudasái. Náka o mitái desu.

KIMURA: Hái, íi desu yo. Íma kara itte mimashóo.

Vocabulary

Kimura　　　(Note there is no **san**. It is not usual to use honorifics
to refer to members of one's own organisation when
speaking to outsiders.)

... ni yoru	*it depends on*
fukúmete	*including* (from **fukuméru** *to include*)
nozoite	*except, excluding* (from **nozoku** *to exclude*)
... to betsu ni	*apart from, in addition to*
reikin	*key money* (non-refundable fee paid to landlord)

Exercise 13.6

Test your comprehension of Dialogue 2 by answering these questions.

1. Where is Mr Kimura's desk?
2. Why did Mary come to the International Centre?
3. Which is the most expensive accommodation?
4. What is 'geshuku' like?
5. What did Mary ask Mr Kimura to do for her?
6. Why did she do so?

Exercise 13.7 ▮▮

First, listen to the dialogue. You may want to read the notes before you play it a second time.

Mary has decided to take a room in a student boarding house. We join her as the landlord is showing her around on her first day in her new lodgings.

大家_{おおや}さん： これはあなたの部屋_{へや}になります。

メアリー： 明るくて大きい部屋_{へや}ですねえ。

大家_{おおや}さん： ええ、南向_{むむ}きの八畳_{じょう}の部屋_{へや}です。日当_{あた}りもいいし、道路_{どうろ}から離_{はな}れているんで、とても静_{しず}かです。この窓_{まど}から公園_{こうえん}とお寺_{てら}の屋根_{やね}が見えます。ちょっとご覧_{らん}下さい。眺_{なが}めがいいでしょう?

メアリー： ええ、庭_{にわ}もきれいですね。ところで、食堂_{どう}はどこですか。

大家_{おおや}さん： 一階_{かい}にあります。玄関_{げんかん}を入って、すぐ左の広_{ひろ}い洋間です。

メアリー： お風呂_{ふろ}は?

大家さん： 共同の大浴場は別館にあります。このビルの後ろにあって通路でつながっています。

メアリー： 門限はありますか。

大家さん： 門限はありませんが、夜は静かにしてもらわないと近所に迷惑をかけますから十一時すぎにはできるだけテレビの音を小さくして、音楽を流さないように気をつけてください。

メアリー： はい、わかりました。これから一年間どうぞよろしくお願いします。

Vocabulary

–joo	*numeral classifier for* **tatami** *mats* (approx. 0.8 m x 1.9 m)
hiatari ga íi	*sunny, good sunny aspect*
ofúro	*bath, bathroom* (elegant form of **furó**)
daiyókujoo	*large bath, communal bath*
méiwaku o kakéru	*to be a nuisance, to cause trouble to others*
dekiru dake	*as far as possible, as … as possible* (followed by an adjective in **–ku** form)
nagásu	*to play* (music on the radio, CD player etc.), *let flow, pour*

Now use the information you have gained from the previous dialogue between Mary and her landlord to answer true or false to the following statements.

1. 部屋が小さかったので、メアリーはがっかりしました。
2. メアリーの部屋は広くて眺めもいいです。
3. 道路の音が気になりました。
4. 窓からきれいな庭と公園が見えます。
5. 食堂はメアリーの部屋の直ぐ上にあります。
6. メアリーの部屋にバス・トイレが付いています。

7. お風呂は別館にあります。

8. 門限がないので、ほっとしたでしょう。

Exercise 13.8

Read these sentences aloud then translate them into English. If you are having trouble following the Japanese script refer to the Key to Exercises (p. 285).

1. 牛肉と豚肉とどちらがお好きですか。

2. 映画館の前で友だちと待ち合わせました。

3. 親切な人がおとしたさいふを持ってきてくれました。

4. 友人の家の近くに日本刀を売る店が有ります。

5. 左右の出口をご利用下さい。

6. 秋に外国に旅行した時色々な物を買ってかえりました。

7. 小さいのに力が有ります。

8. 言語学者に言わせると日本語にはたくさんの方言が有ります。

Useful expressions

Watakushi wa koo yuu monó de gozaimásu
Here is my business card (literally, 'I'm this kind of person')

Sakihodo wa shitsúrei itashimáshita
Sorry to trouble you just now.

Goshoochi no yóo ni
As you know

Ossháru toorí desu
That's right, It's as you say

Otómo shite mo yoroshii désu ka
Would you mind if I join you?

–te sashitsukae arimasén ka.
Would it be all right if …?
(literally, 'Is there any objection to…?')

Kanji

Kanji	Reading	Meaning/Examples	Kanji	Reading	Meaning/Examples
色	**SHOKU** **iró** 6 strokes #13.143	colour どんな色 dónna iró what colour 茶色 chairo brown 色々な iroiro na various	物	**BUTSU,** **MOTSU** **monó** 8 strokes #13.144	thing 食べ物 tabemonó food 飲み物 nomimóno drink 動物 doobutsu animal
牛	**GYUU** **ushi** 4 strokes #13.145	cow, bull, ox 子牛 koushi calf 水牛 suigyuu water buffalo	肉	**NIKU** 6 strokes #13.146	meat 牛肉 gyuuniku beef 肉じゃが nikujága beef and potato stew
映	**EI** **utsú(ru)** 9 strokes #13.147	reflection, to reflect 月が海に映る tsukí ga úmi ni utsúru the moon as reflected on the sea 上映する jooei s. show (a film), be screened	画	**GA, KAKU** 8 strokes #13.148	picture; stroke (in kanji) 映画 éiga film, movie 画の数え方 kaku no kazoekáta how to count the strokes
館	**KAN** 16 strokes #13.149	building 映画館 eigákan cinema 洋館 yookan western building	店	**TEN** **misé** 8 strokes #13.150	shop 高い店 takái misé an expensive shop 売店 baiten shop, store, kiosk
待	**TAI** **má(tsu)** 9 strokes #13.151	wait お待たせしました omatases. Sorry I kept you waiting. 少々お待ち下さい shóoshoo o machi kudasai Please wait a moment.	力	**RYOKU, RIKI** **chikará** 2 strokes #13.152	strength 力いっぱい chikaraíppai with all one's strength 火力 karyoku thermal energy
刀	**TOO** **katana** 2 strokes #13.153	sword 長い刀 nagái kataná a long sword 日本刀 Nihontoo a Japanese sword	切	**SAI, SETSU** **kí(ru)** 4 strokes #13.154	cut 小刀で切る kogatána de kíru cut with a knife 一切 íssai (not) at all, in the least
親	**SHIN** **oyá** 16 strokes #13.155	parent 父親 chichioya father 親切な shínsetsu na kind	友	**YUU** **tómo** 4 strokes #13.156	friend 親友 shin'yuu close friend 友だち tomodachi friend 友人 yuujin friend
右	**U, YUU** **migi** 5 strokes #13.157	right 右手 migite the right hand; on/to the right 右側 migigawa the right-hand side	左	**SA** **hidari** 5 strokes #13.158	left 左きき hidarikiki left-handed 左右 sayuu left and right 左右する sayuu s. to control, influence
有	**YUU** **á(ru)** 6 strokes #13.159	have, exist, be located 有名な yuumei na famous 有田 Árita a place in Kyushu famous for its porcelain	言	**GEN** **yu(u)** 7 strokes #13.160	say 言語 géngo language 言語学 gengógaku linguistics 言うまでもなく yuu made mo náku it goes without saying
近	**KIN** **chiká(i)** 7 strokes #13.161	near 近親 kinshin a close relative 近い友だち chikái tomodachi a close friend	家	**KA** **ié** 10 strokes #13.162	house; person (as a suffix) 家の外 ie no sóto outside the house 画家 gaka artist 音楽家 ongakka musician

14 もしもし秋元先生いらっしゃいますでしょうか。

Móshimoshi, Akimoto sensei irasshaimásu deshóo ka.

Hello, may I speak to Professor Akimoto?

In this unit you will learn how to:

- Use verb forms to show respect to the subject of a sentence
- Use verb forms to show respect to the object of a sentence
- Use formal language to indicate politeness
- Use compound verbs
- Use particles indicating extent and degree
- Form abstract nouns from adjectives
- Use the plain imperative form.

You will also acquire:

- 20 more **kanji**: 音 楽 暗 持 病 強 町 県 太 平
  両 昼 晩 勉 所 場 工 広 馬 駅

Dialogue 1 ■■

Mr Nakamura of the Kaigai Shinbun newspaper makes a telephone call to Professor Akimoto, a researcher in Chinese studies.

中村： もしもし。秋元先生のお宅ですか。

秋元宅： はい、そうです。

中村： 中村と申しますが、先生、いらっしゃいますで
しょうか。

秋元宅： はい、少々お待ち下さい。

After a short pause

秋元： もしもし。秋元ですが...

中村： 私は海外新聞の中村と申します。現在、日中関係につ
いての記事を書いています。それで是非先生に一度お目
にかかりたいのですが、ご都合はいつがよろしいでしょ
うか。

秋元： 今度の金曜日からベトナムの方に行くので、その後
になりますが...

中村： 結構です。ベトナムからいつお帰りになりますか。

秋元： 三月九日に戻ります。

中村： そうですか。では十四日の月曜日はいかがでしょうか。

秋元： ちょっと手帳を調べてみます。えーと、午後の
三時なら空いています。

中村： 申し訳ございません、三時はちょっと... 午前中で
空いているお時間がございませんか。

秋元： 朝の九時なら何とかなりますが...

中村： 結構です。では十四日の九時にそちらに伺います。

秋元： はい、分かりました。

中村： では、宜しくお願い致します。

NAKAMURA: Móshimoshi. Akimoto senséi no otaku désu ka.
AKIMOTO TAKU: Hái, sóo desu.
NAKAMURA: Nakamura to mooshimásu ga, senséi, irasshaimásu
deshóo ka.
AKIMOTO TAKU: Hái, shóoshoo omachi kudasái.

AKIMOTO:	Móshimoshi. Akimoto désu ga…
NAKAMURA:	Watakushi wa kaigaishínbun no Nakamura to mooshimásu. Génzai, Nitchuu-kánkei ni tsuite no kíji o káite imasu. Sore de zéhi senséi ni ichido ome ni kakaritái no desu ga, gotsugoo wa ítsu ga yoroshii deshóo ka.
AKIMOTO:	Kóndo no kin'yóobi kara Bétonamu no hóo ni ikú no de, sono áto ni narimásu ga…
NAKAMURA:	Kékoo desu. Bétonamu kara ítsu o kaeri ni narimásu ka.
AKIMOTO:	Sángatsu kokonoka ni modorimásu.
NAKAMURA:	Sóo desu ka. Déwa, juuyokka no getsuyóobi wa ikága deshóo ka.
AKIMOTO:	Chótto techoo o shirábete mimasu. Éeto, gógo no sánji nára aite imásu.
NAKAMURA:	Mooshiwake gozaimasén, sánji wa chótto… Gozenchuu de aite iru ojikan ga gozaimasén ka.
AKIMOTO:	Ása no kúji nara nántoka narimásu ga…
NAKAMURA:	Kékkoo desu. Déwa, juuyokka no kúji ni sochira ni ukagaimásu.
AKIMOTO:	Hái, wakarimáshita.
NAKAMURA:	Déwa, yoroshiku onegai itashimásu.

Vocabulary

móshimoshi	*hello* (over the telephone)	**taku**	*house, residence*

Respect language

Although respect language, or **keigo,** has its origins in the hierarchical feudal society of pre-Meiji Japan, it continues to play an important role in the modern, egalitarian, middle-class society of contemporary Japan, as 'the lubricating oil' of harmonious social interaction.

For the foreign learner the acquisition of **keigo** comes gradually after long periods of exposure to its use within Japanese society. Usually, you will find that if you stick to the polite **désu/–másu** style and use the honorific expressions you have learnt in the formal set routines for greetings, apologies and thanks, you will have no difficulty communicating and you will not cause offence. You cannot neglect **keigo**, however, as you are likely to hear a lot of it from all sorts of people who want to make you feel welcome in their country and ensure that you leave with a good impression of Japan.

Japanese respect language falls into two main categories, 'referent honorifics' which show respect to the person you are referring to, and 'addressee honorifics' which show politeness to the person you are talking to. The addressee honorifics, characterised by the use of **désu** or **–másu** at the end of the sentence, are the forms you have been learning in this book and should present few problems at this stage. You have also already met some honorific verbs, such as **irassháru**, meaning '*a respected person comes, goes*' or '*is*'. Within the referent honorifics, the verb **irassháru** belongs to a category known as 'subject honorifics' in which the 'socially superior referent' (i.e. the person to whom you wish to show respect) is the subject of the verb. **Irassháru** joins a small group of subject-honorific verbs ending in **–áru** which lose the final **–r** of the root before adding **–másu**. For example:

Ítsu Nihón ni irasshaimáshita ka.   *When did you arrive in Japan?*

The other verbs in the group are **kudasáru** '*to give*', **ossháru** '*to say*' and **nasáru** '*to do*'.

The **–r** of the root also drops in the imperative form of these verbs, as we have seen in the request form **–te kudasái**. Be careful, however, when using the imperative forms as, even though they derive from honorific verbs, they have only a mildly honorific connotation. **Irasshái**. '*Come!*' or '*Go!*', for example, is most often used for addressing children, junior workmates or close friends.

Although **meshiagaru**, the honorific verb '*to eat*', ends in **–aru** it has the regular **–másu** and imperative forms, **meshagarimásu** and **meshiagare**. (See p. 241 for the formation of the plain imperative forms.)

The regular subject honorific form for verbs is formed by using the honorific nominal prefix **o–** followed by the verb stem and **ni náru**. The verb **káku** '*to write*', for example, produces **okaki ni náru** '*an honoured person writes*'. There is an alternative form of the regular subject-honorific construction in which **ni náru** is replaced by a form of the copula, **da**. This latter construction seems to be used to describe present states or actions in progress and is therefore more equivalent to the **–te iru** ending.

Móo okaeri desu ka.   *Are you leaving* (going back) *already* (so soon)?

Odekake désu ka.   *Are you going out somewhere* (a common greeting)?

A polite imperative form can be made with the honorific prefix **o–** plus the verb stem and **kudasái.**

Gojúusho to onamae o koko ni okaki kudasái.	*Please write your name and address here.*

There is also a category of elegant or euphemistic verbs which usually replace the expected regular form.

Náma no káki mo meshiagaremásu ka.	*Can you also eat raw oysters?*
Dóchira ni osumai désu ka.	*Where do you live?*
Kono óoba o omeshi ni narimásu ka.	*Will you try on this overcoat?*

The subject-honorific equivalent of **shitte iru** '*to know*' is **gozónji da**, and the subject-honorific form of the copula, **da**, is **de irassháru**.

Matsuzaki senséi o gozónji desu ka.	*Do you know Mr Yamazaki?*
Matsui senséi wa Nihon-búngaku no kyooju de irasshaimásu.	*Dr Matsui is a professor of Japanese literature.*

If the respected person is not the subject of the verb but the direct or indirect object, the object-honorific verb form is used. The subject of the object-honorific construction, though rarely explicitly expressed, is usually, 'I' or 'we'. The regular object-honorific verb is formed with the honorific prefix **o–** plus the verb stem and part of the verb **suru** '*to do*', or its formal equivalent **itásu**. There is an example in Dialogue 1 of this unit.

Dóozo yoróshiku onegai itashimásu.	*I am very grateful for your help.*

Here are some more common uses of the object honorific form:

Okaban o omochi shimashóo ka.	*Shall I carry your bag for you?*
Kinóo katta konpyúuta o omise shitái desu.	*I'd like to show you the computer I bought yesterday.*

There are several object-honorific verbs which either replace, or occur alongside, their regular counterparts. An example here should suffice to give you an idea how these verbs behave.

Séngetsu haishaku shita hón o   *Tomorrow I'll return the book I bor-*
ashita okaeshi shimásu.   *rowed last month.*

Note that in this last example, the regular form **okari shita** could be used instead of **haishaku shita** with little change in the meaning.

Exercise 14.1

Can you answer these comprehension questions on Dialogue 1?

1. Why does Mr Nakamura ring Professor Akimoto?
2. Why isn't this Friday convenient for the professor?
3. What date does Mr Nakamura suggest for their meeting?
4. Why doesn't Professor Akimoto reply immediately?
5. When do they finally agree to meet?

Honorifics with nouns and adjectives

We have had many examples of nouns with the prefix **o–** or **go–** attached to them. In some cases this prefix has lost its original honorific force and simply forms an elegant alternative to a common word. This usage occurs frequently with a number of very common nouns, many of them the names of foods and beverages, and is employed particularly often by women. Examples include, **oyu** '*hot water*', **osake** '*rice wine*', **ocha** '*tea*', **okome** '*rice*' (uncooked), **góhan** '*rice*' (cooked), **okane** '*money*', **oháshi** '*chopsticks*', **otsuri** '*change*' (money), **oteárai** '*lavatory*', etc. Elsewhere these prefixes are attached to nouns to indicate that they are owned by, or in some way connected to, a respected person. So **otaku** or **ouchi** means '*an honorable house*', often '*your house*', **gohón** means '*your book*', and so on. Originally the prefix **o–** was used with nouns of native Japanese origin and **go–** with compounds borrowed from Chinese, but the situation has become very confused with some original Japanese words taking **go–**, as in **goyukkúri** '*please take your time, please relax*' and Chinese loans taking **o–** as in **odénwa** '*your telephone call*' (or '*my telephone call to you*'). Some words like, **henjí** '*answer*', seem to occur with either prefix, so that you might hear **ohenji** '*your answer*' one day then **gohenji** with the same meaning the next.

o–		go–	
ohima	*spare time*	**gojúusho**	*address*
oikutsu	*how old?*	**gojibun**	*yourself,* etc.
ogénki	*fit, well*	**gokenson**	*modest*

Sometimes the honorific prefix indicates not that the noun is owned by a respected person but that it is a verbal noun or the like directed towards someone to whom respect is shown.

Tookyoo o goannai shimásu.	*I'll show you around Tokyo.*
Odénwa o sashiagemásu.	*I shall telephone you.*

True adjectives and descriptive nouns make their honorific forms with the addition of the honorific prefix **o–** or **go–** in the same way as that described above for nouns.

Sensei no ókusan wa taihen outsukushíi katá desu né.	*Your wife is a very beautiful lady, Sir.*
Oisogashíi tokoro o dóomo sumimasén deshita.	*I'm sorry to have troubled you when you were so busy.*

There is one adjective **íi** (or **yói**) '*good*' which has a separate honorific form, **yoshíi**. It is generally used to indicate that someone in a respected position approves or endorses a particular situation. In practice it is frequently used in questions seeking the approval of a respected superior.

Móo káette mo yoroshíi desu ka.	*May I go home now?*
Kore de yoroshíi desu ka.	*Is this all right?*

Polite and formal styles

In Japanese there are three speech styles, plain, polite and formal, which show increasing degrees of politeness to the person being addressed. All final verbs in Japanese carry an indication of the degree of politeness to the addressee and the degree of respect shown to the subject or object of the main verb. So far in this book you have become very familiar with the polite **desu/–másu** style. You also know the plain style as it occurs in non-final verbs and you have heard a few dialogues between close friends with final plain-form verbs. The formal style too, is not altogether new to you as it occurs in a number of greetings and formal routines with the verb **gozaimásu**. This verb along with a small number of verbs listed below are characteristic of the formal style which is used mainly in greetings, speech making and over the telephone. Other verbs used in the formal style are **móosu** '*to say, to be called*', **itású** '*to do*', **máiru** '*to come*' or '*to go*', **óru** '*to be*' and **itadaku** in the sense of '*to eat*'. These verbs usually have the speaker, or someone close to the speaker, as subject.

Watakushi wa Nakamura to mooshimásu.	*My name is Nakamura.*
Itte mairimásu.	*Goodbye.*
Súgu itashimásu.	*I'll do it straight away.*
Róndon ni rokúnen súnde orimáshita.	*I lived six years in London.*
Móo juubún itadakimáshita.	*I've already had sufficient.*

Perhaps you have noticed that adjectives in the formal style have a long vowel before the final **gozaimásu**. We have already met **arígatoo gozaimásu** from the adjective **arigatái** '*grateful*' and **ohayoo gozaimásu** from **hayái** (or rather its honorific form **ohayai**). Adjectives with roots ending in –**a** or –**o** have formal forms ending in –**oo**, those with roots in –**u** become –**uu** and those with roots ending in –**ki** or –**shi** become –**kyuu** or –**shuu** respectively. The adjective **íi** '*good*' becomes **yóo** (from **yóku**) and the honorific **yoroshíi** becomes **yoroshúu**.

Kyóo wa oatsúu gozaimásu né.	*It's hot today isn't it* (both honorific and formal).
Yuube no éiga wa taihen omoshiróo gozaimáshita.	*Last night's film was very interesting.*
Kono séki de yoroshúu gozaimásu ka.	*Is this seat all right?*

The formal style also uses certain vocabulary items, usually of Chinese origin, in place of the more common native Japanese words. **Ashita** '*tomorrow*', for example, is likely to be replaced by **myóonichi** and **kinóo** '*yesterday*' by **sakújitsu**. The noun **monó** '*person*' is also frequently used in this style to refer to oneself. For example as you hand over your business card you might say.

Watakushi wa koo yuu monó de gozaimásu.	'*Here is my card.*' (literally, 'I am this kind of person.')

Exercise 14.2

Complete the sentences on the left by choosing the most appropriate ending from the list on the right.

1. 黒_{くろ}いペンで   a. 御利用_{ごりよう}下さい。
2. おたばこを   b. ごゆっくりお休み下さい。
3. エレベーターを   c. ご遠慮_{えんりょ}下さい。
4. お疲_{つか}れのようですから   d. どうぞおかけ下さい。
5. この席_{せき}が空_あいていますから   e. お書き下さい。

Exercise 14.3

The honorific verb **irassháru** replaces a number of different verbs. Identify the meaning of **irassháru** in each of these sentences and give the neutral (i.e. non-honorific) polite-style equivalent. Look through the **kanji** introduced in this unit before you tackle this exercise.

1. いつここにいらっしゃいましたか。
2. 来月の音楽会へいついらっしゃいますか。
3. 先生は今 研究室_{けんきゅうしつ} にいらっしゃいます。
4. 皆_{みな}さんお元気でいらっしゃいますか。
5. もしもし、ブラウンですが、小林先生いらっしゃいますか。
6. 何かお仕事をしていらっしゃいますか。

The passive as an honorific

Generally, not every verb in an honorific sentence need carry an honorific suffix. As long as one verb near the end of the sentence is marked as honorific, the sentence is interpreted as an honorific sentence. Often only the auxiliary verb carries an honorific suffix. For example, it is possible to say, **Sensei, íma náni o nasátte irasshaimasu ka** '*What are you doing now, Sir?*', but in practice it is usual to use just one honorific verb, **Sensei, íma náni o nasátte imasu ka** or the more common, **Sensei, íma náni o shite irasshaimásu ka**.

The passive voice ending can also be used as a regular subject-honorific construction. This is perhaps a little less respectful than the full

o– verb stem **–ni náru** form. It seems to be used more by men and is used as a matter of personal preference more by some individuals than others. It can be distinguished from a true passive by the lack of an agent marked by the particle **ni**.

Matsuzaki senséi wa kinóo	*Mr Matsuzaki returned home*
Yooróppa kara kaeraremáshita.	*from Europe yesterday.*
Ototói Tanaka san no okáasan ga	*Mrs Tanaka's mother passed*
nakunararemáshita.	*away the day before yesterday.*

Exercise 14.4 ■■

Imagine you are a student talking to an eminent university professor, Dr Yamamoto. Using the respect language you have learnt and the cues in parentheses supply the questions which drew these responses from the Professor.

1. 来週の金曜日に旅行にでかけます。(your question ends in **désu ka**)
2. 環境問題に関する研究をしています。(your question begins with **dónna**)
3. 渋谷に住んでいます。(your question ends in **désu ka**)
4. では、お願いします。(you offered to carry his bag)
5. 今月の末アメリカから帰ってきます。(your question ends in **–másu ka**)

Abstract nouns from adjectives

There is a very convenient suffix, **–sa**, which attaches to the adjective root (the bit left when you chop off the final **–i**) to form an abstract noun. Here are some examples of abstract nouns formed with **–sa**. The adjective from which each is derived is given in parentheses; **takása** '*height*' (**takái**), **nagása** '*length*' (**nagái**), **óokisa** '*size*' (**ookíi**), **yósa** '*value*' (**yói** '*good*'), **nása** '*absence*' of (**nái**), **subaráshisa** '*splendour*' (**subarashíi**), **kireisa** '*cleanliness*' (**kírei** '*clean*'), **shizukása** '*tranquillity*' (**shízuka**). There is another similar suffix **–mi**, which is also used to form abstract nouns. It is far less frequent than **–sa** and seems to be used to convey a more figurative or metaphorical meaning. From the adjective **omoi** '*heavy*', for example, we get both **omosa** '*weight*' and **omomi** '*gravity*', '*significance*'. Another common abstract noun in –**mi** is **umami** '*deliciousness*', '*wonderful taste*' from **umái** '*delicious*'.

Particles of extent and degree

We have learnt that Japanese has no equivalents to the comparative degree of adjectives in English. You will recall that to compare the attributes of two things, Japanese uses the noun **hóo** '*side, direction*' and the particle **yori** '*than, from*', but the form of the adjective concerned remains unchanged.

Taihéiyoo to Taiséiyoo to de wa dóchira no hóo ga hirói desu ka.	*Which is larger the Pacific or the Atlantic?*
Taihéiyoo wa Taiséiyoo yori hirói desu.	*The Pacific Ocean is larger than the Atlantic.*
Taihéiyoo no hóo ga hirói desu.	*The Pacific is larger.*

We did not learn, however, how to say, for example, that A is not bigger than B or that A is about the same size as B. To do this we need to call into service two more particles, **hodo** and **gúrai**.

Taiséiyoo wa Taihéiyoo hodo híroku arimasén.	*The Atlantic is not as large as the Pacific.*
Otootó wa bóku hodo omoku nái desu.	*My younger brother is not as heavy as I am.*
Áni wa chichi gúrai se ga takái desu.	*My elder brother is as tall as my father.*
Kore wa Pári de tábeta ryóori gúrai oishii desu.	*This is as good as the food we ate in Paris.*

Exercise 14.5

Use the data in parentheses to fill in the gaps in these sentences.

1. Chikatetsu wa _____ tákaku arimasén. (**densha ¥360; chikatetsu ¥280**)
2. Bíiru wa _____ tsúyoku arimasén. (**bíiru, 5do; osake, 12do**)
3. Wáin wa _____ tsuyói desu. (**wáin, 12do; osake, 12do**)
4. Oosaka wa _____ óoku nái desu. (**oosaka, jinkoo 500mannin; Tookyoo, jinkoo 1,000mannin**)
5. Otootó wa _____ sé ga takái desu. (**otootó 181 sénchi, chichi 178 sénchi**)

Vocabulary

–do *degrees* (measure of alcohol content) **sénchi** *centimetre*

Compound verbs

Japanese has a large number of compound verbs, most of which will be acquired as separate vocabulary items. However, it is useful to learn some of the common endings with wide application, so you can form compounds from many of the verbs you have already learnt. Compound verbs are formed by adding a verb to the stem of another verb. Here we have set out some of the most common second elements with example sentences.

–dásu	*to begin, start suddenly, to break out*
furidásu	*to start raining*, e.g. **Áme ga furidashimáshita.**
nakidásu	*to burst into tears*, e.g. **Akanboo ga nakidashimáshita.**
waraidásu	*to burst out laughing*, e.g. **Okíi kóe de waradashimáshita.**
iidásu	*to start saying, to speak out*, e.g. **Kyuu ni iidashimáshita.**
–hajiméru	*to begin*
yomihajiméru	*to begin to read*, e.g. **Sensoo to Heiwa** (*War and Peace*) **o yomihajímeta bákari desu.**
narihajiméru	*to begin to become*, e.g. **Kuraku narihajimemáshita.**
naraihajiméru	*to begin to learn*, e.g. **Obáasan wa saikin Eigo o naraihajimemáshita.**
–owaru	*to finish*
kakiowáru	*to finish writing*, e.g. **Yatto kono hón o kakiowarimáshita.**
tabeowáru	*to finish eating*, e.g. **Tabeáwótte kara mata benkyoo shihajimemáshita.**
–naosu	*to redo, to do again*
yarinaósu	*to redo*, e.g. **Moo ichido saisho kara yarinaoshimashóo.**
kangaenaósu	*to rethink*, e.g. **Kangaenaóshite kudasai.**
–tsuzukéru	*to continue*

arukitsuzukéru	*to keep walking*, e.g. **Ashí ga ítaku náru made arukitsuzukemáshita.**
hanashitsuzukéru	*to keep talking*, e.g. **Nanjíkan mo hanashitsuzukemáshita.**
–sugíru	*to overdo, to be too much* (also used with adjective roots)
nomisugíru	*to drink too much*, e.g. **Uísukii o nomisugimáshita.**
tabetoosugíru	*to eat much*, e.g. **Shoogatsú** (*New Year*) **ni náru to ítsumo tabesugimásu.**
takasugíru	*to be too high, too expensive*, e.g. **Keitai-dénwa no ryóokin** (*fees, charges*) **wa takasugimásu.**

The plain imperative

In your dealings with Japanese, or anyone else for that matter, you will probably get greater cooperation if you avoid ordering people around. The –**te kudasái** request form will suffice for most everyday purposes. You should know, nevertheless, that Japanese has a plain imperative form, which you will hear used from time to time in conversation between close friends and within the family. The plain imperative of consonant-root verbs is formed by adding –**e** to the verb root, e.g. **ike** '*go!*', **nóme** '*drink!*', **warae** '*laugh!*'. With vowel-root verbs the suffix –**ro** is generally added, though –**yo** is also quite common in western Japan and in written Japanese, e.g. **tabéro** '*eat!*', **míro** '*look!*', **tsugi no mondai ni kotaeyo** '*answer the following questions*' (written instruction). The plain imperative forms of the irregular verbs, **kúru** and **suru** are **kói** and **shiró** (or **séyo**) respectively, e.g. **Póchi, kotchí e kói** '*Come here, Pochi!*' (calling a dog), **háyaku shiró** '*do it quickly!*', **20 péeji o sanshoo séyo** '*refer to page 20*' (written instruction). The in-giving verb **kureru** '*someone gives me*' also has an irregular imperative, becoming **kuré** '*give me!*', without the anticipated –**ro** suffix. This also applies when **kureru** is used as an auxiliary verb, e.g. **tasukete kuré** '*Help me!*'

The plain negative imperative is formed by adding the particle **na** to the plain form of the verb, e.g. **ikú na** '*don't go!*', **míru na** '*don't look!*'. Often in the plain style the request forms are used without **kudasái** or, put differently, the –**te** form alone is used as a request. Sometimes **choodai** '*accept with thanks*', '*please*' is added to the –**te** form to make a casual, friendly request in the plain style.

Kore o yónde.	*Read this* (please).
Sore o mísete choodai.	*Show me that* (please).

In practice these brusque plain imperatives are often softened with the addition of the sentence final particle, **yo**.

Ki ni surú na yo.	*Don't worry about it!*
Kyóo wa sore de íi ni shiró yo.	*Leave it at that for today!*
Oshiete choodái yo.	*Please tell me* (pleading tone).
Joodan yuú na yo.	*Stop kidding! Don't make jokes!*

The brusque imperatives are used even in polite-style speech when reporting instructions that have been made to oneself.

Iké to iwaremáshita.	*I was told to go.*
Súgu dáse to iimáshita.	*He said to send it straight away.*
Míru na to okoraremáshita.	*I was angrily told not to look.*

Direct requests with **kudasái** can be changed to reported speech with the imperative of **kureru, kuré**.

Yóji ni kite kuré to	*I was told to come at 4 o'clock.*
tanomaremáshita.	

Of course, reported commands can also be expressed with the plain form of the verb followed by **yóo ni**.

Iku yóo ni iwaremáshita.	*I was told to go.*

Exercise 14.6

In the following sentences replace the indirect imperative in **yóo ni** with the plain imperative form, then translate into English. We give you an example to help you get started.

Cue: Osoku naranái yoo ni iwaremáshita.
A: **Osoku náru na to iwaremáshita.**   I was told not to be late.

1. Ashita kúru yoo ni iwaremáshita.
2. Róbii de mátsu yoo ni iimáshita.
3. Senséi wa séito ni yóku benkyoo suru yóo ni iimáshita.
4. Densha no náka de keitai-dénwa o tsukawanai yóo ni to yuu anaúnsu ga arimashita.
5. Asoko de chuusha shinai yóo ni to káite arimashita.

Dialogue 2 ▄▄

At the restaurant

ウェーター:	いらっしゃいませ。何名様ですか。
客 <small>きゃく</small>:	四人です。
ウェーター:	少々お待ち下さい。(the waiter goes to look for a table for four) どうぞこちらへ。(after he has seated the guests) ワイン・リストとメニューでございます。
客 <small>きゃく</small>:	どうも。
ウェーター:	お飲み物は何になさいますか。
客 <small>きゃく</small>:	先ず、生ビールの中ジョッキ二つとミネラルウォーター二つ下さい。
ウェーター:	はい、かしこまりました。(after a while he brings the drinks) お食事の方はお決まりでしょうか。
客 <small>きゃく</small>:	はい。この茹でた蟹料理ですが、蟹はどの位の大きさですか。
ウェーター:	そうですねえ、この位です。
客 <small>きゃく</small>:	では、それを一つお願いします。メインは蟹と伊勢海老で、みんなで分けて食べます。そして前菜はこの野菜スープを四人前お願いします。
ウェーター:	ワインは何になさいますか。
客 <small>きゃく</small>:	(looking at the wine list) この中で辛口の白ワインはどれですか。
ウェーター:	こちらのオーストラリアのワインは中々好評です。
客 <small>きゃく</small>:	ではそれにします。
ウェーター:	かしこまりました。ご注文は以上でよろしいですか。
客 <small>きゃく</small>:	ええ、取りあえずそれで結構です。足りなかったら後で追加します。
ウェーター:	はい、かしこまりました。しばらくお待ち下さい。 (after they have finished the main course)

ウェーター:　お下げします。(he returns a few moments later)
　　　　　　デザートはいかがですか。
客：　　　　デザートは結構です。お勘定をお願
　　　　　　いします。

WEITAA:　Irasshaimáse. Nánmeisama desu ka.

KYAKU:　Yonin désu.

WEITAA:　Shóoshoo omachi kudasai. Dóozo kochira e. Wain rísuto to
　　　　　ményuu de gozaimásu.

KYAKU:　Dóomo.

WEITAA:　Onomímono wa náni ni nasaimásu ka.

KYAKU:　Mázu, namabíiru no chuujókki futatsu to mineraru uóotaa
　　　　　futatsú kudasái.

WEITAA:　Hái, kashikomarimáshita. Oshokuji no hoó wa okimari
　　　　　deshóo ka.

KYAKU:　Kono yúdeta kani-ryóori desu ga, kani wa dóno gurai no
　　　　　óokisa désu ka.

WEITAA:　Sóo desu née, kono gurai désu.

KYAKU:　Déwa, sore o hitótsu onegai shimásu. Méen wa kani to iseebi
　　　　　de, minná de wákete tabemasu. Soshite zensai wa kono
　　　　　yasai-súupu o yoninmae onegai shimásu.

WEITAA:　Wáin wa náni ni nasaimásu ka.

KYAKU:　Kono náka de karakuchi no shíro wa dóre desu ka.

WEITAA:　Kochira no Oosutorária no wáin wa nakanaka koohyoo
　　　　　désu.

KYAKU:　Déwa, sore ni shimásu.

WEITAA:　Kashikomarimáshita. Gochúumon wa íjoo de yoroshii
　　　　　désu ka.

KYAKU:　Ée, toriáezu sore de kékkoo desu. Tarinákattara áto de tsuika
　　　　　shimásu.

WEITAA:　Hái, kashikomarimáshita. Shibáraku omachi kudasái. Osage
　　　　　shimásu. Dezáato wa ikága desu ka.

KYAKU:　Dezáato wa kékoo desu. Okanjoo o onegai shimásu.

Vocabulary

–mei	numeral class (for counting people)
nánmeisama desu ka	*How many of you are there, Sir/Madam?* (honorific)

óokisa	*size* (**–sa**, suffix to form abstract noun from adjectives)
yoninmae	*four portions/servings* (**–ninmae** counter for servings)
gochúumon wa íjoo de yoroshii désu ka	*will that be all for your order, Sir/Madam?*
toriáezu	*for the time being, first, for a start*
osage shimásu	*I'll clear the table for you*
okanjoo	*bill* (also **kanjóo**)

Exercise 14.7

Answer the following questions on Dialogue 2.

1. What drinks did they order before the meal?
2. What entrées did they have?
3. What was ordered for the main meal?
4. Why were only two main meals ordered?
5. What wine did they settle on and why?

Exercise 14.8 ■■

After studying the list of new **kanji** for this unit translate the following sentences into English. Then read the sentences aloud. Finally, see if you can reproduce the Japanese script from the English translation.

1. 昔、東京の下町の芸術大学で西洋音楽を勉強したことがあります。
2. この紙に書いてある四字の駅名をどう読みますか。ああ、これはたかだのばばです。高田馬場は東京の山手線の駅で、有名な早稲田大学のある場所です。
3. あの広い野原を馬に乗ってかけて見たいですねえ。
4. 御両親の御住所とお名前をここにお書き下さい。
5. 昼も夜も工場で仕事をするのは楽ではありません。
6. 大西洋は太平洋ほど広くありません。

7. 病気なのにちっとも暗い気持ちを人に見せません。
8. 青森県と秋田県は冬が長くて雪が何ヶ月も降ります。

Vocabulary

Yamanotesen	*the Yamanote* (or Yamate) *line* (main loop-line for trains in Tokyo)
sén	*line*
Omedetoo gozaimásu	*Congratulations*
Dóozo yói otoshi o.	*I hope you have a Happy New Year.*
Akemáshite omedetoo gozaimásu.	*Happy New Year.*
Kánben shite kudasai.	*Please bear with me, please excuse me.*
Okotoba ni amaete.	*That's very kind of you* (literally, 'I'm taking advantage of your kind words').
Zéhi yorasete itadakimásu.	*I'll certainly be dropping in.*

See next page for Kanji table.

Kanji

Kanji	Reading	Meaning	Kanji	Reading	Meaning
音	**ON OTÓ** 9 strokes #14.163	sound, noise 雨の音 **áme no otó** the sound of the rain 発音 **hatsuon** pronunciation 騒音 **soo'on** noise, racket	楽	**RAKU, GAKU** **tano(shíi)** 13 strokes #14.164	pleasure; music 音楽 **óngaku** music 楽な仕事 **rakú na shigoto** easy work 楽しい旅 **tanoshíi tabí** a pleasant trip
暗	**AN** **kurá(i)** 13 strokes #14.165	dark 暗い部屋 **kurai heyá** a dark room 暗記 **ánki** learning by heart	持	**JI** **mó(tsu)** 9 strokes #14.166	to hold 気持ち **kimochi** feeling, mood お持ちしましょうか **omochi shimashóo ka** shall I carry it?
病	**BYOO** **yamai** 10 strokes #14.167	illness, sick 病気 **byooki** sickness, disease 病人 **byoonin** sick person	強	**KYOO** **tsuyó(i)** 11 strokes #14.168	strong 強力な **kyooryoku** powerful 力が強い **chikará ga tsuyói** strong
町	**CHOO** **machi** 7 strokes #14.169	town, district; block 下町 **shitamachi** down town 町長 **chóochoo** town mayor	県	**KEN** 9 strokes #14.170	prefecture 青森県 **Aomoríken** place n. 高知県 **Koochíken** place n. 秋田県 **Akitáken** place n.
太	**TAI** **futó(i)** 4 strokes #14.171	large, vast; fat 太い足 **futói ashí** fat legs 太陽 **táiyoo** sun	平	**HEI, BYOO** **taira** 5 strokes #14.172	flat, level; fair 太平洋 **Taihéiyoo** Pacific Ocean 平らな部分 **taira na búbun** the flat part
両	**RYOO** 6 strokes #14.173	two, both 両方 **ryoohóo** both 両親 **ryóoshin** parents	昼	**CHUU** **hirú** 9 strokes #14.174	midday, daytime 昼食 **chuushoku** lunch お昼 **ohíru** lunch 昼間 **hirumá** daytime
晩	**BAN** 12 strokes #14.175	night, evening 今晩 **kónban** tonight 明晩 **myóoban** tomorrow night	勉	**BEN** 10 strokes #14.176	diligence 勉強 **benkyoo** study 勉強家 **benkyooka** a hard worker, a studious type
所	**JO** **tokoro** 8 strokes #14.177	place 近所 **kínjo** neighbourhood 台所 **daidokoro** kitchen	場	**JOO** **ba** 12 strokes #14.178	place, site 場所 **basho** place 会場 **kaijoo** conference room 市場 **íchiba** market
工	**KOO** 3 strokes #14.179	work, make 工場 **koojoo** factory 人工 **jinkoo** artificial	広	**KOO** **hiró(i)** 5 strokes #14.180	wide, broad, large 幅が広い **haba ga hirói** wide 広大な **koodai na** vast, extensive
馬	**BA** **uma** 10 strokes #14.181	horse 馬に乗る **umá ni noru** to ride a horse 馬力 **bariki** horsepower 競馬 **keiba** horse racing	駅	**EKI** 14 strokes #14.182	station 東京駅 **Tookyoo-éki** Tokyo station 駅ビル **ekibiru** station

15 上達の秘訣はこれです。
Jootatsu no hiketsu wa kore desu.
The secret road to progress!

In this unit you will learn how to:

- Increase your comprehension skills
- Discuss current events
- Recite the list of 12 zodiac animals
- Increase your vocabulary with **kanji** compounds
- Recognise some common **kanji** signs and notices.

You will also acquire:

- 20 more **kanji:** 内 屋 室 美 術 芸 者 員 市 道
  晴 的 化 無 不 便 利 文 寺 詩

Dialogue 1 ■■

After working your way through this course you decide to talk to a Japanese teacher about what you should do to progress further in your study of Japanese. This is primarily an exercise in vocabulary building.

先生： このコースの最後のユニットまで勉強してきましたが、
　　　 いかがでしょうか。

生徒： そうですねえ、もう大体基礎文法も身につきました
　　　 し、簡単な会話もできますが、これから上達するのに
　　　 はどうすれば一番いいでしょう。

先生： 先ず、語彙を増やすことですね。

生徒： そうですか。知っている単語の数がまだまだ足りないとよく感じます。

先生： 初級のレベルでは、挨拶、自分の家族や趣味、数字、時刻、天候、旅行や乗り物等についての会話で使うような単語を導入しました。

生徒： そうですね。ある程度その位の会話に自信がありますが、中級、上級の日本語はどんなものですか。

先生： もう既に中級の会話もいくつかこの本で紹介してあります。例えば、健康の話とか、ホテルでのチェックインとか、競馬の話等がそうです。もっと長い文章やかなり複雑な文型が分かったり、自分で利用できたりすると、中級のレベルに達したと言えます。

生徒： 上級まで進むのは難しいでしょうねえ。

先生： いいえ、決してそんなことはありません。続けて努力することが大切です。

生徒： ああそうですか。

先生： 上級まで進む秘訣は漢字を沢山覚えることです。そうすると辞書を引きながら新聞や雑誌や小説が読めるようになります。

生徒： 早くそうなりたいですね。

先生： 読むことによって徐々に進歩しますよ。国際政治や経済、世界の各地の戦争、宗教争い、飢餓などの現状に関する語彙を知っていれば話題が豊富になります。

生徒： そうですか。考えてみれば、よく世界の事情の会話を交わしますね。

先生： それから、よくテレビの番組に出てくるような社会問題の語彙も知っておくと便利ですよ。

生徒：　法律、教育、福祉関係　等といった
　　　　問題ですか。

先生：　そうです。また、老人問題、離婚率の上
　　　　昇、いじめ、自殺、麻薬の乱用という
　　　　問題と殺人事件、強盗、収賄、
　　　　汚職その他の犯罪もよく話題にのぼります。

生徒：　ああ、そうですねえ。

先生：　ええ。それに、、地震、台風、洪水、火山の噴火
　　　　等の天災と、大気汚染、地球の温暖化、
　　　　密林の伐採等の自然環境を取り囲む諸
　　　　問題もあります。加えて、　IT　、つまり情報通信
　　　　技術とか、株の取引、投資、保険などの金融
　　　　関係の知識も必要ですね。

生徒：　聞いただけで気が遠くなりそうですね。これから
　　　　漢字を一生懸命勉強しなければなりません。

先生：　五百字位覚えれば大分分かるようになります
　　　　よ。毎日一、二字ずつ覚えたら早く上達しま
　　　　すよ。頑張ってください。

Vocabulary

sáigo	*last*
sai–	*most –* (prefix. cf., **saikoo** 最高 *highest, best*; **saisho** 最初 *first*)
–tari –tari suru	*to do such things as…and…, do frequently or alternately*
…kotó ni yotte	*by –ing, through –ing*
kákuchi	*everywhere, all places throughout…*
shuukyoo-árasoi	*religious strife*
shúukyoo	*religion*
arasói	*fight, struggle, strife*
sonóta	*and other*, etc.
wadai ni noboru	*become a topic of conversation*
aitíi	*I.T.*

tsúmari	*that is, in short*
joohoo	*information*
tsuushin	*communications*
gíjutsu	*technology*
ki ga tooku náru	*faint away, feel dizzy*

Exercise 15.1

Translate the following sentences, based on Dialogue 1, into English.

1. 簡単な会話もできますが、まだ基礎文法が身についていません。
2. 上達するのに語彙を増やすのが一番いいです。
3. 初級のレベルでは会話で使うような単語を導入しました。
4. 上級まで進むのに、続けて努力することが大切です。
5. 世界の事情に関する語彙を知っていれば話題が豊富になります。

Dialogue 2 ■■

メアリーさんは何年ですか。　　　　What animal sign were you born under, Mary?

There are people in Japan who believe a person's personality is determined by the sign of the animal for the year in which he or she was born. Even those who don't believe like to go along with the game. Don't be surprised if you are asked what your animal sign is. After this unit you should know. Here is a conversation between Mary and her Japanese friend, Haruo.

春男:　　メアリーさんは何年ですか。

メアリー:　何年って。どういう意味ですか。

春男:　　干支のことですよ。十二支を知っているでしょう?

メアリー:　聞いたことがありますが忘れました。十二匹の動物だということだけ覚えています。どんな動物なのか、どんな順序なのか分かりません。

春男: 　教えて上げましょうか。

メアリー: 　ええ、お願いします。

春男: 　じゃ、最初は「子」— それは「ねずみ」の「ね」
　　　　　ですよ。それから「丑」、「寅」、「卯」、

メアリー: 　「う」は何ですか。

春男: 　そうですねえ。これも分かりにくいです。「うさぎ」
　　　　　を略して「う」と言います。

メアリー: 　じゃ、「ね、うし、とら、う」それから何が来ますか。

春男: 　「辰」、「巳」…

メアリー: 　ええ?たつみって。竜は古代中国の架空の動物で西洋の

春男: 　ドラゴンに当たるようなものです。

メアリー: 　ああ、そうですか。十二支はみんな本当の動物
　　　　　だと思っていましたよ。

春男: 　まあね。でも、古代の人たちは竜が本当
　　　　　に存在すると信じていたみたいですよ。

メアリー: 　そうでしょうねえ。ところで、「み」
　　　　　は何ですか。

春男: 　これは十二支で言う蛇のことです。

メアリー: 　ああそうですか。その次は?

春男: 　そうですねえ。ね、うし、とら、う、たつ、み、
　　　　　うま...そ、そう「午」です。「午」、「未」、
　　　　　「申」、「酉」、「戌」、「亥」。「い」は
　　　　　「猪」のことです。

メアリー: 　よく覚えていますね。

春男: 　ええ。子供の時からずっとやっていますから。
　　　　　幾つかのグループに分けて覚えると簡単
　　　　　ですよ。メアリーさんもきっと直ぐ覚えられると思
　　　　　いますよ。私がもう一度言いますから、その後
　　　　　メアリーさんが言ってください。いいですか。

メアリー: 　はい。

春男:　　　　じゃ、行きますよ。ね、うし、とら、う、　たつ、
　　　　　　　み　うま、ひつじ、さる、とり、いぬ、い

メアリー:　　よく分かりました。ところで、私は何年
　　　　　　　でしょう。

春男:　　　　何年生まれですか。

メアリー:　　1982 年です。

春男:　　　　じゃ、僕より三つ下ですから、戌年
　　　　　　　でしょう。

Vocabulary

nanidoshi	*what zodiac animal sign*
eto	traditional Chinese calendrical system with 10 stems (arranged in five pairs) and 12 branches combining to produce a cycle of 60 years
juuníshi	*12 branches; 12 animals of the Chinese zodiac*
… ni ataru	*to be equivalent to*
mítai na	*like, as; it seems that*

The following chart shows the zodiac animals with below the Zodiac names and the normal conversational terms for these animals.

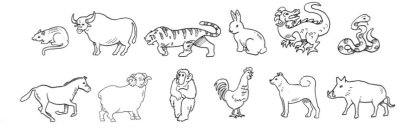

Zodiac name	Zodiac character	Common name (where different)	Common character	English	Dates
ne	子	**nezumi**	鼠	*rat*	1924 1936 1948 1960 1972 1984 1996 2008
ushi	丑		牛	*ox*	1925 1937 1949 1961 1973 1985 1997 2009
tora	寅		虎	*tiger*	1926 1938 1950 1962 1974 1986 1998 2010
u	卯	**usagi**	兎	*rabbit*	1927 1939 1951 1963 1975 1987 1999 2011
tatsu	辰		竜	*dragon*	1928 1940 1952 1964 1976 1988 2000 2012
mi	巳	**hébi**	蛇	*snake*	1929 1941 1953 1965 1977 1989 2001 2013
umá	午		馬	*horse*	1930 1942 1954 1966 1978 1990 2002 2014
hitsuji	未		羊	*sheep*	1931 1943 1955 1967 1979 1991 2003 2015
sáru	申		猿	*monkey*	1932 1944 1956 1968 1980 1992 2004 2016
tori	酉	**niwatori**	鶏	*cock*	1933 1945 1957 1969 1981 1993 2005 2017
inú	戌		犬	*dog*	1934 1946 1958 1970 1982 1994 2006 2018
í	亥	**inoshíshi**	猪	*boar*	1935 1947 1959 1971 1983 1995 2007 2019

Kanji

内	**NAI** **uchi** 4 strokes #15.183	inside 内外 **náigai** internal & external その内 **sono uchi** meanwhile 年内 **nénnai** within the year	屋	**OKU** **ya** 9 strokes #15.184	house; small shop 肉屋 **nikúya** butcher /–'s shop 屋外 **okúgai** outdoor 屋上 **okujoo** rooftop
室	**SHITSU** **muró** 9 strokes #15.185	room 室内 **shitsúnai** interior 室町時代 **Muromachi–jídai** Muromachi period (1336–1573) 病室 **byooshitsu** sick room	美	**BI** **isó(gu)** 9 strokes #15.186	sudden; steep; to hurry 急に **kyuu ni** suddenly 急ぎましょう **isogimashóo** let's hurry
術	**JUTSU** 11 strokes #15.187	technique, practical art 美術 **bíjutsu** art, the fine arts 手術 **shújitsu** surgical operation	芸	**GEI** 7 strokes #15.188	skill, performance; art 芸術 **geijutsu** (an) art 工芸 **koogei** craft
者	**SHA** **monó** 8 strokes #15.189	person 芸者 **geisha** geisha 学者 **gakusha** scholar なまけ者 **namakemono** lazybones; sloth (the animal)	員	**IN** 10 strokes #15.190	member 会社員 **kaishain** office worker 店員 **ten'in** shop assistant
市	**SHI** **ichi** 5 strokes #15.191	city, municipal market 青森市 **Aomoríshi** A. city 市内 **shínai** within the city 市場 **íchiba, shijoo** market	道	**DO** **michi** 12 strokes #15.192	road; way; art of 北海道 **Hokkáidoo** place n. 近道 **chikámichi** short cut 空手道 **karatédoo** karate
晴	**SEI** **ha(réru)** 12 strokes #15.193	clear; fine; to become fine 晴時々曇り **hare tokidoki kumóri** fine with occasional cloud 晴天 **seiten** fine weather	的	**TEKI** **máto** 8 strokes #15.194	target; adjectival suffix 私的 **shiteki** private 目的 **mokuteki** goal, objective 知的 **chiteki** intellectual
化	**KA** **ba(kéru)** 4 strokes #15.195	change; -ation, -ize etc. (suffix) 化学 **kágaku** chemistry 美化 **bíka** beautification 強化 **kyóoka** strengthening お化け **obáke** ghost, apparition	無	**MU, BU** **ná(i)** 12 strokes #15.196	not 無名 **mumei** unknown 無事 **búji na** safe 年中無休 **nénjuu-mukyuu** open all year round
便	**BIN, BEN** **táyo(ri)** 9 strokes #15.197	convenient; letter, post 便所 **benjó** toilet, lavatory 郵便局 **yuubínkyoku** post office 便りがない **táyori __** we've had no letter /news	利	**RI** **ki(ku)** 7 strokes #15.198	便利 **bénri na** convenient 利口 **rikoo na** clever 左利き **hidarikiki** left-handed 金利 **kinri** interest rate
不	**FU** 4 strokes #15.199	not 不便 **fúben na** inconvenient 手不足 **tebúsoku** lack of staff 不安 **fuan na** uneasy, worried	文	**BUN** **fúmi** 4 strokes #15.200	writing; literature; letter 文学 **búngaku** literature 英文 **eibun** English (written) 文芸 **bungei** literary arts
寺	**JI** **tera** 6 strokes #15.201	temple (Buddhist) 東大寺 **Tóodaiji** the Todaiji temple in Nara 山寺 **yamádera** mountain temple	詩	**SHI** 7 strokes #15.202	poetry 詩的 **shiteki** poetic 詩人 **shijin** poet

Exercise 15.2

1. Work out you own zodiac animal.
2. Explain in Japanese what the zodiac animal is for this year and next year.
3. Say in Japanese how many of these animals can be found outside zoos in your country?
4. Explain in Japanese why the dragon is included in the list.
5. Ask your Japanese friend (in Japanese, of course) what are the characteristics (**tokuchoo**) of people born under the sign of the tiger.

More useful kanji

Although the emphasis in this book has been on the spoken language, by the end of this unit you will have learnt the two syllabaries, **hiragána** and **katakána**, and about 200 **kanji**. Most of the **kanji** introduced in this unit have considerable generative force, combining with other **kanji** to form a large number of **kanji** compounds.

In addition to those characters introduced specifically for writing and recognition, you have seen a large number of **kanji** with their readings given in **furigana** and you have **kanji** transcriptions for most of the vocabulary items in the glossaries. By now you have acquired a sound knowledge of how **kanji** characters are formed and how to write and count the strokes in each character correctly. When you feel you have mastered the 200 basic characters introduced for reading and writing, you can go back and tackle those characters that have been introduced with **furigana** annotation. Learn each character or character compound as it occurs and white out the **furigana** reading when you feel you have learnt it. Finally, you will have erased all the **furigana** in this text and you will be well on the way to reading Japanese. At this point, however, we feel you should learn at least to recognise these few extra characters often seen on signs in public places.

非常口	**hijóoguchi**	*(emergency) exit*
改札口	**kaisatsúguchi**	*ticket gate, turnstile*
窓口	**madóguchi**	*counter, window*
危険	**kiken**	*danger*
注意	**chúui**	*attention, be careful*
避難所	**hinanjo**	*evacuation point*
案内所	**annaijo**	*information counter*
禁止	**kinshi**	*forbidden*

駐車禁止	**chuusha-kinshi**	*no parking*
禁煙	**kin'en**	*no smoking*
一方通行	**ippootsúukoo**	*one-way traffic*
右側通行	**migigawatsúukoo**	*keep right*
工事中	**koojichuu**	*under construction; men at work*
営業中	**eigyoochuu**	*open for business*
定休日	**teikyuubi**	*regular holiday* (shop closed)
化粧室	**keshooshitsu**	*powder room, toilet*

Exercise 15.3 ■■■

Translate into English the following sentences which contain **kanji** introduced in Unit 15.

1. 東京芸術大学では美術も勉強できます。
2. この町の文化的 水準 はかなり高くておどろきました。
3. 夏には東京の屋上のビヤガーデンで生ビールを飲むのが好きです。
4. このごろ日本の国内も外国へもよく旅行します。
5. 今朝北海道からアイヌ文化の学者が無事に着きました。
6. そのお寺は非 常 に不便な所にありました。
7. 日本の文学や詩に芸者の話がよく出てきます。
8. 駅前の市場の野菜は新鮮で安いです。
9. あの店の店員はほとんどアルバイトをしている若者です。
10. 明日晴れたらとなりの町まで行ってみましょう。

Vocabulary

Tanoshími ni shite orimásu.	*I'm looking forward to it.*
Taihen kékoo na monó o itadaite…	*Thank you for the lovely gift.*
Tsumaránai monó desu ga, dóozo.	*It's nothing much, but please…*
Ohisashiburi désu né.	*It's been a long time, hasn't it?*
Gobúsata shite orimásu.	*Sorry I've been out of touch.*
Mata ome ni kakarimashóo.	*Let's meet again.*

Key to the Exercises

Unit 1

Exercise 1.1

(from right to left) hamachi, úni, kazunoko, ika, kani

Exercise 1.2

1 a yama no ue   **2** j kawá to ta   **3** h yama no shita   **4** b kawa no náka   **5** g yama no hón   **6** i hón no yama   **7** d yama no shita no kawá   **8** e yama no ue no ta   **9** c yamá to kawá   **10** f kawa no ue no yamá

Exercise 1.3

1 Ueda Sachie   **2** Yamamoto Máchiko   **3** Shimoda Kánoko
4 Kawada Sátoko   **5** Honda Chie   **6** 田山 ますえ   **7** 田中 はまこ
8 中山 そのこ

Exercise 1.4

1 (Watashi wa) [your name] desu. Or, Watashi no namae wa [your name] desu.   **2** Hajimemáshite (dóozo yoroshiku).
3 Dóo itashimashite.   **4** Sayonara. Mata ashita.   **5** Oyasumi nasái.

Exercise 1.5

1 Tanaka san desu ka. Hái, sóo desu. Tanaka désu.   Are you Ms
  (Mr, Mrs, etc.) Tanaka? Yes, that's right. I'm Tanaka.
2 Kawamoto san désu ka. Iie, chigaimásu. Yamamoto désu.   Are you
  Mr Kawamoto? No, I'm not. (literally, 'that's not right') I'm Yamamoto.
3 Yamá to kawá to tá.   Mountains and rivers and rice fields.
4 Yama no náka no tá.   The rice fields in the mountains.
5 Honda san to Táyama san.   Mr Honda and Mr Tayama.

Exercise 1.6

1 c   2 a   3 d   4 e   5 b

Exercise 1.7

Part A Comprehension

Mr Ueda is a teacher, Ms Tanaka is a student, Honda is a doctor and
Yamada is a civil servant.

Part B Practice

1 Oshígoto wa nán desu ka. oshi ごとは　na ん ですか。   2 Kaishain
desu ka. かい sha いん ですか。   3 Shúfu desu ka. Shúfu ですか。
4 Súmisu san wa shachoo desu ne. スミスさんは shacho うです ne。
5 Yamada san wa gakusei desu ka. 山田さんは が kuse いですか。

Exercise 1.8

1 Ohayoo gozaimásu. おは yo う ございます。   2 Konnichi wa.
こんにちは。 3 Konban wa. こんばんは。 4 Oyasumi nasái.
お ya す mi na さい。 5 Sayoonara さ yo う nara   6 katagaki
(*credentials*, details of company and rank on business card); nigori
(*voicing mark*, which turns **t**– into **d**– etc.); izakaya (*pub*); myóoji
(*family name*); ojígi (*bow*); itamae (*sushi chef*)

Unit 2

Exercise 2.1

1 川田さんは日本人です。　**2** ラリー・ミラーさんは中国
にすんでいます。　**3** 日本語も 中国語も できます。　**4** リーさんは
いま 英語を ならt ています。　**5** 山本さんはアメリカに
すんでいます。

Exercise 2.2

Páku san to Ríi san wa Kankokujín desu. Kánkoku no Sóuru kara
kimáshita. Íma, Amerika ni súnde imasu. Futaritomo Eigo ga yóku dekimásu. Nihongo mo sukóshi dekimásu. Páku san wa rókku to supóotsu ga
sukí desu. Ríi san wa rokku-óngaku ga amari sukí dewa arimasén.
Kurásshikku to dókusho ga sukí desu.

　Páku san to Ríi san wa íma, Rárii Míiazu san no uchi ni súnde imasu.
Míiazu san wa Amerikájin desu. Arasuka ni súnde imasu. Íma, Nihongo o
narátte imasu. Míiazu san no shúmi wa Amerikan-fúttobooru to aisuhók-
kee desu. Ténisu mo sukí desu.

Mr Park and Mr Lee are Koreans. They came from Seoul in South Korea.
Now they are living in America. Both of them speak English well. They
also know a little Japanese. Mr Park likes rock music and sport. Mr Lee
does not like rock music much. He likes classical music and reading.

　Mr Park and Mr Lee are now living in Larry Mears's house. Mr Mears
is an American. He lives in Alaska. Now he is learning Japanese.
Mr Mears's hobbies are American football and ice hockey. He also likes
tennis.

Exercise 2.3

1 Yamagawa san wa dóchira kara kimáshita ka. Watashi wa Nihón
kara kimáshita.　**2** Ari san wa dóchira kara kimáshita ka. Indo
kara kimáshita. (*Note*: watashi can be omitted.)　**3** Han san wa
dóchira kara kimáshita ka. Kánkoku kara desu.　**4** Míraa san wa
dóchira kara désu ka. Watashi wa Eikoku kara kimáshita.
5 Méarii san wa dóchira kara kimáshita ka. Arasuka kara kimáshita.
6 Ríi san wa dóchira kara désu ka. Watashi wa Chúugoku kara desu.

Exercise 2.4

1 Kochira wa Wán san desu. Wán san wa Chuugokújin desu. Nihongo mo dekimásu. **2** Kochira wa Béeka san désu. Béekaa san wa Igirisújin (Eikokújin) desu. Furansugo mo dekimásu. **3** Kochira wa Buráun san désu. Buráun san wa Doitsújin desu. Chuugokugo mo dekimásu. **4** Kochira wa Ránii san désu. Ránii san wa Indójin desu. Taigo mo dekimásu. **5** Kochira wa Góodon san désu. Góodon san wa Amerikájin desu. Roshiago mo dekimásu.

Exercise 2.5

1 Yamamoto san wa dóko (or 'dóchira' which is more polite) ni súnde imasu ka. Nágoya ni súnde imasu. **2** Kunimoto san wa dóchira ni súnde imasu ka. Sapporo ni súnde imasu. **3** Súmisu san wa dóko ni súnde imasu ka. Róndon ni súnde imasu. **4** Ríi san wa dóchira ni súnde imasu ka. Pékin ni súnde imasu. **5** Rukuréeru san wa dóko ni súnde imasu ka. Pár ni súnde imasu. **6** Káa san wa dóko ni súnde imasu ka. Shídonii ni súnde imasu. **7** Mekari san wa dóko ni súnde imasu ka. Róma ni súnde imasu. **8** Kímu san wa dóko ni súnde imasu ka. Sóuru ni súnde imasu.

Exercise 2.6

Helena – Sweden, Eric – Germany, Peter – New Zealand, Mr Kim – Korea, Mary – America, Edwina – UK, Bob – Australia.

Exercise 2.7

1 Máikeru san no shúmi wa sáafin to basukétto desu. **2** Robáato san no shúmi wa jooba to sákkaa desu. **3** An san no shúmi wa óngaku to háikingu desu. **4** Káaru san no shúmi wa dókusho to ryokoo désu. **5** Góodon san no shúmi wa suiei to yakyuu désu. **6** Anáta no shúmi wa kaimono (shóppingu) to ténisu desu.

Exercise 2.8

1 China **2** No (In Thailand) **3** Chinese **4** No **5** Sport, especially golf

Unit 3

Exercise 3.1

1 taxi **2** Italy **3** ice **4** pasta **5** bar **6** colour TV **7** maker (manufacturer) **8** camera **9** lighter **10** 'cooler' (air-conditioner) **11** イタリアの pa スタ **12** カメラのメーカー **13** 日本の カラー・terebi **14** アメリカのライター **15** タク shi一のクーラー

Exercise 3.2

1 六 (rokú) (*6*) **2** 五 (gó) (*5*) **3** 十八 (juuhachí) (*18*) **4** 二十七 (níjuunana) (*27*) **5** 六十二 (rokujuuní) (*62*) **6** yón (*4*) **7** yónjuugo (*45*) **8** júuku (*19*) **9** nanájuuroku (*76*) **10** júusan (*13*)

Exercise 3.3

1 九九四九 の 二〇〇七 (kyúu kyúu yón kyúu no níi zéro zéro nána) **2** 四時半 (yóji hán) **3** 三百六十八 (sánbyaku rokujuuhachí) **4** 三二 九一 の 五六〇二 (sán níi kyúu ichi no góo rokú zéro níi) **5** ごぜん 七時 (gózen shichíji) **6** 3461-2708 (sán yón rokú ichi no níi nána zéro hachí) **7** 3594-7702 (sán góo kyúu yón no nána nána zéro níi) **8** 3208 (sán níi zéro hachí) **9** 二六の三四六五の八七九一 (níi rokú no sán yón rokú góo no hachi nána kyúu ichi) **10** 〇三の九七八六の 三三四二 (zéro sán no kyúu nána hachí rokú no sán sán yón níi)

Exercise 3.4

1 Chichí wa rokujuugósai desu. **2** Ane wa nijuukyúusai desu.
3 Háha wa yonjuuhássai desu. **4** Áni wa sanjuunísai desu.
5 Otootó wa nijuusánsai desu. **6** Sófu wa kyúujuunisai desu.
7 Sóbo wa hachijuunána desu. (Note that the suffix **–sai** is not essential in conversion when the context is clear.) **8** Imootó wa juunána (sai) desu.

Dialogue 2 (transliteration)

SÚMISU: Tanaka san, okosan wa nánnin irasshaimásu ka.
TANAKA: Uchi wa sannin désu. Otokónoko futari to onnánoko hitóri imásu. Otaku wa?

SÚMISU: Uchi mo sannin désu. Onnánoko ga futari to otokónoko ga hitóri imásu. Ue no ko wa otokónoko de, shita to mannaka wa onnánoko desu. Tanaka san no ue no okosan wa dóchira desu ka.

TANAKA: Ue wa onnánoko desu. Daigákusei desu. Mannaka no otokónoko wa kookóosei desu. Shita no ko wa máda chuugákusei desu.

SÚMISU: Uchi no kodomo wa máda chiisái desu. Ue no otokónoko wa shoogákusei desu. Futari no onnánoko wa máda yoochíen desu.

TANAKA: Sore jáa, ókusan wa máinichi oisogashíi deshóo né.

SUMISU: Soo desu. Watashi mo taihen désu.

Exercise 3.5

HONDA KAZUO: Uchi no kázoku wa sófu to sóbo, chichí to háha, áni to ane, imootó to otootó, sore ni watashi désu. Zénbu de kunin désu. Chichí wa koomúin de, háha wa shúfu desu. Áni wa kaisháin desu. Ryokoogáisha no sháin desu. Ane wa daigákusei desu. Kaimono ga sukí desu. Imootó wa chuugákusei desu. Otootó wa shoogákusei desu. Imootó mo otootó mo supóotsu ga sukí desu.

HÁRII KURÁAKU: Takusán desu né.

HONDA KAZUO: Ée. Kuráaku san wa kyóodai ga imásu ka.

HÁRII KURÁAKU: Iie, imasén. Hitoríkko desu.

1 9   **2** 1 (Harry Clark is an only child)   **3** sport   **4** civil servant
5 in a travel company   **6** shopping   **7** home duties (she is a housewife)
8 primary school

Exercise 3.6

1 Sóbo no shúmi wa ryokoo désu.   **2** Chichi no shúmi wa kéndoo desu.   **3** Háha no shúmi wa ténisu desu.   **4** Áni no shúmi wa sákkaa desu.   **5** Otootó no shúmi wa sáafin desu.   **6** Ane no shúmi wa kaimono désu.   **7** Sófu no shúmi wa dókusho desu.   **8** Imooto no shúmi wa basukettobóoru desu.

Exercise 3.7

1 Ginkoo wa nánji kara nánji made desu ka. (Ginkoo wa) gózen júuji kara gógo yóji hán made desu. 2 Mise wa nánji kara nánji made desu ka. (Mise wa) gózen júuji hán kara gógo shichíji made desu. 3 Súupaa wa nánji kara nánji made desu ka. (Súupaa wa) gózen shichíji kara gógo hachíji made desu. 4 Depáato wa nánji kara nánji made desu ka. (Depáato wa) gózen júuji hán kara gógo kúji made desu. 5 Konbíni wa nánji kara nánji made desu ka. (Konbíni wa) gózen rokúji kara gógo juuichíji hán made desu.

Exercise 3.8

1 おとうさんの　たんじょうびは　何月ですか。ちちの
たんじょうびは　四月です。　2 山川せんせいの　たんじょうび
は　何月ですか。山川せんせいの　たんじょうびは　八月です。
3 クラークさんの　おくさんの　たんじょうびは　何月ですか。
かないの　たんじょうびは　十月です。　4 お子さんの
たんじょうびは　何月ですか。こどもの　たんじょうびは
六月です。　5 おばあさんの　たんじょうびは　何月ですか。
そぼの　たんじょうびは　九月です。

Unit 4

Exercise 4.1

1 Kono hón wa tákaku nai desu. 2 Ano sukáafu wa kírei ja arimasen. 3 Kono monó wa yóku nai desu. 4 Sono hón wa watashi no dewa arimasén. 5 Háha wa génki ja arimasen. 6 Kono iro wa mezuráshiku nai desu. 7 Górufu wa sukí ja arimasén. 8 Ano kámera wa yásuku arimasén. 9 Ríi san wa Chuugokújin dewa arimasén. 10 Otooto no shúmi wa karaóke ja arimasen.

Exercise 4.2

1 Ano kiiroi nékutai o mísete kudasai. 2 Kón no sebiro o mísete kudasai. 3 Ano akai sukáato o mísete kudasai. 4 Midori no booshi o mísete kudasai. 5 Sono chairo no zubón o mísete kudasai. 6 Ano aói waishatsu o mísete kudasai. 7 Haiiro no sebiro o mísete kudasai.

8 Shirói jíinzu o mísete kudasai. **9** Sono kírei na sukáafu o mísete kudasai. **10** Moo sukóshi yasúi no o mísete kudasai.

Exercise 4.3

1 でんかせいひんうりばは　何がいに　ありますか。わかりました。
五かいですね。　**2** カメラうりばは　何がいにありますか。
わかりました。六かいですね。　**3** とけいうりばは　何がいですか。
わかりました。四かいですね。　**4** かぐうりばは　何がいにありますか。
わかりました。七かいですね。　**5** スポーツようひんうりばは
何がいですか。わかりました。三かいですね。　**6** コンピュータ
うりばは　何がいにありますか。わかりました。五かいですね。
7 ふじんのくつうりばは　何がいですか。わかりました。二かいですね。
8 しょくりょうひんうりば　は何がいですか。わかりました。
ちか一かいですね。　**9** ちゅうしゃじょうは　何がいにありますか。
わかりました。ちか二かいですね。　**10** うえきうりばは
何がいにありますか。わかりました。おくじょうですね。

Exercise 4.4

1 shoogákkoo: primary school　**2** kookoo: high school
3 yasúi hón: an inexpensive book　**4** Eigo no senséi: an English teacher
5 daigákusei: a university student

Exercise 4.5

Tanaka san to Yamamoto san wa tomodachi désu. Futaritomo Nihonjín desu. Keredomo íma wa Pári ni súnde imasu. Tanaka san wa Pári no Nihonjin-gákkoo no senséi desu. Yamamoto san no goshújin wa Nihon no ginkoo no Pári shiténchoo desu. Tanaka san mo Yamamoto san mo kaimono ga dáisuki desu. Pári ni kírei na misé ga takusán arimásu. Takái misé mo yasúi misé mo arimásu. Kyóo wa Yamamoto san wa búutsu o kaimáshita. Totemo íi búutsu desu. Itaria no monó desu.

Miss Tanaka and Mrs Yamamoto are friends. Both of them are Japanese. But they live in Paris. Mrs Tanaka is a teacher at the Japanese School in Paris. Mrs Yamamoto's husband is the manager of the Paris branch of a Japanese bank. Both Miss Tanaka and Mrs Yamamoto love shopping. In Paris there are many beautiful shops. There are both expensive and inexpensive shops. Today Mrs Yamamoto bought some boots. They are very fine boots. They are Italian ones.

Exercise 4.6

1 g 2 d 3 n 4 l 5 a (**tsuaa**, tour) 6 b 7 o 8 e 9 k
10 m 11 s 12 c 13 p (**bahha**, Bach) 14 i 15 q 16 j 17 r
18 t (**pan**, bread) 19 f 20 h

Unit 5

Exercise 5.1

1 Ashita Tanaka san ni aimásu. 2 Rainen Nihón ni ikimásu.
3 Mainichi góhan o tabemásu. 4 Sengetsu atarashíi kuruma o
kaimáshita. 5 Kinóo wa mokuyóobi deshita or Kinóo wa suiyóobi
deshita (depending on how you interpret the question).

Exercise 5.2

1 Otótoshi Róndon kara kimáshita. 2 Sarainen Chúugoku ni ikimásu.
3 Asátte wa doyóobi desu. 4 Ototói wa kayóobi deshita. 5 Kyóo wa
naniyóobi desu ka. Áa sóo desu. Mokuyóobi desu.

Exercise 5.3

1 Íma kaerimashóo ka. Shall we go back (home) now? 今かえりまし
ょうか。 2 Aói no o kaimashóo. Let's buy the blue one. あおいのを
買いましょう。 3 Nánji ni aimashóo ka. What time shall we meet?
何時に　あいましょうか。 4 Hachíji ni tabemashóo. Let's eat at
eight o'clock. 八時に　たべましょう。 5 Súgu ikimashóo ka. Shall
we go straight away? すぐ　いきましょうか。

Exercise 5.4

1 Imada senséi wa Nihon Dáigaku no Eigo no senséi desu. Professor
Imada is an English teacher at Nihon University. 2 Raishuu no
doyóobi hachíji hán ni kite kudasái. Please come next Saturday at half
past eight. 3 Yamanaka san no shita no onnánoko wa kookoo
sannénsei desu. Mr Yamanaka's youngest girl is a third-year high

school student.   4 Maishuu gétsu, ká, súi ni Nihongo no kúrasu ga
arimásu. Every week on Mondays, Tuesdays and Wednesdays I have a
Japanese class.   5 Mizu o kudasái. Please give me some water.
6 Kyóo wa okane ga arimasén. Today I don't have any money.
7 Yasúi uísukii wa amari sukí ja arimasén. I don't like cheap whisky
very much.   8 Senshuu no mokuyóobi ni Kaneda san wa Shikóku kara
kimáshita. Last Thursday Mr Kaneda came from Shikoku.

Exercise 5.5

1 Today's English class.   2 He is going skiing with his friends.
3 On Wednesday of next week.   4 At 7:30 p.m.   5 Pretty cheesed off,
I should imagine.

Exercise 5.6

1 ¥380   2 apple pie and vanilla ice cream   3 whisky   4 ¥360
5 ¥830

Unit 6

Exercise 6.1

1 Íma náni o shite imásu ka (question omitted below). Kuruma o aratte
   imásu. 今何をしていますか。くるまを あらっています。
2 Tegami o káite imasu. てがみを 書いています。
3 Nihongo o benkyoo shite imásu. 日本語を べんきょうしています。
4 Heyá o sooji shite imásu. へやを そうじしています。
5 Térebi o míte imasu. テレビを みています。
6 Tomodachi o mátte imasu. ともだちを まっています。
7 Rájio o kiite imásu. ラジオを 聞いています。
8 Shoosetsu o yónde imasu. しょうせつを 読んでいます。
9 Koohíi o nónde imasu. コーヒーを のんでいます。
10 Kéeki o tsukútte imasu. ケーキを つくっています。

Exercise 6.2

1 b   2 d   3 e   4 a   5 c

Exercise 6.3

1 Roomáji de káite kudasai. ローマじで　書いてください。
2 Chotto mátte kudasai. ちょっと　まってください。
3 Moo ichidó itte kudasái. もう一ど　いってください。
4 Sánji ni denwa shite kudasái. 三時に　でんわしてください。
5 Chízu o káite kudasai. ちず　を書いてください

Exercise 6.4

1 Q: Dóo yatte yuubínkyoku e ikimásu ka. どうやって　ゆうびん
きょくへ　行きますか。
   A: Kono michi o massúgu itte, hitotsume no shingoo o watatte
kudasái. Yuubínkyoku wa migigawa de, shingoo no kádo kara
súgu desu. このみちを　まっすぐ行って、一つめの　しんご
うを　わたってください。ゆうびんきょくは　みぎがわで、
しんごうの　かどから　すぐです。

2 Q: Dóo yatte gakkoo e ikimásu ka. どうやって学校へ行きますか。
   A: Kono michi o massúgu itte, mittsume no shingoo o migi e
magatte kudasái. Mata massúgu itte, tsugi no michi o watatte
kudasái. Suru to, gakkoo wa súgu máe ni arimásu. このみちを
まっすぐ行って、三つめの　しんごうを　みぎへ　まがって
ください。また　まっすぐ行って、つぎの　みちを　わたっ
てください。すると、学校はすぐまえ　にあります。

3 Q: Dóo yatte takushii-nóriba e ikimásu ka. どうやってタクシー
のりばへ　行きますか。
   A: Kono michi o massúgu itte, yottsume no shingoo o migi e
magatte súgu desu. Tákushii noriba wa éki no chuushajoo no máe
ni arimásu. このみちを　まっすぐ行って、四つめの　し
んごうを　みぎへ　まがってすぐです。タクシーのりばは
えきの　ちゅうしゃじょうの　まえにあります。

4 Q: Dóo yatte kooen e ikimásu ka. どうやって　こうえんへ
行きますか。
   A: Kono michi o massúgu itte, futatsume no shingoo o hidari e
magatte kudasai. Mata sono michi o massúgu itte kudasai. Kooen
wa tsukiatari desu. このみちを　まっすぐ行って、二つ
めの　しんごうを　ひだりへ　まがってください。またそのみち
を　まっすぐ行ってください。こうえんは　つきあたりです。

5 Q: Dóo yatte byooin e ikimásu ka. どうやって　びょういんへ
行きますか。

A: Kono michi o massúgu itte, hitotsume no shingoo o migi e magatte kudasái. Tsugi no kádo made arúite, oodanhódoo o watatte kudasái. Suru to byooin wa súgu máe ni arimasu. このみちを　まっすぐ行って、一つめの　しんごうをみぎ　へ　まがってください。つぎの　かどまで　あるいて、おうだんほどうを　わたってください。すると　びょういんは　すぐまえにあります。

6 Q: Dóo yatte kusuriya e ikimásu ka. どうやって　くすりやへ　行きますか。

A: Kono michi no hidarigawa o arúite, hitotsume no toorí o watatte súgu desu.このみちの　ひだりがわを　あるいて、一つめのとおりを　わたってすぐです。

7 Q: Dóo yatte hanáya e ikimásu ka. どうやって　はなやへ　行きますか。

A: Kono michi o massúgu itte, futatsume no shingoo o migi e magatte kudasái. Tsugi no shingoo máde arúite, hidari e michi o watatte kudasái. Suru to, hanáya wa manmáe ni arimasu. このみちを　まっすぐ行って、二つめの　しんごうを　みぎへ　まがってください。つぎの　しんごうまで　あるいて、ひだりへ　みちを　わたってください。　すると、はなやは　まんまえにあります。

8 Q: Dóo yatte résutoran e ikimásu ka. どうやってレストランへ　行きますか。

A: Kono michi o massúgu itte, futatsume no shingoo o migi e magatte kudasái. Tsugi no michi máde arúite, oodanhódoo o watatte kudasái. Résutoran wa sono kádo ni arimásu. このみちを　まっすぐ行って、二つめの　しんごうを　みぎへ　まがってください。つぎの　みちまで　あるいて、おうだんほどうを　わたってください。　レストランは　そのかどに　あります。

9 Q: Dóo yatte éki e ikimásu ka. どうやって駅へ行きますか。

A: Kono michi o massúgu itte, tsukiatari máde arúite kudasái. Éki wa hirói toori no mukoogawa ni arimásu. この道をまっすぐ行って、つきあたりまで歩いてくだ　さい。えきは　ひろいとおりの　むこうがわにあります。

10 Q: Dóo yatte konbini e ikimásu ka. どうやってコンビニへ行きますか。

A: Kono michi no hidarigawa o massúgu, mittsume no shingoo máde itte kudasái. Mata sono michi o massúgu itte kudasái. Soko de wataru to konbini ga arimásu. このみちの　ひだりがわを　まっすぐ、三つめの　しんごうまで　行ってくだ

さい。またそのみちをまっすぐ行ってください。そこで　わ
たると　コンビニがあります。

Exercise 6.5

1 OKYAKUSAN: Oteárai wa dóko desu ka.
  TEN'IN: Hái, josei no oteárai wa kono saki ni arimásu.
    Mázu, koko o massúgu itte kudasái.
    Soshite tsukiatari o hidari ni magatte kudasái
    Josei no oteárai wa migigawa ni arimásu.
  OKYAKUSAN: Dansei no wa?
  TEN'IN: Ha!?
  OKYAKUSAN: Dansei no oteárai no máe de tomodachi ga mátte
    imasu kara.

  CUSTOMER: *Where is the toilet?*
  SALES ASSISTANT: *Yes. The women's toilet is up this way.*
    First, go straight along here.
    And turn left at the end of the aisle.
    *Then you will find the women's toilet on your
    right.*
  OKYAKUSAN: *What about the men's?*
  TEN'IN: *Uh!?*
  OKYAKUSAN: *A friend of mine is waiting in front of the men's
    toilet.*

2 Koko o massúgu itte, tsukiatari o migi e magatte kudasái. Suru to
dansei no oteárai wa hidarigawa ni arimásu.

Exercise 6.6

1 Asako: Chuuka-ryóori ga tabetái desu.
  You: Já, issho ni tábe ni ikimashóo.
2 Asako: Éiga ga mitái desu.
  You: Já, issho ni mí ni ikimashóo.
3 Asako: Keitai-dénwa ga kaitai désu.
  You: Já, issho ni kai ni ikimashóo.
4 Asako: Róndon de Eigo o benkyoo shitai désu.
  You: Já, issho ni (Róndon e) benkyoo shi ni ikimashóo.
5 Asako: Rókku o kikitai désu.
  You: Já, issho ni kiki ni ikimashóo.

Exercise 6.7

1 all connected with music (clarinet, castanets, trombone, flute, Christmas carol) **2** food and drink (cocktail, nougat, celery, yoghurt, chocolate) **3** all connected with boats (canoe, kayak, yacht, oar, boat) **4** place names (Kenya, Senegal, Europe, Brazil, Rome) **5** not sure, perhaps because they are all enjoyable (Valentine's Day, a sale, cake, roulette, present)

Exercise 6.8

1 At the company cocktail party. **2** On Friday night last week. **3** Because he spent four years working in London. **4** He is a journalist working for the Yomiuri Shimbun. **5** They both used to work in Europe. **6** He is writing a book about cooking Italian pasta and desserts.

Senshuu no kin'yóobi no ban ni, kaisha no kakuteru páatii de Takayama san to Yasuda san ni aimáshita. Takayama san wa kisha de, Yomiuri Shinbun ni tsutómete imasu. Yasuda san wa ginkoo-man de, watashi no uchi no chikáku ni súnde imasu. Futaritomo mukashi Yooróppa de shigoto o shite imashita. Takayama san wa yonenkan Rondon ni imashita. Eigo ga totemo joozu desu. Yasuda san wa nagaku Itaria no inaka ni súnde imashita. Itari ryóori ga daisuki de, jibun de yóku tsukurimasu. Ima Itaria no pasuta to dezáato ni tsuite hón o káite imasu.

Unit 7

Exercise 7.1

1 d I'm turning in early because I'm tired. **2** b I'm hungry so I'm going to eat. **3** e I'm thirsty, so let's have a beer. **4** c I've got no money so please lend me ¥1,000. **5** a I'll take some medicine because I've got a stomach ache.

Exercise 7.2

1 Kaisha e dekakéru máe ni chooshoku o tabemásu. (I'll have breakfast before leaving for the company.) **2** Okane o irete kara botan o

oshimásu. (You press the button after putting in the money.)
3 Botan o oshite kara nomímono ga déte kimásu. (The drink comes out after you press the button.) 4 Denwa o suru máe ni denwa-bángoo o shirabemáshita. (I checked the phone number before ringing.)
5 Jogingu o shite kara sháwaa o abimásu. (I have a shower after I've been jogging.) 6 Neru máe ni sutóobu o keshite kudasái. (Please turn off the heater before you go to bed.)

Exercise 7.3

1 Básu de keitai-dénwa o tsukatte mo íi desu. Eigakan de (keitai-dénwa o) tsukatte wa damé desu. (You may use your mobile phone on the bus. You mustn't use your mobile phone in the cinema.) 2 Pén de káite mo íi desu. Enpitsu de káite wa damé desu. (You may write in pen. You mustn't write in pencil.) 3 Eigo de hanáshite mo íi desu. Nihongo de hanáshite wa damé desu. (You may speak in English. You mustn't speak in Japanese.) 4 Dóru de harátte mo ii desu. Én de harátte wa damé desu. (You may pay in dollars. You must not pay in yen.) 5 Ása sháwaa o abite mo íi desu. Yóru sháwaa o abite wa damé desu. (You may have a shower in the morning. You mustn't have a shower at night.)
6 Each of these pairs of sentences can be combined into a single sentence using ga 'but' e.g. Básu de keitai-dénwa o tsukatte mo íi desu ga, eigakan de (keitai-dénwa o) tsukatte wa damé desu. (You can use your mobile phone on the bus, but you can't in the cinema.) 7 This exercise is self-explanatory. Make your own dialogues along the lines of the model in the book.

Exercise 7.4

1 Térebi ga <u>kowárete imasu.</u> (The TV is broken.) 2 <u>Róbii no misé ga íma aite imásu ka.</u> (Are the shops in the hotel lobby open now?)
3 Iie, íma wa <u>shimátte imasu</u>. (No, they are closed now.) 4 Shokuji wa moo <u>dékite imasu ka</u>. (Is the meal ready yet?) 5 Iie, máda <u>dékite imasen</u>. (No, it's not ready yet.) 6 Ja, <u>jidoohanbáiki ga arimásu ka</u>. (Is there an automatic vending machine, then?) 7 Hái, dansei no ofúro no máe <u>ni arimásu.</u> (Yes, there is one in front of the men's bathroom.)

Exercise 7.5

Tanaka san wa Tookyoo-umare de, kotoshi nijuugo ni narimásu. Se wa hikúkute futótte imasu. Daigaku de sumóobu ni háitte imashita.

Shúmi wa íma ténisu to górufu de, ténisu wa maishuu shimasu. Sannen máe ni Tookyoo-dáigaku o sotsugyoo shite. Mainichi Shinbun-sha ni hairimáshita. Íma wa Shikóku ni tsutómete ite, rainen kara Oosaka ni kawarimásu.

1 Tokyo   2 24 (he will be 25 this year)   3 He's short and fat.   4 Sumo   5 Tokyo University   6 3 years ago   7 Every week   8 Mainichi Shinbun Company   9 Shikoku   10 He's being transferred to Osaka.

Exercise 7.6

1 E   2 F   3 A   4 D   5 C   6 B

Exercise 7.7

1 Yamamoto san to Honda san wa máinichi juuníji júugofun ni kaisha no tonari no résutoran de átte, issho ni shokuji shimásu. Mr Yamamoto and Mr Honda meet in the restaurant next door to the company everyday at 12:15 and have lunch together.   2 Aro shirói supootsukáa wa Edowáado Vinsento no atarashíi kuruma désu. That white sports car is Edward Vincent's new car.   3 Kyóo wa kuruma de kimáshita kara, arukooru o nónde wa damé desu. Today I came by car so I mustn't drink any alcohol.   4 Aóyama san wa óoki na ginkoo n tsutómete imasu. Mr Aoyama works in a large bank.   5 Yásuka san wa kírei na té oshite imasu. Yasuko has beautiful hands.   6 Watashi wa konogoro máinichi Nihonshoku o tábete imasu. These days I've been eating Japanese food every day.   7 Kyóo wa dónna shokuji ni shitai désu ka. What kind of food do you want to eat today?   8 Koko de tabako o nónode wa damé desu. You must not smoke here.

Unit 8

Exercise 8.1

1 Kinóo no shokuji wa totemo oíshikatta desu.   2 Senshuu no éiga wa amari omoshíroku nakatta desu.   3 Nihongo no shikén wa sengetsu muzukáshikatta desu.   4 Yuube no páatii wa tanóshikatta deshoo née.   5 Kinóo no okyakusan wa amari óoku nakatta desu.

Exercise 8.2

1 Ée, koko de mátta hoo ga íi desu yo.   **2** Ée, móo hajimeta hoo ga íi desu yo.   **3** Ée, háyaku ókita hoo ga íi desu.   **4** Ée, takái no o katta hoo ga íi desu.   **5** Ée, Nihongo de hanáshita hoo ga íi desu.

Exercise 8.3

1 Anóhito wa senshuu Méari san no páatii de átta Suzuki san desu.
2 Kore wa ototoi depáato de katta booshi désu.   **3** Íma yónde iru shinbun wa Asahi-shínbun desu.   **4** Kore wa watashi ga Nihongo de káita tegami désu.

Exercise 8.4

1 きのう買った本はベストセラーだそうです。   **2** きものを きている人は　だれですか。   **3** そうだんしたいことがあります。
4 きのう見たえいがは　おもしろかったですよ。   **5** 中国にもって行くもの はどれですか。

Exercise 8.5

APPLICANT: Hái, dekimásu. Jidóosha no ménkyo mo ootóbai no ménkyo mo mótte imasu.

APPLICANT: Hái, ryóori mo dekimásu. Máe ni wa Pári no hóteru de hataraita kotó ga arimásu.

APPLICANT: Itaria-ryóori ga dekimásu. Chuuka-ryóori to Tai-ryóori mo tsukúru kotó ga dekimásu.

APPLICANT: Iie, háha kara naraimáshita.

APPLICANT: Iie, Chuugokújin de wa arimasén. Nihonjín desu.

APPLICANT: Iie, hiragána to katakána dake desu. (*Or*)
Iie, hiragána to katakána shika káku kotó ga dekimasén.

APPLICANT: Hai, konpyúuta mo tsukau kotó ga dekimásu.

Exercise 8.6

1 Yamada san wa Nakagawa san yori se ga takái desu.
2 Yamamoto san wa Tanaka san yori futótte imasu.   **3** Honda san wa

Maeda san yori toshiue désu.   **4** Tákushii yori chikatetsu no hoo ga
hayái desu.   **5** Kóora wa bíiru yori yasúi desu.   **6** Tenpura wa ráamen
yori takái desu.   **7** Kyóo wa kinóo yori atatakái desu.
8 Raishuu no hoo ga tsugoo ga íi desu.

Exercise 8.7

1 New Zealand   **2** 1980   **3** she came to Japan   **4** at a small newspaper
company in Tokyo   **5** an English language newspaper for travellers
6 backpackers visiting Japan from America, Britain and Australia
7 to travel overseas   **8** she is going to Beijing

Jeen Róbaatsu san wa sén kyúuhyaku hachijúunen ni Nyuujíirando de
umaremáshita. Daigaku de yonenkan Nihongo o benkyoo shimáshita.
Daigaku o sotsugyoo shite súgu Nihón ni kimáshita. Íma wa Tokyo ni
áru chíisa na shinbunkáisha ni tsutómete imasu. Ryokoosha no tame
no eiji-shínbun desu. Ómo ni América ya Igirisu ya Oosutorária
nádo kara Nihón ni kúru wakái bakkupákkaa no hitotachi ga
yomimásu. Jeen san mo rainen kaigai-ryókoo o shitai to itte imásu. Máda
Chúugoku ni itta kotó ga nái kara, kúgatsu ni Pékin ni iku tsumori da sóo
desu.

Exercise 8.8

1 先週京都へ行って来ました。   **2** 来月田中先生と花見に行きます。
3 目の前にたくさんのきれいな花がありました。
4 午後五時半に東京駅の前でまっていてください。
5 東京は京都より大きいです。

Unit 9

Exercise 9.1

1 g   **2** h   **3** d   **4** e   **5** b   **6** a   **7** c   **8** f

Exercise 9.2

1 If you leave straight away now you will be in time.   **2** If I don't have
the car I'll walk there.   **3** If you want Japanese friends I'll introduce

you (to some).   **4** After ten o'clock the trains are empty (this is a euphemism for 'not impossibly crowded').   **5** If you are cold put on an extra blanket.   **6** If you exercise every day you'll soon lose weight.

Exercise 9.3

1 朝子さんはポテトチップスを食べながら新聞を読んでいます。
2 ゆうべ母はテレビを見ながらいねむりをしました。
3 トラックのうんてんしゅはいつもラジオを聞きながらトラックを
うんてんします。   **4** つとむさんは　うたをうたいながら　おふろに
はいっています。   **5** うちのむすこは　よく　おんがくを
聞きながら　べんきょう　します。

Exercise 9.4

1 Enpitsu ga juuníhon irimásu. I need twelve pencils.
2 Tishupéepaa sánmai kudasai. Please give me three tissues.
3 Máinichi gyuunyuu o sanbai nomimásu. Every day I drink three glasses of milk.   **4** Inú o níhiki kátte imasu. I have two dogs.
5 Doobutsúen de kirin ga nítoo umareta sóo desu. I hear two giraffes were born at the zoo.   **6** Sakanaya de chíisa na sakana sánbiki kaimáshita. I bought three small fish at the fish shop.   **7** Wáin ga nánbon nokótte imasu ka. How many bottles of wine are left?
8 Yuube tegami o santsuu kakimáshita. Last night I wrote three letters.   **9** Kinóo kuruma nándai uremáshita ka. How many cars did you sell yesterday? **10** Kamí ga nánmai hoshíi desu ka. How many sheets of paper do you want?

Exercise 9.5

1 3rd October, 1991   **2** 6th August, 1945   **3** 8th December, 1941
4 Sunday, 4th September, 1905   **5** Children's day is 5th May.

Exercise 9.6

1 Koko wa furobá desu. Koko de ofúro ni háittari, sháwaa o abitari shimásu.   **2** Koko wa oosetsuma désu. Koko de osháberi o shitári, okyakusan o séttai shitári shimasu.   **3** Koko wa daidokoro désu. Koko de tábetari, ryóori o shitári shimasu.   **4** Koko wa toshóshitsu desu. Koko de shinbun o yóndari, benkyoo shitári shimasu.   **5** Koko wa sentakuba désu. Koko de sentaku shitári, áiron o káketari shimasu.

Exercise 9.7

1 Dáre mo takarákuji ni ataranakute gakkári shimashita. We were disappointed because nobody won anything in the lottery.   **2** Uchi ni nánimo tabéru mono ga arimasén kara résutoran de shokuji shimashóo. Because there is nothing to eat at home let's eat out at a restaurant.   **3** Dáreka dóa o nókku shite imásu kara mí ni itte kudasái. Please go and have a look. There's someone knocking at the door.   **4** Dókoka shízuka na tokoro de ocha démo nomimashóo. Let's have some tea or something in a quiet spot somewhere.   **5** Ítsuka hima na toki ni uchi ni asobi ni kite kudasái. Some time when you are free please come around to my place.   **6** Ano misé wa ítsumo kónde imasu. That shop is always crowded.   **7** Nánika komátta kotó ga áttara ítsudemo itte kudasái. If you have anything worrying you please tell me any time at all.   **8** Kóndo no shuumatsu wa dókoemo ikimasén. I'm not going anywhere this weekend.

Exercise 9.8

1 Késa Yamanaka san wa Tookyoo ni tsúita sóo desu. I hear Mr Yamanaka arrived in Tokyo this morning.   **2** Shirói kamí o sánmai kudasai. Please give me three sheets of white paper.   **3** Ashita no ryokoo ni básu o nídai yoyaku shimáshita. I reserved two buses for tomorrow's trip.   **4** Eigo no senséi wa daigaku no món no máe de gakusei to hanáshite imashita. The English teacher was talking with a student in front of the university gate.   **5** Ashita no gógo úmi e doráibu ni ikimashóo ka. Shall we go for a drive to the seaside tomorrow afternoon?   **6** Ríi san, jikan ga áttara ítsuka Chúugoku no hanashí o shite kudasái. Mr Lee, when you have time please talk about China.   **7** Nihón de wa ichínen ni juugonichi no kyuujitsu ga arimásu. In Japan there are fifteen public holidays a year.   **8** Shóoto san wa kón no sebiro o kite kúru soo desu. Apparently Mr Short will come wearing a navy blue suit.   **9** Ashita kaisha o yasumítai desu. I'd like to take a day off from the company tomorrow.   **10** Mukoo ni tsúitara denwa o kudasái. When you get over there give me a ring.

Unit 10

Exercise 10.1

1 Haruo kun wa jáanarisuto ni náru tsumori désu.   2 Rie san wa Eigo no kyóoshi ni náru tsumori désu.   3 Jun kun wa isha ni náru tsumori désu.   4 Sachie san wa shéfu ni náru tsumori désu.   5 Tomoko san wa óngaku no sensei ni náru tsumori désu.

Exercise 10.2

1 Shéfu ni naritákereba minarai ni itta hóo ga íi desu.   2 Okane ga takusán hoshíkereba, úmaku tooshi o shita hóo ga íi desu.   3 Jikan ga nákereba áto ni shitára dóo desu ka.   4 Jibun de dekinákereba hito ni tanóndara ikága desu ka.   5 Nedan ga tákakereba betsu no misé ni mo itta hóo ga íi deshoo.

Exercise 10.3

1 フランコさんは中国語が話せますか。   2 フランコさん、こんばんパスタガつくれますか。   3 木よう日にパンダを見に、どうぶつえんへ行けますか。   4 しおからやうめぼしが食べられますか。
5 日本語が読めますか。

Exercise 10.4

1 Q: Okyakusama no handobággu wa dónna iro desu ka.
　A: Kuró desu.
2 Q: Dónna katachi desu ka.
　A: Shikakú desu.
3 Q: Dónna mono ga háitte imashita ka.
　A: Hyaku póndo ga háitte iru saifu to kurejitto-káado to teikíken ga háitte imasu.

Exercise 10.5

1 A: My throat hurts and I have a cough so I'd like to leave (literally, 'go home') early. Would that be all right?
　B: Yes. Perhaps it's a cold. Take care.
　A: Thank you very much.

2 A: I slipped and fell over. See how swollen it is (literally, 'it has swollen up this much').

   B: Perhaps it's a break. Let's take an X-ray and have a look.

3 A: I need some medication for a headache in a hurry. Where would they sell it, I wonder?

   B: Hm, today's a holiday, isn't it. But perhaps they sell it at the convenience store.

   A: Then, I'll just go and see.

Exercise 10.6

1 Do you know young Yamaguchi's mother and father?   2 No I don't know them. Where do they live?   3 Can you go in from the side? No, that's the exit.   4 The front entrance is not open.   5 In that case, there is nothing for it but to wait until the time when the front gate opens.
6 The '**bun**' character in **shinbun** (newspaper) is a character in which '**mon**' (gate) and '**mimi**' (ear) are written together.   7 Yasuko's small, white ears looked like flowers.   8 Open your mouth wide and stick out your tongue.

Unit 11
Exercise 11.1

1 Amari átsuku nai kísetsu ni itta hóo ga íi desu.   2 Densha ga amari kónde inai toki ni notta hóo ga íi desu.   3 Amari amaku nái desáato ga sukí desu.   4 Jímu ni ikanai hi wa doyóobi to nichiyóobi desu.
5 Kónban kónai hito ga nanninka imásu.

Exercise 11.2

2, 4, 5, 8

Exercise 11.3

1 f   2 d   3 e   4 b   5 c   6 a

Exercise 11.4

1 Tabako o suwanai kotó ni shimásu. **2** Amai mono no kawari ni kudámono o tabéru kotó ni shimásu. **3** Osake no ryóo o herasu kotó ni shimásu. **4** Máinichi undoo (o) suru kotó ni shimásu. **5** Mótto sakana ya yasai o tabéru kotó ni shimásu.

Exercise 11.5

1 すべら **2** おくれない **3** わすれ

Exercise 11.6

1 c **2** a **3** d **4** e **5** b

Exercise 11.7

1 Miss Abe is looking for something a bit out of the ordinary. **2** She is worried about safety because she has never flown in a helicopter before. She also thinks a helicopter flight might be too expensive. **3** The concierge said the helicopter flight was (1) great fun, (2) safe and (3) the best way to see the scenery. **4** It was too expensive and she had not had the opportunity to fly in Japan. **5** Because it was half the price of a similar flight in Japan.

Exercise 11.8

1 Let's walk back (home) through the snow. **2** Southern Japan is hotter than the north. **3** Let's decide not to go if the weather is bad. **4** I'm thinking of travelling through western Japan in the spring holidays. **5** From the evening the wind became stronger and it started to rain. **6** It's cold so you had better wear a slightly warmer sweater. **7** (Literally) Apparently in summer the people who come to the sea in this area are extremely numerous. **8** The high mountain opposite looks beautiful bathed in the sunlight of the setting sun in autumn. **9** As there wasn't much snow this winter I didn't go skiing. **10** About how many minutes does it take to walk from the southern entrance to Tokyo station to the northern entrance?

Unit 12

Exercise 12.1

1 agemáshita **2** kudasaimáshita **3** itadaki **4** moraimáshita
5 yarimáshita

Exercise 12.2

1 フランスの香水をもらいました。 Kaya got some French perfume
from Hiroshi. **2** ネックレスをあげました。 Akio gave Kaya a
necklace. **3** お金をくれました／くださいました。 My parents gave
me money. **4** きれいな花をもらいました。 She got some beautiful
flowers (from her boyfriend). **5** つくってくれました／くださいました。
My mother made me a birthday cake.

Yóoko san,
Ogénki desu ka. Shídonii wa dandan haruméite kimashita. Niwa niwa
iroiro na haná ga saite ite taihen kírei desu.
　　Kyóo wa kúgatsu yokka de, watashi no nijússai no tanjóobi desu.
Uchiwa sannin kyodai desu. Watashi wa mannaka de ue to shita ni ani to
otooto ga arimasu. Ani no namae wa Hiroshi de, kotoshi nijuusan sai
desu. Otooto wa juuku de, Akio to yuu namae desu. Tanjóobi ni kázoku
kara iroiro na purézento o moraimáshita. Ryóoshin kara wa okane o
moraimáshita. Áni wa Furansu no koosui o kuremáshita. Otootó no Akio
wa nékkuresu o kuremashita. Watashi no boifuréndo wa kírei na haná o
motte kite kuremáshita. Háha wa tanjoobi kéeki o tsukútte kuremashita.
Watashi no sukí na chokoreeto-kéeki deshita. Yuru wa, kazoku to issho
ni chuuka-ryoori o tabeni ikimashita. Totemo íi tanjóobi deshita. Ashita
wa chichi no hi desu. Nihon nimo chichi no higa arimasuka? Watashi no
chichi wa itsumo furui shatsu bakari kite iru node atarashii shatsu o katte
agemashita. Ki ni itte kureru ka doo ka chotto shinpai shite imasu. Saizu
wa tabun daijoobu da to omoimasu.
　　Watashi no daigaku wa raishuu kara hajimarimásu. Sukóshi
isogáshiku narisóo desu.
　　Sore dé wa, mata tegami o kakimásu. Minásama ni yoroshiku.
Kaya

Exercise 12.3

1 How did you respond when asked if you would like to go to Kyoto?
2 Have you ever eaten sashimi? **3** What work you said you would
like to do in the future. **4** Would like to try some sake. **5** What
kinds of things do you want to see in Japan?

Exercise 12.4

1 c **2** e **3** b **4** a **5** d

Exercise 12.5

1 Iie, potetochíppusu wa móo katte arimásu. **2** Ée, tomatosóou
wa máda katte arimasén kara katte oite kudasái. **3** Iie, kyúuri
mo máda katte arimasén. **4** Arígatoo gozaimásu. Rémon wa
katte arimasén kara motte kite kudasái. **5** Ée, sutéeki wa móo katte
arimásu.

Exercise 12.6

sagáshite iru ('*you are looking for*'); **oite oita** ('*I left it on the table to
use later*'); **itte kúru** ('*I'll go and get something*', literally 'I'll go and
come back'); **katte koyóo** ('*shall I buy?*'); **to omótte** ('*I think I will…*'
sentence incomplete to give time for wife to respond); **irete átta** ('*had
been put in*'); **nónde shimatta** ('*we drank it all up*'); **shimátte iru** ('*are
closed*'); **utte iru** ('*they sell*' – habitual state); **itte míru** ('*I'll try going
there*'); **katte kite** ('*buy and bring back*'); **itte kúru** ('*I'm going [and
coming back]*'); **itterasshái** (short for **itte irasshái**) '*goodbye*' – literally,
'please go and come back'. I make it fourteen –**te** forms. How many did
you find?

Exercise 12.7

1 hazu **2** béki **3** hazu **4** béki **5** hazu **6** béki

Exercise 12.8

1 Today the weather is superb with not a single cloud in the blue sky.
2 The chief of the overseas division of Yamashita Electrical is now

travelling around Aomori and Akita.   **3** As the sky suddenly clouded over and it looked as if it was going to rain we hurried home.   **4** I think the name of the person standing behind Company President Morita is Kobayashi Yooko.   **5** Although the sky is cloudy they say there is no fear of rain.   **6** Professor Oobayashi looks well, doesn't he? **7** Apparently this is a famous sake from Akita.   **8** The foreign students in national universities have been increasing every year.

Unit 13

Exercise 13.1

1 She hurt her neck and lower back. Kubi to koshi ga ítaku narimáshita.   **2** She is attending a clinic for regular treatment. Chiryoo ni kayotte imásu.   **3** No, she has put it in for repair. Iie, shúuri ni dashimáshita.   **4** She thinks the other party will pay everything. Aite ga zenbu haráu to omótte imasu.   **5** She says it is inconvenient not having the car for shopping. Kaimono no toki kuruma ga nái to fúben da to itte imásu.   **6** She offers to give her a lift next time she goes shopping. Tsugí ni kaimono ni iku toki tsurete itte ageru to itte imásu.

Exercise 13.2

1 e I was caught in the rain on my way to work.   **2** d I was told by the doctor to take more exercise.   **3** a Sake is made from rice.   **4** b I was praised for my Japanese.   **5** c I had my wallet stolen when I was abroad.

Exercise 13.3

1 Jón san wa joodan o itte hito o warawasemásu. John tells jokes and makes people laugh.   **2** Yuushoku no shitaku wa watashi ni sasete kudasái. Please let me prepare the evening meal.   **3** Shinpai sasete sumimasén. I'm sorry I made you worry.   **4** Tsugí wa boku ni harawásete kudasái. Next time please let me pay.   **5** Kono konpyúuta o chótto tsukawasete kudasái. Please let me use this computer for a minute. **6** Háisha de ichijíkan íjoo matasaremáshita. I was kept waiting for more than an hour at the dentist's.   **7** Kodomo no toki ni múri ni tabesaseráreta no de, yasai ga kirai ná n' desu. I don't like vegetables because I was forced to eat them as a child.   **8** Konogoro osoku máde shigoto o saseraremásu. Lately I've been made to work until late.

Exercise 13.4

1 Yumi and Yoshie are friends. They are looking at clothes together in the clothing department of a department store.
YUMI: Would this coat suit me, I wonder?
YOSHIE: Yes, it looks as if it would suit you. Why not just try it on?

2 Yumi and Yoshie are feeling hungry. They are discussing what to eat as they peruse the display window in the department store restaurant.
YUMI: Let's see, that looks good. I'll have *tenpura*.
YOSHIE: I'll have eel.

3 Yumi is looking for an apartment. She is talking to Yoshie about the apartment she saw yesterday.
YOSHIE: How was the apartment you saw yesterday?
YUMI: It has its own bath and toilet and is conveniently located near the station.
YOSHIE: That sounds good. Are you going to settle on that?
YUMI: I think I'll make up my mind after I've looked around a little more.

4 Yumi and Yoshie are choosing a present for their teacher.
YUMI: How would this scarf be, I wonder?
YOSHIE: Ah, that's very tasteful. It looks like the sort of thing the professor would like.
YUMI: A bit conservative, don't you think?
YOSHIE: Yes, perhaps a slightly brighter one would be better.
YUMI: Oh! It looks like rain. Shall we head home in a minute?

Exercise 13.5

1 He thought perhaps she had forgotten about the appointment.
2 Takeo rang Akiko's home.
3 Nobody was home to answer the phone.
4 They waited for over an hour.
5 A: Chótto sumimasén. Kore no yarikata o oshiete kudasái.
   B: Ée, íi desu yo. Sukóshi fukuzatsu désu ga…
6 A: Chótto sumimasén. Éki e no ikikata o oshiete kudasái.
   B: Ée, íi desu yo. Sukóshi yayakoshíi desu ga…
7 A: Chótto sumimasén. Makizúshi no tsukurikata o oshiete kudasái.
   B: Ée, íi desu yo. Kotsu o oshiete agemásu.
8 A: Chótto sumimasén. Kippu no kaikata o oshiete kudasái.
   B: Ée, íi desu yo. Koko ni okane o irete, kono botan o osu dake désu.

Exercise 13.6

1 Mr Kimura's desk is the second desk from the window over there.
2 She wants to discuss accommodation with someone at the centre.
3 Self-catering apartments are the most expensive.   **4** Geshuku is a
boarding house with shared bathroom facilities and two meals a day
provided six days per week.   **5** She asked him to take her to see the
boarding house (geshuku).   **6** She wanted to see what the
accommodation was like inside.

Exercise 13.7

1 False   **2** True   **3** False   **4** True   **5** False   **6** False   **7** True
8 True

1 Heyá ga chiisakátta no de, Méarii wa gakkári shimashita.   **2** Méarii
no heyá wa hirókute nagamé mo íi desu.   **3** Dóoro no otó ga ki ni
naramáshita.   **4** Mádo kara kírei na niwa to kooen ga miemásu.
5 Shokudoo wa Méarii no heya no súgu ue ni arimásu.   **6** Méarii no
heya ni basutóire ga tsúite imasu.   **7** Ofúro wa bekkan ni arimásu.
8 Mongén ga nái no de, hotte shita deshóo.

Exercise 13.8

1 Which do you prefer, beef or pork?   **2** I met my friend in front of the
cinema.   **3** A kind person brought (back) the wallet I dropped.   **4** Near
my friend's house there is a shop which sells Japanese swords.   **5** Please
use the exits to your left and right.   **6** When I made a trip abroad in the
autumn I returned with all sorts of things I had bought.   **7** Although she
(he) is small she (he) is strong.   **8** According to linguists there are many
dialects in Japanese.

Unit 14
Exercise 14.1

1 Mr Nakamura rings Professor Akimoto to seek information for a story
he is writing on Sino-Japanese relations.   **2** Because the professor is
leaving for Vietnam on Friday.   **3** Monday, 14th March.   **4** He needs

to go away to check his appointment diary.   **5** The agree to meet at 9:00 a.m. on Monday, 14 March.

Exercise 14.2

1 e   **2** c   **3** a   **4** b   **5** d

Exercise 14.3

1 kimáshita (imáshita is also possible if we assume the sentence could mean, '*When were you here?*')   **2** ikimásu (kimásu is also possible if the sentence is taken as an invitation)   **3** imásu is most likely (but given the right context ikimásu or kimásu are also possible)   **4** désu   **5** imásu   **6** shite imásu

Exercise 14.4

1 Ítsu goryokoo ni odekake désu ka.   **2** Dónna (go)kenkyuu o shite irasshaimásu ka.   **3** Dóchira ni osumai désu ka.   **4** Okaban o omochi shimashóo ka.   **5** Ítsu (goro) Amérika kara káette irasshaimásu ka.

Exercise 14.5

1 densha hodo   **2** osake hodo   **3** osake gúrai   **4** Tookyoo hodo jinkoo ga   **5** chichí yori

Exercise 14.6

1 Ashita kói to iwaremáshita. I was told to come tomorrow.   **2** Róbii de máte to iimáshita. He said to wait in the lobby.   **3** Senséi wa séito ni yóku benkyoo shiro to iimáshita. The teacher told the pupil to study hard.   **4** Densha no náka de keitai-dénwa o tsukau na to yuu anaúnsu ga arimáshita. There was an announcement (saying) not to use mobile phones on the train.   **5** Asoko de chuusha suru na to káite arimashita. There was a sign (literally, 'it was written') that you should not park there.

Exercise 14.7

1 Two medium mugs of beer and two glasses of mineral water.   **2** They all had vegetable soup.   **3** Steamed lobster and boiled crab.   **4** They decided to share the lobster and crab between four.   **5** They settled on a dry Australian white to go with the seafood because the waiter said it was highly regarded.

Exercise 14.8

1 It was a long time ago when I studied western music at the University of the Arts in downtown Tokyo.   **2** 'How do you read the four character station name written on this piece of paper?' 'Oh, this is Takadanobaba. Takadanobaba is a station on the Tokyo Yamanote line and is the place where the famous Waseda University is.'   **3** How I'd love to be on a horse galloping over that broad field.   **4** Write you parents' names and address here please. (*Note*: in Japanese it is usual to put address before name.)   **5** It is not easy working day and night in the factory.   **6** The Atlantic Ocean is not as wide as the Pacific.   **7** Although she is ill, in company she never shows the slightest sign of being depressed. (literally, 'does not show people the slightest dark feeling'.)   **8** In Aomori and Akita prefectures the winters are long and it snows for many months.

Unit 15

Exercise 15.1

1 I can hold a simple conversation, but I still have not mastered the basic grammar.   **2** To advance, the best thing to do is increase your vocabulary.   **3** At the elementary level we introduced the kind of words you use in everyday conversation.   **4** To move up to the advanced level it is important to put in sustained effort.   **5** If you know the vocabulary pertaining to current world events, your topics of conversation become richer and more varied.

Exercise 15.2

1 Watashi wa sarudoshi désu. (I was born under the sign of the monkey, how about you?)   **2** Kotoshi wa umadoshi dé, rainen wa hitsujidoshi désu.   **3** Tora to sáru to tatsu no hoka no doobutsu wa minna watashi no kuni ni imásu.   **4** Mukashi no hitóbito wa tatsu ga hontóo ni sonzai suru doobutsu da to shínjite ita kara désu.
5 Toradoshi no hito no tokuchoo wa nán desu ka.

Exercise 15.3

1 You can also study fine art at the Tokyo University of the Arts. **2** I was surprised to find the cultural level of this town is quite high. **3** In summer I like drinking draft beer in Tokyo's rooftop beer gardens. **4** These days I often travel both within Japan and abroad. **5** This morning the scholar of Ainu culture arrived safely from Hokkaido. **6** The temple in question (**sono**) was located in an extremely inconvenient (inaccessible) place.
7 Stories of geisha often appear in Japanese literature and poetry. **8** The vegetables from the market in front of the station are cheap and fresh.
9 The shop assistants in that shop are almost all young people doing part-time work. **10** If it clears up tomorrow, let's try going to the next town.

Grammar summary

Summary of the verb, adjective and copula

Verb: suffixes attached to the root[1]

Suffix	Accented consonant-root kák– 'to write'	Unaccented consonant-root ka(w)[2]– 'to buy'	Accented vowel-root tábe– 'to eat'	Unaccented vowel-root ake– 'to open'	Irregular verbs su–/shi– 'to do'	kú–/kó– 'to come'
INDECLINABLE[3]						
–(r)u present	káku '(I) write'	kau '(I) buy'	tabéru '(I) eat'	akeru '(I) open it'	suru '(I) do'	kúru '(I) come'
–(r)éba conditional	kákeba 'if (I) write'	kaéba 'if (I) buy'	tabéreba 'if (I) eat'	akeréba 'if (I) open it'	suréba 'if (I) do'	kúréba 'if (I) come'
–(y)óo propositive/ conjectural	kakóo 'let's write'	kaóo 'let's buy'	tabeyóo 'let's eat'	akeyóo 'let's open it'	shiyóo 'let's do (it)'	koyóo 'let's come'
–e brusque imperative	káke 'Write!'	kaé 'Buy!'				
–ro/–yo imperative			tabéro/ tabéyo 'Eat!'	akeró/ akeyo 'Open it!'	shiró/séyo 'Do it!'	(kói) 'Come!'
DECLINABLE[4]						
–e potential	kakéru '(I) can write'	kaeru '(I) can buy'	uses passive	uses passive	uses dekíru	uses passive

Suffix	Accented consonant-root kák– 'to write'	Unaccented consonant-root ka(w)[2]– 'to buy'	Accented vowel-root tábe– 'to eat'	Unaccented vowel-root ake– 'to open'	Irregular verbs	
					su–/shi– 'to do'	kú–/kó– 'to come'
–(r)are– passive	kakaréru '(it) is written'	kawareru '(it) is bought'	taberaréru '(it) is eaten'	akerareru '(it) is opened'	sareru '(it) is done'	koraréru '(I'm) put out when someone comes'
–(s)ase–/ –(s)as– causative	kakaséru 'make/let write'	kawaseru 'make/let buy'	tabesaséru 'make/let eat'	akesaseru 'make/let open'	saseru 'make/let do'	kosaseru 'make/let come'
–(s)aserare– –(s)asare– passive of causative	kakase-raréru '(I) am made to write'	kawase-rareru '(I) am made to buy'	tabesase-raréru '(I) am made to eat'	akesase-raréru '(I) am made to open it'	saserareru '(I) am made to do it'	kosase-rareru '(I) am made to come'
–(a)na– negative	kakánai '(I) don't write'	kawanai '(I) don't buy'	tabénai '(I) don't eat'	akenai '(I) don't open'	shinai '(I) don't do it'	kónai '(I) don't do it'

Notes:

1. Suffixes with an initial consonant lose that consonant when the root ends in a consonant. Suffixes with an initial vowel lose that vowel when the root ends in a vowel.
2. The root consonant –w is only written before **a**.
3. The indeclinable suffixes come at the end of the verb and have no further suffixes attached to them. They may, however, be followed by clause-final or sentence-final particles.
4. The declinable suffixes occur in combination with other suffixes. Here they appear in the examples combined with the present-tense suffix, –(r)u, for suffix verbs and –i for suffix adjectives.

Verb: suffixes attached to the stem[1]

Suffix	Accented consonant-root kák– 'to write'	Unaccented consonant-root kaw– 'to buy'	Accented vowel-root tábe– 'to eat'	Unaccented vowel-root ake– 'to open'	Irregular verbs	
					su–/shi– 'to do'	kú–/kó– 'to come'
INDECLINABLE[2] (none) connective	káki '(I) write and…'	kai '(I) buy and…'	tábe '(I) eat and…'	ake '(I) open and…'	shi '(I) do and…'	kúru '(I) come'

	kaki-	kai-	tabe-	ake-	shi-	ki-
-agara Simultaneous action, 'while'	kakinágara 'while (I) write'	kainagara 'while (I) buy'	tabenágara 'while (I) eat'	akenagara 'while (I) open'	shinagara 'while (I) do'	kinágara 'while (I) come'
-e[3] Gerund	káite 'writing'	katte 'buying'	tábete 'eating'	akete 'opening'	shite 'doing'	kite 'coming'
-a Past	káita 'wrote'	katta 'bought'	tábeta 'ate'	aketa 'opened'	shita 'did'	kita 'came'
-ára[3] Conditional	káitara 'if (I) wrote'	katára 'if (I) bought'	tábetara 'if (I) ate'	aketára 'if (I) opened'	shitára 'if (I) did'	kitara 'if (I) came'
-ári[3] Frequentative/alternative	káitari 'writing' etc.	kattári 'buying' etc.	tábetari 'eating' etc.	aketári 'opening' etc.	shitári 'doing' etc.	kitari 'coming' etc.
-sái Imperative	kakinasái 'Write!'	kainasái 'Buy!'	tabenasái 'Eat!'	akenasái 'Open it!'	shinasái 'Do it!'	kinasái 'Come!'
-oo (da) 'look as if something will happen'	kakisóo 'looks about to write'	kaisoo 'looks about to buy'	tabesóo 'looks about to eat'	akesoo 'looks about to open'	shisoo 'looks about to do'	kisóo 'looks about to come'
-ata 'way of ...ing'	kakikatá 'way of writing'	kaikata 'way of buying'	tabekatá 'way of eating'	akekata 'way of opening'	shikata 'way of doing'	kikatá 'way of coming'
INDECLINABLE[4]						
-násu Polite address	kakimásu '(I) write'	kaimásu '(I) buy'	tabemásu '(I) eat'	akemásu '(I) open it'	shimásu '(I) do it'	kimásu '(I) come'
... ni náru Subject honorific	okaki ni náru 'a respected person writes'	okai ni náru 'a respected person buys'	otabe ni náru[5] 'a respected person opens'	oake ni náru 'a respected person opens'	nasáru 'a respected person does'	(oide ni náru) 'a respected person comes'
... suru Subject honorific	okaki suru '(I) write to/for a respected person'			oake suru (?) '(I) open it for a respected person'		
-wáru etc. Compound verbs	kakiowáru '(I) finish writing'	kaiowáru '(I) finish buying'	tabeowáru '(I) finish eating'			
-ai Desiderative	kakitái 'I want to write'	kaitai 'I want to buy'	tabetái 'I want to eat'	aketai 'I want to open'	shitai 'I want to do it'	kitái 'I want to come'

Suffix	Accented consonant-root kák– 'to write'	Unaccented consonant-root kaw– 'to buy'	Accented vowel-root tábe– 'to eat'	Unaccented vowel-root ake– 'to open'	Irregular verbs	
					su–/shi– 'to do'	kú–/kó– 'to come'
–yasúi 'easy to'	kakiyasúi 'easy to write'	kaiyasúi 'easy to buy'	tabeyasúi 'easy to eat'	akeyasúi 'easy to open'	shiyasúi 'easy to do it'	kiyasúi 'easy to come'
–nikúi 'difficult to'	kakinikúi 'difficult to write'	kainikúi 'difficult to buy'	tabenikúi 'difficult to eat'	akenikúi 'difficult to open'	shinikúi 'difficult to do it'	kinikúi 'difficult to come'

Notes:

1. The stem is formed by adding –i to the root of consonant-root verbs, but verbs with final –t and have stems ending in –chi and –shi respectively, e.g. mát– 'to wait' has the stem máchi and haná 'to talk' becomes hanáshi.
2. The indeclinable suffixes come at the end of the verb and have no further suffixes attached to them. They may, however, be followed by clause-final or sentence-final particles.
3. These suffixes, all beginning with –t, fuse with the final syllable of the verb stem undergoing sou change in the process. These changes can be seen, for example, in the formation of the –te form, gerund, as follows:-

   káki + –te becomes káite   writing
   isógi + –te becomes isóide   hurrying
   kai + –te becomes katte   buying
   máchi + –te becomes mátte   waiting
   káeri + –te becomes káette   returning home
   yómi + –te becomes yónde   reading
   tobi + –te becomes tonde   flying
   shini + –te becomes shinde   dying

   The vowel-root verbs, irregular verbs and consonant-root verbs with stems ending in –shi simply a these suffixes without change, e.g. tábete 'eating', kite 'coming', shite 'doing', hanáshite 'talking', e
4. The declinable suffixes occur in combination with other suffixes. Here they appear in the exampl combined with the present-tense suffix –(r)u, for suffix verbs and –i for suffix adjectives.
5. This verb, while possible, is usually replaced by the honorific verb meshiagaru 'to eat'.

Adjective

Suffix	Accented root taká– 'high'	Unaccented root aka– 'red'
–i present	takái 'is high'	akai 'is red'
–ku adverbial	tákaku 'high(ly)'	akaku 'red(ly)'
–ku nai negative	tákaku nai 'not high'	akaku nái 'not red'

–kute gerund	**tákakute** *'high and...'*	**akákute** *'red and...'*
–katta past	**tákakatta** *'was high'*	**akákatta** *'was red'*
–kattara conditional 1	**tákakattara** *'if high'*	**akákattara** *'if red'*
–kereba conditional 2	**tákaereba** *'if high'*	**akákereba** *'if red'*

Copula

Tense	Plain	Polite
Present *'is/am/are'*	**dá**[1]	**désu**
Past *'was/were'*	**dátta**	**déshita**
Conditional *'if... were'*	**dáttara**	**déshitara**
Conjectural *'probably is'*, etc.	**daróo**	**deshóo**
Gerund *'is/am/are...and'*	**dé**	**(déshite)**[2]
Negative *'is/am/are not'*	**de (wa) nái** **ja nái**	**de (wa) arimasén** **ja arimasén**

Notes:
1. The formal copula **de áru**, which follows the pattern of **áru**, may occur in either the plain or polite styles, but in spoken Japanese its use is largely confined to speech-making.
2. This form is used where extremely polite language is called for. **dé** is usually sufficient.

Particles

The following phrase-final particles follow nouns.

wa topic marker – *'as for...'*, *'speaking of...'*, *'as far as...is concerned'* (written with **hiragána 'ha'**)

> **Kore wa hón desu.**　　　*This is a book.*

ga subject marker (object marker with stative verbs and adjectives)

> **Dóre ga Tanaka san no hón desu ka.**　　　*Which is your book, Mr Tanaka?*

o object marker; shows path of action with motion verbs (written with **hiragána 'wo'**)

Sono hón o mísete kudasái. *Please show me that book.*

Umibe o arúite imasu. *He is walking along the beach.*

no possessive marker; noun qualifier – '*of*'

Kore wa watashi no hón desu. *This is my book.*

ni indirect object; goal, locative with existential verbs – '*to*', '*in*'

Tanaka san ni hón o agemáshita. *I gave Mr Tanaka a book.*

de locative with action verbs; instrument – '*at*', '*in*'; '*with*', '*by means of*'

Kono hón o Tookyoo de kaimáshita. *I bought this book in Tokyo.*

mo '*too*', '*also*'

Sore mo watashi no hón desu. *That's my book too.*

démo '*even*'

Hón demo tákaku narimashita ne. *Even books have become expensive, haven't they?*

to '*and*'

Hón to bóorupen o kaimáshita. *I bought a book and a ball-point pen.*

ya '*and*', '*such things as…*'. – links items in a logical category or series

Hón ya zasshi o kaimáshita. *I bought books and magazines.*

nádo '*and so on*', '*etc.*'

Enpitsu ya bóorupen nádo o kaimáshita. *I bought pencils, ball-point pens, etc.*

e direction marker – '*to*', '*towards*' (written with **hiragána 'he'**)

Tookyoo e ikimásu. *I go to Tokyo.*

made destination marker; upper extent – '*up to*', '*as far as*', '*until*'; '*even*'

Kádo made issho ni arukimásu. *I'll walk with you up to the corner.*

kara departure marker – '*from*'

Básu wa dóko kara demásu ka. *Where does the bus leave from?*

yóri comparison marker – '*than*'

Tookyoo wa Róndon yori bukka ga takái desu.	*Prices are more expensive in Tokyo than in London.*
Táda yori takái mono wa arimasén.	*There is nothing more expensive than what you receive* (for) *free.*

dake '*extent*'; '*only*', '*alone*'

Sore dake de wa tarimasén.	*That alone is not enough* (literally, 'With that only it does not suffice').

gurai '*about*'

Nikágetsu gúrai koko ni iru tsumori désu.	*I intend to be here for about two months.*

hodo '*extent*'; '*only*', '(not) *that much*'

Kyóo wa kinoo hodo átsuku arimasén deshita.	*Today was not as hot as yesterday.*

bákari '*to the extent of*' , '*as much as*', '*as many as*', '*only*', '*just*'

Sannen bákari Nyuuyóoku ni súnde imashita.	*I lived in New York for three years.*

The particle **no** combines with a number of nouns indicating location to give 'postpositional phrases' equivalent to English prepositions.

no ue ni '*on top of*', '*on*'

Jísho wa tsukue no ue ni arimásu.	*The dictionary is on the table.*

no shitá ni '*under*', '*below*'

Kagí o ishí no shita ni iremáshita.	*I put the key under the stone.*

no máe ni '*in front of*'

Ginkoo no máe ni imásu.	*He is in front of the bank.*

no ushiro ni '*behind*'

Shashin no ushiro ni kakimáshita.	*I wrote it on the back of the photograph.*

no náka ni '*inside*'

Hikidashi no náka ni iremáshita.	*I put it into the drawer.*

no sóto ni '*outside*'

> **Pósuto wa yuubínkyoku no sóto ni arimásu.**
>
> *The post-box is outside the post office.*

no aida ni '*between*'

> **Kánojo wa futari no otokonohitó no aida ni suwatte imáshita.**
>
> *She was sitting between two men.*

no migigawa ni '*on the right-hand side of*', '*to the right of*'

> **Chuuka-ryooríya no migigawa ni arimásu.**
>
> *It's on the right-hand side of the Chinese restaurant.*

no chikaku ni '*near*'

> **Daigaku no chikáku ni hón'ya ga takusán arimasu.**
>
> *There are many bookshops near the university.*

Clause particles (conjunctions)

to '*when*', '*whenever*', '*if*'

> **Tegami o kaku to te ga ítaku narimásu.**
>
> *When (I) write letters my hand gets sore.*

toki '*when*', '*time when*'
('*when*' clauses ending in **toki** are actually adjectival clauses with the verb qualifying the noun **toki**, '*time*').

> **Tegami o káku toki kono pen o tsukaimásu.**
>
> *When I write letters I use this pen.*

máe ni '*before*'

> **Irassháru máe ni denwa o kudasái.**
>
> *Before you come please give me a ring.*

no de '*because*', '*since*'

> **Tegami o kaku no de pen o kashite kudasai.**
>
> *Please lend me a pen because I'm going to write a letter.*

mono no '*although*' (written)

> **Tegami o káita mono no, shoochi shinákatta.**
>
> *Although I wrote a letter he did not agree* (to what I asked).

no ni '*although*'

> **Tegami o káita no ni hénji o**   *Although I wrote a letter he did*
> **shite kuremasén deshita.**   *not give me a reply.*

áto de '*after*' (follows the plain past form of the verb)

> **Tegami o káita áto de shinbun o**   *After writing the letter I read*
> **yomimáshita.**   *the newspaper.*

nára '*if*'

> **Tegami o káku nára kyóo káita**   *If you are writing a letter*
> **hoo ga íi desu.**   *you'd better write it today.*

Verbal suffixes in subordinate clauses

–te '*and*' (gerund). See the section on verbs below for other uses of
the **–te** form.

> **Tegami o káite dashimáshita.**   (I) *wrote a letter and posted it.*

–te wa (ikemasen) '*must not*'

> **Koko de tabako o sutté wa ikemasen.**   *You can't smoke here.*

–te mo íi desu '*may*'

> **Koko de tabako o sutté mo íi desu ka.**   *May I smoke here?*

–te kara '*after*'

> **Tegami o káite kara**   (I) *went out after writing a*
> **dekakemáshita.**   *letter.*

–tara '*when*', '*if*' (conditional)

> **Tegami o káitara yorokóbu deshoo.**   *If* (you) *write a letter*
>   (he) *will be pleased.*

–tari '*doing…over and over*', '*doing A then doing B*' (frequentative/
alternative)

> **Tegami o káitari hón o yóndari**   (I) *wrote letters and read*
> **shimáshita.**   *books and so on.*

–(r)eba '*if*' (conditional)

> **Tegami o kákeba wakátta**   *If* (I) *had written a letter* (she)
> **deshoo.**   *would have understood.*

–nagara '*doing A while also doing B*' (simultaneous action)

> **Tegami o kakinágara rajio o kiite imáshita.** — *While writing the letter I was listening to the radio.*

Verb plus noun plus désu

A number of nouns combine with **désu** (and its related forms) in final predicates to give an added nuance to the main verb.

tsumori desu '*intend to…*'

> **Háyaku neru tsumori désu.** — *I intend to go to bed early.*

yotei désu '*plan to…*'

> **Sánji ni tátsu yotei désu.** — *I plan to leave at 3 o'clock.*

no désu or **n' désu** '*the fact is…*,' (makes a link with the previous sentence)

> **Dóoshite kuruma o urú n' desu ka.** — *Why are you selling your car then?*

wáke desu '*that is to say…*' (adds explanation)

> **Okane ga tarinái wáke desu né.** — *That is to say we don't have enough money, do we?*

házu desu '*the expectation is that…*'

> **Móo Amerika ni itta házu desu.** — *I expect he's already gone to America.*

sóo desu '*it is said that*'

> **Ashita kúru sóo desu.** — *I hear he is coming tomorrow.*

yóo desu '*it looks as if*'

> **Ano ie ni dáremo súnde inai yóo desu.** — *It looks as if there is nobody living in that house.*

hóo ga íi desu '*it is/would be better to…*' (usually follows a verb in the past tense)

> **Ashita háyaku ókita hóo ga íi desu.** — *You had better get up early tomorrow.*

Pronouns

Japanese has a rich array of pronouns which vary according to the degree of formality of the occasion, the relative status of speaker and listener, and the sex of the speaker.

Person	Singular		Plural		Notes
1st	**watakushi**	*I*	**watakushidómo**	*we*	formal form
1st	**watashi**	*I*	**watashitachi**	*we*	polite style
1st	**atashi**	*I*	**atashitachi**	*we*	casual (female)
1st	**boku**	*I*	**bókutachi**	*we*	casual (male)
			bókura		
1st	**ore**	*I*	**orétachi**	*we*	vulgar (male)
2nd	**anáta**	*you*	**anatagáta**	*you*	general polite
2nd	**kimi**	*you*	**kimitachi**	*you*	casual (male)
2nd	**omáe**	*you*	**omáetachi**	*you*	vulgar (male)
			omáera		
3rd	**anóhito**	*he, she*	**anóhitotachi**	*they*	= that person
3rd	**káre**	*he*	**káretachi**	*they* (m)	casual (used by
			kárera		both sexes)
3rd	**kánojo**	*she*	**kánojotachi**	*they* (f)	casual (used by
					both sexes)

Question words

There is a group of nouns which cannot be followed by the topic particle **wa**. They are the interrogatives **náni** '*what*', **dáre** '*who?*', **dónata** '*who?*' (honorific), **dóko** '*where?*', **íkutsu** '*how many?*', **íkura** '*how much?*', etc. **Náni ga muzukashíi desu ka.** '*What is difficult?*' **Dáre ga kimásu ka.** '*Who is coming?*' Note that these question words all have high pitch on the first syllable.

Indefinite pronouns

In addition to the personal pronouns listed above, Japanese has a group of indefinite pronouns and negative pronouns formed from the interrogatives by the addition of the particles, **ka**, **mo** and **demo**.

Interrogative	Indefinite	Definite	Emphatic
náni *what*	**nánika** *something*	**nánimo** *nothing*	**nándemo** *anything at all* *nothing at all*
dáre *who*	**dáreka** *someone*	**dáremo** *no-one/everyone*	**dáredemo** *anyone/no-one* *at all*
dónata *who* (honorific)	**dónataka** *someone* (honorific)	**dónatamo** *no-one/everyone* (honorific)	**dónatademo** *anyone/no-one at* *all* (honorific)
dóko *where*	**dókoka** *somewhere*	**dókomo** (not) *anywhere*	**dókodemo** (not) *anywhere* *at all*
íkutsu *how many*	**íkutsuka** *several*	**íkutsumo** (not) *many*	**íkutsudemo** *any number at all*

Demonstratives

Japanese distinguishes 'this', near the speaker, 'that', near the addressee and 'that' (over there), away from both the speaker and addressee.

	Close		Intermediate		Distant		Interrogative
kore	*this*	**sore**	*that*	**are**	*that over there*	**dóre**	*which*
koko	*there*	**soko**	*there*	**asoko** **asuko**	*over there*	**dóko**	*where*
kotchí/ **kochira**	*this one* (of two)/ *this way*	**sotchí/** **sochira**	*that one* (of two)/ *that way*	**atchí/** **achira**	*that one* (of two)/ *that way*	**dótchi/** **dóchira**	*which* (of two)/ *where*

In addition to these demonstrative pronouns there is a corresponding set of demonstrative adjectives and adverbs.

Pronoun	Place	Adjective1	Adjective 2	Adverb
kore *this*	**koko** *here*	**kono** *this*	**konna** *this kind of*	**koo** *like this*
sore *that*	**soko** *there*	**sono** *that*	**sonna** *that kind of*	**soo** *like that*

are	asoko	ano	anna	aa
that (over there)	(over) *there*	*that*	*that kind of*	*like that*
dóre	**dóko**	**dóno**	**dónna**	**doo**
which	*where*	*which*	*what kind of*	*how*

Respect and politeness

Every final verb in Japanese tells us something about the degree of respect the speaker shows towards the person being referred to (the referent), usually the subject (or indirect object) of the main verb, and the degree of politeness shown to the person spoken to (the addressee). The system as a whole is known as honorific language, or **keigo** in Japanese. There are three speech styles, plain, polite and formal, which indicate the degree of politeness to the addressee and a number of levels of respect languages shown to the referent. For our purposes, however, it is sufficient to distinguish simply neutral and honorific verb forms and to make a further distinction according to whether the respected referent is the subject or indirect object of the verb. Respect and politeness in the Japanese verb can be expressed in terms of two intersecting axes, as can be seen in the verb 'to write' in the following table.

Respect/politeness	*Plain*	*Polite*	*Formal*
neutral	**káku**	**kakimásu**	**kaku n' de gozaimásu**
subject honorific	**okaki ni naru**	**okaki ni narimásu**	–
subject honorific (alternative present-continuous form)	–	**okaki desu**	–
object honorific*	**okaki suru**	**okaki shimasu**	–

Note: * The object honorific generally has the meaning of '(I) *do something for a respected referent*.'

The same distinctions can be seen in the copula.

Respect/politeness	*Plain*	*Polite*	*Formal*
neutral	**da** (spoken) **de áru** (written)	**désu**	**de gozaimásu**
subject honorific	**de irassháru**	**de irasshaimásu**	–

In addition to the regular forms of verbs there are a number of separate euphemistic verbs used in honorific expressions in Japanese. Some of the more common honorific verbs are given below with their neutral counterparts. In the list below they are given in the plain form, though as main verbs they would most often occur in the polite style.

Neutral	Honorific	Meaning
iu	ossháru	to say
suru	nasáru	to do
iku	irassháru	to go
kúru	irassháru	to come
iru	irassháru	to be, to exist
tabéru	meshiagáru	to eat
nómu	meshiagáru	to drink
míru	goran ni náru	to see
neru	oyasumi ni náru	to sleep
kiru	omeshi ni náru	to wear

Numbers and Numeral classifiers

	1 2	3 4	5 6	7 8	9 10	100 ?
–bai times as much	ichibai nibai	sanbai yonbai	gobai rokubai	nanabai hachibai	kyuubai juubai	hyakubai nanbai
–ban number, ordinals	ichíban níban	sanban yonban	goban rokuban	nanában hachíban	kyúuban júuban	hyakúban nánban
–ban nights	hitóban futában	míban yóban	–	–	–	–
–bun part, fraction	ichibun nibun	sanbun yonbun	gobun rokubun	nanabun hachibun	kubun juubun	hyakubun nanbun
–byoo seconds	ichíbyoo níbyoo	sánbyoo yónbyoo	góbyoo rokúbyoo	nanábyoo hachíbyoo	kúbyoo júubyoo	hyakubyoo nánbyoo
–chakú suits, outfits	itchakú nichakú	sanchakú yonchakú	gochakú rokuchakú	nanachakú hatchakú	kyuuchakú jutchakú	hyakuchakú nanchakú
–dáasu dozens	ichidáasu nidáasu	sandáasu yondáasu	godáasu rokudáasu	nanadáasu hachidáasu	kyuudáasu juudáasu	haykudáasu nandáasu
–dai	ichidai	sámdai	gódai	nanadai	kyúudai	hyakúdai

ehicles, machines	nidai	yóndai	rokudai	hachidai	juudai	nandai
dan rades teps	ichídan	sandan	godan	shichídan	kyúudan	hyakúdan
	nídan	yondan	rokúdan	hachídan	júudan	nándan
dó mes	ichidó	sandó	godó	nanadó	kudó	hyakudó
	nidó	yondó	rokudó	hachidó	juudó	nandó
do egrees	ichído	sándo	gódo	nanádo	kúdo	hyakúdo
	nído	yóndo	rokúdo	hachído	júudo	nándo
en en	ichien	san'en	goen	nanaen	kyuuen	hyakuen
	nien	yon'en	rokuen	hachien	juuen	nan'en
fun inutes	íppun	sánpun	gófun	nanáfun	kyúufun	hyáppun
	nífun	yónpun	róppun	háppun	júppun	nánpun
gatsú ames of onths	ichigatsú	sangatsú	gogatsú	shichigatsú	kugatsú	–
	nigatsú	shigatsú	rokugatsú	hachigatsú	juugatsú	nangatsú
gúramu rams	ichigúramu	sangúramu	gogúramu	nanagúramu	kugúramu	hyakugúramu
	nigúramu	yongúramu	rokugúramu	hachigúramu	juugúramu	nangúramu
hai upfuls, lasses	ippai	sánbai	góhai	nanáhai	kyúuhai	hyáppai
	nihai	yónhai	róppai	háppai	júppai	nánbai
hen umber of imes	ippén	sanbén	gohén	nanahén	kyuuhén	hyappén
	nihén	yonhén	roppén	happén	juppén	nanbén
hiki nimals	ippikí	sánbiki	góhiki	nanáhiki	kyúuhiki	hyappikí
	níhiki	yónhiki	roppikí	happikí	juppikí	nánbiki
hon ylindrical bjects	íppon	sánbon	gohon	nanáhon	kyúuhon	hyáppon
	níhon	yónhon	róppon	háppon	júppon	nánbon
hyakú undreds	hyakú	sánbyaku	gohyakú	nanáhyaku	kyúuhyaku	–
	nihyakú	yónhyaku	roppyakú	happyakú		nánbyaku
ji clock	ichíji	sánji	góji	shichíji	kúji	–
	níji	yóji	rokúji	hachíji	júuji	nánji
juu ens	júu	sánjuu	gojúu	nanájuu	kyúujuu	–
	níjuu	yónjuu	rokujúu	hachijúu		nánjuu
ka essons	íkka	sánka	góka	nanáka	kyúuka	hyákka
	níka	yónka	rókka	hákka	júkka	nánka
ka/ nichi ays	ichinichi	mikka	itsuka	nanoka	kokonoka	hyakunichi
	futsuka	yokka	muika	yooka	tooka	nannichi
kái umber f times	ikkái	sankái	gokái	nanakái	kyuukái	hyakkái
	nikái	yonkái	rokkái	hakkái	jukkái	nankái

	1 2	3 4	5 6	7 8	9 10	100 ?
–kai storeys, floors	ikkai nikai	sangai yonkai	gokai rokkai	nanakai hakkai	kyuukai jukkai	hyakkai nangai
–ken buildings	íkken níken	sánken yónken	góken rókken	nanáken hákken	kyúuken júkken	hyákken nánken
–ki aeroplanes	ikki niki	sánki yónki	góki rókki	nanáki hákki	kyúuki júkki	hyákki nánki
–kiro kilogram/ metre	ichíkiro níkiro	sánkiro yónkiro	gókiro rókkiro	nanákiro hachíkiro	kyúukiro júkkiro	hyákkiro nánkiro
–ko '*a piece*', boxes, fruit, furniture, etc., round or square objects	ikko níko	sanko yónko	góko rókko	nanáko hákko	kyúuko júkko	hyákko nánko
–mai '*sheets*', flat objects, paper, plates, shirts, ties, etc.	ichímai nímai	sánmai yónmai	gomai rokumai	nanámai hachímai	kyuumai júumai	hyakúmai nánmai
–man ten-thousands	ichimán nimán	sanmán yonmán	gomán rokumán	nanamán hachimán	kyuumán juumán	hyakumán nanmán
–nen years	ichínen nínen	sannen yonen	gonen rokunen	shichinen hachinen	kunen júunen	hyakúnen nánnen
–nin/–ri people	hitóri futarí	sannin yonin	gonin rokúnin	shichinin hachinin	kunin juunin	hyakunin nánnin
–sai years of age	issai nisai	sánsai yónsai	gósai rokusai	nanasai hassai	kyuusai jússai	hyakusai nánsai
–satsu '*volume*', books	issatsú nísatsu	sánsatsu yónsatsu	gósatsu rokúsatsu	nanásatsu hassatsú	kyúusatsu jussatsú	hyakusatsu nánsatsu
–seki ships	isseki níseki	sánseki yónseki	góseki rokúseki	nanáseki hasseki	kyúuseki jusseki	hyakuseki nánseki
–sen thousands	sén nisén	sanzén yonsén	gosén rokusén	nanasen hassén	kyuusén –	– nanzén

–soku	issokú	sánzoku	gósok	nanások	kyúusok	hyakúsoku
'pair',	nísoku	yónsoku	rokúsoku	hássoku	jússoku	nánzoku
shoes,						
socks						
–soo	íssoo	sánsoo	gósoo	nanásoo	kyúusoo	hyakúsoo
vessels,	nísoo	yónsoo	rokúsoo	hássoo	jússoo	nánsoo
boats						
–tén	ittén	santén	gotén	nanatén	kyuutén	hyakutén
points,	nitén	yontén	rokutén	hattén	juttén	nantén
marks						
–too	íttoo	sántoo	gotoo	nanátoo	kyúutoo	hyakutoo
'head',	nítoo	yóntoo	rokútoo	háttoo	júttoo	nántoo
large						
animals						
–tsu	hitótsu	mittsú	itsútsu	nanátsu	kokónotsu	–
miscella-	futatsú	yottsú	muttsú	yattsú	tóo	íkutsu
neous						
objects,						
years of						
age						
–tsuu	ittsuu	santsuu	gotsuu	nanatsuu	kyuutsuu	hyakutsuu
letters	nitsuu	yontsuu	rokutsuu	hattsuu	juttsuu	nántsuu
–wa	ichíwa	sánba	gówa	nanáwa	kyúuwa	hyáppa
birds	níwa	yónwa	róppa	hachíwa	júppa	nánwa

Notes:
1. In the above table **yón–** and **nána–** have been used for 4 and 7 where possible, though in most cases **shi–** and **shichí –** can be used instead. With 9 the form which first sprang to mind has been chosen. **Kú–** and **kyúu–** are often not interchangeable, so use the form given here, but be prepared to hear the other as well. In the interrogative expressions it is always possible to place an accent on the first syllable instead of using the accent shown here. For 8 it is usually possible to use the full form **hachi–** instead of the forms with a double consonant.
2. **–jíkan**, '*hours duration*'; **–jóo –tatami**, '*mats, unit of room size*'; **–meetoru**, '*metres*'; **–paasénto**, '*per cent*'; **–péeji**, '*pages*'; **–póndo**, '*pounds*' undergo no sound changes or shift of accent; **–kágetsu**, '*months duration*', retains its accent, but has double consonants in combination with 1, 6, 8, 10 and 100; **–sénchi**, '*centimetres*' and **–shúukan**, '*weeks duration*', retain their original accent, but double the consonant in 1, 8 and 10; **–doru**, '*dollars*', is unaccented and follows the pattern of **–dai**.

Appendix
Hiragána, katakána and kanji

Hiragána

あ a	い i	う u	え e	お o	や ya	ゆ yu	よ yo
か ka	き ki	く ku	け ke	こ ko	きゃ kya	きゅ kyu	きょ kyo
が ga	ぎ gi	ぐ gu	げ ge	ご go	ぎゃ gya	ぎゅ gyu	ぎょ gyo
さ sa	し shi	す su	せ se	そ so	しゃ sha	しゅ shu	しょ sho
ざ za	じ ji	ず zu	ぜ ze	ぞ zo	じゃ ja	じゅ ju	じょ jo
た ta	ち chi	つ tsu	て te	と to	ちゃ cha	ちゅ chu	ちょ cho
だ da	(ぢ) ji	(づ) zu	で de	ど do	(ぢゃ) ja	(ぢゅ) ju	(ぢょ) jo
な na	に ni	ぬ nu	ね ne	の no	にゃ na	にゅ nu	にょ no
は ha	ひ hi	ふ fu	へ he	ほ ho	ひゃ hya	ひゅ hyu	ひょ hyo
ば ba	び bi	ぶ bu	べ be	ぼ bo	びゃ bya	びゅ byu	びょ byo
ぱ pa	ぴ pi	ぷ pu	ぺ pe	ぽ po	ぴゃ pya	ぴゅ pyu	ぴょ pyo
ま ma	み mi	む mu	め me	も mo	みゃ mya	みゅ myu	みょ myo
ら ra	り ri	る ru	れ re	ろ ro	りゃ rya	りゅ ryu	りょ ryo
わ wa				を o			
							ん n

Katakána (basic syllables only)

ア a	イ i	ウ u	エ e	オ o
カ ka	キ ki	ク ku	ケ ke	コ ko
サ sa	シ shi	ス su	セ se	ソ so
タ ta	チ chi	ツ tsu	テ te	ト to
ナ na	ニ ni	ヌ nu	ネ ne	ノ no
ハ ha	ヒ hi	フ fu	ヘ he	ホ ho
マ ma	ミ mi	ム mu	メ me	モ mo
ヤ ya		ユ yu		ヨ yo
ラ ra	リ ri	ル ru	レ re	ロ ro
ワ wa				ヲ o
				ン n

Kanji

The following lists the **kanji** introduced for acquisition throughout this course, arranged in ascending order of the number of strokes. The digits before the decimal point refer to the Unit in which the **kanji** was introduced. The three digit code after the decimal point is the order of introduction of the character. This chart provides a running tally of the number of kanji acquired by any particular point in the course. This is followed by a finder list of Chinese-style **on** readings (in small caps) and native Japanese **kun** readings in lower case with the parts usually written in **hiragána** included in parentheses.

1 stroke
一 3.013
2 strokes
人 2.010
二 3.014
七 3.018
八 3.019
九 3.020
十 3.021
入 10.097
力 13.152
刀 13.153
3 strokes
川 1.004
山 1.005
上 1.006
下 1.007
三 3.015
女 3.023
子 3.024
大 3.025
小 3.026
千 4.033
万 4.034
土 5.051
口 10.092
夕 11.110
工 14.179
4 strokes
中 1.003
日 2.008
五 3.017
六 3.017
月 3.030
円 4.035
今 5.042
火 5.047
水 5.048
木 5.049
分 7.066
手 7.070
午 8.079

父 10.095
北 11.103
方 11.111
少 11.113
少 11.113
天 11.116
心 12.124
元 12.136
牛 13.145
切 13.154
友 13.156
太 14.171
内 15.183
化 15.195
不 15.199
文 15.200
5 strokes
田 1.001
本 1.002
四 3.016
半 3.031
生 4.041
白 7.068
目 8.077
台 9.091
母 10.096
出 10.098
冬 11.109
外 12.123
立 12.141
右 13.157
左 13.158
平 14.172
広 14.180
市 15.191
6 strokes
好 3.027
百 4.032
安 4.037
先 4.040
毎 5.044
年 5.046

行 6.052
会 6.053
早 7.067
休 9.088
耳 10.093
字 10.094
西 11.105
多 11.112
気 11.117
名 12.135
色 13.143
肉 13.146
有 13.159
両 14.173
寺 15.201
7 strokes
男 3.022
何 3.029
来 5.043
売 6.055
社 6.058
車 7.065
私 7.071
花 8.076
見 8.078
住 10.099
言 13.160
近 13.161
町 14.169
芸 15.188
利 15.198
8 strokes
国 2.009
英 2.012
学 4.038
金 5.050
事 7.063
青 7.069
東 8.072
京 8.073
明 9.084
門 9.087

枚 9.090
知 10.100
歩 11.115
雨 11.118
長 12.134
林 12.137
空 12.140
物 13.144
画 13.148
店 13.150
所 14.177
者 15.189
的 15.194
9 strokes
食 7.062
前 8.080
後 8.081
海 9.086
南 11.104
春 11.106
秋 11.108
風 11.120
思 12.125
急 12.126
洋 12.129
降 12.138
映 13.147
待 13.151
音 14.163
持 14.166
県 14.170
昼 14.174
屋 15.184
室 15.185
美 15.186
便 15.197
10 strokes
時 3.028
高 4.036
校 4.039
書 6.059
紙 9.089

夏 11.107   部 12.132   森 12.139   暗 14.165
旅 11.114   強 14.168   雲 12.142   詩 15.202
酒 12.127   術 15.187   晩 14.175   **14 strokes**
配 12.128   **12 strokes**   場 14.178   語 2.011
家 13.162   買 6.054   道 15.192   読 6.056
病 14.167   飲 7.064   晴 15.193   銀 6.057
勉 14.176   間 8.075   無 15.196   聞 6.060
馬 14.181   着 9.082   **13 strokes**   様 12.130
員 15.190   着 9.082   新 6.061   駅 14.182
11 strokes   朝 9.085   話 9.083   **16 strokes**
週 5.045   開 10.101   電 12.131   曇 12.133
都 8.074   寒 11.121   楽 14.164   館 13.149
雪 11.119   暑 11.122   楽 14.164   親 13.155

Kanji on-kun finder list

a(keru) 開 10.101
á(ru) 有 13.159
á(u) 会 6.053
aida 間 8.075
aka(rui) 明 9.084
áki 秋 11.108
ame 雨 11.118
AN 安 4.037
AN 暗 14.165
aó(i) 青 7.069
arú(ku) 歩 11.115
ása 朝 9.085
atara(shíi) 新 6.061
áto 後 8.081
atsú(i) 暑 11.122
ba 場 14.178
BA 馬 14.181
ba(kéru) 化 15.195
BAI 売 6.055
BAI 買 6.054
BAN 晩 14.175
BEN 便 15.197
BEN 勉 14.176
BI 美 15.186

BO 母 10.096
BOKU 木 5.049
BU 部 12.132
BUN 分 7.066
BUN 文 15.200
BUN 聞 6.060
BUTSU 物 13.144
BYOO 病 14.167
CHAKU 着 9.082
CHI 知 10.100
chichí 父 10.095
chii(sái) 小 3.026
chiká(i) 近 13.161
chikará 力 13.152
CHOO 朝 9.085
CHOO 町 14.169
CHOO 長 12.134
CHUU 中 1.003
CHUU 昼 14.174
dá(su) 出 10.098

DAI 台 9.091
DAI 大 3.025
DAN 男 3.022
dé(ru) 出 10.098
DEN 田 1.001
DEN 電 12.131
DO 土 5.051
DOKU 読 6.056
DON 曇 12.133
DOO 道 15.192
EI 映 13.147
EI 英 2.012
EKI 駅 14.182
EN 円 4.035
FU 不 15.199
FU 父 10.095
fú(ru) 降 12.138
fúmi 文 15.200
FUN 分 7.066
futa(tsú) 二 3.014
futó(i) 太 14.171
FUU 風 11.120
fuyú 冬 11.109
GA 画 13.148
GAI 外 12.123

GAKU 学 4.038
GAKU 楽 14.164
–gatá 方 11.111
GATSU 月 3.030
GEI 芸 15.188
GEN 元 12.136
GEN 言 13.160
GETSU 月 3.030
GIN 銀 6.057
GO 五 3.017
GO 午 8.079
GO 語 2.011
GYOO 行 6.052
GYUU 牛 13.145
ha(réru) 晴 15.193
HACHI 八 3.019
háha 母 10.096
HAI 配 12.128
hái(ru) 入 10.097
HAKU 白 7.068
HAN 半 3.031
haná 花 8.076
haná(su) 話 9.083
háru 春 11.106

hayá(i) 早
7.067

hayashi 林
12.137

HEI 平 14.172

hi 日 2.008

hí 火 5.047

hidari 左
13.158

higashi 東
8.072

hiró(i) 広
14.180

hirú 昼
14.174

hito 人 2.010

hitó(tsu) 一
3.013

HO 歩 11.115

hoka 外 12.123

HOKU 北
11.103

HON 本 1.002

HOO 方 11.111

HYAKU 百
4.032

i(ku) 行 6.052

ICHI 一 3.013

ichi 市 15.191

ié 家 13.162

íma 今 5.042

IN 員 15.190

IN 飲 7.064

iró 色 13.143

isó(gu) 急
12.126

itsú(tsu) 五
3.017

JI 事 7.063

JI 字 10.094

JI 寺 15.201

JI 持 14.166

JI 時 3.028

JI 耳 10.093

JIN 人 2.010

JITSU 日 2.008

JO 女 3.023

JOO 上 1.006

JOO 場 14.178

JUTSU 術

15.187

JUU 中 1.003

JUU 中 1.003

JUU 住 10.099

JUU 十 3.021

KA 何 3.029

KA 化 15.195

KA 夏 11.107

KA 家 13.162

KA 火 5.047

KA 花 8.076

ká(ku) 書
6.059

ka(u) 買 6.054

KA, GE 下 1.007

KAI 会 6.053

KAI 海 9.086

KAI 開 10.101

KAKU 画
13.148

kami 紙 9.089

KAN 寒 11.121

KAN 館 13.149

KAN, KEN 間
8.075

kane 金 5.050

katá 方 11.111

kataná 刀
13.153

kawá 川 1.004

kaze 風 11.120

KEN 県 14.170

KEN 見 8.078

kí 木 5.049

KI 気 11.117

ki(ku) 利
15.198

ki(ku) 聞 6.060

kí(ru) 切
13.154

ki(ru) 着 9.082

KIN 近 13.161

KIN 金 5.050

kita 北 11.103

ko 子 3.024

kokóno(tsu)
九 3.020

kokóro 心
12.124

KOKU 国 2.009

KON 今 5.042

KOO 口 10.092

KOO 好 3.027

KOO 工 14.179

KOO 広 14.180

KOO 後 8.081

KOO 校 4.039

KOO 行 6.052

KOO 降 12.138

KOO 高 4.036

kotó 事 7.063

KU 九 3.020

kú(ru) 来
5.043

kubá(ru) 配
12.128

kuchi 口
10.092

kúmo 雲
12.142

kumó(ru) 曇
12.133

kuni 国 2.009

kurá(i) 暗
14.165

kuruma 車
7.065

KUU 空 12.140

KYOO 強
14.168

KYOO, KEI 京
8.073

KYUU 九 3.020

KYUU 休 9.088

KYUU 急
12.126

má(tsu) 待
13.151

machi 町
14.169

mae 前 8.080

MAI 枚 9.090

MAI 毎 5.044

MAN 万 4.034

máto 的 15.194

mé 目 8.077

MEI 明 9.084

MEI 名 12.135

mí(ru) 見 8.078

michi 道

15.192

migi 右 13.157

mimí 耳 10.093

minami 南
11.104

misé 店 13.150

mit(tsú) 三
3.015

miyako 都
8.074

mizu 水 5.048

mó(tsu) 持
14.166

MOKU 木 5.049

MOKU 目 8.077

MON 門 9.087

monó 物
13.144

monó 者
15.189

mori 森
12.139

motó 元 12.136

moto 本 1.002

MOTSU 物
13.144

MU 無 15.196

muró 室
15.185

mut(tsú) 六
3.017

MYOO 明 9.084

na 名 12.135

ná(i) 無 15.196

nagá(i) 長
12.134

NAI 内 15.183

náka 中 1.003

nán 何 3.029

NAN 南 11.104

NAN 男 3.022

nána 七 3.018

naná(tsu) 七
3.018

náni 何 3.029

natsú 夏
11.107

NEN 年 5.046

NI 二 3.014

NICHI 日 2.008

NIKU 肉 13.146

NIN 人 2.010

NIN 人 2.010

nishi 西 11.105

nó(mu) 飲 7.064

nochi 後 8.081

NYO 女 3.023

NYUU 入 10.097

o(ríru) 降 12.138

OKU 屋 15.184

omó(u) 思 12.125

ON 音 14.163

onná 女 3.023

óo(i) 多 11.112

oo(kíi) 大 3.025

otó 音 14.163

otokó 男 3.022

oyá 親 13.155

RAI 来 5.043

RAKU 楽 14.164

RI 利 15.198

RIN 林 12.137

RITSU 立 12.141

ROKU 六 3.017

RYO 旅 11.114

RYOKU 力 13.152

RYOO 両 14.173

SA 左 13.158

SAI 切 13.154

SAI 西 11.105

sake 酒 12.127

saki 先 4.040

sama 様 12.130

samú(i) 寒 11.121

SAN 三 3.015

SAN 山 1.005

SEI 晴 15.193

SEI 生 4.041

SEI 西 11.105

SEI 青 7.069

SEKI 夕 11.110

SEN 先 4.040

SEN 千 4.033

SEN 川 1.004

SETSU 切 13.154

SETSU 雪 11.119

SHA 社 6.058

SHA 者 15.189

SHA 車 7.065

SHI 四 3.016

SHI 子 3.024

SHI 市 15.191

SHI 思 12.125

SHI 私 7.071

SHI 紙 9.089

SHI 詩 15.202

shi(ru) 知 10.100

SHICHI 七 3.018

SHIKI 色 13.143

SHIN 心 12.124

SHIN 新 6.061

SHIN 森 12.139

SHIN 親 13.155

shiró(i) 白 7.068

shita 下 1.007

SHITSU 室 15.185

SHO 所 14.177

SHO 暑 11.122

SHO 書 6.059

SHOKU 食 7.062

SHOO 小 3.026

SHOO 少 11.113

SHOO 生 4.041

SHU 手 7.070

SHU 酒 12.127

SHUN 春 11.106

SHUTSU 出 10.098

SHUU 秋 11.108

SHUU 週 5.045

SOO 早 7.067

sóra 空 12.140

sóto 外 12.123

su(kí na) 好 3.027

sú(mu) 住 10.099

SUI 水 5.048

sukó(shi) 少 11.113

sukun(ái) 少 11.113

SYA 社 6.058

TA 多 11.112

tá 田 1.001

ta(béru) 食 7.062

tá(tsu) 立 12.141

tabi 旅 11.114

TAI 台 9.091

TAI 大 3.025

TAI 大 3.025

TAI 太 14.171

TAI 待 13.151

taira 平 14.172

taká(i) 高 4.036

tano(shíi) 楽 14.164

táyori 便 15.197

té 手 7.070

TEKI 的 15.194

TEN 天 11.116

TEN 店 13.150

tera 寺 15.201

TO 都 8.074

toki 時 3.028

tokoro 所 14.177

TOKU 読 6.056

tómo 友 13.156

TOO 冬 11.109

TOO 刀 13.153

tóo 十 3.021

TOO 東 8.072

toshí 年 5.046

tsu(ku) 着 9.082

tsuchí 土 5.051

tsukí 月 3.030

tsuyó(i) 強 14.168

U 右 13.157

U 雨 11.118

u(mareru) 生 4.041

u(mu) 生 4.041

u(ru) 売 6.055

uchi 内 15.183

ue 上 1.006

umá 馬 14.181

úmi 海 9.086

UN 雲 12.142

ushi 牛 13.145

ushi(ro) 後 8.081

utsú(ru) 映 13.147

utsuku(shíi) 美 15.186

WA 話 9.083

wa(kéru) 分 7.066

watakushi 私 7.071

watashi 私 7.071

ya 屋 15.184

yamá 山 1.005

yámai 病 14.167

yasú(i) 安 4.037

yasú(mu) 休 9.088

yat(tsú) 八 3.019

yó(mu) 読 6.056

yón 四 3.016

YOO 様 12.130

YOO 洋 12.129

yot(tsú) 四 3.016

yu(u) 言 13.160

yuki 雪 11.119

YUU 友 13.156

yuu 夕 11.110

YUU 有 13.159

ZEN 前 8.080

Japanese–English glossary

A

áa ああ — *Ah!* (exclamation)
abiru 浴びる — *to shower, bathe*
abunai 危ない — *dangerous, watch out!*
achira あちら — *over there, that way*
Afurika アフリカ — *Africa*
agaru 上がる — *to go up, rise, enter*
agemásu — see **ageru**
ageru 上げる — *to give, raise up*
agó 顎 — *chin*
ái suru 愛する — *to love*
aida 間 — *between, interval, gap*
aikawarazu 相変わらず — *as usual*
aimásu — see **áu**
áinu アイヌ — *Ainu (the aboriginal people of Hokkaido)*
áiron アイロン — *iron (clothes)*
Áirurando アイルランド — *Ireland*
áisatsu 挨拶 — *greeting, formal conversational routines*
aité 相手 — *the other party, partner, opponent*
aite iru 空いている 開いている — *to be vacant; to be open*
aitíi アイティー — *I.T., information technology*
aiyoo suru 愛用する — *to enjoy using regularly*
aizuchi 合槌 — *chiming in*

aji 味	*taste*
Ájia アジア	*Asia*
ajisai 紫陽花	*hydrangea*
ákachan 赤ちゃん	*baby*
akai 赤い	*red*
akanboo 赤ん坊	*baby*
akarui 明るい	*light, bright*
akemáshite omedetoo gozaimásu 明けましておめでとうございます	*Happy New Year!*
akeru 開ける	*to open* (transitive)
áki 秋	*autumn*
akimásu	see **aku**
akiraméru 諦める	*to give up, abandon, resign oneself to*
akisu 空き巣	*sneak thief*
Ákita 秋田	*place name*
aku 開く	*to come open, open*
aku 空く	*to become vacant, be free*
amai 甘い	*sweet*
amari/anmari 余り	*very, a lot; not very*
amasugíru 甘すぎる	*too sweet*
áme 雨	*rain*
ame 飴	*sweet, candy*
Amérika アメリカ	*America*
Amerikájin アメリカ人	*American*
Amerikasei アメリカ製	*made in America*
–(a)nai ない	negative suffix
–(a)naide ないで	*without* (negative suffix)
–(a)nakerba narimasen なければなりません	*must…, have to…*
–(a)nakute なくて	negative suffix
anáta あなた、貴方	*you*
anaúnsu アナウンス	*announcement*
ane 姉	*elder sister*
áni 兄	*elder brother*
ánki 暗記	*learning by heart*
anmari	see **amari**
anna あんな	*that kind of*
annai suru 案内する	*to guide, show around*
annaijo 案内所	*information counter*
ano あの	*that over there*
anóhito あの人	*he*

anóhitotachi あの人たち	*they*
anokatá あの方	*he* (honorific)
anokatagata あの方々	*they* (honorific)
anóko あの子	*he* (child)
anoo あのう	*um, er* (hesitation form)
anshin suru 安心する	*be free from worry*
anzen na 安全な	*safe, secure*
anzen-kámisori 安全剃刀	*safety razor*
aói 青い	*blue, green*
Aómori 青森	*place name*
aozóra 青空	*blue sky*
apáato アパート	*rented flat*
arasói 争い	*fight, struggle, strife*
Arashiyama 嵐山	*place name*
arau 洗う	*wash*
are あれ	*that over there*
ari 蟻	*ant*
arigatái 有り難い	*grateful*
arígatoo 有り難う	*thank you*
arimásu	see **áru**
áru teido ある程度	*to a certain extent*
áru 或る	*a certain*
áru 有る	*to be located somewhere; to have*
arubáito アルバイト	*part-time work*
arúiwa 或いは	*or*
arukitsuzukéru 歩き続ける	*to keep on walking*
arukimásu	see **arúku**
arúku 歩く	*to walk*
ása 朝	*morning*
asa-góhan 朝御飯	*breakfast*
ásahi 朝日	*morning sun*
Asahishínbun 朝日新聞	*a major daily paper*
asanéboo o suru 朝寝坊	*… sleep in late in the morning*
asátte 明後日	*the day after tomorrow*
–(a)seru	see **–(s)aseru**
ashí 足	*leg, foot*
ashita 明日	*tomorrow*
asobu 遊ぶ	*to play, have free time*
asoko あそこ	*over there*
asu 明日	*tomorrow*
ataeru 与える	*to give*
atamá 頭	*head*

atamá ga íi 頭がいい   *intelligent*
atarashíi 新しい   *new*
ataru…ni ___ に当たる   *be equivalent to*
atashi あたし   *I* (feminine)
atatakai 暖かい   *warm*
atchí あっち   *that way, over there*
áto 後   *later, afterward;* 跡 *remains*
áto de 後で   *after*
atsugáru 暑がる   *to feel the heat, be hot*
atsui 厚い   *thick*
atsúi 暑い   *hot*
astumáru 集まる   *to collect, gather* (intransitive)
astuméru 集まる   *to collect, gather* (transitive)
atsuryoku 圧力   *pressure*
attakái 暖かい   *warm*
áu 会う   *to meet, come together, fit*
awaséru 合わせる   *to bring together*
–(a)zu ず   negative suffix = **–(a)nai**

B

báa バー   *bar*
báabekyuu バーベキュー   *barbecue*
báai 場合   *occasion, time, if, when*
báka 馬鹿   *fool, bloody idiot* (very abusive)
bakageta kotó 馬鹿げた事   *stupid thing, ridiculous thing*
bakarashíi 馬鹿らしい   *foolish, stupid*
bákari ばかり   *only, to the extent of*
bakkupákkaa バックパッカー   *back-packer*
ban 晩   *night, evening*
ban 番   *number*
bánana バナナ   *banana*
ban-góhan 晩御飯   *dinner, evening meal*
bangoo 番号   *number*
bangumí 番組   *radio, TV programme*
bánsen 番線   *track number*
banzái   *hooray, long live* (literally, 'ten thousand years')

bara 薔薇   *rose*
báree バレー   *ballet; volley* (ball)
basho 場所   *place*

bassai 伐採	*felling, cutting down*
básu バス	*bus*
basu-nóriba バス乗り場	*bus terminus/depot, bus station*
basuketto(bóoru) バスケットボール	*basketball*
basútei バス停	*bus stop*
basutoire-tsuki バストイレ付き	*with bath and toilet*
báta/bátaa バター	*butter*
batta 蝗	*grasshopper*
béiju ベージュ	*beige*
bekkan 別館	*annex, separate building*
bengóshi 弁護士	*lawyer, solicitor*
benjó 便所	*toilet, lavatory*
benkyoo suru 勉強する	*to study*
benkyooka 勉強家	*a hard worker, a studious type*
bénri na 便利な	*convenient, useful*
bentóo 弁当	*lunch box*
béruto ベルト	*belt*
Bétonamu ベトナム	*Vietnam*
betsu na/no 別	*separate, different, another*
betsu ni 別に	*in particular*
bétto (béddo) ベット	*bed*
bidánshi 美男子	*handsome man*
bíiru ビール	*beer*
bíjin 美人	*a beauty, beautiful woman*
bíjutsu 美術	*art, the fine arts*
bijútsukan 美術館	*art gallery*
bíka 美化	*beautification*
bín 瓶	*bottle*
bíru ビル	*building*
biyagáaden ビヤガーデン	*beer garden*
bodii-súutsu ボディースーツ	*body suit*
boku 僕 (or **bóku**)	*I*
booeki 貿易	*trade*
booeki-gáisha 貿易会社	*trading company*
booifuréndo ボーイフレンド	*boyfriend*
booringu ボーリング	*bowling* (ten pin)
booru ボール	*ball; bowl*
bóorupen ボールペン	*ball-point pen*
booshi 帽子	*hat, cap*
bótan ボタン	*button*
–bu 部	*copy of document* (numeral classifier)

–**bu** 部	*division of company,* etc.
búbun 部分	*part*
buchoo 部長	*division head*
búdoo 武道	*martial arts*
budoo 葡萄	*grapes*
búji na 無事な	*safe*
bukka 物価	*prices*
búkkyoo 仏教	*Buddhism*
bunbóoguya 文房具屋	*stationer/'s*
búngaku 文学	*literature*
bunka 文化	*culture*
bunkateki na 文化的な	*cultural*
bunkei 文型	*sentence pattern*
bunpoo 文法	*grammar*
búnshoo 文章	*sentence; writing*
Burajiru ブラジル	*Brazil*
buróochi ブローチ	*brooch*
buta 豚	*pig*
butsurígaku 物理学	*physics*
búutsu ブーツ	*boots*
byóo 秒	*second* (numeral classifier)
byooin 病院	*hospital, clinic*
byooki no 病気の	*sick, ill*
byooki 病気	*illness, disease*
byoonin 病人	*sick person*
byooshitsu 病室	*sickroom*

C

cha 茶	*tea* (see **ocha**)
chairo 茶色	*brown*
–**chaku** 着	*suit, outfit* (numeral classifier); *arrival*
chanto ちゃんと	*properly*
–**chau**	see –**te shimau**
chawan 茶碗	*rice bowl, tea-cup*
chekkuín チェックイン	*check in*
chi 血	*blood*
chichí 父	*father*
chichioya 父親	*father*
chigau 違う	*to differ, to be wrong, no*

chíisa na 小さな	*small*
chiisái 小さい	*small*
chíizu チーズ	*cheese*
chika 地下	*underground*
chikái 近い	*near*
chikáku 近く	*vicinity, near*
Chikámatsu 近松	*Chikamatsu,* Japan's greatest playwright (1653–1724)
chikámichi 近道	*short cut*
chikará 力	*strength*
chikatetsu 地下鉄	*underground railway*
chikazúku 近付く	*to approach*
chikyuu 地球	*earth, globe*
–chimau	see **–te shimau**
chíri 地理	*geography*
chirí 塵	*dust, dirt*
chiru 散る	*to scatter, fall* (blossoms, etc.)
chiteki 知的	*intellectual*
chittómo ちっとも	*in the least* (not) *at all*
chiryoo 治療	*medical treatment*
chishiki 知識	*knowledge*
chízu 地図	*map*
chokoréeto チョコレート	*chocolate*
–choo 長	*head, chief* (suffix)
chóochoo 町長	*town mayor*
choodai 頂戴	*please, give me*
choodó 丁度	*exactly, just*
chóohoo na 重宝な	*useful, precious*
choohookei 長方形	*rectangular*
choonán 長男	*eldest son*
Choosen 朝鮮	(North) *Korea*
chooshi ga ii 調子がいい	*to run well, go smoothly*
chooshoku 朝食	*breakfast*
chótto ちょっと	*a little*
–chuu 中	*in the course of*
chuugákusei 中学生	*junior high-school student*
Chúugoku 中国	*China*
Chuugokugo 中国語	*Chinese* (language)
Chuugokújin 中国人	*Chinese* (person)
chúui 注意	*attention, be careful*
chuujókki 中ジョッキ	*medium-sized tankard*
chúuka 中華	*Chinese* (food)

chuukaryóori 中華料理 — *Chinese cuisine*
chuukyuu 中級 — *intermediate*
chuumon 注文 — *to order*
chuunen 中年 — *middle age*
chuuoo 中央 — *central*
chuusha suru 駐車する — *to park* (a car, etc.)
chuushajoo 駐車場 — *car park*
chuusha-kinshi 駐車禁止 — *no parking*
chuushi suru 中止する — *to call off, stop doing*
chuushoku 昼食 — *lunch*

D

dáburu ダブル — *double* (room)
daenkei 楕円形 — *oval, elliptical*
dái 台 — *stand, dais*
daibu 大分 — *considerably, very many times*
daibutsu 大仏 — *great Buddha* (image)
daidokoro 台所 — *kitchen*
Daiei-hakubutsukan 大英博物館 — *British Museum*
daigaku 大学 — *university*
daigákusei 大学生 — *university student*
daihyoo 代表 — *representative*
dáiichi 第一 — *first, number one*
daijóobu 大丈夫 — *all right, OK*
dáiku 大工 — *carpenter*
dairiten 代理店 — *agency, agent*
dáisuki na 大好きな — *to love, be very fond of*
daitai 大体 — *approximately, generally, for the most part*
daitóoryoo 大統領 — *President*
daiyokujoo 大浴場 — *large bath*
dákara だから — *so, therefore*
daké だけ — *only, extent*
dakuten 濁点 — *voicing marks*
damé 駄目 — *no good; stop it!*
dandan だんだん — *gradually*
dansei 男性 — *male, man*
dánshi 男子 — *man, male* (**dánshi no** *men's …*)
dánsu ダンス — *dance*
dantairyókoo 団体旅行 — *group travel, tour*

dáre 誰   *who?*

dáredemo 誰でも   *anyone at all*

dáreka 誰か   *someone*

dáremo 誰も   *no one*

darusóo だるそう   *listless looking, tired looking*

dashimásu   see **dásu**

dasu 出す   *take out, put out*

dayígai 以外   *besides, outside*

de áru である   *is, are, etc.* (written-style copula)

de gozaimásu でございます   *is* (formal)

de irassháru でいらっしゃる   *is* (honorific)

de で   *'agent', by means of, with*

de で   *in, at*

déguchi 出口   *exit*

dekakeru 出かける   *to go out*

dekimásu   see **dekíru**

dekiru dake ... できるだけ   *as much as possible, as ... as possible*

dekíru 出来る   *to be done, be ready, be made; be able to, can*

demásu   see **déru**

démo でも   *even*

dengon 伝言   *message*

dénki 電気   *electricity, light*

densha 電車   *train (electric)*

denshi-méeru 電子メール   *electronic mail*

denwa 電話   *telephone*

denwa-bángoo 電話番号   *telephone number*

depáato デパート   *department store*

déru 出る   *to go out, come out, appear*

deshóo でしょう   *probably is*

désu です   *is, are, am* (copula)

dezáato デザート   *dessert*

–do 度   *degrees* (measure of alcohol content)

–do 度   *times* (numeral classifier)

dóa ドア   *door*

dóchira どちら   *which one, where* (honorific)

dóchiramo どちらも   *both, either*

dóchirasama どちら様   *who* (honorific)

Dóitsu ドイツ   *Germany*

dóko 何処、どこ   *where*

dokú (o-ki no____) お気の毒   *what a shame, I'm sorry to hear that*

dokú 毒   *poison*

dokushin 独身   *unmarried man or woman, bachelor*

dókusho 読書   *reading*

dónata どなた   *who* (honorific)

dónatasama どなた様   *who* (honorific)

dóndon ドンドン   *rapidly, quickly*

dónna どんな   *what kind of*

dónna kanji desu ka どんな感じですか   *what's it* (he, she, etc.) *like?*

dono kurai/gurai どのぐらい   *how long, how far, how much?*

dóno どの   *which?*

dóo どう   *how?*

dóo itashimashite どういたしまして   *don't mention it, not at all*

dóo shimashita ka どうしましたか   *What happened? What's the matter?*

doo shiyoo mo nai どうしようもない   *hopeless, impossible*

dóo yuu どういう   *what kind of?*

dóo yuu fuu na どういうふうな   *what kind of?*

dóo yuufuu ni どういうふうに   *how?, in what way?*

dooaku 獰悪   *fierce, wild* (literary word)

doobutsu 動物   *animal*

doobutsuen 動物園   *zoo*

dóomo どうも   *Thanks! Sorry! very*

doomoo 獰猛   *fierce, wild, savage*

doonyuu suru 導入する   *introduce, bring in*

dóoro 道路   *road*

dooro-hyóoshiki 道路標識   *road sign*

dóose どうせ   *anyway*

dóoshite どうして   *why, how*

dooshitémo どうしても   *no matter what, without fail*

dóozo yoroshiku どうぞよろしく   *how do you do? Please do what you can for me*

dóozo どうぞ   *please*

doráiibu ドアライブ   *drive*

doráiibu suru   *to drive*

doragon ドラゴン   *dragon*

dóre どれ   *which one?*

doroboo 泥棒 — *robber, thief*

dóryoku suru 努力する — *make an effort, endeavour, take pains*

dótchi どっち — *which one?*

doyóobi 土曜日 — *Saturday*

E

–e — brusque imperative suffix

e へ — *to, toward*

é 絵 — *picture*

–eba — see **–(r)eba**

ebi 蝦、海老 — *prawn, shrimp*

Edomae 江戸前 — *fresh from the sea in front of Edo (Tokyo)*

ée ええ — *yes*

eetto ええっと — *let me see* (hesitation form)

eibun 英文 — *English* (written)

éiga 映画 — *film, movie*

eigákan 映画館 — *cinema*

eigakantoku 映画監督 — *film director*

eigo 英語 — *English*

eigyoochuu 営業中 — *open for business*

eiji 英字 — *English language* (newspaper)

Eikoku 英国 — *England, Britain*

Eikokújin 英国人 — *Englishman, Briton*

eikyoo 影響 — *influence*

éki 駅 — *station*

ekibíru 駅ビル — *station building*

ekimáe 駅前 — *in front of the station*

ekimei 駅名 — *station name*

én 円 — *yen*

enpitsu 鉛筆 — *pencil*

enryo 遠慮 — *reserve, holding back*

erábu 選ぶ — *to choose*

erái 偉い — *great, praiseworthy, well done!*

erebéetaa エレベーター — *lift, elevator*

–eru える — *potential suffix*

éru 得る — *to get, gain*

esá 餌 — *feed, bait*

esukaréetaa エスカレーター   *escalator*
eto 干支   *traditional Chinese calendar system*

F

fákkusu ファックス   *fax, facsimile*
fóoku フォーク   *fork*
fuan na 不安   *uneasy, worried*
fúben na 不便な   *inconvenient*
fuchúui 不注意   *carelessness*
fude 筆   *writing brush*
fuéru 増える   *to increase*
–fújin –夫人   *Mrs…*
fujin 婦人   *lady, woman*
Fújisan 富士山   *Mt Fuji*
fújiyuu 不自由   *disabled, inconvenienced, handicapped*

fuku 吹く   *to blow*
fuku 拭く   *to wipe*
fukú 服   *clothes*
fukuméru 含める   *to include*
fukúshi 福祉   *welfare*
fukuúriba 服売り場   *clothing department*
fukuzatsu na 複雑な   *complicated*
–fun 分   *minutes*
funabin 船便   *sea mail*
fúne 船   *ship, boat*
funka 噴火   *eruption*
Furansu フランス   *France*
furidasu 降り出す   *to start raining*
furó 風呂   *bath*
furobá 風呂場   *bathroom*
fúru 降る   *to fall* (rain and snow)
furúi 古い   *old*
furúsato 故郷   *hometown, native place*
futarí 二人   *two people*
futatsú 二つ   *two*
futói 太い   *fat, thick*
futorimásu   see **futóru**
futorisugi 太りすぎ   *too fat, overweight*

futóru 太る   *to get fat*
futsuka 二日   *two days, 2nd of the month*
futsukayoi 二日酔い   *hangover*
futsuu 普通   *usual*
futtobóoru フットボール   *football*
fúudo フード   *hood*
fúukei 風景   *scene, scenery*
fuyásu 増やす   *increase* (transitive)
fuyu 冬   *winter*

G

ga が   *but* (clause-final particle)
ga が   subject particle
ga ご迷惑ですが   *sorry to bother you, but…*
gáado ガード   *railway arch*
gáido ガイド   *guide*
gaijin 外人   *foreigner, westerner* (colloquial)
gaikoku 外国   *foreign country, abroad*
gaikokújin 外国人   *foreigner*
gaishoku 外食   *eating out*
gaka 画家   *artist*
gakkári suru がっかりする   *to be disappointed*
gaku 額   *a frame*
gakusei 学生   *student*
gakuse'iryoo 学生寮   *student dormitory*
gakusha 学者   *scholar*
ganbáru 頑張る   *to persevere, stick to a task*
ganbátte kudasai 頑張って下さい   *keep at it, give it all you've got!*
garasu ガラス   *glass*
–gáru がる   *to act in a…way* (suffix forms verb from adjective)

gasorin ガソリン   *gasoline*
gasorinsutándo ガソリン・スタンド   *petrol station*

gásu ガス   *gas; cooker; petrol* (colloquial)
–gata がた   plural suffix (honorific)
géi an 芸   *an art, accomplishment; trick*
geijutsu 芸術   *art, artistic performance*
geisha 芸者   *geisha, traditional professional entertainer*

gekijoo 劇場	*theatre*
gen'in 原因	*cause*
géndai 現代	*modern, present times, current*
gendáibyoo 現代病	*diseases of the modern lifestyle*
gengo 言語	*language*
gengogakusha 言語学者	*linguist*
genjoo 現状	*conditions, state of affairs*
genjúumin 原住民	*aborigine, original inhabitant*
génkan 玄関	*entrance porch, vestibule*
génki na 元気な	*healthy, fit, well*
geshuku 下宿	*boarding, lodging*
génzai 現在	*now, at present*
getsuyóobi 月曜日	*Monday*
gíjutsu 技術	*technology, skill*
gín 銀	*silver*
ginkoo 銀行	*bank*
Gírisha ギリシャ	*Greece*
gítaa ギター	*guitar*
go 五	*five*
–go 語	*language* (suffix)
go…desu ご…です	*is…* (subject honorific construction)
gobusata shite imásu ご無沙汰しています	*I have not been in touch, I have been neglectful*
gochisoosama déshita ご馳走様でした	*thank you for the wonderful meal*
goenryo kudasai 御遠慮ください	*please refrain from…*
goenryo naku ご遠慮なく	*please don't stand on ceremony, don't just be polite*
goenryo nasaránaide kudasai ご遠慮なさらないで下さい	*don't stand on ceremony, don't just be polite*
gógatsu 五月	*May*
gógo 午後	*afternoon*
góhan ご飯	*cooked rice, a meal*
gói 語彙	*vocabulary*
goissho ご一緒	*together, with you* (honorific)
gokenson ご謙遜	*modest* (honorific)
gokúroosama deshita ご苦労様でした	*thanks for your help*
gokyoodai ご兄弟	*brothers and sisters* (honorific)
gomeiwaku desu ご迷惑です	*it's an imposition* (on…)

gomen kudasái ご免下さい — *excuse me, anyone home?;
  goodbye* (on telephone)

gomen nasái ご免なさい — *I'm sorry*

gomi ごみ — *rubbish*

gomibáko ごみ箱 — *rubbish bin, dustbin*

gookaku 合格 — *passing* (exam), *making the grade*

Góoshuu 豪州 — *Australia*

gootoo 強盗 — *robbery*

goran kudasái/nasái
  ご覧下さい — *please look* (honorific)

goran ni ireru ご覧に入れる — *to show to a respected person –
  object* (honorific)

goran ni náru ご覧になる — *to look, see* (honorific)

gorippa ご立派 — *splendid* (honorific)

goriyoo kudasái ご利用ください — *please use*

góro 頃 — *about, around*

górufu ゴルフ — *golf*

goryooshin ご両親 — (your) *parents* (honorific)

goshinpai náku ご心配なく — *please don't worry*

goshinsetsu ni ご親切に — *thank you for your kindness*

goshoochi no yóo ni ご承知のように — *as you know*

goshookai shimásu ご紹介します — *let me introduce …*

goshújin ご主人 — *husband* (honorific), *your
  husband*

goshúmi 御趣味 — *hobby* (honorific), *your hobby*
  (**shúmi**)

goyóo ご用 — *business, something to do*
  (honorific)

goyukkúri ごゆっくり — *at leisure, slowly* (honorific)

gozaimásu ございます — *is, are* (formal)

gózen 午前 — *morning, ハ a.m.*

gozenchuu 午前中 — *all morning, throughout the
  morning*

gozónji desu ka ご存じですか — *do you know?*

gozónji 御存じ ご存じ — *know* (honorific)

gurai 位 — *about, as … as*

gúramu グラム — *gram weight*

gurée グレー — *grey*

guuzen 偶然 — *by chance*

gyuuniku 牛肉 — *beef*

gyuunyuu 牛乳 — *milk*

H

ha 歯	*tooth*
haba 幅	*width*
haba ga hirói 幅が広い	*wide*
haba ga semái 幅が狭い	*narrow*
hachi 八	*eight*
hachi 蜂	*bee*
hadashi 裸足	*bare-footed, bare feet*
hadé 派手	*bright, loud, showy*
háha 母	*mother*
hái はい	*yes*
hai 杯	*cupfuls, glassful*
haiiro 灰色	*grey*
haiken shite mo yoroshíi desu ka 拝見してもよろしいですか	*may I have a look?*
haiken suru 拝見する	*to look at object* (honorific)
háikingu ハイキング	*hiking*
hairimásu	see **háiru**
háiru 入る	*to enter, go in, fit*
háisha 歯医者	*dentist*
haishaku suru 拝借する	*to borrow from a respected person* (honorific)
haitatsu suru 配達する	*to deliver*
haiyuu 俳優	*actor*
hajimaru 始まる	*to start, begin* (intransitive)
hajime 初め 初め	*first, beginning*
hajime…o _____…mo …を初め…も	*not only but …, from … to …*
hajimemáshite 初めまして	*how do you do?*
hajimemásu	see **hajimeru**
hajimeru 始める	*to begin*
hajímete 初めて	*for the first time*
hákase 博士	*doctor, PhD*
hakken 発見	*discovery*
hakkíri はっきり	*clearly*
hako 箱	*box*
hakobu 運ぶ	*transport, carry* (transitive)
haku 履く	*to wear shoes, socks, skirt, trousers,* etc.
hakubútsukan 博物館	*museum*

hamachi はまち	*kingfish, yellowtail*
hameru はめる	*to wear/put on* (gloves, ring, etc.); *insert*
hán 半	*half past, – and a half*
haná 花	*flower*
hana 鼻	*nose*
hanamí 花見	*cherry-blossom viewing*
hanaréru 離れる	*separate from, move away from*
hanashí 話	*story, talking*
hanashimásu	see **hanásu**
hanasu 放す	*to let go*
hanásu 話す	*to speak*
hanátaba 花束	*bunch of flowers*
hanáyome 花嫁	*new bride*
hanbai-búchoo 販売部長	*sales manager, head of the sales section*
hanbáiki 販売機	*vending machine*
hanbún 半分	*half*
handobággu ハンドバッグ	*handbag*
hanga 版画	*woodblock-print*
hangaku 半額	*half price*
hánsamu na ハンサムな	*handsome*
hansei suru 反省	*reflect, think over, reconsider*
hantai 反対	*opposite, against*
hanzai 犯罪	*crime*
hanzúbon 半ズボン	*shorts, short pants*
happa 葉っぱ	*leaf*
hará 腹	*belly*
haráu 払う	*to pay*
hare 晴れ	*fine weather*
haremásu	see **haréru**
hareru 腫れる	*to swell*
haréru 晴れる	*to fine up*
háru 春	*spring*
haruméku 春めく	*become like spring*
haru-yásumi 春休み	*spring holiday*
hashí 橋	*bridge*
háshi 箸	*chopsticks*
hashirimásu	see **hashíru**
hashíru 走る	*to run*
hatá 旗	*flag*
hátachi 二十歳	*twenty years old*

hatarakimásu	see **hataraku**
hataraku 働く	*to work*
–hatsu 発	*leaving at/from* (suffix)
hatsuka 二十日	*twenty days*
hatsuon 発音	*pronunciation*
hayái 速い	*fast, quick, early* 早い
hayamé ni 早めに	*early, on the early side*
hayashi 林	*forest*
hayásu 生やす	*to grow* (beard, etc.)
hazu はず、筈	*should be, is expected to be*
hazukashigáru 恥ずかしがる	*to act shyly, be shy*
hazukashíi 恥ずかしい	*ashamed, shy, embarrassed*
hébi 蛇	*snake*
heisei 平成	*year period, 1989–*
heitai 兵隊	*soldier*
heiwa 平和	*peace*
hén na 変な	*strange, peculiar*
hen 辺	*place, area*
hénji 変じ	*answer, reply*
herasu 減らす	*reduce, decrease* (transitive)
herikóputa ヘリコプタ	*helicopter*
hetá na 下手な	*poor at, weak at*
heyá 部屋	*room*
hi 日	*day; sun*
hiatari 日当たり	*exposure to the sun*
hiatari ga íi 日当たりが好い	*to be sunny*
hidari 左	*left*
hidarigawa 左側	*left-hand side*
hidarikiki 左利き	*left-handed*
hidói 酷い	*cruel, severe*
hidói me ni áu 酷い目に会う	*have a terrible experience*
higashí 東	*east*
hige o sóru 髭を剃る	*to shave*
hige 髭	*beard, moustache*
hijoo ni 非常に	*extremely, very*
hijóoguchi 非常口	*(emergency) exit*
hiketsu 秘訣	*secret* (method)
hiki 匹	*counter for animals*
hikidashi 引き出し	*drawer*
hikóoki 飛行機	*aeroplane*
hiku 引く	*to catch a cold; to pull; look up in a dictionary*

hiku 弾く — *to play piano, guitar,* etc.
hikúi 低い — *low, short*
hima 暇 — *spare time*
hinanjo 避難所 — *evacuation point*
hiragána 平仮名 — **hiragána** *syllabary*
hirói 広い — *broad, wide, vast*
hirú 昼 — *midday, lunchtime*
hirugóhan 昼御飯 — *lunch*
hirumá 昼間 — *daytime*
hisashiburi 久しぶり — *after a long time*
hísho 秘書 — *secretary*
hitó 人 — *person, someone else*
hitobanjuu 一晩中 — *all night*
hitogomi 人混み — *crowd of people*
hitóri 一人 — *one person*
hitóri de 一人で — *alone, by oneself*
hitori mo + negative 一人も — *no one, nobody*
hitoríkko 一人っ子 — *only child*
hitótsu 一つ — *one*
hitsuji 羊 — *sheep*
hitsuji 羊 — *sheep;* 未 (calendar sign)
hitsuyoo na 必要 — *necessary*
híyoo 費用 — *cost*
hodo 程 — *extent;* (not) *as … as*
hoka 外 — *other, another*
hoken 保険 — *insurance*
hokengáisha 保険 — *insurance company*
Hokkáidoo 北海道 — most northerly of Japan's four main islands
hókkee ホッケー — *hockey*
homéru 誉める — *to praise*
–hón 本 — (numeral classifier) *for cylindrical objects*
hón 本 — *book*
hóndana 本棚 — *bookshelf*
hontóo/hontó 本当 — *true*
hón'ya 本屋 — *book shop*
hóo ga íi 方がいい — *be better to …*
hóo 方 — *direction, side*
hóofu na 豊富な — *rich, abundant*
hoogén 方言 — *dialect*
hookokusho 報告書 — *report*

hóomu ホーム	*railway platform*
hooritsu 法律	*law*
hoosoo suru 放送する	*to broadcast*
hoshi 星	*star*
hoshigáru 欲しがる	*to want, appear to want*
hoshíi 欲しい	*to want*
hosói 細い	*thin, fine, narrow*
hóteru ホテル	*hotel*
hotóndo ほとんど	*almost all, nearly*
hotto suru ほっとする	*to be relieved*
hyakkáten 百貨店	*department store*
hyakú 百	*hundred*
hyakubun 百聞	*hearing one hundred times*
hyoogen 表現	*expression* (in speech or writing)

I

í 亥	*boar* (calendar sign)
ichi 一	*one*
íchiba 市場	*market*
ichíban 一番	*first, no. 1, most*
ichíbu 一部	*one part; one copy*
ichído 一度	*once, sometime*
ichidó wa 一度は	*once, just once, at least once*
ichigatsú 一月	*January*
ichigo 苺	*strawberry*
ichinichijuu 一日中	*all*
ichioo 一応	*tentatively, as a start, somehow*
ié 家	*house, household; family*
igai to 意外と	*unexpectedly, surprisingly*
iidásu 言い出す	*begin to say; come out with*
Igirisu イギリス	*England, Britain*
Igirisújin イギリス人	*Englishman, Briton*
íi 好い	*good*
iie いいえ	*no*
iimásu	see **yuu**
íimeeru E メール	*E-mail*
ijime 苛め	*bullying*
íjoo 以上	*all, above, up to here*
ika 烏賊	*squid, cuttlefish*
íka 以下	*less than, from … down*

ikága 如何	*how?* (honorific)
ikága desu ka 如何ですか	*how are you?*
ikébana 生花	ikebana, *flower arrangement*
ikemasén いけません	*won't do; Don't do that!*
ikimásu 行きます	see **iku**
ikken 一見	*one look*
íkoo 以降	*after, since, from … onwards*
iku 行く	*to go*
íkutsu 幾つ	*how many*
íkura 幾ら	*how much*
íma 今	*now*
imada 未だ	*still*
imásu	see **iru**
ími 意味	*meaning*
imootó 妹	*younger sister*
inaka 田舎	*countryside*
Índo インド	*India*
Indonéshia インドネシア	*Indonesia*
inemúri 居眠り	*dozing off; falling asleep* (at the wheel)
infure インフレ	*inflation*
inku/inki インク	*ink*
inóru 祈る	*to pray*
inoshíshi 猪	*wild boar*
inshoo 印象	*impression*
inshooteki 印象的	*impressive, striking, moving*
inú 戌	*dog* (calendar sign)
inú 犬	*dog*
ippai いっぱい	*full*
íppai 一杯	*one glassful, cupful*
ippen ni 一遍に	*at once, at a time*
íppo 一歩	*one step*
ippootsúukoo 一方通行	*one-way traffic*
irasshái いらっしゃい	*welcome!*
irasshaimáse いらっしゃいませ	*welcome* (honorific)
irasshaimásu	see **irassháru**
irassháru いらっしゃる	*to come, go, be* (honorific)
iremásu	see **ireru**
ireru 入れる	*to put in*
iriguchi 入り口	*entrance*
irimásu	see **ir-u**
iró 色	*colour*

iroiro na 色々な	*various*
iru いる	*to be*
íru 入る	see **háiru**
ir-u 要る	*need*
iséebi 伊勢海老	*lobster*
isha 医者	*doctor*
ishí 石	*stone*
isogashíi 忙しい	*busy*
isogimásu	see **isógu**
isógu 急ぐ	*to hurry*
issho 一緒	*together*
ísshoo 一生	*life, throughout one's life*
isshookénmei 一生懸命	*for all one is worth, desperately*
isshu 一種	*a kind of*
isshuu suru 一周する	*to do a circuit of, to go around*
isu 椅子	*chair*
itadaku 頂く	*to receive* (object (honorific)), *to eat* (formal)
itái 痛い	*painful, to hurt*
itamae 板前	*cook, chef* (Japanese food)
Itaria, Itarii イタリア、イタリー	*Italy*
itású 致す	*to do* (object (honorific))
itóko 従兄弟	*cousin*
ítsu 何時	*when*
itsudémo 何時でも	*any time at all*
ítsuka いつか	*sometime, one day*
itsuka 五日	*five days; 5th of the month*
ítsumo 何時も	*always*
itsútsu 五つ	*five*
ittai 一体	*(what) on earth!*
iu 言う	see **yuu**
iya いや	*no* (when contradicting)
iyá na 嫌な	*unpleasant, disagreeable*
iyagáru 嫌がる	*to dislike, find repugnant, be unwilling to*
izakaya 居酒屋	*tavern, pub* (Japanese style)

J

já/jáa じゃあ	*well then, in that case*
jaanarísuto ジャーナリスト	*journalist*

jama 邪魔	*hindrance, nuisance* (see **ojama**)
jí 字	*character, letter*
ji 時	*o'clock* (suffix)
jibikí 字引	*dictionary*
jibun de 自分で	*by oneself*
jidóosha 自動車	*car*
jigi	see **ojigi**
jíinzu ジーンズ	*jeans*
jijoo 事情	*circumstances, the state of things*
jikan 時間	*time; hour*
jíken 事件	*incident, case, affair*
jíko 事故	*accident*
jíko 自己	*self*
jikogénba 事故現場	*scene of an accident*
jíkoku 時刻	*time*
jikoshóokai 自己紹介	*self-introduction*
jímen 地面	*ground*
jimí 地味	*subdued, conservative, plain*
jímu ジム	*gym*
jimúsho 事務所	*office*
–jin 人	*person;* suffix of nationality
jinja 神社	*shrine* (Shinto)
jinkoo 人口	*population*
jisatsu 自殺	*suicide*
jishin 自信	*confidence*
jishin 地震	*earthquake*
jísho 辞書	*dictionary*
jissai ni 実際に	*really, actually, in reality*
jisui 自炊	*cooking for oneself*
jiténsha 自転車	*bicycle*
jitsú ni 実に	*really, honestly*
jitsú wa 実は	*actually, in fact*
jiyúu 自由	*freedom;* **–na** *free*
jizake 地酒	*local sake*
jógingu ジョギング	*jogging*
jójo ni 徐々に	*gradually*
jókki ジョッキ	*jug, mug, tankard*
–joo 錠	*tablet* (numeral classifier)
jooba suru 乗馬する	*to ride a horse*
joodan 冗談	*joke*
jooei 上映 F	*showing* (a film), *screening*
joohoo 情報	*information*

jookyuu 上級	*advanced class/level*
jooshoo 上昇	*increase, rise*
jootatsu 上達	*progression, advancement*
joozú na 上手な	*to be skilful; to be good at*
josei 女性	*woman*
jóshi 女子	*woman; women's* (sporting event)
joshigákusei 女子学生	*female student*
júnbi 準備	*preparations*
júnjo 順序	*order*
–juu 中	*all through* (suffix)
júu 十	*ten*
juubún 十分	*sufficient, enough, plenty*
júudoo 柔道	*judo*
juugatsú 十月	*October*
juuichigatsú 十一月	*November*
juunigatsú 十二月	*December*
juuníshi 十二支	*12 branches; 12 animals of the Chinese zodiac*
júusho 住所	*address*
júusu ジュース	*orange juice*
juuyokka 十四日	*14th day of the month*

K

ka か	interrogative particle*; or*
káado カード	*card*
kaban 鞄	*bag, briefcase*
kabe 壁	*wall*
kabin 花瓶	*vase*
kabu 株	(stocks and) *shares*
kabuki 歌舞伎	*Kabuki traditional theatre*
kabúru 被る	*to wear a hat; put on the head*
kachimásu	see **kátsu**
kachoo 課長	*head of a section or department*
kádo 角	*corner*
kaeri 帰り	*the way home; going home*
kaerimásu	see **káeru**
káeru 帰る	*to return home, go back*
kaeru 蛙	*frog*
káesu 返す	*to return, give back*

kágaku 化学	*chemistry*
kágaku 科学	*science*
kagamí 鏡	*mirror*
kage 影	*shade, shadow*
–kágetsu ヶ月	*months* (numeral classifier)
kagí 鍵	*key*
kago 籠	*basket; cage*
kagu 嗅ぐ	*to smell*
kágu 家具	*furniture*
kai 'in 会員	*member*
kaidan 階段	*stairs, steps*
kaigai-ryókoo 海外旅行	*overseas trip*
kaigan 海岸	*coast, seaside*
kaigí 会議	*conference; also* **káigi**
kaigichuu 会議中	*in conference*
kaigíshitsu 会議室	*conference room*
kaiin 会員	*member*
kaijoo 会場	*conference room*
kaimásu	*see* **kau**
kaimono 買い物	*shopping*
kaisatsúguchi 改札口	*ticket gate*
kaisha 会社	*company*
kaishain 会社員	*company employee*
kaiwa 会話	*conversation*
káji 火事	*fire*
kakarimásu	*see* **kakáru**
kakaríchoo 係長	*chief clerk, project manager*
kakáru かかる	*to cost*
kakáru かかる	*to take time, cost; be hanging;* **denwa ga kakáru** *to be rung up*
kakéru かける	*to hang, attach*
kakéru 駆ける	*to run, gallop*
kaki 柿	*persimmon*
káki 牡蠣	*oyster*
kakimásu	*see* **káku**
kakiowáru 書き終わる	*to finish writing*
kakkoo 格好	*form, shape, appearance*
káku 書く	*to write*
kákuchi 各地	*everywhere, all places throughout…*
kakuu no 架空の	*imaginary, fictitious*

kamá 窯   *kiln*

kamaimásén 構いません   *it doesn't matter*

kámera カメラ   *camera*

kami 紙   *paper*

kaminári 雷   *thunder*

kaminóke 髪の毛   *hair*

kámo shiremasen かも知れませ   *perhaps*
ん

kamoku 科目   *subject, course*

–kan 間   suffix indicating duration

kanaboo 金棒   *metal rod, iron rod*

Kánada カナダ   *Canada*

kánai 家内   *wife; my wife*

kanarazu 必ず   *certainly, surely, without fail*

kánari かなり   *fairly*

kanashii 悲しい   *sad*

kanban 看板   *signboard, sign*

kánben shite kudasái 勘弁して下   *please forgive me; please excuse*
さい   *me*

kane 金   *metal, see* **okane**

kanemochí 金持ち   *rich person*

kangaekatá 考え方   *way of thinking*

kangáeru 考える   *to think, consider*

kangei suru 歓迎する   *to welcome*

kangei 歓迎   *welcome*

kangófu 看護婦   *nurse*

kani 蟹   *crab*

kanja 患者   *patient*

kanji 感じ   *feeling*

kanji 漢字   *Chinese characters*

kanjiru 感じる   *feel*

kanjóo 勘定   *bill, account*

kankei 関係   *relations, connection*

Kánkoku 韓国   *South Korea*

Kankokugo 韓国語   *Korean* (language)

Kankokujín 韓国人   *Korean* (person)

kankoo 観光   *tourism*

kankyoo 環境   *environment*

kánojo 彼女   *she*

kanpai 乾杯   *a toast, cheers*

kanreki 還暦   *sixtieth birthday*

kannrinin 管理人   *caretaker, janitor*

kánsuru 関する	*about, concerning*
kantan na 簡単な	*simple, easy, brief*
kao 顔	*face*
kaoiro 顔色	*complexion*
kaori 香り	*smell, fragrance*
kara から	*because* (clause final particle)
kara から	*from* (phrase final particle)
kara これから	*now, from now on*
kará 空	*empty*
kara, –te____	see **–te kara**
karada o kowásu 体をこわす	*to harm one's health*
karada 体	*body; health*
karakuchi 辛口	*dry* (of wine, etc.)
karaoke カラオケ	*karaoke, singing to musical accompaniment* (literally, 'empty orchestra')
karate 空手	*karate* (a martial art)
karatédoo 空手道	*the way of karate, teachings of karate*
káre 彼	*he*
karimásu	see **karu** and *kariru*
kariru 借りる	*to borrow*
karu 刈る	*to mow, cut*
karui 軽い	*light; not heavy*
kása 傘	*umbrella*
kashikói 賢い	*clever*
kashikomarimáshita 畏まりました	*certainly sir/madam* (object honorific)
kashimásu	see **kasu**
káshira かしら	*I wonder if …* (feminine sentence-final particle)
kasu 貸す	*to lend*
kata 方	*person* (honorific)
káta 肩	*shoulder*
katachi 形	*shape, form*
katagaki 肩書き	*credentials, title* (writing beside the name on a business card)
katai 固い	*hard*
katakána 片仮名	*a Japanese syllabary*
katákori 肩凝り	*stiffness in the shoulders*
katana 刀	*sword*
katazukéru 片付ける	*to tidy up, put away*

kátsu 勝つ	*to win*
káu 飼う	*to keep* (an animal); *have* (a pet)
kau 買う	*to buy*
kawá 川	*river*
kawaíi 可愛い	*cute, appealing; precious, beloved*
kawaku 乾く	*to dry up*
kawari ni 代りに	*instead of*
kawaru 変わる	*to change*
kawasu 交わす	*exchange* (conversations)
kawatta 変わった	*strange, peculiar; weird*
kayóobi 火曜日	*Tuesday*
kayou 通う	*to attend; go regularly between, ply*
kayui 痒い	*itchy*
kázan 火山	*volcano*
kaze 風	*wind*
kaze 風邪	*a cold*
kazoeru 数える	*to count*
kázoku 家族	*family*
kázu 数	*number*
kazunoko 数の子	*salted herring roe*
ke 毛	*hair, fur*
kedo けど	*but* (casual speech)
kegá 怪我	*injury*
keiba 競馬	*horse-racing; race-horse*
keigo 敬語	*respect language*
keijiban 掲示板	*notice board*
keikaku 計画	*plan*
keiken 経験	*experience*
keikoo 傾向	*tendency*
keimusho 刑務所	*prison, gaol*
keisatsu 警察	*the police*
keitai-dénwa 携帯電話	*mobile phone, cell phone*
keiyaku 契約	*contract*
kéizai 経済	*economy, economics*
keizaiséichoo 経済成長	*economic growth*
kekkon suru 結婚する	*to marry*
kekkón-shiki 結婚式	*wedding ceremony*
kékkoo desu 結構です	*it's fine; it's all right; no thank you; I've had enough*
kékkoo na 結構な	*fine, wonderful*

kemuri 煙	*smoke*
kén 券	*ticket*
ken 県	*prefecture*
–ken 軒	(numeral classifier for buildings)
kenbutsu 見物	*sightseeing*
kenchikka 建築家	*architect*
kenchiku 建築	*architecture*
kéndoo 剣道	*Japanese fencing*
kenka 喧嘩	*argument*
kenkoo na 健康な	*healthy*
kenkoo 健康	*health*
kenkyuu 研究	*research, study*
kenkyúushitsu 研究室	*office* (of a university academic)
kenson na 謙遜な	*modest, humble*
kentóo ga tsukánai 見当がつか ない	*have no idea, be unable to guess*
keredomo けれども	*but, however*
késa 今朝	*this morning*
keshiki 景色	*scenery*
kesshite 決して	(definitely) *not; never*
kesu 消す	*to put out, extinguish*
ki ga suru 気がする	*to feel, think*
ki ga tooku náru 気が遠くなる	*faint away, feel dizzy*
ki ga tsuku 気がつく	*to notice, realize*
ki ni iru 気に入る	*to like, be pleased*
ki ni náru 気になる	*to be a worry, weigh on one's mind*
ki ni suru 気にする	*to worry*
ki o tsukéru 気をつける	*to be careful*
kí 木	*tree; wood*
ki 気	*mind, spirit, energy*
kieru 消える	*to go out, disappear*
kíga 飢餓	*famine*
kíji 記事	*article* (newspaper, etc.)
kikai 機会	*opportunity*
kikái 機械	*machine*
kikaseru 聞かせる	*to tell, relate*
kiken 危険	*danger*
kiken na 危険な	*dangerous*
kikimásu	see **kiku**
kikoeru 聞こえる	*to be able to hear, be audible*
kikoeru 聞こえる	*to be audible; can hear*

kiku 利く	*to work, be effective, function*
kiku 聞く	*to hear, listen; ask*
kiku 菊	*chrysanthemum*
kimaru 決まる	*to be decided*
kimásu	see **kúru**
kimeru 決める	*to decide, fix, settle*
kimi 君	*you* (familiar)
kimochi 気持ち	*feeling; mood*
kimono 着物	*kimono, garment*
kín 金	*gold*
kinchoo suru 緊張する	*to be tense, to be strained*
kindókei 金時計	*gold watch*
kin'en 禁煙	*no smoking*
kinen 記念	(in) *commemoration, souvenir, keepsake*
kíngyo 金魚	*goldfish*
kínjo 近所	*neighbourhood, nearby*
kinmédaru 金メダル	*gold medal*
kinóo 昨日	*yesterday*
kinshi 禁止	*forbidden*
kin'yóobi 金曜日	*Friday*
kin'yuu 金融	*finance*
kiósuku キオスク	*kiosk*
kippu 切符	*ticket*
kirai na 嫌いな	*to dislike*
kírei na 綺麗な	*beautiful; clean*
kirimásu	see **kír-u**
kirin キリン	*giraffe*
kiro キロ	*kilometre, kilogram*
kíru 切る	*to cut*
kiru 着る	*to wear*
kísetsu 季節	*season*
kisha 汽車	*train*
kisó 基礎	*basis, foundation*
kisobúnpoo 基礎文法	*basic grammar*
kisóku 規則	*rule, regulation*
kisoku-tadashíi 規則正しい	*regular, regulated*
kissáten 喫茶店	*tea shop, coffee shop*
kitá 北	*north*
kitai 期待	*expectation, hopes, anticipation*
kitanai 汚い	*dirty, filthy*
kitte 切手	*postage stamp*

kitto きっと	*surely, certainly*
kke っけ	retrospective question particle
ko 個	(numeral classifier) *for miscellaneous objects*
ko 子	*child*
kochira kóso こちらこそ	*me too; the pleasure is mine*
kochira こちら	*this one, this way*
kódai 古代	*ancient period; ancient*
kodomo 子供	*child*
kóe 声	*voice*
kóe ga suru 声がする	*to hear a voice*
kokki 国旗	*national flag*
koko ここ	*here*
kokonoká 九日	*nine days; 9th of the month*
kokónotsu 九つ	*nine*
kokóro 心	*heart; feelings; mind*
kokuritsu 国立	*national*
kokuritsu-dáigaku 国立大学	*a national university*
kokusai 国際	*international* (as prefix)
kokusaikóoryuu 国際交流	*international exchange*
kokusaiteki 国際的	*international* (adjective)
komáasharu コマーシャル	*commercial, advertisement*
komáru 困る	*to be in trouble; become distressed; be at a loss*
kome 米	*rice* (uncooked)
koméya 米屋	*rice merchant; rice shop*
kómu 込む	*to get crowded*
kón 紺	*navy blue*
kónban 今晩	*this evening*
konban wa 今晩は	*good evening*
konbíni コンビニ	*convenience store*
kondákutaa コンダクター	(tour) *conductor*
kóndo 今度	*this time; next time*
kóngetsu 今月	*this month*
konna こんな	*this kind of*
konnichi wa 今日は	*hello!; good day*
kono この	*this*
kono aida/konaida この間	*recently, the other day*
konogoro このごろ	*these days*
konpyúuta コンピュータ	*computer*
konshéruje コンシェルジェ	*concierge* (in a hotel)
konshuu 今週	*this week*

koo こう	*like this*
koo yuu こういう	*this kind of*
koo yuu fuu na こういうふうな	*this kind of*
koo yuu fuu ni こういうふうに	*like this*
kooban 交番	*police-box*
Koochíken 高知県	*Kochi Prefecture*
koodai na 広大な	*vast, immense*
kooen 公園	*park*
koofun 興奮	*excitement*
koogai 公害	*pollution; public nuisance*
koohai 後輩	*junior* (student, etc.)
koohíi コーヒー	*coffee*
koohyoo 好評	*popular, well received, highly praised*
koojichuu 工事中	*under construction; men at work*
koojoo 工場	*factory*
kookan 交換	*exchange*
kookan-ryúugakusei 交換留学生	*overseas exchange student*
kookoku 広告	*advertisement; announcement*
kookoo 高校	*high school* (abbr.)
kookóosei 高校生	*high-school student*
kookúuken 航空券	*airline ticket*
kóokyo 皇居	*the imperial palace*
koomúin 公務員	*civil servant, government employee*
koonétsuhi 光熱費	*heating and lighting costs*
koori 氷	*ice*
kooryuu 交流	*cultural exchange*
koosoku 高速	*high speed*
koosoku-básu 高速バス	*highway bus*
koosoku-dóoro 高速道路	*highway, motorway*
kóosu コース	*course*
koosui 香水	*perfume*
kóoto コート	*coat*
kootoogákkoo 高等学校	*high school*
kootsuu 交通	*traffic*
kootsuu-jíko 交通事故	*traffic accident*
kooyoo 紅葉	*autumn leaves*
koozui 洪水	*flood*
koppu コップ	*a glass*
kore これ	*this*
koro 頃	*time; about when; about*

korobu 転ぶ	*to fall over*
korosu 殺す	*to kill*
koshi 腰	*hips, lower back*
koshiraeru こしらえる	*to make; manufacture*
koshoo suru 故障する	*to break down, malfunction*
koshóo 胡椒	*pepper*
kóso こそ	*the very one* (emphatic particle)
kossetsu 骨折	*broken bone*
kotáeru 答える	*to answer*
kotchí こっち	*here; this way; this one*
koten-óngaku 古典音楽	*classical music*
kotó 事	*thing; fact*
kotó ga aru ことがある	*to have done; to have experienced*
kotó ga dekiru ことができる	*to be able*
kotó ni suru ことにする	*to decide to*
kotó ni yotte ことにいよって	*by …ing, through …ing*
kotobá 言葉	*words; language*
kotoshi 今年	*this year*
kotsu こつ	*knack, trick*
kowagáru 怖がる	*to be frightened*
kowái 怖い	*to be frightened; frightening*
kowareru 壊れる	*to get broken*
kowásu 壊す	*to break*
kozutsumi 小包	*parcel*
–ku く	adverb suffix
kú 九	*nine*
–ku nai くない	negative suffix
kubáru 配る	*to distribute*
kubi 首	*neck*
kuchi 口	*mouth*
kuchihige 口髭	*moustache*
kudámono 果物	*fruit*
kudasái 下さい	*please give me*
kudasáru 下さる	*to give*
kugatsú 九月	*September*
kúmo 雲	*cloud*
kumóru 曇る	*to cloud over; become cloudy*
kumorí 曇り	*cloudy weather*
kun 君	familiar form of address for men and boys
kuni 国	*country; one's native place*

kurai 暗い	*dark*
kurasu 暮らす	*to live*
kurejittokáado クレジットカード	*credit card*
kureru 呉れる	*to give*
kuríininguya クリーニング屋	*dry cleaner's*
kurísumasu クリスマス	*Christmas*
kurói 黒い	*black*
kúru 来る	*to come*
kuruma 車	*cart; car*
kusá 草	*grass*
kusái 臭い	*smelly*
kusáru 腐る	*to rot; go bad*
kusuri 薬	*medicine; medication*
kusuriya 薬屋	*chemist's*
kutabiréru くたびれる	*to get tired; exhausted*
kutsú 靴	*shoes*
kutsu-úriba 靴売場	*shoe department/counter*
kúu 食う	*eat* (vulgar)
kúuki 空気	*air*
kuukoo 空港	*airport*
kuwáete 加えて	*in addition*
kyaku 客	*guest; customer*
kyónen 去年	*last year*
kyóo 今日	*today*
kyóoshi 教師	*teacher*
kyóodai 兄弟	*brothers and sisters*
kyoodoo 共同	*in common, shared*
kyoogijoo 競技場	*stadium, sports ground*
kyooiku 教育	*education*
kyóoju 教授	*professor*
kyóoka 強化	*strengthening*
kyóomi 興味	*interest*
kyóomi o mótsu 興味を持つ	*to be interested* (in = **ni**)
kyóoshi 教師	*teacher*
kyóri 距離	*distance*
kyúu 九	*nine*
kyuujitsu 休日	(public) *holiday*
kyúuri 黄瓜	*cucumber*
kyúuryoo 給料	*salary*
Kyúushuu 九州	*Kyushu* (southernmost of Japan's four main islands)

M

ma ni áu 間に合う   *to be in time* (for = **ni**); *to be enough*

máa máa まあまあ   *so so; not bad*

máajan 麻雀   *mahjong*

machí 町   *town; district*

machiawaséru 待ち合わせる   *to meet, arrange to meet*

machigaeru 間違える   *to mistake* (transitive)

machigai 間違い   *mistake, error*

machigatte 間違って   *by mistake*

machigau 間違う   *to be wrong; make a mistake*

machimásu   see **mátsu**

máda 未だ   *still, not yet*

máde まで   *as far as, until*

máde ni までに   *by, before*

mádo 窓   *window*

madóguchi 窓口   *counter, window*

máe 前   *front;* ____ **no máe ni** *in front of*

máfuraa マフラー   *muffler*

magaru 曲がる   *to turn; go around*

máhi 麻痺   *paralysis*

–mai 枚   (numeral classifier for flat objects)

mai- 毎   *each, every* (prefix)

máiasa 毎朝   *every morning*

maigetsu 毎月   *every month*

mainen 毎年   *every year*

máinichi 毎日   *every day*

máiru 参る   *to go, come* (formal)

maitoshi 毎年   *every year*

maitsuki 毎月   *every month*

makikomaréru 巻き込まれる   *to be caught up in, be swept along with*

makizushi 巻寿司   *sushi roll*

mama まま   *way, fashion, as it is* (see **sono mama**)

mamóru 守る   *to protect; observe* (rules, etc.)

mángaichi 万が一   *just in case*

mannaka 真ん中   *right in the middle*

mánshon マンション   *flat; apartment*

mánzoku suru 満足する	*to be satisfied*
marude まるで	*just like, just as if*
marui 丸い	*round*
másaka まさか	*surely not, nonsense!*
–masén ません	polite negative ending
–masén deshita ませんでした	polite past negative ending
–máshita ました	polite past ending
–mashóo ましょう	polite hortative ending, *let's…*
massúgu 真っ直ぐ	*straight ahead*
mata dóozo またどうぞ	*please come again*
mátchi マッチ	*matches*
mata また、又	*again; further*
mátsu 待つ	*to wait*
mátsu 松	*pine*
matsuri 祭り	*festival*
mattaku 全く	*completely, absolutely*
mawari 周り	*surrounding area, around*
mayaku 麻薬	*narcotic drugs*
mázu 先ず	*first* (adverb)
mé 目	*eye*
–me 目	*ordinal suffix*
méeru メール	*mail* (E-mail)
méetoru メートル	*metre*
mégane 眼鏡	*spectacles, glasses*
–mei 名	numeral classifier for people
Méiji 明治	*year period* (1868–1912)
Meijijínguu 明治神宮	shrine in Tokyo commemorating the Emperor Meiji
meirei suru 命令する	*to order*
méin メイン	*main meal, main dish*
meishi 名刺	*business card, name card*
meishu 銘酒	*fine sake*
meetoru メートル	*metre*
méiwaku 迷惑	*trouble, nuisance*
mekata 目方	*weight*
Mekíshiko メキシコ	*Mexico*
mémo メモ	*memo; memo pad*
ménbaa メンバー	*member*
mendóo na 面倒	*bothersome; difficult*
ménkyo 免許	*licence* (qualification)
ményuu メニュー	*menu*
menzéiten 免税店	*tax-free store*

meshiagaru 召し上がる	*to eat* (honorific)
meshita 目下	*socially inferior* (i.e. below oneself in age, position or status)
meue 目上	*socially superior* (i.e. above oneself in age, position or status)
mezurashíi 珍しい	*rare; unusual*
mi ni tsuku 身につく	*to absorb, acquire, learn* (intransitive)
mi 巳	*snake* (calendar sign)
miai 見合い	*marriage meeting*
michi 道	*road*
mídori 緑	*green*
miéru 見える	*to come on a visit* (honorific)
miéru 見える	*to be able to see; be visible*
migaku 磨く	*to polish; shine; clean*
migi 右	*right*
migigawa 右側	*right-hand side*
migigawatsúukoo 右側通行	*keep right*
mígoto na 見事な	*splendid*
mijikái 短い	*short*
míkan 蜜柑	*mandarin orange, satsuma*
mikka 三日	*three days; 3rd of the month*
mimai 見舞い	*visit to the sick, get-well visit*
mimásu	see **míru**
mimí 耳	*ear*
miná 皆	*all, everyone*
minami 南	*south*
minamimuki 南向き	*facing south*
minásama 皆様	*everyone; all of you; ladies and gentlemen* (honorific)
minásan 皆さん	*everyone; all of you; ladies and gentlemen* (honorific)
minato 港	*harbour, port*
mineraru-wóotaa ミネラル・ウォーター	*mineral water*
minna みんな	*all, everyone*
minshuku 民宿	*bed and breakfast, guesthouse*
minshushúgi 民主主義	*democracy*
min'yoo 民謡	*folk song*
mínzoku 民族	*ethnic group, people*
miokuru 見送る	*to see off; send off*
míru 見る	*to see, look, watch*

míruku ミルク	*milk* (condensed)
misé 店	*shop*
misemásu	see **miséru**
miséru 見せる	*to show*
mítai na みたいな	*like, as*
míte morau 診てもらう	*to have oneself examined* (by a doctor)
mitsukaru 見つかる	*to be found; be able to find*
mitsurin 密林	*jungle*
mittsú 三つ	*three*
miyage 土産	*souvenir; gift*
miyako 都	*capital*
mizu 水	*water*
mizuúmi 湖	*lake*
mo も	*also, too; even*
mo…mo も…も	*both…and*
mochiagéru 持ち上げる	*to lift up*
mochíron 勿論	*of course*
modan na モダンな	*modern*
modóru 戻る	*to return* (intransitive)
modósu 戻す	*to put back; bring up, vomit* (transitive)
mokuyóobi 木曜日	*Thursday*
momo 桃	*peach*
momoiro 桃色	*pink*
món 門	*gate*
Monbúshoo 文部省	*Ministry of Education*
mondai 問題	*problem, question*
mongén 門限	*curfew, closing time*
monó 物	*thing*
monó 者	*person* (formal)
móo もう	*already*
moo もう	*more*
mooshiagéru 申し上げる	*to say* (object honorific)
mooshiwake arimasén 申し訳ありません	*I'm terribly sorry; there's no excuse*
móosu 申す	*to say; be called* (formal)
morau 貰う	*to receive, be given*
mori 森	*wood; grove*
móshi(ka) もし(か)	*if*
móshimoshi もしもし	*hello* (telephone)
motoméru 求める	*to seek; to buy* (honorific)

mótsu 持つ — *to have; hold*
motte iku 持っていく — *to take*
motte kúru 持ってくる — *to bring*
mótto もっと — *more*
móttomo 最も — *most*
moyori no 最寄りの — *nearest*
muchiuchishoo 鞭打ち症 — *whiplash injury*
muda na 無駄な — *useless; a waste*
múgamuchuu 無我夢中 — *frantically; like mad*
muiká 六日 — *six days, 6th of the month*
mukaeru 迎える — *to meet, welcome*
mukashi 昔 — *the past; long ago; formerly*
mukau 向かう — *to face; go towards*
mukoo 向こう — *opposite; over there; abroad*
muku 向く — *face* (intransitive), *turn towards; suit*

mumei 無名 — *unknown*
murá 村 — *village*
murásaki 紫 — *purple*
múri na 無理な — *unreasonable, fruitless, useless*
muró 室 — *room*
Muromachi-jídai 室町時代 — *Muromachi period (1336–1573)*

mushi 虫 — *insect, worm, bug*
mushiatsúi 蒸し暑い — *humid, sultry*
músu 蒸す — *to steam*
musubu 結ぶ — *tie, link, join*
musuko 息子 — *son*
musumé 娘 — *daughter*
muttsú 六つ — *six*
muzukashíi 難しい — *difficult*
myóo na 妙な — *odd, strange, peculiar*
myóoban 明晩 — *tomorrow night* (formal)
myóoji 名字 — *family name, surname*
myóonichi 明日 — *tomorrow* (formal)

N

'n desu んです — *the fact is*
na no de なので — *because it is*
na no ni なのに — *although it is*

ná な	..., *isn't it?* etc. (sentence-final particle)
na な	negative imperative particle
náa なあ	same as **ná** above
nadakái 名高い	*famous*
nádo 等	*et cetera, and so on*
nagái 長い	*long*
nagamé 眺め	*view, outlook*
–nágara 一ながら	*while...ing* (verbal suffix)
nagareru 流れる	*flow*
nagasu 流す	*to wash away; play* (music)
–nai ない	see **–(a)nai**
nái ない	*to be not; to have not*
–naide	see **–(a)naide**
náifu ナイフ	*knife*
náigai 内外	*internal and external; home and abroad*
náikaku 内閣	*cabinet, ministry*
náka 中	*inside, middle*
nakanáka なかなか	*very, considerably*
nakámi 中身	*contents*
nakidásu 泣き出す	*burst out crying*
nakigóe 鳴き声	*cry; song of bird,* etc.
naku 泣く	*cry*
nakunaru 亡くなる	*to die, pass away*
nakusu なくす	*to lose*
náma 生	*raw; live entertainment*
namabíiru 生ビール	*draft beer*
namae 名前	*name*
namatámago 生卵	*raw egg*
nán 何	*what*
nána 七	*seven*
nanátsu 七つ	*seven*
nándaka 何だか	*somehow*
nandémo 何でも	*anything at all; somehow, anyhow*
nandomo 何度も	*any number of times; very often*
náni 何	*what*
nanidoshi 何年	*what zodiac animal sign*
nánika 何か	*something*
nánimo 何も	*nothing*
nankai mo 何回も	*any number of times; very often*

nánmeisama desu ka 何名様です か	*how many people, Sir/Madam*
nanoka 七日	*seven days, 7th of the month*
nánte なんて	*and the like, the likes of…, what (exclamation)*
nántoka 何とか	*somehow or other*
naóru 直る	*be cured; get better; be fixed*
naósu 直す	*mend; cure*
–naósu 直す	*re-…*
nára なら	*if*
naraihajimeru 習い始める	*begin to learn*
naráu 習う	*learn*
naréru 慣れる	*become accustomed* (to = **ni**)
narimásu	*see **náru***
náru 成る	*become*
–nasái なさい	*imperative ending*
nasáru なさる	*do* (honorific)
natsú 夏	*summer*
natsukashigáru 懐かしがる	*to feel nostalgic about*
natsukashíi 懐かしい	*nostalgic*
natsuyásumi 夏休み	*summer vacation*
náze 何故	*why*
né ね	*isn't it?, etc. (sentence-final particle)*
ne 子	*rat (calendar sign)*
nedan 値段	*price*
née ねえ	*isn't it?, etc. (sentence-final particle)*
néesan	*see **onéesan***
negáu 願う	*to request, see **onegái***
nékkuresu ネックレス	*necklace*
néko 猫	*cat*
nékutai ネクタイ	*tie*
nemuru 眠る	*sleep*
–nen 年	*years*
nénjuu-mukyuu 年中無休	*open all year round*
nenrei 年令	*age*
neru 寝る	*go to bed; lie down; sleep*
netsú 熱	*heat; temperature; fever*
nezumi 鼠	*rat, mouse*
ni kánshite に関して	*about, concerning (adverb)*
ni kánsuru に関する	*concerning, about (adjective)*

ni tótte にとって	*for*
ni tsúite no について	*about, concerning*
ni yoru to によると	*according to*
ni yotte によって	*by* (agent of passive)*; in accordance with* (see also **kotó ni yotte**)
ni に	*indirect object particle*
ni 二	*two*
niáu 似合う	*suit, become*
–nichi 日	*-days* (numeral classifier)
Nichiei 日英	*Japan and Britain*
nichiyóobi 日曜日	*Sunday*
nigái 苦い	*bitter*
nigatsú 二月	*February*
nigorí 濁り	*voicing marks; muddiness*
Nihón 日本	*Japan*
Nihongo 日本語	*Japanese language*
Nihonjín 日本人	*Japanese person*
Nihonsei 日本製	*Japanese manufacture, made in Japan*
Nihonshu 日本酒	*Japanese rice wine, sake*
Nihontoo 日本刀	*Japanese sword*
nikú 肉	*meat*
–nikúi にくい	*be difficult to …* (suffix)
nikujága 肉じゃが	*beef and potato stew*
nikúya 肉屋	*butcher, butcher's shop*
nímotsu 荷物	*luggage; parcels*
ningen 人間	*human being; person*
ningyoo 人形	*doll*
ninja 忍者	*ninja, a feudal-period spy-commando*
ninki 人気	*popularity*
Nippón 日本	*Japan* (formal pronunciation), see **Nihón**
niru 似る	*take after; come to resemble*
nishi 西	*west*
nishiguchi 西口	*western gate, western exit*
Nitchuu– 日中	*Japan and China*
nite iru 似ている	*resemble, look like*
niwa 庭	*garden*
niwatori 鶏	*cock, hen, chicken*
no の	*'s of …* (possessive particle)

no の	*the fact; the one* (nominalizing particle)
no de ので	*because*
no désu のです	see **'n désu**
no ni のに	*although*
noboru 上る	*climb, go up, come up in* (conversation)
nochihodo 後程	*later, afterwards* (formal)
nódo 喉	*throat*
nódo ga kawakimáshita 喉が渇いた	*I'm thirsty*
nokóru 残る	*remain*
nomimásu 飲みます	see **nómu**
nomímono 飲み物	*drink, beverage*
nomisugiru 飲み過ぎる	*drink too much*
nómu 飲む	*drink*
noo 能	*the Noh theatre*
nóoto ノート	*exercise book, notebook*
noriba 乗り場	*boarding place; taxi rank; bus station*
norikaeru 乗り換える	*change trains, buses,* etc.
norimásu	see **noru**
norimono 乗り物	*transport*
noriokuréru 乗り遅れる	*miss* (bus, etc.), *be late for…*
noru 乗る	*get on; ride,* **ni** after object; *appear in newspaper,* etc.
noseru 乗せる	*put on, place on; give a ride to*
nozoku 覗く	*to peep at, glance at, look at*
nozoku 除く	*to exclude*
nozoite 除いて	*excluding*
núgu 脱ぐ	*take off* (clothes)
nureru 濡れる	*get wet*
nusúmu 盗む	*steal*
nyuugaku-shikén 入学試験	*entrance examination*
nyuuin suru 入院する	*go to hospital*
Nyuujíirando ニュージーランド	*New Zealand*
nyúushi 入試	*entrance examination* (abbr.)
nyúusu ニュース	*news*

O

o を	object particle*; along, through*, etc.
o– お	*honorific prefix* (if a word is not listed here look it up without the initial **o–**)
o…ni náru お…になる	(honorific) *verb*
oagari kudasai お上がり下さい	*please come in; please eat*
oari désu ka お有りですか	*have you got …?*
oba 叔母	*aunt*
obáasan おばあさん	*grandmother, old woman* (honorific)
obasan 叔母さん	*aunt* (honorific)
óbi 帯	*sash, belt* (judo, etc.)
oboemásu	see **obóeru**
obóeru 覚える	*to remember; learn*
oboosan お坊さん	*Buddhist priest*
ocha お茶	*tea*
ocha no yu お茶の湯	*tea*
ocha o ireru お茶を入れる	*to make tea*
ochíru 落ちる	*to fall; fail examination*
ochitsuku 落ち着く	*to settle down; be calm*
odaiji ni お大事に	*take care of yourself*
odekake désu ka お出かけですか	*are you going out?*
odoróita 驚いた	*Oh! You frightened me!* (exclamation of surprise)
odoróku 驚く	*to be surprised*
odoru 踊る	*to dance*
ofúro お風呂	*bath*
ogénki desu ka お元気ですか	*How are you? Are you well?*
oháshi お箸	*chopsticks*
ohayoo gozaimásu お早うございます	*good morning*
ohima お暇	*spare time* (honorific)
ohíru お昼	*midday; lunch*
oide ni náru お出でになる	*to come; go* (honorific)
oikutsu お幾つ	*how old? How many?* (honorific)
oishasan お医者さん	*doctor* (honorific)
oishii 美味しい	*delicious, tasty*
oisogashíi 忙しい	*busy* (honorific)
ojama shimáshita お邪魔しました	*goodbye; sorry to have bothered you*

ojama shimásu お邪魔します   *hello; may I come in? Sorry to bother you*

oji 叔父   *uncle*
ojigi suru お辞儀する   *to bow*
ojíisan おじいさん   *grandfather, old man* (honorific)
ojisan 叔父さん   *uncle; middle-aged man* (honorific)

ojóosan お嬢さん   *miss; young lady; daughter* (honorific)

oka 丘   *hill*
okáasan お母さん   *mother* (honorific)
okaeri désu ka お帰りですか   *are you leaving, are you going home?*

okaeri nasái お帰りなさい   *welcome back; hello*
okagesama de お陰様で   *yes, thank you; fortunately; thanks to you*

okake kudasái おかけ下さい   *please sit down*
okane お金   *money*
okanemochí お金持ち   *rich person*
okáshi お菓子   *cakes*
okanjoo お勘定   *bill* (also **kanjóo**)
okáshi お菓子   *cakes, sweets*
okashíi おかしい   *funny, strange*
okáwari wa ikága desu ka お代わりはいかがですか   *would you like another helping?*
okazu おかず   *side dishes eaten with rice*
–oki 置き   *at intervals of* (numeral suffix)
oki ni iru お気に入る   *to like, be pleased* (honorific)
oki ni meshimáshita ka お気に召しましたか   *did you like it? Were you satisfied?*
oki ni mésu お気に召す   *to like, be pleased* (honorific)
oki no doku désu お気の毒です   *what a pity, I am sorry to hear that*
okiki shimásu お聞きします   *excuse my asking; would you mind telling me*

okimásu   see **óku** and **okíru**
Okinawa 沖縄   *Okinawa*, Japan's southernmost prefecture

okíru 起きる   *to get up*
okóru 怒る   *to get angry, be offended*
okóru 起こる   *to happen*
okosan お子さん   *child* (honorific), *your child*
okósu 起こる   *to cause; suffer* (heart attack)

óku 億	*one hundred million*
oku 置く	*to place, put*
okuchi ni awánai deshoo ga お口 に合わないでしょうが	*I hope you like it* (of food), *it might not be to your liking*
okujoo 屋上	*rooftop*
okureru 遅れる	*to be late* (for = **ni**)
okurimásu	see **okuru**
okurimono 贈り物	*present*
okuru 送る	*to send*
ókusan 奥さん	*wife* (honorific), *your wife*
okyakusama お客様	*guest, customer, audience* (honorific)
okyakusan お客さん	*guest; customer, audience*
omachidoosama déshita お待ち どうさまでした	*sorry to have kept you waiting*
omae お前	*you* (very familiar; used by men only)
omatase shimáshita お待たせし ました	*sorry to keep you waiting*
omáwarisan お巡りさん	*policeman*
ome ni kakáru お目にかかる	*to meet object* (honorific)
omiai お見合い	*marriage meeting*
omimai お見舞い	*visit to a sick person* (honorific)
omiyage お土産	*souvenir; gift*
ómo na 主な	*main*
ómo ni 主に	*mainly*
omócha 玩具	*toy*
omochi désu ka お持ちですか	*have you got …?*
omochi shimashóo ka お持ちし ましょうか	*shall I carry it for you?*
omói 重い	*heavy*
omoidásu 思い出す	*to recall, remember*
omoshirogáru 面白がる	*to find interesting or amusing*
omoshirói 面白い	*interesting; amusing*
omote 表	*front, outside*
omóu 思う	*think*
omówazu 思わず	*unintentionally, spontaneously*
onaji 同じ	*same*
onaka お腹	*stomach, abdomen*
onaka ga sukimásu お腹が空き ました	*get hungry*
onamae お名前	*name* (honorific)

onamae wa nán to osshaimásu ka お名前は何とおっしゃいますか — *what is your name?* (honorific)

ondanka 温暖化 — *warming*

onéesan お姉さん — *elder sister* (honorific)

onegai shimásu お願いします — *please; I'd be obliged if you would do it for me*

óngaku 音楽 — *music*

ongakka 音楽家 — *musician*

oníisan お兄さん — *elder brother* (honorific)

onnanohitó 女の人 — *woman*

onnánoko 女の子 — *girl*

onnarashíi 女らしい — *feminine*

onsen 温泉 — *hot spring*

óoame 大雨 — *heavy rain*

óoba オーバ — *overcoat*

óoi 多い — *many, numerous*

ookíi 大きい — *big, large*

óoki na 大きな — *big, large*

ookisa 大きさ — *size*

Oosaka 大阪 — *Osaka*

oosetsuma 応接間 — *sitting room, lounge room*

Oosutoráriya オーストラリア — *Australia*

oosugíru 多過ぎる — *to be too many, too numerous*

ootóbai オートバイ — *motorbike, motorcycle*

óoyasan 大家さん — *landlord*

ópera オペラ — *opera*

ópushonaru tsúaa オプショナル・ツアー — *optional tour*

Oranda オランダ — *the Netherlands, Holland,*

orénji オレンジ — *orange* (fruit)

orenjiíro オレンジ色 — *orange* (colour)

orígami 折り紙 — *paper folding*

orinpíkku オリンピック — *the Olympic Games*

oríru 降りる — *to get off; go down; come down*

óru おる — *to be* (formal)

óru 折る — *to bend; to fold; to break; to weave*

osage shimásu お下げします — *I'll clear the table*

osake お酒 — *rice wine, sake*

osaki お先 — *in front; first* (honorific)

osára お皿 — *plate, saucer*

osátoo — see **satóo**

osawagase shimáshita お騒がせ
しました — *sorry to have caused so much bother/fuss*

osen 汚染 — *pollution*

oséwa ni náru お世話になる — *to be looked after*

oséwa suru お世話する — *to take care of*

osewasamá deshita お世話様で
した — *thank you for your help*

osháberi o suru お喋りをする — *to chatter, talk, gossip, chat*

osháre おしゃれ — *fashionable; smart dresser*

oshiemásu — see **oshiéru**

oshiéru 教える — *to teach*

oshoku 汚職 — *corruption*

osoi 遅い — *late, slow* (adjective)

osoku 遅く — *late* (adverb)

osómatsusama deshita お粗末様
でした — *sorry it was such a simple meal*

osóre irimasu 恐れ入ります — *excuse me, I'm sorry*

osowaru 教わる — *to learn, be taught*

ossháru 仰る — *to speak, say* (honorific)

ossháru tóori desu 仰る通りです — *it is as you say*

osu 押す — *to push, press*

osumai wa dóchira desu ka お住
まいはどちらですか — *where do you live?*

otaku お宅 — *house* (honorific)*; you*

otéarai お手洗い — *lavatory, toilet*

otésuu desu ga お手数ですが — *sorry to trouble you, but…*

otera お寺 — *a temple*

otétsudai san お手伝いさん — *maid, household help*

otétsudai shimashóo ka お手伝い
しましょう — *shall I help you*

otó 音 — *sound, noise*

otokonohitó 男の人 — *man*

otokónoko 男の子 — *boy*

otómo shite mo yoroshii désu ka
お供してもよろしいですか — *may I accompany you?*

otonashíi おとなしい — *gentle; mild; meek; obedient*

otóosan お父さん — *father* (honorific)

otootó 弟 — *younger brother*

otoshi お年 — *age* (honorific)

otósu 落とす — *to drop, let fall*

ototói 一昨日 — *the day before yesterday*

otótoshi 一昨年 — *the year before last*

otsukarésama deshita お疲れさまでした   *you must be tired, thanks for your efforts*

otsuri お釣り   *change*

ouchi お家   *house* (honorific)

owakari désu ka お分かりですか   *do you understand?*

owaru 終わる   *to finish*

oyá 親   *parent*

oyasumi お休み   *holiday; rest* (honorific)

oyasumi nasái お休みなさい   *good night!*

oyasumi ni náru お休みになる   *to go to bed, sleep* (honorific)

oyogimásu 泳ぎます   see **oyógu**

oyógu 泳ぐ   *to swim*

oyu お湯   *hot water*

P

páatii パーティー   *party*

paináppuru パイナップル   *pineapple*

pán パン   *bread*

pánfuretto パンフレット   *pamphlet*

pánya パン屋   *baker, bakery*

Pári パリ   *Paris*

pasupóoto パスポート   *passport*

péeji ページ   *page*

Pékin 北京   *Peking, Beijing*

pén ペン   *pen*

pénki ペンキ   *paint*

pianísuto ピアニスト   *pianist*

piano ピアノ   *piano*

pínku ピンク   *pink*

pósuto ポスト   *post-box*

potetochíppu ポテトチップ   *potato chip*

puréeyaa プレーヤー   *player CD/record,* etc.

purézento プレゼント   *present*

R

rágubii ラグビー   *rugby*

rai– 来–   *next-, coming-* (prefix)

ráigetsu 来月   *next month*

rainen 来年   *next year*

rainichi 来日	*coming to Japan*
raishuu 来週	*next week*
rájio ラジオ	*radio*
rakú na 楽な	*easy, comfortable*
ran'yoo 乱用	*abuse*
–(r)areru られる	*passive ending*
–rashíi らしい –	*-like*
rárii ラリー	*rally* (car)
–(r)éba れば	*conditional suffix*
–(r)eba…–(r)u hodo…	*the more …the more …*
réberu レベル	*level*
réesu レース	*race; lace*
réi 零	*zero*
réi 礼	*bow, salutation; courtesy*
reikin 礼金	*key money, non-refundable deposit*
reizóoko 冷蔵庫	*refrigerator*
rekóodo レコード	*record*
rémon レモン	*lemon*
renraku suru 連絡する	*to contact*
renshuu suru 練習する	*to practise*
resépushon レセプション	*reception*
resépushon レセプション	*reception* (party)
ressha 列車	*locomotive, train*
résutoran レストラン	*restaurant*
rikon 離婚	*divorce*
rikónritsu 離婚率	*divorce rate*
ringo リンゴ	*apple*
rippa na 立派な	*splendid, fine*
–rítsu 率	*rate* (cf., **shibóoritsu** *death rate*, **shusshóoritsu** *birth rate*)
riyoo suru 利用する	*use, make use of, utilise*
–ro ろ	*imperative suffix*
róbii ロビー	*lobby, foyer*
rokkotsu 肋骨	*rib*
roku 六	*six*
rokugatsú 六月	*June*
rókku ロック	*rock* (music)
romanchíkku ロマンチック	*romantic*
Róoma ローマ	*Rome*
rón 論	*argument, debate*
Róndon ロンドン	*London*

roojin 老人	*old person*
roojinmóndai 老人問題	*problems associated with the aged*
Róshia ロシア	*Russia*
Roshiago ロシア語	*Russian language*
ryáku suru 略する	*to abbreviate*
ryokan 旅館	*Japanese inn*
ryokoo suru 旅行する	*to travel*
ryokoogáisha 旅行会社	*travel company*
ryokóosha 旅行社	*travel company*
ryokóosha 旅行者	*traveller*
–ryoku 力	*strength* (in compounds)
ryóo 寮	*dormitory, hall of residence*
ryóo 量	*quantity, volume*
ryóo– 両	*both* (prefix)
ryooashi 両足	*both legs*
ryoogae 両替	*money exchange*
ryoohóo 両方	*both*
ryoohóotomo 両方とも	*both*
ryóokin 料金	*fees, charges*
ryóori suru 料理する	*to cook*
ryóori 料理	*cooking; food*
ryóoshin 両親	*parents*
ryúuchoo na 流暢	*fluent*
ryuugaku 留学	*studying abroad*
ryuugákusei 留学生	*overseas student*

S

–sa –さ	*-ness,* forms abstract nouns from adjectives
sa さ	sentence-final particle
sáabisu サービス	*service; complimentary gift*
sáafin サーフィン	*surfing*
sáe... –(r)eba さえ...れば	*if only*
sáe さえ	*even*
sagasu 探す	*to look for*
sagéru 下げる	*to lower, carry; clear away* (dishes, etc.)
–sai 歳	*years* (numeral classifier for age)
saifu 財布	*wallet, purse*
sáigo 最後	*last*

saikai suru 再会する	*to meet again*
saikin 最近	*recently*
saikoo 最高	*best, most, supreme, wonderful*
sáin suru サインする	*to sign*
saisho 最初	*first, beginning*
sáji 匙	*spoon*
sakana 魚	*fish*
sakanaya 魚屋	*fish shop, fishmonger*
sakaya 酒屋	*sake merchant, liquor shop*
sake 酒	*sake, rice wine*
sakéru 避ける	*to avoid*
sakérui 酒類	*alcoholic beverages, liquor*
saki 先	*first, beforehand*
sakíhodo 先程	*just now; a while ago*
sákkaa サッカー	*soccer*
sákki さっき	*just now, a while ago*
sakkyoku suru 作曲する	*to compose* (music)
saku 咲く	*to bloom*
sakújitsu 昨日	*yesterday* (formal)
sakura 桜	*cherry blossom*
sakusen 作戦	*strategy*
samúi 寒い	*cold*
samurai 侍	*warrior*
–san さん	*form of address, Mr, Mrs, Miss*, etc.
san 三	*three*
sánkaku 三角	*triangle*
sánpaku 三泊	*three nights' stay*
sanpo suru 散歩する	*to go for a walk*
sappari さっぱり	*completely; refreshing;* (not) *at all*
sara 皿	*plate, saucer*
sarainen 再来年	*the year after next*
saraishuu 再来週	*the week after next*
sáru 申	*monkey* (calendar sign)
–saseru させる	causative ending
–sasete itadaku	formal verb ending
sasetsu 左折	*left-hand turn*
sashiagéru 差し上げる	*to give* (object honorific)
sashimi 刺身	*raw fish*
sasou 誘う	*to invite*
sassoku 早速	*at once, quickly, immediately*
sásu 刺す、指す	*to sting, poke; indicate*

satóo 砂糖	*sugar*
–satsu 冊	*volume* (numeral classifier)
satsujin 殺人	*murder*
sawaru 触る	*to touch* (**ni** after object)
sayonará/sayoonara さよ(う)なら	*goodbye*
sé 背	*stature, height*
sé ga hikúi 背が低い	*to be short*
sé ga takái 背が高い	*to be tall*
sebiro 背広	*suit*
séeru セール	*sale*
séetaa セーター	*sweater, pullover*
séi 姓	*family name, surname*
séi 性	*sex, gender*
seichoo suru 成長する	*to grow*
séifu 政府	*government*
seigén 制限	*limit*
seihin 製品	*product*
seiji 政治	*politics*
seikatsu 生活	*life, lifestyle*
seikoo 成功	*success*
seiri suru 整理する	*to put in order, tidy up*
seisaku 政策	*policy*
seiseki 成績	*results*
seiten 晴天	*fine weather*
séito 生徒	*pupil, student*
seiyoo 西洋	*the West, the Occident*
sékai 世界	*world*
sekí 咳	*cough*
séki 席	*seat*
sekinin 責任	*responsibility*
sekkaku 折角	*having gone to all this trouble, at great pains*
semái 狭い	*narrow, cramped*
semi 蝉	*cicada*
sén 千	*thousand*
sénchi センチ	*centimetre*
séngetsu 先月	*last month*
senjitsu 先日	*the other day*
senmenjo 洗面所	*washroom, wash basin*
senpai 先輩	*senior* (student, etc.)
senséi 先生	*teacher;* term of address, *Mr, Mrs, Dr,* etc.

sénshu 選手	*competitor, athlete, sportsman or sportswoman*
senshuu 先週	*last week*
sensoo 戦争	*war*
sentaku 洗濯	*washing*
seppuku 切腹	*harakiri, ritual suicide*
–seru	see **–(s)aseru**
setsumei suru 説明する	*to explain*
shabéru 喋る	*to talk, chat*
shachoo 社長	*company director, president*
shákai 社会	*society*
sháko 車庫	*garage*
sharete iru 洒落ている	*stylish, fashionable*
shashin 写真	*photograph*
sháwaa シャワー	*shower*
shéfu シェフ	*chef*
shi し	*and what is more* (clause-final particle)
shi 四	*four*
shi 詩	*poetry; poem*
shiai 試合	*match, bout, game*
shibafu 芝生	*lawn*
shibai 芝居	*play, performance*
shibáraku desu né 暫くですね	*it's been a long time, hasn't it?*
shibáraku 暫く	*for a while*
shibóoritsu 死亡率	*death rate*
shibúi 渋い	*astringent; sober, in good taste*
shichi 七	*seven*
shichigatsú 七月	*July*
shigatsú 四月	*April*
shigéru 茂る	*to grow thickly*
shigoto suru 仕事する	*to work, do a job*
shigoto 仕事	*work*
shihajiméru 仕始める	*to start to do*
shíifuudo シーフード	*sea food*
shíjin 詩人	*poet*
shijoo 市場	*market* (stock market, market trends, etc.)
shíjuu 始終	*all the time, from start to finish*
shika しか	*only* (with negative verb), (nothing) *but*
shika 鹿	*deer*

shikaku 四角	*square*
shikámo しかも	*moreover, what is more*
shikáru 叱る	*to scold*
shikáshi 然し	*but*
shikata 仕方	*way of doing*
shikata ga nái 仕方がない	*it can't be helped, there's no other way*
shiken 試験	*examination*
shiki 式	*ceremony*
shikikin 敷金	*deposit* (for flat, etc.), *surety*
Shikóku 四国	*Shikoku* (smallest of Japan's four main islands)
shimá 島	*island*
shimáru 閉まる	*to close, shut* (intransitive)
shimásu	see *suru*
shimátta! しまった	*damn! blast!*
shimau 仕舞う	*to put away, finish* (see –**te shimau**)
shiméru 閉める	*to close, shut* (transitive)
shimi 染み	*stain*
shimiíru しみ入る	*soak into, sink into*
shínai 市内	*in the city, within city limits*
shinamono 品物	*goods, article*
shínboru シンボル	*symbol*
shinbun 新聞	*newspaper*
shinbúnsha 新聞社	*newspaper company*
shingoo 信号	*signal*
shinimásu	see **shinu**
shinjíru 信じる	*to believe*
shinkan 新館	*new building, new block*
Shinkánsen 新幹線	*Shinkansen,* bullet train lines
shinpai suru 心配する	*to worry*
shínpo suru 進歩する	*progress, advance*
shinseki 親戚	*relation, relative*
shinsen na 新鮮な	*fresh*
shínsetsu na 親切	*kind*
shínshi 紳士	*gentleman*
shinshitsu 寝室	*bedroom*
shintai-kénsa 身体検査	*medical examination*
shíntoo 神道	*Shintoism* (native Japanese religion)
shinu 死ぬ	*to die*
shin'yoojoo 信用状	*letter of credit*

shió 塩	*salt*
shiokara 塩辛	*salted squid guts*
shirabéru 調べる	*to investigate, check, look up*
shiriai 知り合い	*acquaintance*
shirimásu	see **shiru**
shiro 城	*castle*
shirói 白い	*white*
shiru 知る	*to get to know*
shíryoo 資料	*materials, records*
shísetsu 施設	*facilities*
shita 下	*bottom, base, below, under*
shitá 舌	*tongue*
shitagau 従う	*follow, obey, observe*
shitaku 仕度	*preparation* (of meal, etc.)
shitamachi 下町	*down town*
shiteki 私的	*private*
shiteki 詩的	*poetic*
shiten 支店	*branch* (shop or office)
shiténchoo 支店長	*branch manager*
shitsu 質	*quality*
shitsumon 質問	*question*
shitsúnai 室内	*interior*
shitsúrei na 失礼	*rude*
shitsúrei shimasu 失礼します	*goodbye, I must be going*
shiyákusho 市役所	*town hall, city office*
shiyoo ga nái 仕様がない	*it's no good, it can't be helped*
shiyoo 仕様	*way of doing*
shizen 自然	*nature, natural*
shízuka na 静かな	*quiet, peaceful*
shizukésa 静けさ	*stillness, quiet, calm*
sho– 諸	*all, the various* (plural prefix)
shokudoo 食堂	*cafeteria, dining room*
shokugo 食後	*after meals*
shokuji suru 食事する	*to have a meal*
shokuryóohin 食料	*foodstuffs, provisions*
shokúyoku 食欲	*appetite*
shokuzen 食前	*before meals*
shokyuu 初級	*elementary class*
shomóndai 諸問題	*all the problems, various problems*
shóo 小	*small* (noun)
shoochi	see **goshoochi** ~

shoochi suru 承知する	*to consent, agree to*
shoodan 商談	*business discussions*
shoogakukin 奨学金	*scholarship*
shoogákusei 小学生	*primary school pupil*
shóohin 商品	*goods, merchandise, product*
shoojíki na 正直な	*honest*
shookai suru 紹介する	*to introduce*
shookéesu ショーケース	*display window* (for wax models of food, etc.)
shooko 証拠	*proof*
shóorai 将来	*future*
shoosetsu 小説	*novel*
shóoshoo 少々	*a little*
Shóowa 昭和	*year period* (1926–1989)
shorui 書類	*documents, papers*
shosei 書生	*student; houseboy*
shótchuu しょっちゅう	*often, all the time*
shúfu 主婦	*housewife*
shújin 主人	*husband*
shújitsu 手術	*surgical operation*
shukudai 宿題	*homework*
shukuhaku 宿泊	*accommodation, board*
shúmi 趣味	*hobby, pastime, interest*
shuppatsu suru 出発する	*to depart, leave*
shuppatsu 出発	*departure*
shúrui 種類	*type, kind*
shushoo 首相	*prime minister, premier*
shusseki suru 出席する	*to attend*
shusseki 出席	*attendance*
shusshin 出身	*coming from, graduating from, born in*
shusshóoritsu 出生率	*birth rate*
shutchoo 出張	*business trip*
shúukyoo 宗教	*religion*
shuukyoo-árasoi 宗教争い	*religious strife*
shuumatsu 週末	*weekend*
shúuri 修理	*repair*
shuushoku 就職	*finding a job, entering employment*
shuutome 姑	*mother-in-law*
shuuwai 収賄	*taking bribes*
shúzoku 種族	*tribe*

sóba そば	*buckwheat noodles*
sóba 側	*near, beside*
sóbo 祖母	*grandmother*
sochira そちら	*that one, that way; you*
sodatéru 育てる	*to raise, bring up*
sófu 祖父	*grandfather*
soko そこ	*there* (by you)
soko 底	*bottom, base, depths*
sokutatsu 速達	*express delivery*
sonkei suru 尊敬する	*to respect*
sonna そんな	*that kind of*
sono その	*that* (adjective)
sono mama そのまま	*as it is, like that, unchanged*
sono uchi その内	*meanwhile*
sonóta その他	*and other, etc.*
sonzai suru 存在する	*to exist*
–soo そう	*it looks as if it will… (suffix on verb stem)*
sóo そう	*that way, so*
sóo da そうだ	*they say, apparently* (after verb)
sóo desu ka そうですか	*is that so, really?*
soo'on 騒音	*noise*
soodan suru 相談する	*to discuss*
sooji suru 掃除する	*to clean*
sóosu ソース	*sauce*
sootoo na 相当な	*considerable, fit, proper*
sóra 空	*sky*
sore déwa それでは	*then, in that case*
sore jáa それじゃあ	*then, in that case*
sore kara それから	*after that, next*
sore それ	*that* (demonstrative pronoun)
sórosoro そろそろ	*gradually, quietly, soon, about now*
sóru 剃る	*to shave*
sóshite そして	*and*
sotchí そっち	*that one, that way*
sóto 外	*outside*
sotsugyoo suru 卒業する	*to graduate*
subarashíi 素晴らしい	*wonderful*
subéru 滑る	*to slip*
súbete 統べて	*all, everything*
súde ni 既に	*already*

sue 末	*end*
Suéeden スエーデン	*Sweden*
súgata 姿	*figure, form, appearance*
sugí 過ぎ	*past* (the hour)
sugíru 過ぎる	*surpass, exceed, be too…*
sugói 凄い	*terrific, great; tremendous*
sugóku 凄く	*terribly, awfully*
súgu すぐ	*immediately*
suidoo 水道	*water service, water supply*
suiei 水泳	*swimming*
suigyuu 水牛	*water buffalo*
suijun 水準	*level, standard*
Súisu スイス	*Switzerland*
suiyóobi 水曜日	*Wednesday*
suizókukan 水族館	*aquarium*
sukáafu スカーフ	*scarf*
sukáato スカート	*skirt*
sukéeto スケート	*skate, skating*
sukí na 好きな	*to like*
sukí na dake 好きなだけ	*as much as you like*
sukíi スキー	*ski*
sukimásu	see **suku**
sukiyaki すきやき	*beef and vegetable dish*
sukóshi 少し	*a little*
suku 空く	*to become empty*
sukunái 少ない	*few, not many*
sumai	see **osumai**
sumáu 住まう	*to live, dwell* (formal)
sumimásu	see **súmu**
sumimasén すみません	*I'm sorry*
sumoo 相撲	*sumo wrestling*
sumóobu 相撲部	*the sumo club*
súmu 住む	*to live*
suna 砂	*sand*
sunahama 砂浜	*(sand) beach*
supagéttii スパゲッティー	*spaghetti*
Supéin スペイン	*Spain*
supíichi スピーチ	*speech*
supíido スピード	*speed*
supóotsu スポーツ	*sport*
supúun スプーン	*spoon*
suru する	*to do*

súru する	*to pick pockets*
sushí 寿司 (also **súshi**)	*raw fish on vinegared rice*
susumeru 勧める	*to recommend*
susumu 進む	*advance, progress*
sutándo スタンド	*lamp; (petrol) station*
sutéeki ステーキ	*steak*
suteki na 素敵な	*lovely, charming*
sutéru 捨てる	*to throw away, discard*
sutóobu ストーブ	*stove, heater*
sutorésu ストレス	*stress*
sutoresu-káishoo ストレス解消	*relief from stress*
suu 吸う	*to suck; smoke*
suuji 数字	*numbers, numerals*
súupaa スーパー	*supermarket*
súupu スープ	*soup*
súutsu スーツ	*suit*
suutsukéesu スーツケース	*suitcase*
suwarikómu 座り込む	*to sit down*
suwaru 座る	*to sit down* (on the ground)
Suwéeden スウェーデン	*Sweden*
suzushíi 涼しい	*cool*

T

tá 田	*rice field*
–ta た	past-tense suffix
–ta bákari desu –たばかりです	*to have just…*
–ta hóo ga íi –た方がいい	*it would be better to…*
tabako タバコ	*cigarette*
tabemásu	see **tabéru**
tabemonó 食べ物	*food*
tabéru 食べる	*to eat*
tabesugi 食べ過ぎ	*over-eating*
tabí 旅	*journey, trip*
tábun 多分	*probably*
–tachi 達	plural suffix
tachiiri-kinshi 立入禁止	*no entry*
tachippanashi 立ちっぱなし	*standing all the time/way*
táda 只、ただ	*only; free; just*
tadáima ただ今	*I'm back! just now*
tadashíi 正しい	*correct, right*

tade 蓼	*nettles*
–tagáru –たがる	*to want to… (third person)*
Tái タイ	*Thailand*
–tái -たい	*to want to*
tai'in suru 退院する	*to leave hospital*
taifúu 台風	*typhoon*
Taihéiyoo 太平洋	*Pacific Ocean*
taihen na 大変	*very, extreme(ly); terrible; very difficult*
taikiósen 大気汚染	*atmospheric pollution*
taira na 平らな	*flat, level*
Taiséiyoo 大西洋	*Atlantic Ocean*
taisetsu na 大切な	*important*
táishi 大使	*ambassador*
taishíkan 大使館	*embassy*
táishita 大した	*great, important, serious*
Taishoo 大正	*year period* (1912–1926)
taitei 大抵	*generally, as a rule, for the most part*
táiyoo 太陽	*sun*
takái 高い	*high; expensive*
tákaku tsuku 高くつく	*to cost a lot, work out expensive*
tákasa 高さ	*height*
takasugíru 高すぎる	*to be too expensive, too high*
take 竹	*bamboo*
takkyuu 卓球	*table tennis*
táko 凧	*kite*
táko 蛸	*octopus*
taku 宅	*household, residence (see **otaku**)*
takusán たくさん	*a lot*
tákushii タクシー	*taxi*
takushii-nóriba タクシー乗場	*taxi rank*
tama ni たまに	*occasionally, from time to time*
tamágo 卵	*egg*
tamatama たまたま	*by chance*
tamé 為	*for, for the sake of; because*
tango 単語	*word*
tanjóobi 誕生日	*birthday*
tanómu 頼む	*to ask, request*
tanoshíi 楽しい	*fun, enjoyable*
tanoshimí ni suru 楽しみにする	*to look forward to*

tantoo 担当	(person) *in charge*
–tara たら	*if, when*
–tari…–tari suru	*to do such things as …and …, do frequently or alternately*
tariru 足りる	*be enough, suffice*
táshika ni 確かに	*certainly, no doubt*
tassuru 達する	*reach, achieve*
tasu 足す	*to add*
tasukáru 助かる	*to be saved; to be a help*
tasukéru 助ける	*to help; save, rescue*
tatakau 戦う	*to fight*
tatami 畳	*mat, rush mat, tatami* (1.6 m²)
tatémono 建物	*building*
tatóeba 例えば	*for example*
tátsu 発つ	*to leave*
tátsu 立つ	*to stand*
tátsu (yakú ni ＿＿＿) 役に立つ	*to be useful*
tatsu 竜	*dragon, 辰 (calendar sign)*
tatta たった	*only*
té 手	*hand*
té ga hanasenái 手が離せない	*to be occupied*
–te て	*and* ('the **–te** form' ending – joins clauses)
–te agemásu	see **–te ageru**
–te ageru てあげる	*to give* (see **–te áru**)
–te arimásu	
–te áru てある	*to have been…*
–te hoshíi て欲しい	*to want something done*
–te iku て行く	*to go on getting more…*
–te imásu	see **–te iru**
–te iru –ている	*is/are …ing* (present continuous tense or completed state)
–te itadakemasén ka –て頂けませんか	*would you mind …ing for me?*
–te itadaku –て頂く	*to have something done by a respected person*
–te kara –てから	*after*
–te kudasái –て下さい	*please* (request form)
–te kudasáru –て下さる	*a respected person does something for someone*
–te kúru –て来る	*to go and …, to start to …, become more and more …*

–te míru –て見る	*to try …ing; do and see*
–te mo íi desu ka –てもいいですか	*Is it all right?, may I?*, etc.
–te morau –てもらう	*to have someone do something for one*
té ni háiru 手に入る	*to be obtained, get, come by* (intransitive)
té ni ireru 手に入れる	*to get, obtain* (transitive)
té ni tóru yóo ni 手に取るように	*clearly* (literally, 'as if you took into your hands')
–te oku –て置く	*to leave done; do in preparation; do and set aside*
–te wa damé desu –ては駄目です	*must not*
–te wa ikemasén –ては行けません	*must not …*
teárai 手洗い	*lavatory*
téate 手当て	*allowance; medical treatment*
tebúkuro 手袋	*gloves*
techoo 手帳	*notebook, pocket-book, appointment diary*
téeburu テーブル	*table*
tegami 手紙	*letter*
teido 程度	*extent*
teikíken 定期券	*season ticket*
teikyúubi 定休日	*regular holiday* (shop closed)
téinei na 丁寧	*polite*
teiryuujo 停留所	*bus stop*
teishoku 定食	*set meal, fixed lunch or dinner, table d'hôte*
tekitoo na 適当な	*suitable*
temíyage 手土産	*a present* (from visitor to host)
téngoku 天国	*heaven*
ten'in 店員	*shop assistant*
ténisu テニス	*tennis*
ténki 天気	*weather*
tenki-yóhoo 天気予報	*weather report; forecast*
tenkoo 天候	*climate, weather*
tenpura てんぷら	*fish and vegetables in batter*
tensai 天災	*natural calamity*
terá 寺	*temple*
térebi テレビ	*television*
tetsudái 手伝い	*help; helper*

tetsudau 手伝う	*to help*
tíishatsu ティーシャツ	*T-shirt*
tishupéepaa ティシュペーパー	*tissue paper*
to と	*with; and; that, thus* (quotative particle)
to shite として	*as*
tobimásu	see **tobu**
tobu 飛ぶ	*to fly*
tochuu de 途中	*on the way*
todokéru 届ける	*to report; deliver*
todóku 届く	*to reach; be delivered*
tóire トイレ	*toilet, lavatory*
tokei 時計	*watch, clock*
tokí 時	*time; when*
tokoro 所	*place*
tokoróde ところで	*by the way*
tokoróga ところが	*however*
tóku ni 特に	*especially, particularly*
tomaru 止まる	*to stop; stay*
tomaru 泊まる	*to stay* (overnight)
tómato トマト	*tomato*
tomodachi 友達	*friend*
tonari 隣	*next door; neighbouring*
tonneru トンネル	*tunnel*
tonto とんと	*entirely, quite; at all, in the least*
tóo 十	*ten*
toodai 東大	*Tokyo University* (abbreviation)
tooi 遠い	*distant; far*
tooká 十日	*ten days, 10th of the month*
tooku ni 遠くに	*in the distance*
Tookyoo 東京	*Tokyo*
Tookyoodáigaku 東京	*Tokyo University*
Tookyoo-dézuniirando 東京デズニーランド	*Tokyo Disneyland*
toorí 通り	*way; road;* **yuu tóori** *as one says*
tóoru 通る	*to pass; go through*
tooshi 投資	*investment*
tora 虎	*tiger,* 寅 (calendar sign)
torákku トラック	*truck; track*
tori 鳥	*bird; chicken* (meat)
tori 酉	*cock* (calendar sign)
toriáezu 取り敢えず	*for the time being, first, for a start*

torihiki 取引	*dealings, business transactions*
torikáeru 取り替える	*to change, exchange*
torikakomu 取り囲む	*surround, include*
tóru 取る	*to take*
toshí 年	*year; age*
toshiue 年上	*older person, one's elders*
toshiyóri 年寄り	*old person*
toshókan 図書館	*library*
toshoshitsu 図書室	*reading room*
totemo, tottemo とても、とっても	*very*
totsuzen 突然	*suddenly*
tsúaa ツアー	*tour*
tsuchí 土	*ground, earth*
tsugí 次	*next, following*
tsugí kara tsugí e 次から次へ	*one after the other*
tsugoo 都合	*circumstances, convenience*
tsuide ni 序でに	*on the way, taking the opportunity to …*
tsuika suru 追加	*to add, supplement*
tsúin ツイン	*twin* (room)
tsuitachí 一日	*first day of the month*
tsukaremásu	see **tsukaréru**
tsukaréru 疲れる	*to get tired*
tsukau 使う	*to use*
tsukéru 付ける	*to put on, attach*
tsukí 月	*moon, month*
tsukimásu	see **tsuku**
tsúku 着く、つく	*to arrive; to stick, to be attached*
tsukue 机	*desk*
tsukurikatá 作り方	*way of making*
tsukúru 作る	*to make*
tsumaránai 詰まらない	*uninteresting; trifling*
tsúmari つまり	*that is to say, in short*
tsumetai 冷たい	*cold*
tsumori 積もり	*intention*
tsunagaru 繋がる	*to be linked to, to be tied to*
tsunami 津波	*tidal wave*
tsurete iku 連れていく	*to take a person*
tsuri 釣り	*fishing*
tsúru 鶴	*crane* (bird)
tsuushin 通信	*correspondence, communication*

tsutoméru 勤める	*to work* (for = **ni**), *to strive*
-tsuu 通	numerical classifier for letters
tsúuro 通路	*passageway*
tsuwamono 兵	*soldier, warrior*
tsuyói 強い	*strong*
tsuzukeru 続ける	*to keep on …ing; to continue to*
tsuzukete 続けて	*continuously*
tte って	quotative particle

U

u 卯	*rabbit* (calendar sign)
uchi 内	*while; inside*
uchi うち	*house; family*
uchi no うちの	*our, my*
úchuu 宇宙	*space*
uchuuhikóoshi 宇宙飛行士	*astronaut*
ue 上	*top; up; above*
uísukii ウイスキー	*whisky*
ukagaimásu	see **ukagau**
ukagau 伺う	*to ask; visit* (object honorific)
ukéru 受ける	*to receive*
uketoru 受け取る	*to receive a letter,* etc.
uketsuke 受付	*reception desk, reception*
umá 馬	*horse*
umá 午	*horse* (calendar sign)
umái うまい	*to be good at; skilful; tasty*
umare 生まれ	*born in* (year or place)
umareru 生まれる	*to be born*
ume 梅	*plum*
umeboshi 梅干し	*salted plum*
úmi 海	*sea*
umíkaze 海風	*sea breeze*
ún うん	*yes*
unagi 鰻	*eel*
undoo suru 運動する	*to exercise*
undoobúsoku 運動不足	*lack of exercise*
úni 雲丹	*sea urchin*
unten suru 運転する	*to drive*
unténshu 運転手	*driver*

ureshíi 嬉しい	*happy*
uriba 売り場	*sales counter*
uru 売る	*to sell*
urusái うるさい	*noisy, bothersome*
usagi 兎	*rabbit*
usetsu 右折	*right-hand turn*
ushi 牛	*ox, cow, bull*
ushi 丑	*ox* (calendar sign)
ushinau 失う	*to lose*
ushiro 後ろ	*back; behind*
úso 嘘	*lie*
úso o tsuku 嘘をつく	*to tell a lie*
uta 歌	*song, poem*
utagawashíi 疑わしい	*doubtful*
utau 歌う	*to sing*
úten 雨天	*rainy weather*
útsu 打つ	*to hit; send a telegram*
utsukushíi 美しい	*beautiful*
utsúru 映る	*to reflect, show, appear* (in a photograph)
utsúsu 移す	*pass on* (a cold, etc.)

W

wa は	topic particle
wa わ	*feminine sentence-final particle*
wadai 話題	*topic of conversation*
wainrísuto ワインリスト	*wine list*
waishatsu ワイシャツ	*shirt*
wakái 若い	*young*
wakamono 若者	*young person*
wakarimásu	see **wakáru**
wakáru 分かる	*to understand*
wakéru 分ける	*to divide, share*
waraidásu 笑い出す	*to burst out laughing*
warau 笑う	*to laugh, to smile*
wareru 割れる	*to break*
wareware 我々	*we, us*
warúi 悪い	*bad*
wasureru 忘れる	*to forget*

watakushi 私	*I* (formal)
wataru 渡る	*to cross*
watashi 私	*I*
wázawaza わざわざ	*deliberately, expressly*
wéitaa ウェイター	*waiter*
Wíin ウィーン	*Vienna*

Y

–(y)óo ka to omóu ようかと思う	*I think I'll…*
ya や	*and*
–ya 屋	*shop; shopkeeper* (suffix)
yáa やあ	*oh! hey! hi!*
yáchin 家賃	*rent*
yahári やはり	*as expected, to be sure*
yukata 浴衣	*cotton summer kimono*
yakei 夜景	*view at night, night scenery*
yakkyoku 薬局	*pharmacy, chemist shop*
yaku ni tátsu 役に立つ	*to be useful*
yakusoku 約束	*promise, appointment*
yakusoku suru 約束する	*to promise*
yakyuu 野球	*baseball*
yamá 山	*mountain*
yamádera 山寺	*mountain temple*
yámai 病	*illness, disease*
yameru 止める	*to give up; stop; retire; abandon*
yamu 止む	*to stop*
yáne 屋根	*roof*
yappári やっぱり	*too, still, all the same, as expected* (emphatic **yahári**)
yarimásu	see **yaru**
yarinaósu やり直す	*to redo*
yaru やる	*to do; give to an inferior; send on an errand*
yasai 野菜	*vegetable*
yasashíi 優しい	*kind, gentle, considerate*
yasemásu	see **yaseru**
yaseru 痩せる	*to get thin*
yasúi 安い	*cheap*
–yasúi やすい	*to be easy to*

yasumí 休み	*holiday; rest, break*
yasumimásu	see **yasúmu**
yasúmu 休む	*to rest; to go to bed, sleep* (euphemistic honorific)
yatto やっと	*at last, finally*
yattsú 八つ	*eight*
yayakoshíi ややこしい	*complicated, intricate, confusing*
yo よ	sentence-final particle; emphatic
–yo よ	imperative suffix
yoaké 夜明け	*dawn, daybreak*
yói	see *íi*
yóji 四時	*four o'clock*
yókatta よかった	*it was good, good; I'm glad*
yokka 四日	*four days, 4th of the month*
yoko 横	*side; beside*
yóku よく	*well; often*
yokujoo 浴場	*bath, bath-house*
yomihajiméru 読み始める	*to start to read*
yomimásu	see **yómu**
Yomiurishínbun 読売新聞	*the Yomiuri* (a major daily)
yómu 読む	*to read*
yón 四	*four*
yóo na ki ga suru ような	*feel as if…*
yóo na ような	*like, as*
yóo ni ように	*so that* (indirect command)
yóo ni suru ようにする	*arrange to …, make sure that*
–(y)óo to suru ようとする	*to try to* (suffix)
yoochíen 幼稚園	*kindergarten*
yoofuku 洋服	*western clothes*
yóoi 用意	*preparation, provision*
yóoi suru 用意する	*provide, prepare, get ready*
yooji 用事	*business, things to do*
yooka 八日	*eight days, 8th of the month*
yookan 洋館	*a western-style house/building*
yóokoso ようこそ	*welcome*
yooma 洋間	*western-style room*
yooróppa ヨーロッパ	*Europe*
yooshoku 洋食	*western food/meal*
yori より	*than*
yorokobásu 喜ばす	*to delight, make happy*
yorokobi 喜び	*joy*
yorokóbu 喜ぶ	*to be pleased*

yorokónde 喜んで	*with pleasure*
yoroshii よろしい	*good* (honorific)
yoroshii désu ka よろしいですか	*is it all right? Do you mind?*
yoroshiku よろしく	*well, suitably; give my regards; please do what you can for me*
yoru 寄る	*to call at, drop in* (at = **ni**)
yóru 夜	*night; at night*
yoru よる	*to depend*
yoru, ni yoru to よる	*according to*
yósa 良さ	*value, worth, goodness*
yósan 予算	*budget*
yotei 予定	*plan*
yotte, ni ____ よって	*by* (agent of passive)
yótto ヨット	*yacht*
yottsú 四つ	*four*
you 酔う	*to get drunk*
yowai 弱い	*weak*
yoyaku 予約	*reservation, booking*
yozákura 夜桜	*cherry blossoms at night*
yu 湯	*hot water,* see **oyu**
yubi 指	*finger*
yubi (o) sásu 指(を)指す	*to point*
yubiwa 指輪	*ring*
yudéru 茹でる	*to boil*
yude-támago ゆで卵	*boiled egg*
yuka 床	*floor*
–yuki 行き	*bound for …, to …*
yuki 雪	*snow*
yukkúri ゆっくり	*slowly*
yumé 夢	*dream*
yumé o miru 夢を見る	*to dream*
yuu 言う	*to say* (most forms based on **iu**)
yuube 夕べ	*last night*
yuubínkyoku 郵便局	*post office*
yuugata 夕方	*evening*
yuugóhan 夕御飯	*dinner, evening meal*
yuuhi 夕日	*setting sun, evening sun*
yuujin 友人	*friend*
yuumei na 有名な	*famous*
yuushoku 夕食	*dinner, evening meal*
yuzuru 譲る	*to hand over, give up, bequeath*

Z

zannen na 残念な	*unfortunate*
zasshi 雑誌	*magazine*
ze ぜ	emphatic sentence-final particle
zéhi 是非	*certainly, without fail*
zénbu 全部	*all*
zensai 前菜	*entrée, hors d'oeuvre*
zenzen 全然	*not at all*
zéro ゼロ	*zero*
zo ぞ	emphatic sentence-final particle
zonjimasén 存じません	*I don't know* (object honorific)
zonjíru 存じる	*to know* (object honorific)
–zu ず	negative suffix, see –**(a)zu**
zubón ズボン	*trousers*
zúibun 随分	*extremely; quite, very*
zútsu ずつ	*each*
zutsuu 頭痛	*headache*
zutto ずっと	*all the way, all the time*

Index of grammar and language functions

–(a)nákereba narimasen
181–2
–(a)nákute wa narimasen 182
'about', 'about to'
'to be' 166
abstract nouns with –sa 238
'according to'
–te form 220
action in progress 96–8
adjectival clauses 135–6
adjectives 61, 78
adverbial form –ku 62
adversative passive
indirect passive 214
'after … –ing' 118
aizuchi 94
'along', 'through', 'over'
83, 100
'although' 208
'and what is more' 172–3
apologies 11–27
'as … as' 138–40

'because' 115
'before' 118
boku
male pronoun 206
bowing (ojígi) 15
business cards (meishi) 11–13
'but' (see ga)

'can' 136–8
casual conversation
plain style 117, 182
causative 215–17
causative suffix 215–17
chiming in 94–5
'coming' or 'going to do
something' 107
comparisons 138–40
completed state 78, 96
compound verbs 240–1
conditional clauses 148–9
conditions and
consequences 148–9
copula 62–3, 67, 77
counting days 154–5
countries 28–40

dates 48–9, 155
days of the week 85
de
'by means of' 55
place of action 84
degrees of probability 220
dekíru 136–7
demonstratives
adjectives 61–9, 171
adverbs 171
pronouns 41–57, 63
describing people 111–29

descriptive nouns   61–9
deshóo   117–18
désu (*see* copula)
'difficult to'   221–2

e direction marker   107
expectation
  hazu   207–8
explanations   170–1
expressing wishes and desires
  106–7
extent   239

families   41–4, 51–7
female speech   205
feminine final particles   205–6
formal style   235–6
frequentative   156

ga
  as object marker   33–4, 67
  'but'   114, 123–4
giving advice   134, 166–7
giving and receiving   195–9
giving reasons   115, 187–8
go–   97
greetings   11–27

hesitation forms   94–5
hodo   239
honorific prefix   232–5
honorific prefixes **o–**, **go–**
  232–5
honorific verbs   53–4, 232–4
hoo 'side', 'direction'   134, 139,
  239
hoo ga íi   134
hortative   165

imperative   241–2
indefinite pronouns   157–8
indirect imperative   242

indirect or reported speech
  119–20
indirect passive   214
indirect questions   120–1
intention   164–5
introductions   11–27

ka   13, 32, 82
–kan   86
kotó   130–44
kotó ga áru   130–44
–ku form of adjectives   62

likes and dislikes   38–40
listing reasons   172–3

máe   118–19
–mashóo   81–2
–meku 'to seem like'   200
men's language   206
'must not'   171, 183

n' desu   170–1
na adjectives   61–4
–nagara   151
names   14
  girls' given names   20
nára, 'if'   187
nationality   28–40
native Japanese numerals   105
negative forms   62, 179–82
negative requests   99, 185
ni yoru to   220
ni yotte   220
nigori, voicing mark   16
–nikúi 'difficult to'   222
no de, 'because'   187, 208
no ni 'although'   208
no 'the one'   13, 46, 63
numbers   46–57, 70–1
numeral classifiers   47–57,
  67–9, 152–3

o with verbs of motion   100
object honorific   216, 233
objective judgment   219
obligation
   beki   207–8
occupations   26–7

particles
   clause final   187
   direction particles **e** and **ni**
      107
   quotative particle **to**   25
passive   213–15, 216–17, 237–8
past tense
   of adjectives   132–3
   of verbs   97, 116–18
permission   90–110, 122–5
plain form
   formation of   116
   past tense   117
   uses of   117
'please don't', negative
   requests   185
'polite request' **–te itadakemasén
   ka** (*see* 'requests')
polite style   235–6
possession   126
possibility   169–70
potential verbs   168
   with **–rareru**   168–9
prefixes in time expressions   85–6
probability   117–18
prohibition   122–4, 183
pronunciation   1–7
   devoicing of vowels   2–3
   double consonants   4
   long vowels   2
   pitch   4–5

reasons
   –r(éba)   149
reference and address   232

rendaku   14
'reply to thanks'   20, 24–7
'requests'   58–70, 98–102
'respect language'   231–4
   passive as an honorific   234–5

–(s)asete itadakimásu   216
script
   furigana   9–10
   hiragána   8–10
   historical spelling   7–8, 83
   kanji   7–10
   kanji repetition sign   9–10
   katakána   8–9
   kun reading   32, 85
   on reading   32, 48–9, 86
   romanisation   1–2
   writing **kanji**   8
sequences of events   122
sequential voicing   14
shi   31
'should'   202, 207–8
–sóo   200, 218
sóo desu   120, 219
sports   34, 56
stroke order   8
subject honorifics   232
supposition   118
syllables with **b** and **p**   45

–tai   106
talking about plans   107
–tára   148–9
–tári   156
–te form   95
   formation   95–7
   –te áru   202–3
   –te iku   203–4
   –te kara   118–19
   –te kúru   203
   –te míru   201–2
   –te shimau   202

telephone numbers   49–50
tentative, hortative   201–2
the one (*see* **no**)
'this' and 'that'   41–57
time
   clauses of   49, 57, 79–89, 122
   duration   86–7
to quotative particle   14
to 'when'   121
to, 'with' or 'and'   121–2, 25
toki   122
tone, pronunciation
   pitch   4–7
tsumori   164–5

verb plus noun plus **désu**   62
verbs
   conjugations   116
   giving and receiving   195–9
   intransitive verbs   83, 96,
      169, 214

linear motion verbs   83
noun plus verb 'to do'   78
plain form   97, 116–17, 235
transitive verbs   83, 96, 202–3
verb 'to be'   66–8, 126
verb from noun plus 'to do'
   156
verbs for wearing clothes   126
voicing mark (*see* **nigori**)

wa   14
   feminine particle   205–6
'when' or 'whenever'   121–2
'while'   151
'without doing'   188

yóo desu   120
–(y)óo to omou   165
–(y)oo to suru   166
yóri   138–40